Strong Stuff:
Mothers' Stories

Strong Stuff: Mothers' Stories

By

Emily W. Moore

ISBN 1-58500-562-2

1stBooks rev 4/19/00

ABOUT THE BOOK

In <u>Strong Stuff: Mothers' Stories</u> eighty-four American mothers tell their own stories, intimately, candidly, in their own words. These women form a cross section of the mothers in America today: rich and poor; black, white, Hispanic, Native American, and Asian American; Jewish, Catholic, protestant, and Amish; married and single; lesbian and straight; employed in a variety of occupations and at-home-by-choice; mothers in prison; teenage mothers and mothers who are great-grandmothers; Midwest farm mothers, mothers from New England, the South, and the West; homeless mothers; mothers of only children and mothers of many, many children; adoptive mothers and step-mothers.

The individual stories are grouped into seven chapters. Each chapter has a brief introduction, which is followed by the stories. Chapters are:

> Identity
> Lessons and Traditions
> Challenge
> Violence
> Loss
> Mothers and Fathers
> Affirmation

Each story begins with the woman's name (pseudonym), a quote called out from the story, and a few introductory sentences about the mother and her connection to this particular chapter. An index of issues and of mothers' situations makes it easy for anyone to find all references, for instance, to teenage mothers or to managing teenagers.

To my mother and favorite woman
Emily Young Williams

"Teddy"

who taught me the value of listening

ACKNOWLEDGMENTS

Thank you Richard, my husband and life partner, for always encouraging me to do what is important, for being my best critic, and for going the distance.

Thank you Jess and James, my sons, for providing me with the provocation and the inspiration to write <u>Strong Stuff</u>. Your excitement about this project helped it to become a reality.

Thank you to the 143 mothers who told me their stories. I still am in awe of what you know and grateful for your generosity and courage in sharing with me. Even though only some of your stories appear here, all of them, and all of you were part of the great mix which determined the shape of the book.

Thanks also to Joe Danahy, Michael Mars Carr and Barbara, and to John and Cathy Folk-Williams for kindness and contacts; to Kathy Stall, word-woman *par excellence*; and to Kathy Berglund for sharing her heart's reading of the stories.

CONTENTS

INTRODUCTION

My sons Jess and James are now eighteen and sixteen. Mothering them has been the greastest source of joy in my life. However, when they were very small, I was a mother-at-home, and I did not do it as gracefully as I would have liked. I was frequently impatient with them. I questioned myself constantly. Often the days were twelve to thirteen hours long, at the end of a dead-end street, in a small, New England town where I didn't know many young mothers. Often I had no car, and more often, I had nowhere to go. My husband was as interested in and committed to the children as I was, but he was also working full-time. My delight in the children was wrapped in endless cycles of diapers, clutter, and boring meals. There was too little adult companionship and too little brain-food for me. My heart sank every time someone said to me, "These are the best years."

I did not know that it was all right if some of my interactions with the kids weren't terrific. I did not realize how intact each of their personalities already was, or I might have relaxed a little, realizing that I was a guide rather than a creator. I could not yet look at my children and say, "I'm doing a good job," because too much still hung in the balance.

I escaped to my non-mother self once a week, to take a course each semester towards a master's degree in counseling. There I discovered Studs Terkel's book <u>Working</u>. Instantly I wanted to do a book like it about mothers. I wanted to sit at the the kitchen tables of all kinds of mothers and listen as they answered the question, "What's it like for <u>you</u> being a mother?" I wanted to record all those answers, as Terkel had, and let those women speak for themselves, with a minimum of interference from me. I wanted to gather those thoughtful mothers together into a community that any mother could join by reading.

In this book I would ask other mothers what I really wanted to know, and they would speak as they really felt. "How-to" books never seemed helpful to me, but I thought that if I could hear other women telling their own stories, I could wind my own experience in and out of theirs. I could try on other mothers' lives and return to my own with new insight and a fresh perspective.

My husband and I did a few memorable things that worked very well. We did potty-training with M&M's. One for a pee. Two for a poop. "Choose the colors you want." Each of the boys gave and received a gift from his brother on each of their birthdays, so that as each was reveling in what he was going to get, he also was thinking about what he would give. We limited television time to six hours a week and let them choose what they watched.

I began to work part-time. Then, when the boys were seven and five, I went to work full-time. I found Jake's City Kitchen, a local restaurant, and every so often one boy or the other and I would go out to breakfast--just the two of us. "Order whatever you want." Nice, relaxed times over sausage, strawberry waffles, and broccoli eggs benedict. "Hash browns, too, a side order of hash browns, please." And the book idea persisted.

When I turned forty, the future no longer looked infinite. I began to feel that I had to make the book happen or stop thinking that I would ever take on a huge, personal project. I was very fortunate that my husband encouraged me to do the book and was willing for me to cut back to part-time work to do it. Without his support the book would not exist.

The mothers in the book appear under pseudonyms. These women were not hard to find. They are mostly women whom anyone might work with or follow through the grocery store check-out. The first ones responded to a sign I put up at an event in New Hampshire which was attended by about 900 women and a few men. The sign was reminiscent of bandit posters: "WANTED: MOTHERS ... to volunteer to be interviewed ...." There was a blue card to fill out and leave in a box if you were interested. I kept walking past the table to see if there were any cards in the box. I told myself I would be pleased with a dozen cards and would be delighted if I got fifteen. I left the hall with a fistful of blue cards. Twenty-five. Treasure in hand.

Over the course of the three years that I was interviewing, a few mothers heard of the project and boldly said, "I want to be in your book." Many others were suggested to me by someone who knew them. The woman who told me about Julia Cadeau said, "Oh, you must interview this woman in my church. She has eleven children, and she always looks as if she just stepped out of a band box."

I ran a "WANTED: MOTHERS" ad in the Boston Globe once. That turned up some people I was glad to find. Staff people in a county home, a prison, and two homeless shelters suggested the people in those institutions with whom I talked. I did a few road trips and one plane trip to the West and Southwest. I leaned on more than a few friends for contacts all along the way.

When I asked a woman if I could interview her, I frequently got one of two responses: "Yes, but I'm just a normal mother. I don't know what I'd say that you'd be interested in." Or, "Yes, but I'm not a _normal_ mother. You probably wouldn't want to talk to me." What is a "normal mother?" Every mother has a story to tell. Mothering is exquisitely personal.

I wanted mothers to talk about all stages of mothering. I chose to include little about pregnancy and birth. There are many books on those topics, and as one mother, Toni Barraza, said to me, "No one ever talks about what happens _after_ you have that baby. Once you take that baby home and that baby becomes a person, that's when the real stuff starts happening." Birth is a blink at the beginning of mothering time. An intense, awesome blink, but a blink, nonetheless.

Surely there are some kinds of mothers I have not included, but I hope that all mothers will still be able to identify with some of these stories. I talked to 143 mothers. As I did, I was impressed that mothers always seem to be looking for ways to be a better mother. I was also impressed that across different races, classes, and cultures many of the issues mothers face are the same. I hope I have not truly left anyone out.

Many of the interviews lasted two hours or more. After I had interviewed about fifty mothers, I sat with their stories, which I had by then transcribed, and the themes for the chapters emerged. I put later stories into the chapters where they seemed to belong. On only a few occasions did I go to a mother with the intention that her story would go in a particular chapter.

I almost always began the interview by saying something like, "Well, what's your situation as a mother? How many kids do you have? How old are they?" With a little encouragement, each mother made her own decisions about what it was important to talk about. In the beginning I chastised myself for not being more directive in my questioning, but I began to see that what I was doing allowed me to hear their agenda rather than a reflection of my own. One mother told me that "a kid takes eighteen years to do." So, I thought, maybe a book about "doing kids" could evolve out of a slow process as well.

I confess that I love having two teenagers, although it is painful at times being relegated to the sidelines of their lives. I love hearing their ideas, even when we argue about them. Sometimes they talk with me--and with their father--about things that he and I are still trying to figure out for ourselves. They are _interesting_ _people_. James's question, "Did you run today?" helps to keep me running. He's pleased when I set a new personal record, even though he can run almost twice as fast as I can. And how does it occur to Jess to say, teasing me, as I almost burn him with a cookie sheet right out of the oven, "Maybe you're not my real mother"? They are awesome. I love having them in my life. I wish now that I had three children.

I carry all these mothers with me now. They keep me tied into the big picture. They remind me to take nothing for granted.

Emily Moore, 1994

CECILIA SPECK
Age: 38

Cecilia is from Oklahoma. She has been unable to have a child.

I am waiting.

I feel maternal all the time. I find myself do, do, doing for others' children. I worry about the children I see in my physical therapy practice in a way that I might not if I had my own to worry about. It's very frustrating knowing that all this caring energy, all my creativity, is going out NOT to my own children.

A lot of wishful mothers just don't go to functions or places with a lot of children, like baptisms or malls. That doesn't bother me yet. It may never bother me. I'm trying not to make it such a big deal.

My whole life would be totally redirected if I had a child. Not just, "Who should I give this neat toy to?" but I think I would tackle every project with such gusto. When I tackle projects now I don't know really why I'm doing them. I feel guilty for doing a lot of things for myself, jogging or playing tennis. Am I doing it so I'll live longer? For whom? If we have a child, I would feel that I'm going to jog around the block, so that I will live longer for this child, or so I will be in a better mood for this child. I think if I had a child I would just be given a real purpose.

I would like to mold somebody permanently.

We have a wonderful life. We bought this big house thinking it would be full by now. That's the jinx. I think that we would be fabulous parents. We enjoy each other's company, but we would just love to be sharing that with a child. We have singing evenings. We invite musicians over, and we sing and play and have a great time, but I'm beyond that stage of wanting to entertain myself. We'd like children to be the recipient of these times. We have such a ball around here, but after everyone leaves, there's something missing.

1

Identity

When a woman becomes a mother, she is a changed person, forever.

One mother is tired all the time. One loves the slower pace at which babies and little children live; another is frustrated by it and is forever trying to hurry her children along. Mothers discover that they may be interrupted at any time of the day or night, repeatedly, for years. They find that the time they used to share with their partners now has to be split between their partners and their children. Some find that being "just a mother" feels right, like a homecoming. It leaves others feeling guilty or as if something were missing. For some having even a part-time job and a baby is very stressful.

Many are surprised by the personality of the baby. As one mother said, "It's such an adjustment. There's this full-blown personality--a third person--in the house." Another woman is in awe: she is "determining how the next generation will think."

Universally, new mothers seem to feel a tremendous sense of responsibility. With the arrival of a new baby, all of a mother's decisions--from when she goes to the bathroom to where she goes to work--must take this new child into account. For many years to come, it is as if the mother lives a double life.

In the midst of these changes, mothers always seem to be asking questions about how best to raise their children. In quieter voices, they ask questions about themselves, trying to clarify their identities. "Who am I?" "Who will I be in the future?" Sometimes mothers actually ask these questions of partners and friends. More often, the questions are unspoken.

They are buried in complex relationships, swept along by rushing schedules, cut off by interruptions, and shielded by vague apprehensions.

Identity questions can be teased out of the stories in this chapter: Do I have what it takes to be a good mother? How can I be the best mother I can be and also fulfill my own needs? Can I be as close to my son as I would be to a daughter? Am I someone separate, a person in my own right, or am I just a reflection of my children's needs? How am I supposed to know how to be a mother? Can I forego paid work, do all the mundane, care-taking tasks, and still be a thinking person? Without paid work to define me, who am I? How best can I still do my work and also be a mother? Do I have love and patience enough for a second child? How will I cope if that child is "a little monster"? How involved should I be in my children's lives?

Some mothers' questions are more particular to their situations. Between the lines, April Hurley, a teenage mother, asks, "Will it be harder for me to find a husband, since I already have a child? Should I settle for marriage to my baby's father, just so she will have a father?" Kathryne Lennox, a single mother, reflects that for years she tried to be both mother and father to her children. She was never sure how well she was doing. Marney Price, a mother with an unwanted third pregnancy, wonders, "Is it better to keep a baby I may not be able to provide for or to give him away to a couple who wants a child? Can I give up my child? Can I make that decision and go through with it? What will it do to me?"

Although the first child usually changes a woman most dramatically, additional children cause her to keep changing. A second child puts one child in each hand of a single parent. Somehow it is not as easy to just plug a second child into the flow of adult lives. Day-care is more expensive for two children. A mother with limited earning power may find that it costs her more to work than to stay home with her children. With the arrival of a third child, the children clearly outnumber the parents, and the parents must deal with a broader spectrum of children's needs. A fourth child means that instead of <u>four</u>

possible combinations of three children interacting, there are now <u>eleven</u> possible combinations.

With the addition of each child, a mother has to wade through more chaos to accomplish anything. More than one mother has found that when her children are small, there is little or no room for herself in her own life. Even if she feels this way, she is likely also to feel that this suspension of her own needs is "worth it" for the satisfaction she gets out of being a mother. In many of the stories in this chapter the mother eventually finds a way to establish an identity of her own, which is entirely separate from her children's needs and achievements.

As a woman's children get older, their lives expand. Each child's life is like a river that began as a little trickle high in the mountains. It is made wider and deeper, more rich and varied, as it draws from the worlds at its banks over a longer and longer distance.

The mother's life also expands. She quickly realizes that the changing demands of her children will constantly force her to reevaluate and adjust her part of the relationship with each of them. Like other relationships, a relationship with a child is not likely to be static.

It can be a surprise and a comfort for a mother to discover that to some degree her children will teach her how to parent them. They will give her a lot of cues. If she is inclined to listen, her children will let her know what they need, what she is giving them, and when she has gone too far or off the mark. Her children are one of the best, if not the best, sources of information about themselves. They are her teachers, as she is theirs.

She will also learn that a mother does not always know what is really going on with her children. Their lives are always partly hidden.

She may find she has less control over her children's lives than she would like. At times, she will have to make less than ideal choices for her children. Because of limits on time, money, energy, and personality, among other things, a mother may be unable to make the changes she would like to make in her children's lives. She may wish she could change herself, her

3

partner, the school, the courts, and the conditions of her children's lives in ways that are not possible.

She discovers that her experience with her own parents is inescapable. For better or worse, this frame of reference is present on conscious and unconscious levels. Not only can she not escape her childhood, but her children cannot escape it either. If her childhood is a good inheritance, her children are lucky. If she was treated fairly and felt loved, she will probably be fair and loving with her children. If her childhood was more problematic, an aware mother will try to transform its impact as she passes it on to her children. Depending on how she handles the issues to which her childhood gave her an extra sensitivity, her children can either benefit from or be burdened by her experiences as a child.

The cycle continues in the next generation. As her children live through her adult crises and triumphs, watching, questioning, and absorbing, each of them will make a treasure trove of certainties, a path into a secret garden, and a heap of unfinished business.

Each child increases the mother's vulnerability to pain, and ultimately, to death. Broken bones, rejections, failures--her children's pain hurts her also. And once she has a child, that child can be taken from her. She is also vulnerable to the way her children feel about her and to her desire to be loved and respected by them. She is more likely to discover and have to face her own faults. Children of all ages, and especially teenagers, have a way of finding their parents' faults and holding them up to view.

Each child can also increase the mother's joy, and, ultimately, give her a sense of immortality. As a child sees his mother's eyes light up for him, the mother feels that child drawing on her best self. She watches him put her delight-in-him in the center of the great mix of things out of which he is fashioning himself. She knows that her place is unique and lasting.

MICKIE WOOD
Age: 41

Mickie is eight months pregnant. She is a successful costume designer who has been married a year and a half. She had a miscarriage just before this pregnancy. Mickie's thoughts move quickly over the baby, herself, her husband, her career, and the world. How will this child change her?

This child is such a mystery at this point. That's part of the excitement. What crises do I have ahead of me? What do I have to share with my husband? What will the baby have to deal with in terms of us two parents?

Pregnancy is such a convenient packaging device. But it's getting cramped in there. I will always have to remember that the baby needs space. The child will keep needing more space for its own world. I might be possessive--the way my mother was with me.

There are these lovely movements. It's such an extraordinary feeling of seeing my belly ripple, totally out of my control--just as it's doing right now. I think of how much I'm going to miss that. I wonder if I'll ever feel it again.

I am excited about the birth. I am excited about the receiving of my child. For all of my concerns about launching this creature, I am very excited about the birth.

I weep all the time. I feel like this baby is so big it's just pushing tears out of me. So, some antennae are getting tuned up in me. I'm not aware of getting so provoked, so easily, in the past.

What a wonderful year and a half it's been being married to Martin! This is a transition--not that we wouldn't have had a transition anyway whether we had a child or not. I'm concerned that I might be losing some of what we've had. I think it's more likely that the marriage will just be bigger and better in a certain way.

I'll have two months off after the birth. How will I make the transition back to work? How will I still be able to breast-feed? How will I keep from feeling guilty about the baby or about the job? Will I be cheated, or will the baby be cheated in all this? Sometimes I just feel totally incompetent. I don't have any sense of how to do this! I have never changed a diaper in my life. I have looked at newborns. I have held one, maybe two. The list of what I haven't done . . . !

But I am surrounded by people whom I feel comfortable calling and who've given me a lot of advice and reassurance. Also, there's something very comforting about receiving garments worn by other children I have known. I feel very much as if I'm moving into a heritage of some kind. Babies can pass on to other babies these swaddling pieces. It's as if something is going to rub off on me and the baby, from the experience of someone else. The clothes are a bit magical, coming with some history to them.

I can't even anticipate what kinds of decisions I'll have to make in caring for the child. Some of it is very selfish. I allow myself too little time for myself. In a way I sense that this will be a time for me as well as the baby.

Most of what I'm anticipating is the surprise of it all. It's a true adventure.

There are larger world issues. By the year 2010, the population will have doubled from five billion to ten billion. I wonder what I'm doing presuming to bring another one into the world. This one will have some advantages that most of those other billions won't have, but there will be less room, less land, less air, less of everything.

Invariably the things I hope for, for my child, are things I wish had been more firmly developed in myself. A sense of comfort with himself or herself. I'd like to have him or her be able to honestly revel in his own beauty. I hope the child isn't too taken up with comparing himself to others. I like that the child will be brought up in the country, surrounded by cycles of life and people who live on the land. I hope this child can swing

6

between that world and other parts of the world, embracing as much as possible.

I'd like to know how my baby smells. I'd like to know what that head feels like right here under my nose.

APRIL HURLEY
Age: 18

"Everyone thinks that my future is over, but I'll still do what I want, what I plan."

April's daughter Alexandria is sixteen months old. They live with April's mother and five siblings, four of whom are younger than April. April notes, "I am the oldest girl." Her mother is a secretary in a factory.

When we met, April was taking summer school courses in accounting and chemistry. She is determined to make a future for herself and to be a "great mother" too. She is struggling in her relationship with Alexandria's father.

I had Alexandria when I was sixteen, which is very young, but I was very lucky, because I had a lot of support from my family. My mother was really great--different from what I expected. I kind of hid it until I was six months pregnant. When I finally told her, I felt so much better. I don't know why I was so terrified of telling her. I guess I felt she'd be disappointed.

I thought I was going to have to quit school, but everyone at school is really supportive. A lot of people, I feel, look down at me. They think that I won't succeed. This next year I'm going to be a senior. They're surprised that I'm going to college: "Oh, you're going to college!?" I'll be going to college to become a medical assistant. Everyone thinks that my future is over. But, I'll still do what I want, what I plan. It might just take a little longer. I want to be a working mother and still be a great mother, too.

I felt kind of like an outsider, having a daughter and going to school. My friends always were talking about their problems with guys, and I had the baby! One thing I was really afraid of

8

was losing my friends. I was afraid they wouldn't be able to relate to the situation I was in. But they still are with me. They say, "Oh, I want a baby." I say, "No." It's a lot harder than just the way they see it. They see her as just being really sweet. She is sweet, but I have her twenty-four hours a day. My friends don't see all the responsibilities you have to take on. It's been hard. Really I am like a single mother raising her.

I have George. He's my boyfriend, Alexandria's father, but he works all the time. I have all the responsibility. We've been going out for almost four years. We'll probably get married. I tell him I have a job, raising her. He thinks I just sit home all day and play with her. If he could just stay home with her for a week, he would see.

George doesn't understand. He'll come over late at night. I'm always so tired. "You were never like this before," he says. Now I'm tired at nine. I've been tired ever since I had her. I don't mind. I love her. I love watching her grow and learn different things. I play outside with her. We go for long walks.

It's just that George doesn't see that I have all these responsibilities. He doesn't understand how I feel. I feel so tied down and stressed out sometimes. But just seeing her and being with her and seeing how she grows really helps. It makes things seem not so bad. She's so sweet.

The college is an hour away. I'll move closer to the school. George doesn't like that. I tell him, "Well, you don't have to go with me. We'll come and visit." He's worried that I'll find somebody else. His mother understands how he is. She's kind of like on my side: "Stick to your guns." George wants to be married. He's almost twenty-one. But I think it would be harder. It would put more stress on us. Having a baby has really put stress on our relationship as it is. It's been real different. We haven't been getting along. He wants all the attention. I have to give it to her and him. I don't want to shut either one of them out, but it comes down that I put more attention on Alexandria.

Plus, if I'm single, my college will pay for my tuition and for day-care. I'll get reimbursed for driving back and forth to school. It's only a year-long program. Then I would look for a job in a hospital or a clinic. I plan to move out of this area. George works at the track, and he plans to work there forever.

I wish I hadn't grown up taking care of the kids so much when they were young and babies. I was like a little mother. Always cleaning and helping my mother. I don't feel like I had a lot of fun. I started going out with George when I was fourteen. I got too serious, too fast. That was too young. But I'm glad I had Alexandria. I wouldn't want to not have her.

I love Alexandria a lot, but I couldn't stay home and be a housewife or anything like that. I'm not going to let George get in the way of my dreams.

I had planned my life before I had Alexandria. I'm not going to let go of my dreams. I always wanted to go into the medical field. I'm going to pursue my plans and still raise Alexandria. I don't want a relationship with a guy. I hope I can be strong towards George. I can't imagine him changing. We don't have any common interests. We don't do anything together. I do things that he likes, but he won't try anything.

My biggest fear is I'm not going to have somebody else. There are not many guys that would want somebody that already has a baby. We're trying to work things out. I don't think I'll actually marry him if I still feel that he can't understand the responsibilities. We have to have common interests, or we'll just be living together and passing all the time and having two separate lives.

I'm afraid Alexandria won't have a father.

NIECY THOMPSON
Age: 30

"I just said, 'I've got to do this. I don't want my daughter to be adopted out.'"

Niecy is the mother of Shenise, who is almost five. When Shenise was born she tested positive for cocaine, and the hospital took her away from Niecy. Niecy got her back from the state about a year and a half ago. Slowly and powerfully Niecy has changed herself from being a prostitute and a drug addict to being the working mother of a child with special needs. Niecy is black.

I have had such a bad life, and now it's just like so good, and I'm so pleased. I went from the ground down to worst and now I'm okay. I feel real good.

I was in jail for about seven months. I got busted for prostitution.

I started sniffing first. After that I went to smoking. I never did shoot up. I hate needles. I can't stand needles. I was working the streets. These guys were selling out of my house and paying my rent and my bills and everything. It worked for a long time, and then on one particular day, I started to get into crystal. It's stuff you snort and it wires you.

At that time I had a gun. Oh, God. I had a 357, because a lot of people will try to come and rob dope-houses and stuff. I didn't even know how to shoot it. There was a snitch that had come and got some dope, right before the cops busted in. I don't remember this. I was coming down off some crystal and was out of it. The newspaper clipping says that a female that was laying on the couch lifted up with a gun in her hand. An officer shot me five times. I lived. I know that God has me here for something.

After I got that accident, I thought I was going to quit. That's when I got pregnant.

When I was getting high I wasn't even thinking that it was going to hurt my baby. I was getting high, not taking care of business. It was a mess. I knew it was wrong, but I was not even worrying about nothing. I started using at the end, at seven or eight months, you know?

When I went home about a day after the birth of my daughter, I didn't have a daughter. I had to lie, because I didn't want nobody to know my daughter was positive. When I came home everybody was asking me, "Where's your baby?" I told them I had a girl and her birth weight was real low, so she had to be in the hospital a couple days. By the end of two weeks, finally, I had to kinda come up with something else. I said, "My Mom has her. I'm not ready to be a mother right now." I know people probably didn't believe me. I had to lie. I didn't want them to know the reason my daughter was took.

I had my house all fixed up, so when the lady came from the State, she saw the nice clean house. I didn't have very much food, but I had some food in the cabinet. I heard they always go in your cabinets and look. She did do that. We talked. They set up a time for a hearing. I went to the hearing. At that time my daughter was in an emergency shelter. She stayed there for one week. Then she went to a foster mother.

For the first year, I didn't care. I didn't do anything they said. I wanted to continue getting high. They gave me a Reunification Plan. That consisted of I had to go to counseling, I had to go to parenting, I had to do drug testing two or three times a week. If you don't show up, it's considered a dirty test. During the time that I was supposed to be doing all those things in the Reunification Plan, I wasn't.

My Mom knew all this stuff was happening with the foster care where my daughter was. She said, "I'm tired of my granddaughter being from here to here. I'm going to take her myself." She ended up taking my daughter. She kept her for about a year and a half. Every time my daughter was too much for her, she used to call and cuss me out. All the time.

Finally what really did it is, I said, "I can do better than this. I don't want my daughter to be adopted out." I was living on the street. I was living in cars in a junkyard downtown. I didn't have no place to go. I had slept with this guy that I just met that I didn't even know. He had dropped me off at this store. I had these bags in my hands with my things. I kept saying, "This is not it. This is not it. This can't be me."

I called this recovery place to let them know I wanted to try and get clean. I stayed at that center for about six hours and went to a meeting. Someone there sent me to another place. I stayed for three days. Then, I went to a recovery home. I stayed a month and got kicked out, because I was messing around with a guy. I had registered into school for a computer class. (I got my G.E. D. when I was in jail.) I got a loan and a grant. You have to wait about two months, while you're going to school, to get the money. I went to the YWCA and slept in the basketball court on a mat and lived out of a locker.

I had put in an application for a place to live. When I got my money, I moved in. I stayed there a year. I was still going to meetings. I was in recovery. I met this guy, and I've been going with him ever since.

The State gave me six more months to try and get my daughter back. All my tests were clean. At the end of the court when they told me that I could have my baby back, the attorney for the baby came up to me, and she hugged me and told me, "It is rare that mothers get their kids back." I couldn't believe it. From Day One, she was totally against me.

The day I graduated from school I sent my resume to this agency that helps kids and families. They had sent a job announcement to the school. A whole month went by, and they didn't call me. I was crying, because I didn't have a job. Finally the lady called me: Could I come in for an interview? I was wearing this one dress every single day, looking for a job. My interview lasted for two hours. I got the job! It'll be three years next month that I've been here.

13

I have my daughter back. I was living in a one-bedroom. A few months ago I moved to a two-bedroom. I have my daughter back. She's been with me, like I said, almost two years. I have my own car. Never had a car in my life! I have a bank account. Only about twenty-five, thirty dollars in there, but I have a bank account! I don't do any drugs. I've been clean for three years. I don't drink or nothing. My boyfriend's been clean for five years. My Mom understands now. She knows I'm trying to make it. I pay my bills on time. It just feels so good.

My daughter is a special needs child. I think it's because of the cocaine. She'll be five in a few months, but she is kind of like acting on a three-year level. When I first got her back she was driving me crazy. I was wishing that she wasn't there, because I couldn't handle it. But now, it's getting better, because I talked to her teacher. I talk to her. I know how to handle her more. She's very impatient. If she can't do something, oh gosh, she starts screaming and hollering. Kicking her feet. Crying.

She just got potty trained a few months ago. That was driving me crazy, because I had to buy Pampers, and those things are expensive.

She didn't want to do anything. She won't color. I was going crazy. I was like, "You know what? I wish she wasn't here." She was getting on my nerves.

Now it's so much different. Now I know that she's a special needs kid. I'll go, "Shenise, take your time. Just take your time. You're going to do it." I try to play with her a lot. She doesn't want me to read a book to her. She might watch TV for less than five minutes. Her attention span is so short. If she were here, she'd be all over this room. We couldn't even talk. She's getting a little bit better now, and I'm understanding her. And I guess she had to get used to me, too.

I talked to my boss about me starting a little service to type stuff for college kids. I need the extra money. He said I could do that. Do the work here and I'd buy my own paper. I barely can make it from one pay-day to the next. I pay all my bills, and I might have twenty or thirty more. My car takes twenty-eight to fill up. I want extra money, but I want it the legal way. I couldn't afford to have a second job, because there's no one to take care of my daughter.

I don't know. I've had a hell of a life. Now I am so happy. I went through a guilt thing about I shouldn't have been smoking no dope having my daughter. Then I thought, "Well, you know what? What's done is done." I'm living day to day. Not in the past. The present. I messed up when I did it, but it's over. What else can I do?

I'm only a step away from a drug. I go to meetings. I don't have that many friends, because they're all into drugs. I don't want that type of friends. I don't go to clubs, and I don't go out partying. My boyfriend and I talk a lot. My thing is I go play bingo, and I talk on the phone.

Shenise is a difficult kid. She's a handful, but at times she's all right. We talk a little bit. At first she wouldn't even talk. She'd just point at everything. I'd get so pissed: "What are you pointing at?" Now she'll tell me what she needs.

Oh, yes! It's a big, big change.

SWAN LEE
Age: 34

"I am starting a new line. I am going to turn out to be this matriarch. From now on the history will be known."

Swan Lee was adopted as a baby from China and raised by a white American family. She is married now to a white man. Her son Victor Ping is seven; her daughter, Samantha Siu-Ming, three. Swan Lee teaches English composition part-time and does medical transciptions at home. She feels she has family now, for the first time.

There is such an emphasis on ancestry in Chinese culture. You honor the dead on special holidays. You keep little shrines in your house. People have different titles. It's a complex web, but I don't have any of that. Mine was just cut-off. I found out that my birth-mother was also an orphan. There is no telling whether it was during the communist take-over. Were her parents murdered? Did she run away from her village? So, even she didn't have that traditional ancestral background and didn't know where she belonged.

There are legends about dead people being hungry ghosts waiting at the crossroads--always wanting to be appeased. She must have felt like she was always a wandering ghost--for whatever reason. When she got pregnant with me I'm sure there was nobody she could turn to. No help, no money, and giving me up was really the only thing she could do. I feel that, finally, now, in my generation, with my daughter, there is a mother-daughter line in the family. I am starting a new line. I am going to turn out to be this matriarch. From now on the history will be known.

I think it took a lot of courage for my mother to break that pattern of the broken chain, to go through the pregnancy, carry me to term, see that I was placed with a home where I would have some opportunity. I think of us as the missing leaves. Somewhere we do have a family. What happened to the daughter who ran away? There is really no knowing. It is such a mystery.

Now, in China, it is happening more and more, because they are limiting the families more and more to one kid. They want the boys. They are giving away the girls like crazy. So it is like the second wave of what was happening when I was a baby. There are all these unwanted baby girls that are being adopted.

It's funny how a single thing like not knowing your origins can torment you. I am lucky that I even have a Chinese name. It is one of the few things that I have from my beginnings. A lot of adopted people end up with no name. They either were never given one, or they are robbed of their original birth name. There is a lot in that name. It meant that there was somebody who cared enough to think up a name. It's a funny feeling to grow up with a name like "Jessica Smith" and have it not fit your face. My American name never felt right. I actually have a copy of my birth certificate in the Hong Kong registry. I was lucky.

I keep thinking, "I've outgrown all that adoption stuff. I'm a mother now." But it pops up. Just by being a mother, I am constantly reminded of my own past. When Samantha was three months, I thought, "This is how old I was." Actually, I found out later I was only seven weeks old when my mother placed me with a foster mother through an agency. She was supposed to keep in touch and pay for my upkeep. The minute I was placed with this other mother, she just disappeared.

In a way, being a mother is very healing, because I can rewrite history with my kids. I can feel that they are going to have security from my mothering even if I didn't have it. But it is painful sometimes, because I am still mothering myself as I go along.

My kids give me a link to the human race. When you have no resemblance to anybody you know, you seriously wonder if you're human. I can't say that I "take after" someone else.

Grandma or Aunt Suzie. It's an odd feeling. Like being a puzzle piece that doesn't quite fit into the rest of the puzzle.

My earliest memories go back to living in Vermont, where I was the only non-white person in the whole town. Boy, did I feel like an alien. Whenever I went out in public, I was so hyper-self-conscious. I always felt like a freak. I got the strangest looks.

I hated being Chinese. I didn't want to have anything to do with it. There was always this feeling of trying to take off this face, because it's the wrong face.

My father even admitted to me not too long ago that he wanted to make a racial statement. To him, to actually open his home to someone of another race meant a lot. It was okay for him to proudly say, "This is my daughter," but I was sort of the experiment.

I was malnourished and in really bad shape when I came. Way behind in my development. The social workers warned my parents, "She may never be normal. Be prepared." Within a year I had grown six inches, started walking . . . I blossomed under their attention. A lot of things were available to me. I was able to take music lessons. That has been one of my passions. I am eternally grateful. But if they had maybe lived in a city where there was more ethnic diversity. I don't know.

When I am around the Chinese community I feel like I don't fit in there either. It's such a difference being raised American. The Chinese upbringing and values are different. I don't have any of that internal Chinese identity or knowledge of the culture and habits. A Chinese family made fun of me for not knowing how to hold chopsticks, not knowing any Chinese. That was almost as painful as being made fun of for the other.

With our kids, they're going to grow up a little out of sync too, because they do look fairly Asian, although my husband isn't Asian. The difference is that they do have me as a mother, so that they can at least feel like they look like somebody in their family.

I have family now. It was thrilling when Victor was born to see someone who resembled me. Who had my shape of hands, whatever. That has meant a lot. Victor loves to read and I was

18

just crazy about reading. I would get obsessed with a topic and would fall in love with characters in books. They seemed really real to me. He is like that. Samantha loves music. A car radio passing by, she'll just start dancing. That's exciting.

We're part of an Asian-American community and the neighborhood where we live is very diverse. Victor goes to school and fits right in. Sometimes we look at the smaller towns and are tempted to get out of the city. The fresh air, the peace and quiet, letting the kids run free, not having to be in big crowds, but I don't want to repeat what I went through--that feeling of being a bug under glass.

I often ran to my father, and a lot of times he would protect me. That total unconditional love that he gave me is, I think, what got me through as normal as I was, and able to, at least, have a happy marriage later on.

My mother was very much of a martyr and let us walk all over her. She was very resentful. Passive aggressive. I do spend an enormous amount of time, every day even, in every situation, saying things like, "I'm not going to do what my mother did." She cooked beautiful meals and birthday cakes, and she is really the glue that holds the family together, but . . .

I am really completely rewriting being a mother.

MARNEY PRICE
Age: 30

"I try to listen to my heart and make the decision and then stick with it."

Marney is an illustrator and sculptor. When she and I talked the first time, she was a married mother of two small girls. Nina was two and a half, and Constance was six months old. Marney talked about her philosophy of raising children; the threat of violence in herself; and her identity as Marney, separate from her identity as a mother.

When we talked a year and a half later Marney was separated from her husband and was seven months pregnant by another man. She talked candidly about her failed attempts to abort the child, and about how she had decided instead to have the baby and to give him up for adoption.

The last time we talked was five days after the baby was born.

Marney is speaking as the married mother of two small girls:

I'm mostly a mother. That's hard for me . . . I feel so guilty being a mother. You're not doing all your other things. Even when I'm with Nina, there is this voice: "You should be doing something." Sometimes I have to force that thought away and say, "No, right now I'm supposed to be a mother. It's okay to just sit here with my children."

The hardest thing for me is to be honest about my feelings and reactions. A lot of times I feel vulnerable in front of my children. With Nina, I might say, "I'm really sorry I wasn't paying attention." I have to be inferior to her in a way to say that. That's hard, because you're giving them a power over you. So many people are pretending to be something that a child should respect, without earning that respect.

I go crazy trying to figure out right from wrong in every little interaction. You can't. Sometimes Nina will say, "Why?" and I say, "Because it's a decision that I've made." That's the only answer I've got sometimes. There are so many variables. Should I let her do this now? If I don't, is it going to harm her character? I try to listen to my heart, make a decision and stick to it. When I make the decision with Nina now that she can't do something, and she starts to fight me, all these thoughts come in: "Gee, maybe I made the wrong decision." I say to her, "I've made this decision, and you can have a fit if you want, but I've made the decision." It frees me. It might be wrong in certain respects, but that's all I have. Sometimes it's pretty good, and sometimes it's not so good, but it's never that bad.

My mother was divorced when I was five and went through four husbands, one of whom was a bondsman and used to attract a lot of violence to our house. My father went through three wives. A lot of things in my childhood confused me so much that I felt that I didn't really have a set of morals or values by the time I was an adult. The decision to be married is a decision. You're going to meet defects in everyone. So many people don't accept that reality and say, "I deserve better." What do you mean? Whatever's out there is what you're going to get. You're just trading.

I watched my mother trade man after man. She never got better. She just traded. I watched my father trade. They'd get to a point in the marriage, and they'd give up. Now my mother is detached. She's lost something from trading.

When you're in the middle of it, it always looks different. When you step back, you see, and then you have some humility about your life: why couldn't I develop understanding, instead of--pride? Divorce is programmed in my head: "Leave. Divorce." And leave a child. It was horrible. It was devastating for us.

I'm afraid of the violence that comes up in me in being a mother. I think everybody has violence that comes up in them

21

when they're pressed to a certain point. People have different ways of dealing with it. When I get to the point where I feel there are too many demands on me, I just want to lash out and say, "I can't do this!" I get feeling crazy. To just sit in that and feel it and not act on it is so painful. But because I don't want to hit the kids, I either do sit and feel it, and it passes; or else I will pick Nina up and put her in the crib and say, "I'm feeling shaky right now. Give me some space."

My babysitter will say, "I love children." That's not the point. Children are easy to love. What are you going to do when you hate them? That's the real question.

I've seen my mother glaze over. That's her way of sedating the violence. She leaves her body emotionally. To actually feel it and not sedate it or act on it . . . I don't know what it does to your soul, but it's like you're going through a hurricane for a second. For some reason I think that's good to do. At least you're not pushing it away. You're experiencing it. It's as if you're burning it out. If you do it enough times, and face it and remember it, you're going to be more in control the next time.

If a woman's been herself long enough, then she can think about having a child. I did enough things as Marney, and had enough experiences as Marney. I'm not Marney anymore. I'm Mom. I don't think you can really be yourself again until your children are in their teens. Then you reexperience being in control of your life. I haven't felt a separate identity since Nina was born two years ago. That is a loss that I mourn sometimes.

The only time I feel I am Marney is when I am so involved in a piece of art work that nothing else is there but that. I've always felt that when I'm doing my work. That's why I love it. There's only a very thin margin of the brass's ability to take heat without melting, so it's a challenge every time. I <u>have</u> to focus. I lose everything else in that challenge. Everything else is gone. So much of life is distractions. Daily life is not that exciting. It's necessary, and you get a lot of pleasure out of it, but it's nice to be lost in something.

With the children at these ages it's not so much that you don't have free time, it's that you're so vulnerable to being interrupted during that time. So you never feel free. Yes, I can be Marney, but I am never <u>just</u> Marney--and at any moment I might not be Marney.

I think I'll have another child in about five years. I think I'll crave another baby by that time. It's a form of immortality, being a mother. The most important thing about being a mother is you are creating the next generation. You're deciding how the next generation is going to think.

A year and a half later:

Life does not come out like you expect it to. Sam and I separated a couple of months after you and I talked. Constance, who's now two, only had a father for a few months. She doesn't really know the concept of "Daddy." She calls other men "Daddy." Nina is four. She seems to be more affected by the lack of him in the household. I'm worried about what that's going to do to her in the future, to her relationships.

Nick called me in January, out of the blue. I had been in love with him in eighth grade. It was a, "Oh, my true love has found me again" kind of thing. I went to see him in Canada, and I got pregnant right away. Accidental. I wasn't protecting myself.

Right away I thought I would have an abortion. There was just no question. I still wasn't even sure Sam and I were going to get a divorce. I didn't want, by being pregnant, to eliminate the chance that we'd get back together. He didn't want to go for counseling with me, though, and I didn't want to go back with him without it, because he had beat me up twice really bad.

He tried to kill me the second time. He kept telling me that he wanted to kill me. He was choking me. If my father hadn't heard us and pulled him off me, I don't know what would have happened. It was very, very scary.

He just totally disappointed all of us. I feel like everything I believe in has been shattered. I'm trying not to have that man-hate thing. I want to be alone for a while and work out some things, so I'll have a better view to look for in a mate. The key is I have to believe that I deserve someone good.

My mother said to me once, "You're just like me, you like the bad guys. The good guys are always boring." That stuck in my mind. It was a way of pleasing my mother to like the bad boys. I just assumed that that was true from the time she said it. It's not true.

I told Nick that I was going to have an abortion, and he said he didn't want that: "I love you so much. I've been wanting a child for two years." I said, "Okay, but you have to decide for sure if you want me to keep it." I was two and a half months along. I almost aborted Constance because of the problems with Sam. I <u>love</u> Constance, and I would love this baby. I was starting to get attached to the idea of this baby. Nick didn't want to get married, but he wanted us to be a family. I was totally infatuated with him.

I went to see him a few weeks later. I said, "Nick, I'm in <u>no</u> position to have a baby right now if we can't take this as a total commitment thing." He was freaking out.

When I got home I just knew I had to have an abortion. I had the money. I had someone to take my kids for two days. I just assumed Dad would give me a ride. When I told him the day was "tomorrow," he said, "I can't give you a ride tomorrow." He could have done it, but he wouldn't. I needed somebody to wait five hours with me. Nobody would.

Nick finally called in a panic, "You have to have an abortion!" I said, "You come here, you pay for it, give me a ride. Do it next week. We're going into the fourth month here."

So, he came. According to my period the abortion at this point would cost nine-fifty. They said to bring a couple extra hundred dollars in case. So I brought eleven-fifty. Nick didn't have a cent on him. He didn't even have enough money to get back to Canada. He's a schmuck. I didn't want to believe that I was so wrong.

He came with me to Boston. I am sitting there half-naked on the table, looking at the vacuum in front of me. I had to read about how they do it. It's with sort of like an eggbeater. They chop it up first. It's very dangerous. It's very murderous. It's very real. And then they suck it out. It's horrible.

They did an ultrasound. It's totally real then. I was maybe four and a half months pregnant. The baby weighed about a pound, I guess. I saw the head.

They said, "Oh, you're much more pregnant than you think you are. You'll have to pay us six-fifty more." I had already paid them nine-fifty.

"But I don't <u>have</u> six-fifty!" I was in tears. "This thing is rigged to get more money!" It was horrible. I went running out crying and got my money back.

I realized I was going to have this baby. I didn't have a choice.

I was suicidal for about a week. It seemed it would be better to kill myself than to deal with it. Depression. I was alone.

All these dreams were gone. I was left thinking about the reality of life with an infant and two other young children, no father. The idea of Sam picking up Nina and Constance and this little boy saying, "Where's my Daddy? Why can't I go with them?" He would be so shattered, even if Sam were a good enough guy to take him. I would resent the baby too, connecting him with Nick.

I felt, "I have to give this child away. I have to find someone who will love him." He will make somebody very happy. It will be devastating for me, but it will still be better. It kills me.

I was talking to my sister-in-law, who knows a couple who want to adopt. The woman, Sandra, has no uterus. I contacted her. She is extremely personal with me, instead of treating it like a business transaction. I like that. We're alike in a lot of ways.

It's killing me to do this. I'm trying to accept what it's really going to be like, so that I'm prepared. Visualizing the baby and giving it to her, and knowing all its life and all my life from now on, I'm going to think about it. It's so hard. It's <u>so</u> hard. And Nina and Constance, it's their brother.

What's weird is that I care more about this baby for Sandra than I did for me. I was transferring a lot of my anger at Nick to the baby. "Screw it, I'm going to smoke and drink as much as I want. I don't care. If he doesn't care, I don't care." I wanted to kill it. Now this woman and her husband are <u>so</u> happy. She cries on the phone almost every time, "You have no idea what this is going to do, and how much we're going to love the baby." She knows I need to hear that over and over again. I'm doing it for her.

It will be a California adoption. It's only a six-month period when you can retrieve your baby. Can you imagine? They have to live for six months thinking that I might show up any day to get the baby back. Actually, even Nick could show up and claim the baby.

I told Nina that Sandra can't have a baby. She needs someone to have a baby for her. The baby needs a Mummy and a Daddy. She understands to some degree, but she thinks it's sad.

I don't know what my future is going to be like, and it might not be as bad as I think. I certainly could survive, but it would be a boy without a father.

I - still - would - love - to - keep - it. But, the baby stands a better chance of having a whole self by having a mother and father who desperately want a baby. They've got money. They've got a life. Just right now my life is a mess. I'm going to have to be out of here. The bank is foreclosing on the house. I don't know how I'm going to live. I have to go back to work full-time.

That's another thing. My other two children are old enough--I've spent enough time with them every day--but to put an infant in day-care five days a week, so that I can afford to have him--that's no way to come into the world. It wouldn't be enough. He probably would argue when he's eighteen, "It would have been enough." But he'll have a better life. His mother-to-be, his other mother, will be staying home with him for at least two years.

The hardest thing is that I already have kids, and I have to explain it to them. It's like a gift situation. It makes Nina question whether I'm going to give her up. It makes her wonder what money has to do with it. I don't want to put it into her mind either that men are terrible or that women can't live without them.

I couldn't even back out now. I've set it up so that I can't. I don't want to devastate her. And to change my mind to Nina and all of my family? I'm going to probably experience feelings and decisions in my heart like, "<u>No</u>, I can't do this after all," but I'm going to <u>ignore</u> them. It's going to break my heart. That's why I'm trying to visualize it now, every night. I light a candle, and I pray, and I think about it, and my body is just wracked with tears. A little baby boy. I think about how much I love Nina and Constance, and how real they are. This baby is a part of me. It's my baby, and I'm giving him up.... I'll get over it.

I told my mother last night that I was giving the baby up. Typical of her she said, "Oh, good. You've made a decision." That's her way. She's a distancer. I drew in my breath, and thought, "Say something to me." I didn't say anything. Sometimes I can make her come around if I don't react in anger, like, "How could you say that?" I didn't know what to say. I just stood there on the phone. Silent.

She said, "Well, okay" in a voice that I hate.

"You're saying 'Goodbye'?!"

"Oh well, I'm going to go to bed soon."

"Mom. . ."

"Are you irritated with me?"

"No, you just seemed a little distant, and I'm in a lot of pain right now. I'm sorry about this. I'm giving away your grandson."

"Oh, Marney. . ." and she started to cry. I started to cry. At least it was a release. She said, "It feels like a death."

"Yeah, that's what it's like."

I do not want to be intrusive in any way. I do not want to be a constant reminder that their life is not just their life. Sandra was saying I could do whatever I wanted, including having my family visit. I've been wondering if I want to stay in touch. I was thinking maybe a Christmas card with a picture every year. Just to see.

The first thing I usually think about when I light the candles is, "Please forgive me for abandoning you." No matter how you look at it, that's how a child will feel. Why didn't we love him enough to do whatever it was to make it work?

27

Five days after the baby was born:

I think that's the nicest thing I've ever done for anybody in my whole life.

I have absolutely no regrets at all. If I had had the abortion, that would have been a regret for my whole life, because that was totally a real baby to me.

It has been an emotional roller-coaster. It's slowing down now. I thought I was going to face unbearable depression. But I feel so close to these people, and Nina feels good about the baby being with them. They were there to hold him fifteen minutes after he was born. I had to feel secure. I had to see her bonding with that baby.

I told Sandra she can brag about him to me any time.

I gave them that baby. That's their baby. I think they love him more than I did.

It felt like there were angels flying around.

SARAH GOLD
Age: 37

"I don't feel like his mother. I know I'm his mother. I can say the word 'mother,' but what does that mean? I haven't been there to mother him."

Sarah has spent most of the last eleven years in prison for forging checks to support a heroin habit. She is the mother of a ten-year-old boy, Sam, whom her sister has raised, and a nine-year-old girl, whom Sarah gave up for adoption at birth. Sarah will come up for parole in nine months. Her mother is Susan Gold. Her story appears after Sarah's. The Golds are Jewish.

Most of my son's life I have been in and out of prison. When I was arrested with my first prison bit I was six weeks pregnant with him. I went through the whole pregnancy in prison. I was taken to the hospital for three days, and, then, back to the prison. Sam's father's sister came to the hospital and got Sam.

I let my parents know when Sam was born. I sent pictures. They sent them back. It was embarrassing for them. I come from an upper-middle class family and appearances mean a lot to them. I was a big disappointment.

When I got out of prison, I took Sam with me. I started doing the drugs again. I was going city to city, town to town. I couldn't take care of him. I am just now starting to understand a little bit of who I am and what my problems are and what I need to overcome. I was in no way ready to be a mother. I had no idea what a mother <u>was</u>. I was terrified. I couldn't take care of myself, and, then, I had this little person to take care of. There was a part of me when I got pregnant that thought, "I'll have a

29

baby, and then everything will be all right. I won't shoot any more drugs. I'll get stable."

I was in a very addicted, dependent relationship with a man. I had to go out and make the money and make sure that there were drugs, and I had to make sure there was food, clothing, and all kinds of stuff for my son. I remember I would pride myself on the fact that before I would cop any drugs, he was always fed and clean. "At least I have him with me," I'd think. It was so distorted. What's the great sense of having a baby in the car with you when you go from city to city every day, and you're cashing checks? I was sick.

I got arrested again when Sam was about a year old. It was awful. And I was pregnant again. Another horror story. I went to have an abortion. I got all the way to the examining room, and the doctor said, "I can't do it. You're too far along."

Sam was with his father's family, and I was at my wit's end, because I didn't want another baby. I felt like I really never should have had a baby. I didn't know myself well enough. I was screwed up. I was in an awful relationship, and I didn't care what happened to me. I just couldn't give birth to another baby. I could not do it.

They took me to the hospital for an exam. At that time they didn't cuff you, and they left you alone in the examining room. I jumped out of the window in the hospital, first floor window. Seven and a half months pregnant. I took off. I got my son and took him with me and the father again.

When I went into labor I had no idea what I was going to do. It's so bizarre now to think of all this. It's like it's a different person. I don't know what I was thinking. I went into the hospital. I was strung out. I was afraid I was going to get busted, because I had the escape. I saw this little baby girl. I thought, "I can't take her. What am I going to do with her?" I was scared to death. What was I going to do? The next morning I went to look at her in the nursery, and I kept right on walking. That was it. I left.

I had the father call the hospital the next day. He said he would come get the baby when she was ready to go. In the meantime, I got arrested. I got arrested in front of my son, who was a little over a year old. It was awful. There he was in the projects, watching me be taken off. It was terrible.

At first the state had the baby in foster care. Then there was a professional couple that were unable to have children. They were a racially-mixed couple, and this was a racially-mixed baby. Both of my children, the father is black. It just seemed the best thing to give her up.

I spent about two and a half years in prison. When I was ready to come out, I thought that I was done with drugs. I thought, "I can't be around this man. I'm going to go home. This time when I get back to my parents' house, I'm going to have my son with me, and my parents are going to have to accept it." Sam was still with his father's sister. My parents started to see him before I came home. They just fell in love with him, and they moved him right in. Here it starts, supposedly the happy family. Only it wasn't like that.

I was back in my mother's house, in a living situation that didn't work well since I was a kid. The same kinds of problems were there only magnified. Here I was older. I didn't know how to deal with living in their house. They didn't know how to deal with me living in their house all over again. Then on top of it was the paranoia about the drugs and what kind of people I was seeing. Here I am with a three-year-old son. I didn't know how to take care of him. I just didn't know what to do. I didn't know when to say, "That's right," "That's wrong." I just had not the slightest idea.

I equated being a mother with my childhood, and I have nothing but a lot of painful memories about my mother and me. I didn't want to make the same mistakes that I felt she made with me. I didn't want to become the same kind of mother. I didn't know. I didn't know. I was very insecure. He was very testy with me, of course. I didn't even know what to do when he took a tantrum about what color shorts to put on. I had absolutely no idea. We'd get up in the morning, and I'd say, "What do you want to wear?" He'd throw everything on the floor and say, "I'm not wearing any of it." I would let him do anything he did, because I just didn't know. I didn't want to make the wrong decision. I couldn't do it.

31

Then, on top of it, no matter what decision I made, my mother would come right through and say, in front of him, "Oh no, Sarah, you don't do that. This is what you do." It was awful. Then I would just scream at her, "Well, then, you do it anyway. What are you letting me make any decisions for?" It was awful.

One time he, and I, and my sister were in the toy aisle in the grocery store.

"Mom, can I have something?"

"Sure, pick one thing."

"I want two things."

"No, we'll get one thing."

He took a tantrum in this store with all these little old ladies looking on. I know they were thinking, "What did that mother do to her child?" He was down on the floor, hysterical. I didn't know what to do. I said, "Okay, now you won't get anything. We're leaving." I tried to pick him up. He tried to beat me up. He was three years old. He ripped off my necklace. He was screaming, yelling, punching me. It was like my sister was separating two grown people from fighting. This kid was that angry. Of course. He wasn't going to take "no" from me. I had just come home. I'm sure he felt: Who is she anyway? After that I felt, "I don't know how to take care of him. I don't know what to do. What am I going to do? Forget it, take him. I can't. He'll never listen to me."

Before I knew it, I was off again shooting dope and back with the guy. This is always the pattern. The last twelve years I've kind of watched my son grow up from prison bit to prison bit. In between I've seen him for a month or two and then ended up off and running again. It's been painful. It's been painful for him. It's been painful for me.

I think it's more painful now because I'm really getting well. I feel things that I didn't feel before. I don't know my son. I see him. He visits. I talk to him on the phone. I can't explain it. It's like this little kid I know, but it's not like I know him. It's not easy. It's not easy at all.

I'm very honest with Sam. He knows about the drugs. He knows everything I've been through. He has always come to visit me. He's a good kid. He is bright and very sure of himself.

He has a lot of characteristics that I'm glad he has. I did not have these things. But he has a lot of anger too.

He's living in a very suburban, upper-middle class, white household with my sister and her family. He has no connection with his blackness, with his father's side of the family. I think he has lots of troubles. I think he's got a lot of stuff that he doesn't necessarily let out. Every now and then when we talk on the phone if he's had a bad day, or if he's angry at my sister, he'll just kind of lose it and say, "Oh, Mom, I can't stand it, I don't belong here. When are you coming home? I just want you to come home and be with me."

The reality is I don't think I can just go home and be with him. At least not that easily. I don't know if that's good for him, or if that's what I would be able to do. I am the healthiest that I've been in a long, long time, and I'm making gains, but I have a long, long way to go.

I wrote a play, and we put it on here in the prison. It's based on a family, a mother and a son, that I knew in Harlem. I know how these kids grow up. You see a fifteen-year-old kid that's accused of murder, and you wonder, "What kind of animal is he?," but few people know what kind of household the kid came from. I'm very thankful Sam is where he is.

I have never had to worry about the state taking Sam, or if someone was going to adopt him, if I would ever see him again, if he was being abused. I've had contact with him. I have at least been able to know how he is and what he's doing. It's been some kind of on-going communication even when I haven't been there. And he's had a stable home with my sister.

I hope he <u>never</u> has to go through the hell that I've been through. I hope he never has to grapple with drugs. I hope that he can find some kind of peace in his life. Peace within himself. If I had had some kind of peace within me maybe none of this would have happened. I don't want him to ever have to walk into a prison and be locked in a cell. I don't want him to have to go through being addicted to some substance. I would like him to just kind of know who he is and where he wants to go and to try the best he can to get there.

I don't even know why I got up in the morning half the time when I was a kid. I can remember at my son's age I was a mess. When I look at him and talk to him, I realize how much more he has inside at his age than I ever did.

I think I was a real sensitive kid, and somehow in my family I got messages that I was not okay. I had a very domineering mother and a very passive father. If it wasn't done their way, it wasn't done the right way. My thoughts and my feelings and my ideas really were not valid. I was afraid. I was afraid of everything at a very young age. I started with addictive stuff early. Not drugs. Food. Then, relationships. Then, drugs.

Earlier this year some kids asked Sam, "How come you're with your aunt and uncle? Where's your mother and father?" Sam told them, "My parents were killed in a car accident." I guess he kept it inside for about a week. Then he was acting off the wall, and he finally broke down and told my sister what he'd said. I guess he felt really badly about it, but he said that he didn't know what to tell them. I'm sure he's humiliated and embarrassed and ashamed. He's got an ass for a mother and an addict for a father. But I think he doesn't feel free to talk about any of this. I worry about him. I think that he just does not feel that he belongs anywhere.

I think Sam's afraid. I don't think he believes that I'll ever just be there with him on a daily basis. He probably had his hopes, but so many times before it's been here I come and there I go. I think in the back of his mind it's this wonderful thing that could happen but that probably never will.

I have a tremendous amount of guilt. I don't let myself get too close to it. It's like I'm afraid to let myself feel. There's a lot inside that I don't know how to get to yet. I stuffed everything for so long and then covered it with shooting dope all day. But my feelings come through in other ways, like when I write. I'll get caught off guard, and all of a sudden I'll be crying.

With my daughter, I know giving her up was the only thing to do. It was the wisest thing to do for her. There are a lot of days that go by that I think about her. I listen to the pain in my son's voice sometimes, and I think of all the years apart from him, and I see the problems he has, and I say, "If it wasn't for what I put him through, he wouldn't have these problems." I don't have to think that my daughter's thinking the same thing about me somewhere.

The strange thing is that she was, at least when she was adopted, in the same city as my son. Wouldn't it be strange if they were just in the same school a grade apart? Or if they were among the same group of friends? That's his real sister. That's real important to me. No one seems to agree with me, but I just think he has so little he can hold onto that's his own, and here is his real sister. I want them to know each other. They were in the same little town. They could walk up the street and walk by each other and something could click. I don't even know, though, if she's still there. I really don't know anything at all. I don't even know her name.

I wonder, "What does she look like? Is she okay? Is she healthy?" She was born addicted to drugs. I was pissed that I was pregnant. I was doing a lot of cocaine at the time, and heroin. I didn't stop. I was shooting coke the night I went into labor. She was very tiny, under five pounds. It was a horror. I left her crying in the incubator.

It's not easy for me to talk about it. It's not easy for me to face. I am ashamed of a lot of things I've done. I can't take them back. When I think of myself now a lot of times I think of myself just as being bad.

But this last twenty-one months in prison has been probably the most important twenty-one months of my life. It's like there's a Sarah now, someone, a real person, who does have ideas and can speak them and act on them sometimes. Even through all the stuff I go through there is <u>Sarah</u> now.

I want to go back to school when I get out. I want to continue in some way with my writing or the theatre, the creative side of me. I would like to work in some way with kids who see little hope, who're coming out of the kind of houses that I lived in, where their mothers are using and their fathers are using and that's all they know.

I always see the kids, their faces and their eyes, their kind of disbelief that they're living. At my worst I was always running out with extra money to buy shoes for someone or popsicles or breakfast. Whatever I could. Even though I was part of this, I couldn't stand to watch it. They have no choice. They're babies. It's what their world is going to be.

It's a way of me paying back. I can't redo any of Sam's last ten years, but I can do something about maybe someone else. I hope so. I really do.

With my son, I would like to see us know each other. I don't know what a real mother-son relationship is. I don't know what it is to say I want to be a "real mother" to him. I think if we can connect and just stay connected, we can maybe give each other something.

I'd like for him to be proud of me. I'd like for him to someday be able to say, "I'm very proud of my mother." He says, "I love you" now, but, you know, "I love you" is something that you can just get used to saying, and it has no meaning. But to say, "I'm proud of my mother." I think that would do it.

SUSAN GOLD
Age: 64

"I can't tell you the nightmare this produced in this house. I can't tell you what it did to me and to my husband. And to my other daughter. This whole thing. This whole growing up process with Sarah almost destroyed all of us."

More than a year after I talked with Sarah Gold in a state prison, I interviewed her mother, Susan. How did Sarah end up as a heroin addict when she started out in a middle-class family who would do anything for her? Sarah's sister Jane lives in the suburbs, has a master's degree, is the married mother of two children, and has raised Sarah's child since he was six.

I found Susan to be a petite, elegant, delightful woman with no answers.

Sarah broke everybody's heart. My mother never pulled anything that made it harder for me. She never carried on, "What has she done to us? What has she done to you?" She never did that. It was always, "Well, we just have to hope things will work out." It was killing her, but she never made it harder for me. I had a wonderful mother. She was a real savvy lady.

Sarah was in jail. I went to see her, and she told me she was pregnant. I was very careful in what I said to her. I didn't give anything about the fact that she would be a single parent, or the fact that the father was black. I tried to get to her by saying, "Having a child is a commitment. You are not in a position to raise and nurture that child. If you can't take care of a child, you have no right to have that child." I worked on that tack. She said, "Well, I'll have to speak to Eli, because, after all, it's his child too." Eli was also a drug addict. Sarah had told me before this that she was a drug addict.

37

I thought that Sarah should have an abortion. Here she is in jail, facing a long sentence. This is just total irresponsibility! She promised me she would have an abortion. When I visited her on one occasion, she told me that she had had it. I believed her. Then, later, I realized that she hadn't. I said to her, "Sarah, if you're going to show this irresponsibility, then I'm through." I got up, and I walked out.

It is such a horror story, and it goes back so long. We started having real problems when she was in high school. Not heroin problems, but behavior problems. She was never where she should have been. People would see her here or there. It was just a horror. I realized afterwards that there had been some fiddling around with some drugs. At one point I think there was an LSD experience. I don't know. It's a long time ago, and it's just so much.

Anyway, she had that child. I never went to see the baby. I knew exactly what would happen if I saw the baby. I would assume the responsibility of the baby. I knew that.

The second child was born only thirteen months after Sam. Sarah was on the run from the police that time. She walked into the hospital, had the baby, left the hospital. I was called: Would I assume the responsibility of the child? I didn't even know Sarah had been pregnant that time. The baby was still in the hospital. The child was born with a slight addiction. It was like a nightmare in hell that went on forever. I said, "I have to discuss it with my husband. I'll get back to you." Then, I said, "No. I will not take responsibility for the child."

They had a racially-mixed, middle-class couple who wanted to adopt a child. I said it was not up to me. Personally I felt that that would be the best thing for the child. I guess she was adopted by this couple very soon after that.

When I knew Sarah was getting out of prison, I started seeing Sam. He must have been about three years old. I would take him for the day or perhaps overnight. Pick him up, take him to see Sarah. Needless to say, we fell in love with him. It wasn't hard.

I was always willing to take Sarah home. As long as she stayed straight, she could come home, she could go to work, she could stay here until she got on her feet, she could do whatever she wanted--as long as she stayed straight. The minute she was out on the street writing out bad checks and doing drugs, I was not going to support that.

When Sarah got out, she moved in here, and Sam came with her. And truly, she has no understanding, and had no understanding of how to raise a child. Sam is a very strong personality. He had a temper, and he was very physical. I'll never forget it. One day, she wanted him to go somewhere with her, and he didn't want to go. She's dragging him, and he's screaming, and she's dragging him by the arm, and she says, "I'm the mother. I'm your mother." What does this three-year-old child know? She just never had the experience of raising him.

She was here for about six months. Then Eli came around, and she took off. So, I had Sam then for about two and a half years. He was very difficult to manage. He was very physical. We are not young. I loved him. I do love him. He got better. He was difficult in kindergarten--and why wouldn't he be? Really. Stop and think about it. And he's a handful now. He's wonderful. He's fun. He's bright.

My heart breaks for him. When Sarah left that first time, he woke up with so many nightmares. He'd come running out to me crying, and then he'd say, "I want Mommy. I want Mommy. I want Mommy." There was nothing that I could do. I'd pick him up. I'd rock him. I'd sit with him, and I'd say, "I know, Sam. I want Mommy, too." What could I say? I couldn't get her back for him. I couldn't make any promises. My advice to her when she was pregnant was sound, but he is special to me. I'm glad I have him.

This is really the way that it went. Of course, as he got older he's had to bury so much and hide his feelings. Here he is, he's twelve now, a racially-mixed child living in an affluent, white area. He lives with someone he calls "Aunt Jane," instead of someone he can call "Mommy."

He's been very loving to Sarah always. I always felt that he wanted her to get out, so he could live with her. Now that she's out, she feels that he has backed off. It may be true.

39

He was here a couple of weeks ago. We were all going out. The rest of the family went on ahead, and Sam stayed with me a few minutes. I said to him, "I'm glad we're here alone, because it gives us a chance to talk." I'm kind of neutral territory for him. He knows that I love both Aunt Jane and his mother. I said, "Now that your Mom is out of jail, it would seem to me that you may have some kind of concern as to just exactly where you're going to be living. I just want you to understand something. Your mother loves you, Aunt Jane loves you, and I love you. And we are all family. When kids get to be in their early teenage years, their friends and their school, and their games and their dates, become almost more important to them for a time. Right now your Mom can't take you, but the day may come when she can. You don't have to feel uncomfortable that you're leaving Aunt Jane. Or, if you want to stay with Aunt Jane, your Mom will understand that too. All three of these homes are your home." He just listened to me. We all want what's best for Sam. It's very hard. Sarah, though she loves him, has no parenting skills.

He breaks my heart. My husband says to me, "You have to look at it the other way. Look at the position he could have been in." I can't look at it that way. I just know that it has been very, very painful for him. The pain that he went through when he was little was awful, really awful. This has made him very much as aggressive as he is. He's a great kid. He has a wonderful sense of humor. He's tough at home. And he does not like Jane's older child, who is the most benign, sweet, nice eight-year-old kid. Sam is terrible, horrible to him. He's okay with the three-year-old. This is a matter of terrible concern for Jane and a source of resentment on the part of her husband.

I can't make any sense of it. I found myself asking--I don't do it anymore-- "What did I do? Was I too strict? Was I too lenient?" I never did find out the answer. I think my husband thinks that I was too strong, too opinionated. I was very liberal. I don't know.

Sarah was our first child. She was the first grandchild on both sides. You can't imagine how this child was adored. How else would it be? Especially in a Jewish family. She was a big, major event. I don't know.

When she started school, I was told that she had the highest I.Q. in the class. She did very well until about fourth grade, and then things just began to slide.

Sarah had a lot of trouble with eating. It wasn't the weight that bothered me. It was that she hid it. I'd find all these wrappers in her room. It drove me crazy.

She got involved with the wrong kinds of kids in high school. I don't even like the way that sounds when I say it. She fought me on that. She was very disinterested in her school work. She would lie about things that there was absolutely no reason to lie about. I don't know. A lot of things began to develop. It was always difficult with her.

We tried everything. She convinced all the doctors that she was fine. It was the same bullshit over and over again.

I can't tell you the nightmare this produced in this house. I can't tell you what it did to me and to my husband. And to my other daughter. This whole thing. This whole growing up process with Sarah almost destroyed all of us. And I don't know what happened.

It was a horror. She'd go out in the evening. It would be four o'clock in the morning, five o'clock. I'd be walking the floors all night long. I don't know how I survived it. But it changed everything in the house. It changed my personality. My husband got quieter. Jane was so resentful of what this did to her family. And she is still resentful of Sarah. Understandably so. Sarah now would like to have a loving relationship with Jane. Jane doesn't trust it. It took a terrible toll on all of us.

Sarah was lacking in confidence. I don't know if she started out that way. She ultimately was very lacking in confidence.

I tried to figure everything. Jane happened to be exceptionally pretty. Maybe this had something to do with it. In one of Sarah's poems, it was about me. I thought, "Oh my God, it seems like not Jane, but that she's comparing herself to me and coming up short." I don't know.

She's done great things. She's had lots of magazine articles published. Short stories. Lots of poetry published. Her artwork is great. Sarah was more like me in the respect that she was a great reader. She was interested in politics. She was interested in art. My other daughter, finished college and got a master's degree in counseling. She's a much more self-involved person. She couldn't care less about politics, but she's very good to all of her immediate circle: her friends, her children. Never smoked a cigarette. They are entirely different.

I wish I knew the answer. It got to the point where I didn't want to see anybody. I didn't go anywhere. It was just agony. It was really pure agony. My husband was beside himself. He said, "I cannot live this way anymore. I just cannot live this way. It has got to change here. I've got fewer years ahead of me than I've got behind me. I've got to make the most of what we've got left. We just cannot do anymore for her. We have to go on with our lives." I couldn't. I agreed with him, but I couldn't. For years I couldn't concentrate to read. I'd be reading the same page over and over. I just couldn't get her out of my head at any time.

Then, I don't know what happened. It was a gradual process. This whole nightmare had started when she was fourteen. By this time she was in her twenties. I got to the point where I could handle it. I started a small business with a couple of friends. For a few hours a week I was not thinking about Sarah, and it was my salvation. I got out of myself a little bit. In time I got to the point where I knew I had to survive for me and for the rest of my family. And I did. I was just able to remove myself enough to keep my sanity.

I think I've gotten beyond it now. I really do. I want desperately for her to make it, but it's up to her. There's nothing I can do anymore. In the beginning I felt, "There's nothing we can't take care of. We'll get the best doctor, etc. We'll find a way." We didn't find a way. You don't find a way. She's the one who had to find the way.

Right now Sarah is in a half-way house, and she is looking for a job. I hope she makes it this time. I've got my fingers crossed, but I am powerless to change anything for her. In all, she's probably done about nine years in prison. It's been three years now since she's done any drugs. I still can't sit down with her in any way and talk and give any kind of an opinion. She doesn't want an opinion. She doesn't want it. I don't give it.

I don't know how two kids in the same house with the same parents and parents who were always home for the kids . . . All of the factors were those that should have produced--more or less-- a so-called "normal child." Maybe the kids were too important to me, to where I limited my own needs for them. I don't know if that's so. Maybe I was too concerned. Maybe they didn't have enough space. I <u>don't</u> know. I have to say my youngest daughter is also very dependent, very, very attached. I don't think there's a day that goes by that we don't talk to each other on the telephone.

I was always home. That was a big mistake. Really it was. Maybe they didn't have enough independence. I was the PTA President and all that kind of bullshit. I see kids who came from families who had really major problems and none of them turned out like Sarah. In my next life I'll be sure to do it differently.

I didn't have any support. I did not want to talk to friends. I did not. There might have been one or two people that I spoke to somewhat, but not much. I'm very private. I have never lied. I have just never discussed these things. People don't ask. It's nobody's business, and it doesn't help me to discuss it. It's my private personal life. Certainly her name was in the paper often enough under the police log. So what they know they know, but they don't know from me. Just to vomit it out to someone else is no help. Let them think whatever they want.

Whenever she was on the road--so to speak--she would call. She never cut the ties. Every six weeks, every month. She would always call collect. I would always accept the call, and we'd have just a small general conversation. Truly, it was a relief every time she was picked up, because she would have ended up dead. She knew that.

She's very short with me. I don't know. The experts didn't know. It's such a waste. She is so talented. The height of the sixties. Drugs. Really turbulent. The Vietnam War.

But how it happened to her, I don't know.

MAGALI ROMAN
Age: 42

"When I became a mother, all my dreams, I put them aside. Not that I forgot them. No way. But I continued to have my dreams when I was alone of what I wanted to be."

Magali is Peruvian. She has three sons, two by her first husband and one by her second. They are Adam, seventeen; Reuben, sixteen; and Jacob, six. She came to the States because she could not fulfill her dreams in Peru: she wanted to go to college and learn English.

I come from Lima, Peru. I was brought up in a little town that is not far from Lima. But it is a very nice little town, very, very family-type.

My father was brought up to be a professional in my country. He had a lot of schooling. My mother and my father fell in love in poverty, and they never accomplished their dreams. They instilled their dreams in me. My father taught me all about South America. He had traveled everywhere. He taught me about all the customs. I dreamed with him. My grandmother lived with us. She was a pianist. I grew up with opera and books. My world was big--and wide, too.

My father took a lot of time with me. He brought me places, until I was about fourteen. Then I was more with my mother. There were places my mother thought young girls shouldn't go, because there were so many gentlemen. Men talking, and my mother didn't want those little ears to listen. Much to my despair, my mother kept me home. She used to want me to be lady-like. She taught me needlepoint. For coins I used to embroider kerchiefs and pillowcases.

44

I think a mother--now I'm talking only about myself, how I feel--I didn't think I'd feel a woman if I didn't have children. Even if you are rich and famous and successful in many other things, if you don't have a child after you, to know and to share with, your feelings and dreams, and everything else, you're not complete. Like a circle.

My father died when I was not even sixteen years old. I miss him really. He taught me to hop and skip and read, when I was just very young. My mother says that he said that he saw in me something. "This girl is going to be a wonderful mother." I don't know, the way that I cuddled with dolls or played with them . . . not like dolls that you have here in the stores. The dolls that I had were homemade. I like children. Not that I am a very patient person, because I have patience very limited, but I guess with every child God gave you an amount of patience.

There were money problems in my family. To survive. In Peru it doesn't exist welfare or some allowance for the widow. My mother had to go to work, but in those days most mothers stayed home. There were expenses from his sickness and burial. I was almost sixteen. My mother didn't say, "You're going to have to stay home and raise your brothers." I wanted to finish school, but I told her not to worry. What I did, I went to school in nights. In my country it takes more years to do, to make it up.

So, I stayed in the house taking care of my two little brothers. It was responsibility. Meals for the day. I had to go to the market every day to buy fresh. Meat, everything. Otherwise you're going to spoil it. Where are you going to keep it? So, I went in the morning and did that. I bring my children, my brothers, to the school and went to the open market. Go home and prepare the meals, go back and get my brothers, help them with the meals, make their homework with them and do my homework for the night.

I finished my high school. My brothers were bigger. I could do bookkeeping, some of it, Accountant I, but Accountant II still had to sign. Then there was a change in the government that changed the school system. All my schooling was thrown out the door. To go to college I had to stay another three years. The money that I earned didn't cover much. I was always penniless.

I had to help my mother. I never said, "Oh, I'm going to buy this dress, because I feel like it." I never could. I used to penny-pinch for stockings always. I said, "This is not a life."

Some of my cousins came to the States, and they say, "There's opportunities here for the schooling and for work." I looked around me, and I said, "What is for me here? I'm going to marry one Peruvian boy. But what is for me? Just stay home, raising children?" It's not my dream, that. I always see something better. My mother was a dreamer, too. My mother never accomplished her dream, because my father died. My mother wanted to be a nurse, and she never could.

I saved, and I came here. My dream was to continue college and to speak the language. I was in the airport, and I was ready to go back to Peru, because I couldn't talk to anybody. I felt so alone. Finally, some of the people that I came with, they had relatives that picked them up. With them I hitched. I managed after that. It hasn't been easy. I was twenty-one when I came.

Marriage for me when I was growing up was not in my book. Honest. But, you know, sometimes you fall in love--and not with the right person. It changes everything. I became a mother very fast. I don't regret that.

Two times I thought even to maybe kill myself. My children helped me. I saw my children, and I thought I couldn't do it. My children need me. Their father is not a good father. What's going to happen to those children? They'll go in some foster home. One time when I was pregnant with my first son I had a big problem. But I couldn't do it. Abortion to me is a sin to God, to yourself. That was in a way to me to murder two people. I couldn't do it. I said, "I got into this problem. I'm going to get out of this problem."

The second time was when I had my two children, and I had a big argument, and I went out. I stayed out for about three hours, struggling in myself what to do. One neighbor, who was French, who didn't speak English, must have seen my face. I could not face anybody. She came to talk to me in French. She put her hands around me. I will never forget it.

I got a strength just because I wanted to continue, and, whatever happens to me, be the best mother that I could. I was very happy to have my children.

I survived. I got divorced. I started working. My children were growing up very healthy and very much with this environment. I didn't try to raise them as I was raised, because I didn't want to be selfish. I was raised in one way. But I saw that America has a certain charm, also. Independence, self-assurance. Things that I didn't grow up with. When you are in a poor country there are limitations. Here there is so much openness, so much to look for.

My children grew up speaking English more than Spanish. I try to instill in them my morals and my past, the culture of my ancestors. I am very proud of it. Nothing to be ashamed about, being ancestor from the Incas. Since they were little I instilled religion and to respect people. I let them choose their own friends. I always tell them, "In this house you have to go by rules, and everybody who comes here, the same." We don't allow to drink or smoke or swear, no back talk. Never to call elders by their first name. Always say, "Hello." It doesn't take one minute to say, "Hello."

Before I married my husband now--Jean-- I wasn't sure to marry and have another failed marriage. I look him over all sides, all dimensions, because I was scared to get married. There was no only me, there was two children that has to suffer the consequences. They already suffered a lot with their father.

I decided to go to my country and visit my family and put a space. Jean didn't want me to go. I said, "No, first is first. When I come back we'll do things right, if it's meant to be." I went to Peru. I took the children. It was nice! It was maybe ten years since I left home. Two weeks only--ooh, that was so short! I talked to my mother. My mother is very wise. I made up my mind. When I went back we set a date, and he's been a really nice man, father and husband.

My friends tease me and say, "When are you going to look for the little girl." My time for having children is gone, finished. Now I think that I am going to enjoy them. This is now a time for me to look for something else, for something that I didn't finish when I was younger.

I think I can be a social worker. That's what I'm doing now. Right now I'm working for the Latin-American Center doing AIDS awareness. I am the one going home to home. I am using my language, of course. Mostly they are Spanish families, but sometimes it is easier to talk to the children in English. I can talk both. I intend to go to college, but right now my prayer is to put my Adam in college. I have been looking around for maybe some scholarships.

I have dreams, and I put them aside, because, being a mother you are responsible for a life. To me being a mother is a gift from God. Really, it is a precious gift. When I became a mother, all my dreams, I put them aside. No that I forgot them. No way. But I continued to have my dreams when I was alone of what I wanted to be. The most important thing was to be a mother, and to learn English.

I wouldn't be complete. I wouldn't be myself if I didn't have my children.

My children take my breath away.

I am in the middle of my life journey. There's going to be another big chapter in my life.

ROSIE NEWTON
Age: 64

"I think I had a sense of having lost my identity. The three-pound chicken that laid the three-pound egg and disappeared. I just knew I had to do something."

Rosie is the mother of four sons: Matthew, age forty; Tom, thirty-seven; Joshua, thirty-six; and Nathan, thirty-two. She talks about the impact being orphaned in childhood has had on her own life; her need to find an identity outside the home, when her children were quite grown; and the challenge of raising an autistic child.

My mother was sick, so she got a friend of hers to come and take care of the house. This was during the Depression. This woman had no job, so she could just pick up and live with us. She was just wonderful. She had no children of her own. She was a contemporary of my mother's, so that would have made her about forty, and she had an alcoholic husband. I think my mother extracted a promise from her that she would stay on. I think maybe she thought taking care of my sister and me would provide some security. Six weeks after my mother died, my father died also. As it turned out, my parents left nothing. It was a miracle that there was this woman who would take us on. I was thirteen, and my sister was eight.

I can't remember a lot about my mother. I do remember her saying--and I don't know why this stands out so clearly--that she figured that her job was to train the children to be independent. It's a good thing she did.

I think what I missed more than anything was someone teaching me how to be a grown-up. I didn't know, and I'm not sure I still know. What do you do when somebody dies, for instance? I have to school myself. It isn't an immediate reaction. What to do when there's any trouble at all? I remember when one of our boys was suspended from college for importing marijuana. When we got the news some friends of ours just came and sat with us. I wouldn't have known to do that. I would have thought that I was intruding. All these things I've had to take up piecemeal, along the way. Some people learn these things at their parents' knees.

My boys were all born in New York City. I was twenty-three when the first son, Matthew, was born. The next child is Tom. Joshua is my autistic son, who lives across the street from us and works in a workshop in town. Nathan, the baby, still lives in New York. They're all carpenters. My husband always has been very handy and used to spend his summers building and constructing and improving. The kids just fell right in with that. Being carpenters has offered them a way to be independent. They're all their own bosses. They all went to college, except Joshua. Neither my husband nor I is particularly ambitious, so I don't think we could expect our kids to be.

The first child was born in 1949, and I was Mrs. All-American Housewife until 1966 when I just had this growing conviction that if I didn't get very, very busy, I would die, like my mother did, at an early age. I just had this feeling. My mother had always reminded me that her mother died when she was forty-two. My mother thought that was going to be her fate, too, and it was. I was determined that that wouldn't happen to me.

But more than that, I think I had a sense of having lost my identity: the three-pound chicken that laid a three-pound egg and disappeared. I just knew I had to do something.

I had volunteered in the public school, and had a friend who did it also. One day, when my youngest was about eight, my friend and I were talking about what we were going to do with ourselves. I said, "Why don't we go down to NYU and see what they have to offer in the way of graduate programs for people like us?" One course led to another, and, finally, in five years, I had my masters degree, without too much effort.

A woman I knew said, "What are you going to do about getting a job?" I said, "I don't know. What do you do?" She offered to call a friend who was a school principal. She gave me a job. That was my career path. I taught first or second grade for eighteen years after that. I found it very satisfying and very engrossing, and didn't have time to get sick and die.

Autism means, "in a world separated from the real world." It is a brain-damage problem. These people have a very weak self-image. "I" was practically the last word that Joshua ever could add to his vocabulary. In fact, I don't know if I ever hear him say "I," although he does now have a strong personality in terms of what pleases him and what doesn't please him.

Some children are afflicted much worse than Joshua. A lot of them are self-destructive. It's a terrible, terrible affliction for a child to have. Joshua manages to live a fairly independent life. Fortunately, he has it mildly enough so that he can function. We have a sense that Joshua has a kind of mechanical brilliance that we've never been able to tap into and put to its best advantage. He can't read very well at all. His speech is halting. We're also grateful that he's not angry. Some of these kids are so angry all the time, and combative. Joshua is a gentle soul. Fortunately, because he's huge, and strong.

By the time he was three it was clear that he wasn't developing the way the other children were. He was off in this little world of his own. Autism wasn't well understood at that time. You know how you sort of have insights, once in a while, and you're very grateful they came to you, but you don't know where they came from? I thought to myself: "I am not going to limit this person by my expectations for him. We'll just see what he can do." People said, "How did you dare let him do this, or that?" Somehow it was just our instinct to do it. I think it did help him a lot to get a sense of "can do."

Having Joshua did change our lives. He had no sense of caution at all, for instance. We lived in a four-story brownstone. I remember going upstairs one night--it was foolish not to have bars on the window--I came into his bedroom, and all I could see was his legs and the bottom of his bottom! The rest of him was all out the window.

It was sort of a challenge. I mean, what can you do, given the situation, but deal with it the best way possible? It was time-consuming. He would get into the Tide box and eat all the soap. He wasn't toilet-trained until very late. There'd be nights I couldn't get him to bed, or I'd finally get him to bed, and he'd get up--and this would go on for hours.

One helpful thing we were told was to be very consistent, very strong. I think it did help him, but it required an awful lot of concentration. It would have been easier to just let him do his thing. But, we got through. In the long run I think it helped the other kids to be more accepting of other kinds of people.

I think, now, that Joshua sees me as a dependable resource. He's thirty-four. I suppose it has taken some effort of will, but I do see him as a man. Joshua is comfortable with me. You could ask me "How much does Joshua love you?" or "Does he know how to love?" I couldn't answer that question. He doesn't know how to express it. At various stages in his life he's shown a kind of intuition that you would never believe he had, about sensing feelings in other people. Like saying, "I'm sorry if I hurt you." His interior life is just a total mystery.

I think kids are capable of a lot more than we give them credit for. I think the main ingredient is being steadfast, caring. Just being there. If your intentions are good, and you show your kids one way or another that you care, that's the important part.

I had had so much freedom. I had had no surveillance from the time I was thirteen on. I had somehow instinctively known that the standards were up to me. I set them very high. I had confidence that my kids would do the same thing. It's hard to say, in retrospect, how I knew how to cope. There it is. I would call it the grace of God. That's the only way I can understand the concept of grace--these thoughts that come to me that I couldn't possibly describe the source for.

I knew that being a mother was the main thing that I wanted to do in life. That's been my feeling about being a woman. I wanted to have babies. I never was happier than when I was pregnant. Coincidentally, with our finding out that Joshua had this serious problem, our feeling was "we've got to have one more child." It was like plunging in. Joshua was three when

Nathan was born. Our instinct to have another child was very strong.

I just loved having those babies and taking care of them and making a home. Women of our generation were constantly being warned to think of their husbands, and not to let their children be so all-encompassing that their husbands would feel slighted. It was very important for the man to be the most important one, and then the children were sort of little satellites around. I took that seriously. It was not all blissful. It was not. But until that sudden moment when I felt like the three-pound chicken that laid the three-pound egg, it was fine.

I'm just so grateful really. Who knows how long I'll live? It's nice to have had that satisfaction.

DELFINIA ORTIZ
Age: 58

"I think I went through my life in a dream."

Delfinia is Native-American and Hispanic. She is a Catholic and has raised three boys and three girls, who are now between the ages of twenty-five and thirty-five. Delfinia's mother dropped away, vanished because of mental illness. Much of Delfinia's own story is the story of life at her grandmother's side on a poor farm in the pueblo. Like her grandmother, Delfinia did the many things that had to be done. She did not see choices.

When her husband divorced her six years ago, Delfinia's life began to open up. She is now beginning to reflect on her life. Her comments about her children suggest that she gave them more of her goodness than she knows.

My brother and sister and I, all three of us grew up in the pueblo with my grandparents. My father is native American and my mother is a Hispanic, but I'm more native American, because I grew up in the pueblo. We struggled all our life. We were poor in those days. My grandparents didn't have no income of any kind. They survived by raising food, farming. We had maybe sheep, two or three. I remember one cow and one horse. A goat.

In those days we didn't have vehicles. My Dad or my grandfather would go on horseback to the mountains to hunt for deer. That's how they brought the deer down if they got one, on the horse. Or wagon. They can dry meat. They would go for days. Sometimes it would snow while they were there. My grandmother always worried, "I hope they are warm enough. I hope their food lasted."

We as children had to help in the farm, raising vegetables. Corn. Wheat. We had to raise wheat to have flour to make tortillas. We had lots of chile. I loved those days. We knew how to survive.

Chile that hung around the house. When it dries is when you start cleaning it. We cleaned it ourselves. I thought that was the hardest thing, but I did it. You cleaned the chile from the seed and from the pod. Then you save the same seed for the following year that you're going to plant. You have boxes of clean chile. After you finish the chile, you put it in the oven to toast it. We do that according to our boxes. Toasting the chile, toasting the chile. Then we find a mill. Maybe two miles from where we live, there's a big chile grinder. We take all our chile there, and he grinds it, so we have chile for a whole year. We grew up on chile. Chile is our food. For everything, we eat chile.

The same way with our flour. He grinds chile. He grinds flour. Blue corn meal. That lasts a year of eating, then we produce the following year. April is the planting time. We plant again and raise this crop, so we can have another grinding time, with flour, with blue corn meal, with chile, so we can have another year of it. That's the process in the pueblo. You put your corn, hang it on strings to dry, and in the winter when you want to eat corn, you get that whole corn, and you put it in big pots to boil, and that's what our corn is.

My grandparents taught me. You have to work hard for what you need in your home. We went for wood. In wagons. Our grandfather used to take us, to have wood for the winter, to bake bread in the oven. We pile wood. Beginning of fall is when we start bringing wood. We have only wood stoves.

Everything I remember is a process, year 'round, year 'round, year 'round. After school at the grade school, our grandfather would take us in the wagons to go pick corn. We're loading the wagon with corn, and we bring it, and we dump it out in our yard. There's piles and piles of corn out there. The same way with wheat. We go cut wheat, and then we have a big machine that thresh wheat. Right in our pueblo. We separate some of the little stems. We clean it, we wash it, we dry it, then we take it to have it ground for flour. We did all this.

We had no running water. We have a pump right in the pueblo where we get our water in buckets. Not having running water, you have to warm the water to take baths. We put it on the stove. We have tubs, just ordinary tubs where we take our bath. We have buckets sitting, so we have enough water for at least a day. The next day we go haul some more water.

Sometimes I felt I didn't have enough time to play. Five years old, six years old and making tortillas already. My grandmother was blind. My grandfather, he only had one good eye.

But yet he would sit there and make willow baskets. He made the Indian costume, the Indian moccasin. He'd load up his willow baskets in the wagon, and we'd go down to Spanish communities, and he would exchange his baskets for flour or sugar or beans. We had to survive so many ways.

At twenty-two years old my uncle was burnt to death. I was three, four years old then. I remember that. He was someone that took care of us, that was in our lives so much that when we lost him--I still cry about it--it was very sad. So my grandparents lost a son. The only surviving one was my father.

My father married from a very prominent family from the Espanola valley. He married her, but my mother, when my brother was born, became schizophrenic. They tried curing her in our own Indian way, but it didn't work. Nothing helped. My mother was put in a state hospital. My father was an alcoholic. He drank. I knew him only where he drank a lot. He drank and drank. He didn't know what to do with three small children, so he left and went out to work in Colorado.

He left us with our grandparents, yet they were blind. They did their very best in raising us. Seeing, but not really knowing their handicap. My grandmother did everything. When we were younger she did the laundry, but as we grew--we used to go get water or take our laundry to the ditch. In those days you washed on the washboard. God! did we work hard as children. We're washing on the washboard, hanging our clothes. There's a fence going along there. In the afternoon we would go pick up our clothes when it's dry. We did all that.

I was taking the responsibility, because I was the oldest one. I felt, it's my job. Where my Grandma couldn't do, I did. Being blind, she would say, "Making tortillas this is what you do. Get your handfuls. Five. This is how you do it. This is how much you put. This. This." You put by hands. And your baking powder and your salt and your lard. I learned like that. By feeling she did it.

My grandmother didn't know how to speak English. All she spoke was Spanish and Indian. Yet, where in the world did she learn to make cake? She would make the best cake. She was the only person I knew that baked cake in the pueblo. My friends would smell cake when we were coming from school. I would bring them in, and she would have pans of cake already done. That's how my friends remember my grandmother. She was such a strong woman. She did a lot of things that people that don't have a handicap don't do nowadays.

My grandmother had two brothers. They would come in and help and, in turn, she fed them and washed for them. She didn't only take care of her two brothers, but relatives that lived two miles away, they had kids that came to school. In those days you come walking, and you then you go back walking, so a whole week they would stay at my grandmother's house, so they could go home Friday or Saturday. She would have everybody sleeping on the floor. We didn't have any beds. We only had little covers laying all over the floor. She didn't have, but she would share what she had. I am so grateful that I was raised by her, learning her way of life. It was hard, but it taught us responsibility, trust, everything. My friends and I, my sister, we talk. We say, "Those were good old days."

My grandfather died a death that I couldn't understand. This man I remember, I was eleven years old, this man came in from the pueblo with a box of bottles. He had alcohol in it, so I find out, and he gave some to my grandfather. My grandfather was eighty-two then. From that alcohol, he passed out, and he was laying on the floor for a week, just breathing. They didn't take him to the hospital. I didn't know what was going on. I saw people coming in and kneeling down and praying for him. I didn't know what was happening. After a week he died while laying there.

When I was nineteen years old, I got married. I guess I wanted a life, a different type of life. I wanted something. I worked all my life, so I thought I was going to have things a little bit easier maybe. A good life. A home of my own. I never got that.

The person I married didn't want the things I want. But yet I lived with this person thirty-two years. Growing up in the pueblo, I never saw divorces. This is what happened to me six years ago, divorce. You got married by the Church, so I believed that's your life. You stay married. That's the rest of your life, 'til death do you part. I believed that, seeing my grandparents, seeing my relatives. They all grew old together, the husband and wife. Their life was working together, woman and man, side by side. They raised, they farmed, they did everything together. That's what I saw, so that's the way I thought my life's supposed to be.

I didn't know, so it's not going well, there's a way out. I felt guilty, so I stayed in this marriage. My husband was an alcoholic. Abusive.

I think my children were precious to me. They weren't planned. In those days, they were just born. But yet I loved them so dearly. They tell me that I was overly protective. That's how I raised them, but then, I was abused as a child by one of my uncles, so the fear of that was in my mind. I made sure I knew where they were and what they were going to do. I couldn't tell them this happened to me. I wiped that away from my mind.

I knew I had to take care of my children and protect them. That's how my children remember me. I was there constantly. I never did anything anywhere. We raised vegetables. As small as they are, I would take them with lunches. My grandmother used to do that for me, take me with my little tortillas and a jar of water, because it's quite a ways where we farm.

I always made sure that they were dressed clean, that they had food to eat. We were poor. My husband worked at a lumber

58

mill. With six children, it wasn't much. Taking care of my grandmother, we lived in my grandmother's house. We didn't have a home of our own. I grew up in that house. My father grew up in that house. My children grew up in that house.

My children are all close together. From morning to night, my life was so occupied. I remember the last day when I was expecting, I should have been on my way to the hospital, I was on my knees mopping the floor. I wanted to leave the house clean, their clothes washed and ironed for school. I would cook a lot of stuff and have it ready. In those days you were in the hospital three or four days.

I think I went through my life in a dream. I didn't have a chance to do anything.

My oldest ones are girls, so they started helping me. In the cooking. The sharing. I thought that was closeness, but yet, because of my husband's alcoholism, my father's alcoholism, there was always a tense feeling in there. I think where it counts we didn't communicate. They grew up where maybe they had to learn like me at a young age.

By the time they were in high school I would tell them, "I'll do the baking, the bread, outside. You do the cakes and things on feast days on the inside." We did a lot of cooking for our feast days. There's always a feast going on in the pueblo, so they took part in all that, my girls. And the boys had to go for wood and chop wood for the oven. My husband was a hunter too, for deer, so they learned all of that.

We did a lot of doings together, but not a lot of talking. That was missing. I guess I didn't know how. My grandmother didn't have time to sit and talk with us! I always remember work, work, work. My sister and I would be coming to feed the animals, and then we would go home again in the dark. It's kind of scarey along the way. Those trees would be hanging, touching our head. You feel like somebody's touching you. I didn't have time to be a child.

We did go swimming in the river! That's what I enjoyed. We'd have time out from hoeing the garden, or washing the wheat, or irrigating. We'd go to the river, and we'd never want to come home! That's how come we had to come feed the animals in the dark.

My kids grew up as children. They played.

When my father became old, I took care of him until he was seventy-three years old. My grandmother died at ninety-one. I took care of her. I took care of all these people in my life. In '87, my marriage ended in divorce. I would still be married to this day. He was the one that was fooling around, with my neighbor. He left, because he wanted to be with this woman.

I had no skills of any kind. I thought, "How am I going to survive? I have no skills. I never worked in my life." Yet, I continued doing farming. I have fruit trees that I do my own pruning, my own jelly, my own canning. "How will I make it without money? I never had a job." Yet, I sold produce.

I went through something that is unexplainable. I didn't know what was happening to me. I thought I was going crazy like my mother. I couldn't find explanations. So many things happened in my childhood. When this divorce came, all that built up in me burst. It surfaced. A year, I cried and I cried. I started remembering things, pains from my childhood. I still hurt for the things I lost.

Losing my marriage, another loss. Nobody talks about divorces. Nobody talks about separation. Nobody talks about abuse. Nobody talks about anything.

A social worker told me about a two-week workshop in Santa Fe. I met women there that were talking about their lives. God! there are women like me. I couldn't believe it. When the workshop was over, some other women and I started a support group in the pueblo where people will come to talk. We have five in our group. Sometimes it discourages me that women don't see that they need help. They know we're here. It's just that they are afraid to speak of their life. Everything's a secret. Abuse. Alcoholism. Infidelity. It belongs in the house. You can't take it out.

I'm still fearful of the things I do, but I take chances. I am very fearful. I take chances. I learned to drive. My youngest son told me, "Mom, if you want to do things, you have to learn to drive." In two days I learned to drive. My daughter gave me a truck. I joined a choir. We sing in our own language. I'm doing more things than I can handle now. I'm taking G.E.D. classes to get my diploma.

My children all live in the pueblo area, so I do a lot of things with them. They are good children. They all have jobs. I enjoy them. I wish when they were young, it would have been nicer to talk. I hear people say, "The dinner table was our talking time." I wish I had that with my children. Now, at least, we talk.

In the beginning I think they didn't understand me. They saw me in the home all my life. I was always there. Now my younger son says, "I never see you, Mom."

I say, "Isn't that good?!" And I don't cook. All my life I cooked.

So maybe once a month I'll take time and make tortillas and all this good chile. "What's the occasion?" he tells me.

"Well, I felt like cooking today!"

My grandmother couldn't say, "Oh, you look nice today." We were so poor. We wore hand-me-downs. I loved my kids, but yet I didn't say, "You're so pretty. I like your hair today. You look so nice." Nobody ever said those things to me. Nobody told me that.

So, today I say it. I need to say these things to my children. It's just like a new beginning. I am learning all these things that I never learned as a child. Hugging. It feels so good, somebody else hugging you back. I missed all that in my life, and I'm finding it. What love is--and it's so beautiful! I'm finding love. I'm finding friendship. Friends that I never had. I think my children are proud of me, but they don't know how to say it.

I always say that one day I will get my children together, and I'll tell my story. My one son tells me, "Mom, why did you marry Dad? You are two entirely different people. You are so loving, and you are so kind, and Dad is the opposite. Dad only wanted fun in life, and you were the stable one." Now their father does not even acknowledge them.

I couldn't tell them that I was raped by him, and I had to get married. I couldn't to this day bring myself to tell them. I guess I didn't want them to hate their father. So a lot of things they don't know about me. A lot of things I hold in my heart.

KATHRYNE LENNOX
Age: 49

"Mothering changes your life in such a dramatic way. You're always trying to find the best relationship that you can with your children, as babies, as little kids, as young adults."

Kathryne is the mother of twenty-three-year-old, boy and girl twins. As a mother she has been married, divorced, a single parent, and remarried. Although there were stretches of time when Kathryne did not work outside of the home, for the most part she has been a working mother, pursuing a career. As she has tried continually to balance her needs with those of her children, she has struggled with the issue of control; with the contrast between her parenting style and that of her own parents; and with trying to be both mother and father to her children.

Kathryne speaks of the easing of guilt as she sees the kind of people her children are becoming.

You can have a view of what you think you're going to be like as a mother, but you do respond to those children, and you do respond to how your husband responds to his new role. More than anything the success is in the ability to respond.

You have to have a sense of yourself as a person. If the mother doesn't know who she is in the process, the tide does turn. Who's going to be in charge? Is it going to be the child today and you tomorrow? Or the father? Or some passerby? I think I'm sensitive to that because as the mother of twins I was the recipient of more advice.

I remember the second time I ever took them out of our home. It was in March, and they were only a month old, but I thought it was a warm enough day. I went one city block, and a woman stopped and said, "You're going to just smother them. That blanket is too hot." She kind of pulled it down around. I went another block, and a woman said, "You know they're going to catch cold if you don't bundle them up." This went on, and I only managed to walk about eight blocks. I couldn't decide whether they were frozen or sweating. I had started out with what I had thought, using my own judgment, was a reasonable approach.

When I became pregnant I was living overseas and working for a newspaper. I really did think I was Zelda Fitzgerald. I was at a very interesting point in my career. Very involved with my life. I also had a very romantic notion of life. Children, fine. I was just going to go right along. Then, when I found out I was going to have twins, I realized you don't go along quite so easily. I stopped working and stayed home for a while.

I chose to stay home. That was an interesting twist, to go from what I thought was a terrifically exciting life to one that was extremely demanding and regimented. I spent a lot of time feeding, washing, changing, doing laundry. Without thinking very much about it, I returned to the model I had from my mother as a homemaker. I hadn't wanted it.

At first it was automatic. Then, the conflicts arose: who was I? For the first time in my adult life I was not earning my own salary. You don't realize what this means, because you're so tired and so busy and so exhausted. You're really not thinking very big life thoughts. Mostly you're thinking survival.

I was contacted by a university that wanted to do a study on twins. Would I participate? Here was a chance to think again! I responded with great enthusiasm. For several months I filled in blanks on very basic activities. I received a check in the mail at the end of three months -- for $25. My first clue that my life had changed was that I was so excited about this twenty-five dollar check. I began to think that perhaps I had to put together a life that wasn't going to be one way or the other: I wasn't ready to leave the children, but I also wasn't ready to stop thinking.

The challenge goes on for a very long time. How do you balance your own need to make a contribution in your profession with the memory that your family ate breakfast together; you came home from school and your mother had lunch for you at lunch-time; she was there again at three-thirty; and the family ate dinner together? How can you be the very best mother you can be and still fulfill some of your own needs--for yourself?

When my children were seven I was divorced. There I was with twins, and now I owned a newspaper. I still had all the traditional trappings. I never thought I was aiming to be the Super Mother, but I was certainly behaving that way. If I wasn't Super Mother, I sure was on the treadmill.

After my husband and I were divorced, he wasn't an active father. I tried to be both mother and father. I was running around doing it all, and the fact of the matter is, you can't be both. I thought I was doing both, but later in life when my son was growing up, I realized that I guessed I hadn't been such a great father. No matter how many hockey games I went to, I was his mother. I do think there's a difference between having your mother and your father at the hockey game. To me it was a very violent sport. When he checked, I could never say, "Terrific." I wasn't the parent that yelled, even at swimming meets. Well, I did . . . "Sweetie" was a term of endearment, and one time when he was skating hard, I did find myself saying, "Go, Sweetie, Go!" I have a distinctive voice, and people could hear, and he could hear. Much to my horror. I didn't even think about it. But I wasn't his father, and nobody wants to hear "Go, Sweetie, go."

We can laugh. I can laugh, but, you know, at the time it wasn't a terrific thing. I didn't go to the next game. You begin to wonder "who am I?" It became very clear to me that I wasn't a mother and a father no matter how many games I went to. My son would rather his stepfather went to the game. There it was. And if I had gone to twenty games in a row and his real father came to one, it was a very exciting event. I had sat through the freezing cold for twenty, and it didn't much matter. At the time I didn't much like that, but now it's clear as a bell.

My children now live away from home. They've graduated from college. I still think the challenge is there. I find myself still trying to provide the time, still trying to find my way. That's the story of mothering. It changes your life in such a dramatic way. You're always trying to find the best relationship that you can with your children, as babies, as little kids, as young adults.

I took responsibility for problems that weren't all mine. Behavior problems, performance problems. You do, because you think, "If I'd been there," or, "If I'd seen it sooner," or, "If I hadn't been so tired." I now see that it's okay, too.

There are key things that you have to provide. A personal identity. An appreciation for the greater world, beyond yourself. A sense of imagination. Self-reliance and, at the same time, a sense of obligation to other people. Teenagers can really make you wonder if they've ever heard those words. A sense of responsibility to other people? I must have been working on those days when that was learned! A hopefulness, even when money is tight. A willingness to try. I guess that's part of self-esteem. A desire to be happy and a willingness to be content. A willingness to take time to appreciate. A love of learning. A drive to make a contribution.

There are important moments when you have to be there. Now I have a little longer term perspective, I think that the basis of what you're trying to do, you can do and have a profession as well. There may be some low moments. There may be some detours that you think you could have avoided if you'd been there at three-thirty in the afternoon. But I also think you ride them out, and I think it comes out okay. My children are very happy at this moment, so some of those guilty moments are beginning to disappear. I see they are happy. I see they can handle themselves. I see some of the guidance I tried to provide. Maybe it wasn't always on the right day, at the right moment that I dreamed about, but it did come. I did have something to offer. I'm glad I made those choices.

They all weren't luxuries either. There were times when I had to work. Real times. When I was divorced and I did have the responsibility of my children, there wasn't any choice. Working was a necessity. I'll tell you, it's very easy to go to work when it's a necessity. You don't have that upper-middle class question of, "Should I, or shouldn't I?" When you have to work, you have a little less guilt, but you do still miss moments when you would like to be there for your children.

There was a very small crisis in the work life of one of the children just the other day. The pleasing thing now is, and this is one place where working mothers may have an advantage . . . the natural reaction is to call home to the working mother. That's all they need to do: Mrs. Fullcharge has a lot of ideas. But enough wisdom learned over the years of being a mother, to at least catch herself before she's gone too far. You never know. You're still trying to figure out what's too far, what's too much, what's not enough. The pain that your children feel is still, no matter what age they are, pain that you experience.

But today in the mail came the note, "Thank you for the support, and thanks for knowing when not to have the answers." There would have been times when that note might not have come, when I had too many answers, or when that same person might have felt that I didn't have an answer, because I wasn't there. I now have the perspective that you may not always make it work, but over the long haul it does. There's real relief in that. People do live through some very intense times. You have to keep your eye on the longer term. You can't give everything at every moment. I haven't talked about the nightmares, but there were nightmares. The immediate always loomed so large, I wasn't always able to keep my eye further down the road.

I strove hard to have my children treat each other as equals and to respect differences. As the mother of twins, I wasn't always sure that I succeeded. I wondered if one would be so dominant. I've seen my daughter, who was more reticent, assert herself and manage well in very challenging circumstances. There would have been times when she would not have done that. In my son, I look for self-esteem. You have different concerns for each child as they develop. You can't manage everything, and everything was never as tidy as it was in the home I grew up in.

I have very high expectations. Innocently. I have them of myself. They don't seem so high, but they are. That's a problem. That's why I mentioned self-esteem. I'm unaware of my expectations, and it can be wearing to be around me too long.

I took that for granted. It's only now that they're older that we can talk about it in a meaningful way. We kept trying to get at it. It's not so easy, because expectations are elusive. It's not like I said, "A's in class." To me it was just, "Do your best." Well, sometimes, maybe you shouldn't have to do your best. There are areas where maybe you just don't do your best. It was innocent, but it created issues.

I referred earlier to Mrs. Fullcharge. I do feel I'm responsible for the solutions. That's an absurd notion, but if part of the way you think in life is problem-solving by virtue of your professional responsibilities, you start problem-solving everybody else's life. If someone had asked me, "Would you feel better if you didn't have to solve thirty more things in a day?," I would say "YES," but I kept doing it. Coming up with the solutions, quick. It would have been easier on me if I didn't and easier on a whole lot of other people. They weren't always the right solutions, either. Clearly that adds up to a certain kind of personality. Those traits are innocent, but they can be pretty darned destructive.

My husband made a difference in a very different way than I could possibly ever have done. He wasn't appreciated at the time. I think that was my doing. I thought the problems were my problems. There's where Mrs. Fullcharge comes in again. They were my kids, and I thought I had to work it all out. Again, I had the best intentions, but I retarded the benefits a bit. Now the joyous moment is when you get notes, "I love you both." Phone calls are to everyone. It has happened over the course of years, but it could have happened quicker if I had made room.

I think some of those pretty low or pretty tight moments will hold my children in good stead. You hoped they wouldn't ever have to pay some of the prices they've had to pay along the way. But, it's like being a working mother, you have to work a little harder at it. But a little hard work, even when it comes to emotions and feelings pays off in the long run. It's painful. It's hard. But it's worth the work.

2

Lessons and Traditions

Every mother is a teacher. Every child will, some day, go on alone. Each one will have to remember to bring his raincoat home. Each one will have to find a way to put bread on the table and to live alongside others.

Mothers teach by instruction. "Brush your teeth before you leave the house." "Write your grandmother a thank-you note before you wear her gift." They show their children how to feed the ducks and how to cross a city street. They tell them when to do the dishes and when to keep their mouths shut. They tell them what they think is most important. "Always remember where your family came from." An inspired mother can convert a hardship, like having the electricity turned off, into an educational adventure.

Mothers also teach by example. A child will remember the visit to a sick neighbor with a kettle of soup, a handful of flowers. A child will notice a parent who seems to draw others - - to come, to talk, to have their spirits fed. What is this magic? The child would like to have it, too, and will grow toward it all her life once she has felt it.

Mothers teach on purpose as time and wisdom permit. They also teach without intending to. A child learns from the tone of voice as much as he learns from the explanation itself. He may take up his mother's reactions, noticing what strikes fear into her, how her body shifts when she takes in the news of a death, which crises she can step around, and what makes her smile. Children are always watching. They learn from whatever is in front of them.

As a mother listens to her daughter tell her a new joke or takes her daughter out for a breakfast-for-two, or as she rearranges her work so her son can get his driver's license, she conveys her interest in that particular child. She conveys her commitment to be interested in what is important to the child.

When she talks with her children, finds out what they're feeling and what's happening in their lives, she not only teaches them that she is interested, she teaches them that they have something to offer and that others in life will be interested, too. As she spends time discussing society's issues with them as teenagers, she builds a broader base of understanding which makes it easier to discuss issues which come closer to the bone.

Are family and home always the largest influence on a child once he or she is born? Probably. The first years, before school raises its clamor of influences, are the family's opportunity to imprint its children with whatever is most unique, most personal, most precious to the family. It may be black pride and an understanding of black heritage. It may be identity as a member of the Jewish community. It may simply be a sense that you are ours and we are yours. You are next in line. The keeper of our keys.

Each family will have its own ideas about what the next ones in line need to be taught. The difference between right and wrong can be a life-time dialogue, first an external dialogue between parent and child, later an internal dialogue within the grown child, as life becomes increasingly complex. A life-time exploration of what the world has to offer also only begins with exposure of the child to many things -- dance and polo, museums and trains, the ocean and animals -- and to all kinds of people.

As the mother introduces her children to the world, she must teach them to make their way among others -- and in circumstances that are not always benign. "Be positive toward people, but don't be naive." "Take care of your brothers and sisters." "Don't let a person freeze by the side of the road." She may teach them that they are to contribute. "Look for ways to give. Start by doing your chores! And please make breakfast for your grandmother." The children will discover who they are through the commitments they make.

Part of teaching children to make their way is telling them where they may not go. A mother must define limits, and discipline the children to find their pleasure within those boundaries. You can't throw food. You may not bite other children. You can't date drug dealers and have sex with every boy in town. Only a parent can set the limits before damage is done. Also, a parent has to determine how much she can teach and how much the child can learn only by experience.

Each mother has to figure out how much control she needs and how she will get it -- in a constantly changing relationship with each child. Is spanking all right? Perhaps it is even necessary for some children. Can a reward system work? Will hard work keep them out of trouble? The answers don't come easily, especially if one or both of the mother's own parents was missing or made poor choices. A mother's impetus to teach her children certain things may come from a desire to give them something she wished she had had herself. The impetus may come from a desire to spare her children some pain she endured.

Each mother, at her best, enables her children to grapple with some of the ultimate questions:

Is there a God?
Why am I here?
What about death?
Who is my brother?
Where do spark and spirit come from?

MIRIAM TAUB
Age: 87

"The other day there was a robin walking along slowly, and behind it a little one, just in its shadow. Every once in a while the bigger one looked back. That was all. Every once in a while the robin would pick something up from the grass. It's beautiful. It's marvelous. Who trains that robin?

To me it's an unsolved mystery. Where does that love for the baby come from? It's just this little bundle of what? Inconvenience, mostly, but... Adoration creeps in."

Miriam and her husband raised one daughter in New York City a long time ago. Miriam believes that the mother is an artist, molding the soul of the child.

I was a child who never had a doll. So when I had a baby I had a live doll. I was nineteen when I had the child, Lillian. I was going to school myself, and so was my husband, at night. We took turns. When he would come home from school at night, he'd wash the diapers. I nursed her. I gave her what I call the cultural side of things.

Living in New York City, I used to play hopscotch with her on the sidewalk. She came up with the idea she couldn't call me "Mother" anymore. Of course, mothers don't play hopscotch. Mothers don't skate on the streets with children. So she called me "Mug." No babysitters, not because they didn't have them, but because we couldn't afford them. Everywhere we went, she was part of it, not a child, you see. All my friends were single, no children. It was a whole clan of grown-ups. It was a way of life. We liked to go to Jersey on weekends on hikes. I found a place you could go to see polo games for nothing. I always was reaching out. I read her all the good books that I thought could have an effect upon her. Parents give their children what they themselves would like to have had, and didn't. I sent her to a renowned dance school in the city.

Another word for mothering is molding. You can be an artist. The soul, that's what you're molding. Your next-door neighbor can't do it. Your husband somewhat, but not as much as the mother. You can be Michelangelo. Mothers especially, because they have the child most of the day, are the artists. It doesn't always work out. Artists can make a caricature. It's the way you approach it. A child can get frightened if she has a little rash, but if you take it in your stride and pacify the child, the child doesn't react the same way anymore. She takes that reaction from the mother.

I worked in the hospital during the Depression, and Lillian was sick. The hospital took a cold attitude. If you didn't come to work, for any reason whatsoever, you didn't have to come back anymore. I didn't know what to do. I had to leave her alone. I explained it to her. She stayed on the couch. Next to her were water and food and a book to read, a book to color. I told her I'd be home at twelve o'clock for lunch. She was to stay on the couch, except to go to the bathroom. I died a thousand deaths. But I had no alternative. When she saw that I wasn't scared and upset, she took on my attitude. I always tried to be cool, calm and collected.

There was a period in my life when we didn't have money for the electricity, and they were shutting it off. It was a horrible situation. How would this affect my child? That was my first question. I said, "Lillian, maybe for a day or two . . .," I can remember this so clearly, ". . . we're going to live like the pilgrims lived. They didn't have electricity. They didn't have lights. They had candles. So we're going to eat by candlelight tonight. Cooking? The pilgrims had bonfires outside, and we can't make bonfires in New York City, but, we can have cold food--milk and cheese." That was the way it was.

I wouldn't scare her. Parents do a lot of that: "Be careful!" It's the voice thing. I said, "Don't cross over, because there are automobiles coming, and sometimes they don't see the little ones, and they can hurt them. You just wait at the corner, and if

I'm not around, and I usually am, ask some woman to just take you across the street."

I wanted to give her a secure environment. I was young myself and didn't know anything. I didn't know about menses. My mother died before I had it. I went to school with my legs apart the first time. Some kid told me. How did I learn about raising children? I was an orphan. Nobody to advise me. Didn't ask my father about it. I gave birth through a clinic, so there was no real doctor involved. But the government had pamphlets on how to raise children. I did research. I got the pamphlets. They were free. I read them. What I didn't like, I rejected. Confidence is one of the first things they tell you to install. The child has to look up to the parents for everything until they reach a certain age.

Children learn by observation. I'm not a cook. My husband was very modern. We shared women's work. It was nothing for him to wash floors, do diapers, cook. We both worked. It was the right thing to do. I had to leave Lillian quite a bit alone, because I was working. But I didn't work any further than the next street from where we lived. The whole apartment building more or less looked after her. My father had a store a street away. She could go there or to a neighbor's.

One day I came home from work, and my daughter said, "Look at the cookies I made." I thought I'd die. The stove. She was five or six. How could she do that? I said, "How did you make them?" She had a children's cookbook, and she went to the neighbor and asked her to light the stove for her. And they were good! Better than I could have made.

We had a good relationship, Lillian and I, until she went to high school. I was left out in the cold. Other people had the influences on her that I had had. Adults are apt to make a fuss over a bright, good-looking child, and it's no good for the child. When the child gets this kind of artificial attention, it's taking away from the mother who looks upon her more realistically. I went through bad experiences, but now everything is fine. We mature, don't we?

I always made it my business to know different groups of people and to understand what their meaning of life is, versus mine. You have to expose your children to life.

Isn't life interesting? I always wanted something beyond my reach. I always considered myself rich.

SANTANA CORDOVA
Age: 85

Santana comes from one of the old Spanish families in New Mexico which goes back farther than anyone's memory. She lives, alone now, in a small village, where she and her husband raised their eleven children. Her oldest child is sixty, and her youngest is forty-one. The world was a different place when Santana raised her children.

We taught the children to always take care of each other and help each other. People then lived very close. We taught the children to always address people in a kind manner. To honor their parents. To treat everyone like brother and sister. To always attend mass. To take care of your health. To do good. To dress well and wear clean clothes. Take care of their money. Be good workers, be honest. Don't ever take anything that's not yours. Don't be fussy, don't be picky, and don't feel sorry for yourself. Don't waste your time, and don't be lazy. Don't ever speak badly of people. Always be ready. We had many jobs on the farm which we had to be ready with: bushels for apples, wood for the winter, hundreds of jars for canning. Always be ready. Ready with stacks of clean sheets and towels, to give hospitality.

Work, keep going, is what I do. *Caminar.*

It's hard work to have too many. You stayed hours in the kitchen. I made bread .... We taught the children to work. My husband taught the boys to work, and my daughters helped in the house, the kitchen. And keep going. It was hard to support so many. We were poor. My husband worked in the mines.

We raised animals. Pigs and cows. Chickens. My husband liked to have a lot of meat from the farm, not from the store. We had all our vegetables--*todo muy bueno*--all very good. People in those days were friendly. If you had a friend, she'd come and help you, and then you help her. We did a lot of work together and were happy. Today they say, "Pay me money and I'll help you."

My husband planted a lot. We have a very nice orchard. Apples, cherries, pears, all kinds of fruit. But now the weeds grow and grow, and the trees are old.

Before we came here we didn't have electricity in the house. When we came here, I had a washing machine. Only four rooms in the whole house and four or five children. They slept two together in the bed. We didn't have any place. Then my husband built two rooms. The others were born here. They came little by little. *No puede hacer nada*--you couldn't do anything about it.

I worked hard all my life. I tried to keep the house peaceful.

My family likes to be together. This is good. They like to see the children. If they need help, they get together. It is good. I am happy with my children.

It's hard to raise a lot of kids. I took the little one--*chiquito*-- in bed near with me when they were small, and the older one in the crib, beside of my bed. I gave them milk from my breast until they were maybe five months or more, and then I gave canned milk. They were never sick. Sometimes they fought, but they never hurt each other. The older ones kept the little ones. They lived with us all the time, in the same house, until they grew up and, like the birds, they flew.

WANDA SUTLER
Age: 47

"They got the things that they needed and some of the things they wanted, but I didn't go way out to get them everything--they got to be able to strive for something."

Wanda is a nurse. She's black. She and her husband live in Florida and have raised five children, four boys and a girl, who are now between the ages of nineteen and twenty-nine. She believes that the most important teaching of each child takes place with a parent in the home before the child is school-age.

We lived in Alabama, in the deep South. I came from a large family and kids was like, to me, a part of what life is all about. I'm a religious person--I'll put it that way--and I think that it's a blessing to have children. I was very fond of my children. I kept them all home. I wouldn't have five kids now. But at that time, five kids was not that bad. I had more time, and we could live on less.

I just loved taking care of my children. Each one of them all was a different precious child. I'm very proud of them. The kids were not a burden to me. Where I went, to church or the movies, the kids would all go. It was just a big, happy family for us. I didn't work. At that time it cost more for somebody else to sit with them. Salary wasn't that high at that time. Especially in the South, wages were very low. Very few jobs. I always felt like that a child needed to be home with a parent until he gets school-age. That way you can have your background. You can be there to mold that child and have it where it can then be in society.

The most important thing I tried to teach is responsibility, using their own judgment, being responsible for their own actions. When they was little I would kind of like see what they was going to do. I could tell them, "Well, why is it that way? Why don't you try this way?" So they'd get a bearing on what's one way and what's another way. They're using their own minds. Because in the world, you got to deal here. You know? You got to use your head. When they go out, and when things go wrong, or things don't go their way, they at least know what I feel like is the right way. They know the difference. If you're never taught anything, and then you get out there, whatever you see goes, because you don't know the difference.

A child--they're easy to learn. They may not talk a lot, but they know a lot! Everything is not going to be good. If you give them everything, what have they got to look forward to? They're going to look to you for it!

I feel kind of bad for my grandchildren, because things are changing. My children and their wives have to work, and they're not home. I think it's bad, but it takes two of them to survive. The economy has gone up so high and the wages have been kept so low, especially for my people. My children are in professions, but they're not way up here. Like me, they started from scratch. I believe that you should work for what you get, and they are on their way up, but they're not there, and they're having kids now. When the parents get off work, they're tired. The kid is tired. How much can you give?

When we were coming up, Alabama is one of the states where the black people just did not do anything but work for the white man. You did field work, or you did house work. Civil Rights. I'm in that time. I'm in the end of that, so, yes, there were very few opportunities for a black person in Alabama. It was just hard. That's one reason why I left that place. I got married in Alabama, and my husband and I left home and went out to California where the opportunity was much better.

In Alabama at the end of high school I couldn't even go work in a department store. They didn't hire a black person. You could maybe get a part-time job working at a filling station, or maybe baby-sit a white kid, work in the fields, or work in the home. Later on, they had factories. That's where most of the blacks in Alabama are now, working in factories. Now it has changed a lot. They can work in department stores. They don't have to look for the back side for the restaurant. In a doctor's office they took care of the whites before they took care of the blacks. I was in that time.

I think that's one thing what helped me to embetter in my kids: to be strong and struggle for what you could do and how you can make something and be what you are and not just what somebody else wants you to be. They come at me now, and they say "Ma, what do you think?" I say, "What do <u>you</u> think?"

The only thing that I really kept worrying about was that education. I always felt that they would be mistreated when they was coming up or getting into the system or into the world. I was always very mindful of that. It seemed like sometimes I kind of like overreacted because of where I came from. It was <u>there</u>. It's part of your life. You can't get rid of part of your life. I made them aware of it. They are very well aware of it -- how it used to be and what it is now.

Let your kid know that somebody loves him. Even if he doesn't have a good pair of pants to put on, just make them clean. They don't have steak on the table, give them veggies. It's good for them. You don't have to go out and spend all this money on toys. Give him a paper and pencil and draw. They love it. The way they do now is they give them stuff now, so they don't have to worry with them; it's all self-entertained.

Talk to the kids. Sing a song.

PAT LARKIN-WOODS
Age: 28

"We stretch out on the bed and talk about the day. 'Oh, Mom, I love this part. It's such a good part.' He'll snuggle down in his pillow and say, 'So, tell me about your day first.'"

Pat's children are Nate, eight, and Hannah, four. Two years ago Pat left her husband George. She and her children now live with her parents, and Pat is in her final year of nursing school. Pat takes special delight in teaching her children about the outdoors and about relationships. She also has a keen awareness that society does not value the work she does as a mother.

I want to have my own home and make my own nest. I'd like to have things more relaxed and not be so rigid about schedule. My mother is very concerned that they be in bed at 7:30 or 8:00. Sometimes it's a clear night, and we're going to go star-watching. We'll wait until 8:30 to go, and you can feel the tension. It makes me feel that she thinks I'm fifteen and babysitting. The children aren't really quite mine; they're a little more hers.

Yet, in many ways, I do need her. If George is late getting the children, I need her to be there, so that I can get to class on time. Also, it has freed me up financially. My parents pay for everything. We'd be on welfare if I didn't have their help. I made a choice to leave George, and I can't work full-time, go to school full-time, study and take care of two children.

Living with my parents is teaching Nate how to cope with people who have different personalities and different ways of living. There's a lot of innuendos that he picks up on, and he and I talk about at night. We stretch out on the bed and talk about the day.

"Oh, Mom, I love this part. It's such a good part." He'll snuggle down in his pillow and say, "So, tell me about your day first." I feel that's one of the best parts of my mothering. He can tell me whatever he wants to tell me.

Every once in a while I'll say something like, "Well, I remember when . . . ." He loves that.

He'll say, "Mom, tell me when . . ." or, "Does this ever happen to you, Mom?"

I wonder how long this will last. When he's thirteen will he still do this? Even now, I can see some of the innocence going.

The little girl next door and Nate were playing tag one day, when I was gone and my father was minding Nate. They were near the wall that has about a two-foot drop to the grass. Nate came up and tagged Missy, just enough so she fell to the grass. A few hours later Missy's father came to the door and said,

"I need to speak to Nate." "I have a question for you, 'Did you push Missy?'"

"Yes, I did."

"Girls are delicate, and you're not supposed to be pushing them."

Nate said to me later, "I tried to explain to him that I didn't shove her. I tagged her, and I pushed her by mistake, and it made her fall off the wall. But, Mom, he wouldn't listen. He really didn't care about the whole thing. You know how you have to just stand there and listen even though you don't want to? Do you know what I wanted to do? I wanted to slam his nose in the screen door. That really makes me mad at Missy. Those are the rules of the game. I'm not mean. I don't hurt anybody. Missy didn't need to get her father involved."

"Would you like me to speak to Mr. Schultz?"

"No, he's the one that's caused the problem, anyhow. Missy and I will get all this straightened out in the morning."

Cool as a cucumber, he was. He saw through the whole thing. He had the sense to just stand there and keep his mouth shut. I told him, "I'm really proud of you for standing there and just listening, even though you didn't want to. That's really hard."

"It was <u>wicked</u> hard."

We have these wonderful moments. Sometimes I feel that I'm telling him, "This is how I would have told my mother things, if she would have listened." She always just responded, "It's all your fault. You should have known better, etc." I try to listen and not be judgmental.

I like bike-riding with the children. I like to sit and read with them. I love to bathe them and put clean pajamas on them. I like to go on excursions with them, in the car, to museums, wherever. To see things and to talk, and to just hang out together. I like to be out with them.

We talk about "the sweet smell of spring" that we wait for all winter. One evening after dinner, we rode out on our bikes. Spring had just arrived. They were playing on the swings in the park, and Nate ran to me and said, "Mom, I can smell it!"

I didn't clue in for a minute. "What?"

"The sweet smell of spring."

I thought, "Oh, that's wonderful, you get it, you get it!"

It is women and children last in the United States. Work that's not seen is not valued and is not paid for. Mothering is work that's not seen. Unless you've lived it, you don't understand it. My husband would comment, "I've been out all day working."

"So have I, and my time counts just as much as yours." Even if I'm rolling down the hill with the children to feed the ducks, that's my job. I'm the adult who is slowly introducing the world to these children. I kept saying to George, "Who else would do this? Does that mean you don't value the children?"

Mothers who are home with children all day don't have those getting-yourself-back-together-times that a father does, as he drives home from work and feels the wind in his face and listens to the news of the world.

Everyone's happy to see the father. They're sick of the mother's face. They've been with her all day long. Dad's had conversations with outside people. He's maybe had a chance to have a cup of coffee in the car that the mother didn't have time to fix while she was doing dinner. Mothers have that tired feeling of being with the kids all day long.

When my daughter was new and my son was a toddler, I was trying to explain to my husband about my frustration and overwhelming anxiety about having to be with her constantly and not getting very much done. He told me that I just wasn't organized enough. That made me angry. Then he said, "I'll take a week off, and I'll stay home, and I'll show you how to do it."

I said, "Here's a deal. When this baby's weaned, I'll take a week off, and you take a week off at the same time. I'm going to my grandparents in Florida. When I come back, you can tell me how to do it better."

The months went by. I weaned her at twelve months. She was hysterical. I was hysterical, but I said, "I have to go, or I'll shoot somebody." I went to Florida for nine days, left him with the children, did not call home once.

When I got home, the house was immaculate. That was his big thing. But he did say to me, "I was up every night. She wanted a bottle. Then she didn't. She wanted to nurse. I couldn't. I'm exhausted. I don't know why, but I'm exhausted."

I said, "Well, you should get a little more organized." Things chilled out quite a bit after that. A week wasn't even long enough for him to experience what it was like being home all the time, because it's the build-up of the time. The monotony, the stress--all the time--no breaks, no money, no talking to another adult, never feeling as though you've accomplished anything, because it all gets undone anyhow.

When Nate was born, I did day-care for money for our mortgage. Mothers would drop off children in the morning, and I would bathe and feed and change them. Then at the end of the day, the mothers would pick them up. I would have had no one to talk to all day.

Even when we got a phone I didn't feel I could call anyone, because I had so many small children in the house. If someone did call I would be interrupted constantly, and I couldn't remember what I was talking about. It was as if my brain would run out the back of my head. I couldn't wait to get them down for naps, so I could just close my eyes and forget about everything. It was depression. It was. I think a lot of mothers battle with depression, and it's not talked about. The alienation, "Oh, you're a mother," that kind of thing. People hear that, and they don't want to talk to you any further.

George takes them two nights a week and every other weekend. They seem to be more tired when they come back, and fussier. Recently, Nate said, "I don't want to go to Robert's anymore."

"Who's Robert?"

"Julie's boy."

"Who's Julie?" I didn't know.

"Julie is Dad's friend."

"Oh." Then, "Why don't you want to go to Robert's?"

"Julie and Dad kiss." We had gotten an ice cream, and we were in one of our favorite places where the trees make a tunnel. We rolled our windows down, smelled the woods, licked ice cream, and talked.

JACQUELINE WHITE
Age: 37

"I think Hassan watches me a lot to see what kind of reactions I have."

Jacqueline is black. She has one child, a son, Hassan, who is thirteen. She is in a job-training program. At the end of the program, she will look for a job in a dialysis center. She and Hassan live just outside of Boston. Her story is full of events in which she has made decisions about how to guide her son.

Hassan has mild cerebral palsy. He plays basketball. He rides his bike. He runs like a flamingo--his knees are sort of scissored. You want your child to be normal, like other children. Every mother wants a perfect child. He's perfect to me! In school he's in regular classes, and he's a B-average student. We do our homework together. In a way, the handicap doesn't restrict him from anything. He's very unorganized, physically. His coat will hang off him. Now that's the style, so he blends right in with the rest of them.

The children, when he was growing up, made fun of his legs. He used to come home crying. I'd sit down with him and talk to him. I said, "They don't understand. Maybe if you explain to them, they will understand a little better, and it won't be so rough." He got through it. He's a good kid, pleasant, like me, and like his father. He's deceased now.

Sometimes Hassan's like the man of the house. Sometimes he's my baby --"Mummy" this and "Mummy" that. We'll go out, like on a little date, to a movie and out to eat, and I'll let him pay the check and get the tickets at the movie. He likes that.

We have a very good relationship. He knows, when he does something wrong and I yell, I'm just yelling to correct him for the thing that he did. I'll tell him, "I want you home at seven-thirty."

He'll say, "Aww, Mummy, all the other kids stay out until eight-thirty."

"But Hassan, it's getting dark outside now. I tell you to watch the news. There's people getting molested and killed and kidnapped. I'm telling you because I love you. If I didn't care, you could stay out there all night. So, I want you home at this time, and I don't want no argument, and I'm the mother!" Then, he understands. His whole attitude changes.

I worry about the city all the time. I worry about him going to high school. I ask kids I see when I'm riding the bus, "How's your high school? Is there any violence in it? A lot of fighting? Any weapons?" Hassan is my only son, and it took a long time getting him here. Altogether I lost six children, two stillborns and four miscarriages. He finally got here, a premie, at three pounds and eleven ounces. I don't want anyone to come and snatch him from me. We ride the bus together. We visit relatives, and bicycle-riding we do together. I'm mainly a home person. I like him not to go too far. He doesn't go into Boston alone.

Hassan acted so mature when his father died. He was about nine. His father and I had been split up for about two years, but we were very close. He just wasn't living here. I got a phone call in the morning, saying that his father was murdered. I was upset. But I adjust to what I have to adjust to. My family, everybody, came over. My sister said, "How is Hassan going to deal with this?"

Hassan got off the bus around two o'clock. He could see that I'd been crying, but he didn't say anything. He's very close with my sister. I felt that the best way was just to come right out and tell him. My sister told him, "Somebody hurt your father, and he's not living." I think it was like that. He looked a little sad. He didn't cry. He didn't cry at the funeral. He just kind of stood in the background, close to me. I think it was a couple of months later that he did break down and cry. I think Hassan watches me a lot to see what kind of reactions I have. We often

87

talk about his father. We look at pictures. I tell him little stories about his father and myself.

I want Hassan to do what he wants to do. I encourage him. I always stress that a good education is the most important thing. Almost the most important thing in the whole world. Later on I would like him to find a wonderful woman who loves him very much and gives him a whole houseful of kids! If he sees a nice car, be able to afford it. Don't have to worry about, "Gee, I don't have enough money for dinner next week." I tell Hassan, "You never depend on anybody. You depend on yourself." He knows how to sew. He knows how to cook.

He loves it that I'm going to school. He's very proud of me. One of his teachers told me that Hassan told her, "My mother said that you can always learn. There's no stop point. You never know enough." I felt pretty good!

Sometimes I'm too sensitive, and sometimes I fly off too quickly. I should sit back and take a good look before I start in. Hassan did something that got me so mad the other day. "Hassan!" I was chasing at him. He ran up the hallway, and I was running after him. I just had to stop and laugh. Then he peeked around his door and saw me laughing!

I have no major complaints about my son.

My mother lives with me. She had two cancer surgeries. I said, "That's it. You're coming to live with me." So she is there for Hassan, and Hassan's there for her. It's good for him. He cooks her breakfast sometimes.

Once in a while he'll get it from me--he'll get that strap right on his butt. She'll say, "Don't you hit him!" And she hit me! I was reared with a really strict hand. I used to get right under that bed. She couldn't get me under there. (I sent my sisters to get me food!)

I could tell my mother anything coming up. When I took my first drink I even told my mother. She was like a friend. My mother used to put the other kids to bed. Me and her would sit up and have grilled cheese sandwiches and cocoa and watch TV.

I want to do the right things. I want to encourage Hassan in the right way. I want him to see all kinds of people in a good light, but yet, I don't want him to be too naive.

I brought Hassan out to eat. Me, Hassan and my boyfriend. My boyfriend and I are using the Tabasco sauce on our steak. Hassan says, "I want to put some of that on my steak." I says, "Hassan, this is hot. You're too young to have Tabasco sauce on your steak." So he starts pouting. He knows better. I don't stand for that. I said, "Hassan, what did I just say? Why don't you fix your face and finish your dinner. You can't have none." He's mumbling. I gave him a little slap. Nothing like slap your head off. A little slap, just to fix his face. He's got little tears rolling down his cheeks. Then two big police officers walk in and walk right up to our table.

"Did you see a mother in here abusing her child?"

"No," I said, "but I just slapped my son, because he wanted some Tabasco sauce on his steak, and I said that was too hot for his stomach."

"Okay, well, we just came in to check."

When the cops came in, the guy--he was white--that was sitting across from us got up and left. I was furious. I can see it if I was beating my kid, but just to fix the face. Not hard.

I teach Hassan that racism is always going to be here. I tell him to pick and choose his friends. Not everybody is racist. You treat people how they treat you. If you can't treat them good, then just stay away from them. I'm a very religious person, and I tell him, "God takes care of them." Somewhere down the line they might need a black doctor to operate on them. It might change their whole outlook on things. Some people just have bad experiences. I can get mad at somebody of my own color, too.

TRACY WEISS
Age: 29

"We have reward systems. Positive reinforcement is the basis of it. If they don't behave, they don't get what they want."

Tracy has two boys: Drew is nine, and Todd is four. She is from Florida, and is a partner in a telecommunications firm, where she does the finances. Tracy had Drew "out of wedlock," and her husband Ray has adopted him. Tracy talks about juggling full-time work with being a mother, differences she sees in styles of discipline in the North and the South, and the ways she uses to get her children to behave.

I wish I could stay home all the time with them. If we could financially do it, I would. It's hard juggling the responsibilities and stresses of work and being a mother. As a partner in the firm, I take problems home from work. I've gotten pretty good at juggling the time and getting things done. I don't mind rushing home and cooking dinner. If I'm too tired, I'll just take the kids out to eat. Ray is usually working then. But, it's the mental stuff that's hard. I don't have the patience. It's hard to have pressures on me all day at work and then be able to really spend good time with the kids. Sometimes I want to just sit on the couch, because I'm so tired.

I don't care if they don't get a bath that night. I'd rather spend time with them. If the dishes don't get done, I don't care. I let the house go, and I catch it all up on the weekend, while they're taking a nap or playing with their friends. I play outside with them, but I can run back in and stick the laundry in.

You have to take time for yourself. That's probably the biggest thing that's sacrificed during all this juggle. Not that you need that much of it, but you do need some time. When the kids are asleep, I take a bath. Get a book. Put the bubble bath in.

I see a big difference in discipline between the South and the North. Up North, physical discipline, spanking and that sort of thing, is definitely out of the picture. If people do it, they don't talk about it. Down South that's talked about openly. People use discipline. You spank. I know my brothers were taken outside. You got talked, and if it was something really bad, you got spanked. I was a girl, so I didn't get spanked outside, but I was spanked once, with a belt.

I'll never forget this. I was only seven years old. A friend of mine and I crossed a major highway. That was the first wrong thing that we did! We climbed up onto the roof of this building, and we were throwing pebbles off the roof. The police brought us home. My father went crazy. I had crossed the highway and was brought home by the police--and I was a good kid. That's what he couldn't understand. He took me outside and, with a belt, spanked me three times, with my pants down. I remember. I was humiliated.

A lot of the girls that I grew up with, they tell me now, "I just had to spank those kids." It's a form of discipline. It's not like my one-time shot. This is something they do. If they have a problem, that's their solution: spanking. They don't know there are other ways. Some of their children are well-behaved most of the time, but when they get out of control, it takes a lot to get them back into control. Sometimes I can't even stand to be in a room with them.

A girl that I worked with had a little boy that she spanked from day one. Almost immediately, if he cried, she spanked. I went to her house for dinner once. Her kid must have been two or three. He was doing something. She reached up onto the top of the refrigerator and pulled down a paddle.

I said, "What's that for?!"

"I'm going to spank him. He's driving me crazy."

"You're going to spank him with THAT?!"

"He just doesn't listen to my hand any more."

So, it just progressively gets worse. They start with their hand, and the kid laughs at the hand, so they go to a paddle. Then, they go to whatever is next.

With our kids, we have reward systems. Positive reinforcement is the basis of it. If they don't behave, they don't get what they want.

For example, we went to get ice-cream this week. Before we got there, Todd was being completely obnoxious. We said to him, "You either sit down and eat your dinner, or you're not getting ice-cream. You can watch us all get ice-cream, and you're not going to eat any. You make the choice." A lot of people tell me he's too young to make the choice, but it works. He was upset that he didn't get any ice-cream. Now, the next time, he will remember that he was upset.

With Drew we have different problems. We have a rule that his room has to be cleaned every Friday for the weekend, because I see it on the weekend. If you learn the right way, you'll learn that if you keep it clean throughout the whole week, it's not such a big deal on Friday. He's learned that, but sometimes, he'll let it go. I'll say, "Golly, the rule is, 'You can't play with your friends on Saturday until you clean your room.'" He likes to spend time with his friends, so he'll make sure it's clean. And I don't have screaming. I don't have tears. I don't have to spank him. If kids do something wrong, they need to make amends for it. If someone deliberately breaks something, he has to clean up the mess. I'm not going to make you go sit in a chair while I clean it up. That's for sure! That's not going to teach you anything.

We have a rule that they are not to jump around in my room. The other day, they were jumping up and down, from the bed to the chair. The house was shaking. All the pillows were off. It had been a long day. I said, "Please stop. Please stop. Please stop." On and on. They wouldn't stop. Finally, I said, "Get the hell out of my room. I am very angry. You better go away from me before I--." I went downstairs. I had a cup of coffee.

Both kids came down about fifteen minutes later, "Mom, we have something for you . . ." They had cleaned my whole room. They had made my bed again, put the pillows up. They fixed it all on their own. They have learned: if you're wrong, you try to make amends.

Children aren't born with a sense of what is right and wrong. Even though you tell them over and over again what you think is right and wrong, you need to show them by positive and negative reinforcement. In order to teach them, you have to show them by your actions and your reactions to them.

You have to help them come to terms with their emotions. They don't understand what anger is. I always talk to them and explain things. I respect their feelings.

How did you learn these things?

My mother.

IMANI KUZU
Age: 39

"I'm going to at least communicate, find out how my kids are feeling, find out what's happening in their lives."

Imani is married and is in the process of becoming a Muslim. She is black. She has twin boys: Anthony and Edward, who are twelve, and a seven-year-old daughter, Truwork, whose name means "pure gold" in Ethiopian.

Imani has done office work but wanted to do something that will be better economically. She is in a program that will train her as a phlebotomist. Imani talks about raising children in the city, discipline, teaching the children about their black heritage, and racism.

I talk to them. A lot. I talk to them about drugs, about talking to strangers. They are pretty street-smart. We don't deal with guns, water-guns, toy guns, no kind of guns. I always talk to them, "What would you do if someone was playing with a gun? Would you stand around and play with him?"

I'd be more afraid to live in the suburbs than in the city. At least you know what the city is all about. There's always somebody around. You know there's violence; you know there's crime; you know there's drugs. It's out there. This is what's happening.

In the suburbs there's too much space. It's too quiet. Boring. There's a lot of racism. Everyone tries to act like everything is perfect, but it's not. I'd need to find out what's going on. The kids don't hang on the streets and the corners. They get together at somebody's house and smoke herb and drink beer. They're more inclined to get into drugs, being with a group of people and just going over to so-and-so's house. In the city nothing's hidden. That's part of how you survive.

The key is to know your children. Explain things to them. When my kids come home, and one of them is sleeping in the middle of the afternoon, I'm like, "What's wrong with him? Is he doing drugs?"

"Oh, Mom, you're going nuts again!"

"It's two o'clock in the afternoon, and you're asleep. What's wrong with you? Did someone touch you?"

That's how I deal with it. I think knowledge is the key of life. As long as you keep talking with these kids and making them feel comfortable enough to talk to you, they'll come to you. They'll tell you, "Guess what so-and-so is doing?"

"That's why I told you to stay away from him. He has problems, and you can't be a part of that. You have to weed out your friends and know where they're really coming from."

I think half these kids know me now, because all summer that's all I did was come out and interrupt fights. They know me. I'm right in there, "What is going on?"

I tell my kids, "Mind your business. Don't be a third party to anything. Don't get involved. Don't get in the middle. This is how people get killed. Do you guys have dreams and goals to go to college, or are you going to be hoods? What? What?"

Discipline. White people are saying, "You can beat your kids, now, you know? You can spank your child every now and then. It's good for them." We've been kicking our kids' asses since the beginning! When it comes to discipline, especially for black males, it's very important. "This hurts me more than it hurts you." I love that line. If I don't enforce this on you so you understand, I don't want to be standing before some judge--or standing over your casket.

I worked in a day-care center. This little white girl went off on her dad, because he was a little late. She kicked him. She bit him: "I hate you." If that was a black family, she would have gotten her ass kicked. She would have been in that bathroom being told, "If you ever do that to me, it will be your last." A threatening kind of thing. She would have come out of that bathroom subdued.

I can't hit my boys now with my hand. They're too hard. Somebody go get me a stick out here! Bill Cosby talked about the difference of black children being disciplined and white children being disciplined. You can intellectually talk to a white child about what he did wrong, but, he said, "With black kids, you got to get that stick!"

How much control do you want to have over your children? Because they are going to get out of control. A lot of times they are begging for discipline.

We had rules in the center, like, "You can't take toys from other kids." If they broke rules, we had time-out. You have to do that with other people's children. You can't hit them. I do that sometimes with my kids, but with real major, major bad stuff, I just have to do something. I have to let them know when they have pushed their luck.

I have to tell my kids the realities. There are a lot of racist people in the world, of all kinds. It's not just white with black. Everybody has their own little prejudices. You just don't be a part of it.

My kids came home during Black History Month and asked about the bus and Rosa Parks, Martin Luther King.

"How come you couldn't stay on the bus?"

"It was racist. They didn't think black people should sit next to a white person. They thought we should sit in the back."

The other day little radical Truwork came home and said, "Mom, I had a terrible day."

"What happened?"

"Ming said, 'All black people are stupid.'" Ming is her best friend. She's Chinese.

"No! What did you do? What did you say?"

"Well, we had a big meeting with Mrs. Gildae and discussed it. She tried to say that I misunderstood. I didn't misunderstand her. She said it!"

I talked to Mrs. Gildae. She is young. She didn't know how to fix it. She asked me, "How do you deal with things like that?"

I said, "A lot of times you have to show pictures, give examples. Show Bill Cosby's face. Show Magic Johnson. Show black women that they might see on TV." They might not

96

have any other contact with a person of color in their lives. Ask them:

"Is this person stupid?"

"No."

"Is this person stupid?"

"No."

"Well, then, it wasn't a nice thing to say." Ming repeated something she had heard from someone. It wasn't vicious. She didn't really know what she said. She didn't say that from her heart. But, it got to Truwork, because she is very conscious of her blackness and her beauty as a black child.

Somehow the two girls dealt with it and resolved it between themselves. Truwork does things very well. She pinpoints them and nips them in the bud. She's likes to read, and she's always writing. She's Miss Social Butterfly. She's real smart. I think she'll do well.

I'm not going to do what my mother did. I'm going to at least communicate, find out how my kids are feeling, find out what's happening in their lives.

I think having a daughter has especially helped me. I was afraid. I thought, "I don't want a girl. She'll be all fucked up like me." She's a _nice_ girl! She's very into like, "just us women." We go and have a Coke out together on a Sunday. It helps me as a woman. It makes me stronger. Makes me more sure of myself. I have made an extra effort to really have a relationship with her.

Everything was suppressed when we were little, because we were girls. Now it's, "Family meeting, family meeting! Let's talk about it!"

NANCY GILDER
Age: 44

"Dana: 'Mom, what's oral sex?'
Gail: 'Mom, she thinks that means talking about it.'"

Nancy is a painter and the mother of two teenage girls. Gail is fifteen; Dana, fourteen. For Nancy life with her girls is one long, positive conversation.

From the start I've enjoyed those girls. When I was pregnant my mother said, "A happy child has a happy mother." Just always maintaining that little phrase in my mind. I wanted to have those happy children.

We're all sort of busybodies. We've kept always talking to each other. There was a real strange incident when they were about four and five. They had a baby-sitter that told them not to tell me something. Dana told me. She said, "Mom, Ann said that I shouldn't tell you something."

I said, "Well, you know that we don't keep secrets, and especially if it's something that's bothering you. Is it something that you want to talk to me about?"

"Yes."

Then she told me what had transpired, and it was a sexual thing, with the baby-sitter. She must have been four, and she knew that this was wrong, and that I wasn't going to get mad at her. That was one of those pivotal points in our relationship when I realized that we had established something.

Talking about the things that are bothering them has been the key as they reached eleven, when girls start going weird. Gail started being kind of weird first. One day Dana and I were discussing Gail, and Dana said, "Don't worry, Mom, I'll never be like that."

About a year later when Dana was eleven, I said, "Dana, remember last year when you said you wouldn't be like this?"

She said, "Mom, I have no control!"

I laughed. It was wonderful. I just said, "I know--it's true."

They're eighteen months apart and just one year apart in school, which is living dangerously, but it's worked out wonderfully. They're very close. They come to each other's defense. I think they're always going to be good friends.

Gail will all of a sudden announce, "I can't do that. I can't obey this rule. I'm going to do it this way, and that's it."

I'll say, "All right, now, which one of us is the parent? I'm the one that's giving the guidelines." It's a test. I've never backed down. I've never wavered. Ron usually isn't here to make the call. I've never said, "Wait until your father gets home." I always have been able to make the call and stand firm. Maybe in my mind I would say, "Maybe I shouldn't have done that," but once it's done, it's done.

Gail is so articulate. Recently she said, "Do you know what you just did to me? You just insulted me."

It made me stop. I had to think over what I had just said to her, and on this particular occasion I said, "You're right. If you had done that to me, I would feel insulted." I apologized, and we were fine.

It hasn't been tough at all. It hasn't. I think we're through the crazy ringers that the hormonal stuff throws at you. I don't know. People say, "You have two girls? Oh, my God!" I don't even feel that way.

Recently I was going out to do phoning for the National Abortion Rights League, and as I was going out the door, Gail said, ". . . well, Mitzie and Bob are sexually active . . . ." Mitzie is Gail's age, fifteen.

My first reaction was, "Here I am going to do this NARAL telephoning . . . ." I asked, "Is she using birth control?" Then, I immediately gave the ten-minute lecture on responsibility and what that means and how if you become sexually active at age fifteen what that can do to you emotionally. Gail and Dana were both so good, "We know, Mom, don't worry."

I said, "Let's just address the subject a little closer. When you feel like--let's be realistic about this, if Mitzie is becoming sexually active--if either one of you ever wants to become sexually active, what will you do?"

"We'll come to you."

"Thank you so much. And what will we talk about?"

"We'll talk about birth control."

"<u>Thank</u> <u>you</u> <u>so</u> <u>much</u>!" I felt that we had connected again. The fact that they threw that out at me was giving me an opportunity to give them the Nancy Gilder ten-minute lecture on sexual responsibility. I was blown away on that one. Fifteen!

Gail and Dana and I had the oral sex lecture/discussion maybe two months ago. I came home, and Gail said, "Dana has something she wants to ask you, Mom."

"Oh?," and Dana is being kind of fidgety and funny.

Gail is saying, "Go on, Dana, ask her, ask her."

I'm thinking that this is going to be good.

Dana says, "Mom, what's oral sex?"

Then Gail pipes in, "Mom, she thinks that means talking about it."

I said, "Well, Dana you know what 'oral' means, and you know what sex is."

"Ugh!"

"You may say 'ugh,' but in a loving situation, there are things that you want to do with other people that make you feel good and aren't "ugh," but can be very loving."

There are those moments. But things are at a great level now, and I feel like it's always going to stay there.

DILLY MARTINEZ
Age: 60

"Not only older people, but the young kids were in our house all the time. Just to talk to Dad. I started asking myself, 'What makes this person different from the other person? How come he's so well-liked?'"

Dilly is Hispanic. Her mother lives just down the road from her and is still weaving beautiful pieces at age ninety-five. Dilly is also a weaver. She was warping a loom as we talked. The sun threw a patch of light through the open door of her studio. Bees worked their way through flowers beneath the windows. Customers and a baby grandchild were in and out, alternating politeness with howling. Dilly has more time to give to her weaving now that her eight children are grown and she is retired from being Postmaster in her small town in New Mexico.

After twenty-five years of marriage, Dilly felt she had to choose between being a wife and being the kind of mother her children needed her to be.

She has taught her children to reach out to anyone in need. She has taught them, by example, that what they do--not what they say--is what counts.

As they grew up they were integrated right into the chores of everyday. Some were cooking, some were washing, some were in the garden. I was always Postmaster, since I was twenty-one, but it was close to home. I always had two or three acres of garden. It helped the kids out. They made a little money, and they didn't have time to get in trouble. I found out what each one liked to do. Some are good bakers, good cooks, some liked working in the garden. I made it a point to teach them all aspects, not only of living, but of housekeeping.

You have to push sometimes. A young child does not know the consequences of doing something bad. A lot of the parents say, "We're going to let them grow up free and let them choose." How are they going to choose if they don't know the difference? It's like a pot. You start molding the clay. The pot is not going to happen by itself. You can leave the clay outside forever, and it's going to be a clump of clay. But if you start molding, it will take shape. And then it'll be a very proud pot!

I think that the most important thing for a child to know is that there is a reason that they are here. Sometimes it takes a lifetime to find out why. There is a reason. One of the main reasons we are here is to support each other. I hope that my kids will recognize that they are there to support the next-door person. Whether it is here at home, whether it be out on the highway. We belong to one big human family. I don't care what color, what size, what shape we are, we are one family. If we are not available to our neighbors, to whomever, then we're worthless. We should not exist.

I think that all my kids have learned that. It happened every once in a while that I would wake up and I'd see a boy sleeping on the floor or the couch. "Well, Mom, I found him on the highway last night. It was too cold. I couldn't just leave him there." After a good breakfast, he'd be on his way.

My vehicles have the keys in the ignition at all times. If anybody in the neighborhood, anybody, needs a car for an emergency, they go. They're very good. There have been instances where they do take them. I get up in the morning and there's no car. Twenty minutes later it drives up. If we are not available to each other, we are very poor people. And by doing that, we are enriched.

The faith just gives them support to carry this out. Any faith will do that. It just so happens that we were born into the Catholic faith. It really shouldn't have anything to do with religion. If by my actions I cannot prove that I am a worthwhile person, then my words are not going to do it. You have to show it. I tell my kids, "When you come and you help me change the oil in my tractor and you help me hang the door, then I believe you love me." Gifts are great. They are the frosting on the cake, but you need the cake first.

We have very large, extended families, so we really don't have a lot of the problems that people do that come from very small families. We always have access to some kind of counseling, to someone's experience. You have to make your own decisions, but you have a lot to glean from. My mother had ten children. When my kids were first born and growing up it was mostly my sisters who helped me out. Mom was still busy. There's always someone to go to. When you start having your own children, your aunts start telling you about all these other things that you had no inkling about when you were a child. Things about being a mother, being a wife, being a part of this family. Another child of the same mother doesn't always feel the same about the mother, for instance.

My father was a very warm and open person. A person that was able to sit down and discuss with you all aspects of life. Whether it was work, religion, a personal thing. Whatever it was, he was really open. I kept seeing that he had so many friends. Not only older people, but the young kids were in our house all the time. Just to talk to Dad. I started asking myself, "What makes this person different from the other person? How come he's so well-liked?" I loved him. I found out that what it was was that he didn't make any distinction between people. Whether they were Hispanic, Anglos, Negroes -- he treated them all with the same warmth and the same openness. I thought, "I want to be like him." I think that so far I've achieved some of it.

Being a woman, it's sort of hard--and I'm not what you call 'a feminist'--but .... My kids started growing up, and my youngest was about eight years old, my oldest about seventeen. My husband is from Mexico. The Hispanic male is a very possessive person, especially of females. We had all these boys and just the two girls. He treated them <u>very</u> differently. The girls were out of school. They wanted to go out. Do whatever people do at that age. He was getting very picky and wouldn't allow them, or they would come home at ten minutes after ten, and the doors would be locked.

He and I personally had never had any problems. We were married twenty-five years, but when I saw my kids going through all this stuff, I couldn't stand it. I said, "Look, I have to make a choice. Either I'm going to raise these children to be responsible, well-rounded, happy people, or else I'm going to stay with you and pay attention to you." I asked him to leave.

So, I raised half those kids since they were very small. We are not angry at each other. It's just that I needed to get him out of the house to be able to deal with his children! He couldn't change. It was a hard choice. For a whole year afterwards, I felt so guilty and in doubt. Of course, I didn't have any children when I married him, right? So, he should have come first. But then when I saw the anguish in my children's faces, I couldn't decide that way.

My husband could not understand. "Why aren't these children doing exactly what I say?" "Because they're individuals. They have different ideas. They want to try new things."

KATE MAXWELL
Age: 44

Of Betsy:
"The youth officer knew that what we wanted wasn't unreasonable. We wanted our child to go to school, to be loving toward us, and not to date drug dealers and have sex with every boy in town."

Of Jill:
"I didn't want her to feel like an Indian person who lives with us. I wanted her to feel like a Maxwell who happens to be Indian."

Kate is from Illinois. She works in a bookstore. Her two daughters, Betsy, twenty-five, and Jill, twenty-one, have given her two radically different experiences of being a mother. Betsy was a wild, difficult teenager, who would not respect limits on her behavior. Jill is a native American. She was adopted at birth and has been an easy child to raise.

Jill's situation raises the question, "When you adopt a child from another culture, what do you teach her about her identity?"

Ever since I was a child I wanted to adopt a child. It just seemed to make sense to me that if everyone did that there would be no homeless children. I flew to Arizona and picked her up when she was three months old. She's been delightful.

The idea of adopting was a philosophical thing, but the act of adopting is one of pure love. The philosophy goes out the window, because you're enamored with this child, who instantly becomes yours. She is very beautiful and sweet. We had one minor incident when she was getting teased by a boy in school. My other daughter straightened him out. As far as I know we haven't had any other problems. She has done fine.

We have a library of books, and we certainly talk about her heritage, but not a great deal. When we adopted Jill we brought her into our family. She became part of us. I just feel by constantly showing a heritage or making her feel tremendously different, you're separating her in a way from our group. Her heritage certainly was never hidden. A lot of our art is native art. We have some friends who are Indian. This is the nineties. I feel people need to join the world. Be proud of who you are, but don't dwell on it. The days of the Indians roaming the plains are over. In order to be a successful, happy person you have to be part of the world and feel part of it.

I hope I've balanced it so that she feels comfortable. She has never shown a great interest in her roots. Maybe there will come a point when she does. I see a very happy, successful person who is very involved in the world, who mentions her Indianness. We talk about it when it seems appropriate. We have little jokes, like when she gets angry someone will say, "Oh, oh, Jill is on the warpath." Keeping it light. She's a Maxwell. She's us. Being Indian is an interesting feature of her life, but it's not all of her.

It was very interesting when the movie "Dances With Wolves" came out. Everyone in the world wanted to know if she had seen it. She did not want to see the movie. I thought, "Well, there are some feelings there then."

I asked her, "How come?"

"I don't know. It just makes me uncomfortable."

I have bought a lot of Native American music tapes from the Smithsonian. She loves music, and she hated these. When she was about eleven or twelve she asked me not to play them. "They embarrass me," she said. "They sound like dogs that are barking, and I don't like it." I felt badly about that reaction. I'm not sure she feels that way any longer.

I said, "I think we should go see *Dances With Wolves*. It's sort of silly not to see it. We see all the movies." Well, she loved it. In fact we bought a copy, and she has watched it several times. I know there's interest there. I'm not trying to squash any interest.

I didn't want her to feel like an Indian person who lives with us. I wanted her to feel like a Maxwell who happens to be

Indian. I did not adopt her as a scientific experiment or as an anthropologist. She became my child. She's just Jill to us.

With Betsy we had very difficult teenage years. It was just tremendously painful. She just went wild. I don't know how to put it. At twelve she was part of a group that was the clique that was bright and wore the nice clothes. They were pure trouble as far as I was concerned. They were out of control, but everyone was treating them with kid gloves, because they were these "cream of the crop" kids. I thought they were a pain in the ass. Those children knew they were privileged, and they acted it.

When Betsy got to junior high the teacher said, "These kids can't do math." I said, "Well, I don't doubt that. They would get excused from classes to do a report on 'Ghosts in Bavaria' or some really way-out thing. They would go do this fun little report and the basics sort of went by the wayside."

I really can't explain it. I don't know what, if anything, I did wrong. I feel guilty about what happened with Betsy. My husband gets mad when I say that, because he doesn't know what we could have done differently.

At thirteen Betsy wanted to go to Jamaica with a girlfriend and couldn't understand why she couldn't do that. "I don't understand why not. I've saved money. Her father has a condominium, and they said we could go." Other children did go. That made it even more difficult. We did look contrary and difficult compared to many of the other parents. It would have been easy to say, "Yes." It was always hard to say, "No," but it was often the right thing to do.

When she was thirteen we had a party at our house. I was so excited. Rick's sister made a big cake with all these decorations. We bought all this food. It was just going to be this rite of passage, neat thing. We stayed in our bedroom. Betsy didn't want us there. We said we'd stay out of her way. When the third Coke can hit our door, Rick said, "I'm going out there!"

He had been saying that, and I was saying, "No, Rick, you're going to ruin her socially." He stopped the party at about 9:45. It was completely out of control. Their sneakers were in the fireplace, being burned. My dining room was covered with Coke, an inch deep. The hand stenciled wallpaper was covered with Coke. The beautiful cake had cans and junk pushed into it. They didn't eat it. We had girls in the bathtub sobbing over who knows what. All my houseplants were pulled out by the roots. I could not believe it.

When I finally realized something was going on that wasn't good, I went out into the dining-room, and I said, "All right, I want you guys to knock this off."

One of the boys came up to me and whined at me, "I want you guys to knock this off." It was unreal.

We lined them all up and said, "Call your parents." They were sitting on our kitchen table, sitting on our kitchen counter. Rick said to them, "Off the table. Don't sit on the table." They wouldn't move.

Two of the girls were supposed to be spending the night, and we sent them home. Now, if your children were supposed to be spending the night with a friend, and then the parents sent them home, wouldn't you call to find out what happened? We never got a phone call. We called every parent the next day and told them what had happened. I found out I did a lot of things wrong. I should have had fewer kids, because "you know things like that happen."

It was so sad. Rick and Betsy and I were cleaning it all up. I thought Rick was going to have a heart attack. Betsy was sobbing, "But you don't understand. They've got to be my friends." I just felt a failure.

Sexually it was just unbelievable. Thank God there wasn't AIDS then. I know she would have had AIDS. She was simply out of control, starting at about twelve. For the next five, six years, it was just hell. It was as if we had a race horse by the tip of its tail. We had a little tiny grip on her, but she was down the track.

I went to all my friends, and I got all these different opinions. If I could go back and do it over again, I would not ask advice of so many people. I would go with my gut reaction. I also would trust Rick's instincts a lot more. I felt, "I'm the mother. I know." But I didn't know everything. In retrospect I feel I should have had more faith in Rick. I had a tendency to try to fix it myself. But I couldn't fix it, and it just got more and more difficult. It was very hard on our marriage. Very hard.

The police called, a man Rick had grown up with, and said, "Your daughter is dating a drug dealer. We want you to know. He is going to be arrested very soon, and if she's with him, she'll be arrested." But telling your daughter not to date someone is not all that easy. Well, telling her is easy. Getting her to stop doing it is something else.

She was very angry. She was very resentful. She hated school. Her curfew would be eleven o'clock, and she'd drift in at three-thirty, drunk. At fifteen, sixteen. She would offer a sullen look, no explanation. Outrageous.

She would go to school, check in, and walk out the back door. We would get phone calls from friends saying they had seen her in different places. It was just unbelievable. We're such little straight arrows, and yet we're very liberal. It's not like I'm some crashing fundamentalist.

The nurse at the high school counseled the girls for birth control. I was very resentful. I did not want Betsy having indiscriminate sex. There's a whole argument that they will anyway, so we might as well protect them. I understand that. But I felt they were being encouraged to do things that they might not necessarily do. That nurse suggested that Betsy go to the feminist health center. I was very angry about that. I felt I was being usurped as a mother. This person stepped in because she knew "really" what Betsy needed. I was made out to be this fuddy-duddy who was being difficult. And I wasn't. I did not want Betsy having sex with ten different boys. Put the physical stuff to the side, the emotional stuff is just incredibly damaging. I think Betsy had a low self-esteem, and I don't think that that helped it. When you get passed around and you get crabs and you get herpes and you have genital warts by the time you're fifteen ...

You want to cry. Then you go talk to the people who are those of responsibility in her life. They act like it's my problem and Rick's problem, and that, in fact, they're the responsible ones, because they're giving her birth control. I'm still very angry.

Betsy was not talking to us. She went to the doctor and was being treated for I did not know what, because I was not allowed to know. I went up to his office, and I said, "I want to know what my daughter is being treated for. What is wrong? She's fifteen. I have the right to know."

"No, you don't have the right to know. This is her medical history. Young girls won't come for help if they have to deal with their parents."

It was horrendous dealing with this. Yet, you know, they sent me the bill. It just said, "For services rendered." I went up there with the bill. I said, "I'm not paying this bill. If Betsy is so responsible that she can't divulge her medical history to her mother, then she's responsible enough to pay this bill."

It wasn't the money. I'm very angry at the feminist health center. I'm a woman too, and I need support too. They were hostile toward me. They would support me if I went and had a career and got mad at my husband. They would support me if I was fourteen and wanted contraceptives or an abortion. Why wouldn't they support me? I'm a nice person. I am trying to be a good parent. All I'm really wanting is to love my child. And not in a suffocating way. Not, "You be home at 8:01. If you're home at 8:02, that's it for a year." I wanted what I felt were very normal, healthy, good desires for my child. I was treated like I was some kind of a kook.

We went to private counseling. That was a disaster. It was more of the same kind of people. "Will you make a contract with Betsy that if she goes to a party and has only three beers and two joints, it's okay?"

Rick and I both said, "No." Really. "Are you going to come to her funeral when she's dead from hitting a tree? Are you going to sit up all night with me to see if she comes home? Are you going to mourn the rest of your life if my child is killed?" I said, "Absolutely not" to that contract. I love my child.

We went to another counselor, also highly recommended. He blamed everything on me. I was hanging over Betsy. I needed to leave her alone. She was a mature, responsible, young person. This was when she was fourteen! He had not even talked to her.

110

I felt like hell as we were leaving. You do blame yourself. I felt, "It must be my fault."

The counselor said as we were walking out the door, "You know, you guys are really amazing. You've had a relationship for how long? How long have you been married? I've never been able to maintain a relationship more than six months. I just am so envious, and I admire you so much."

I said, "You know, I've come to talk to you and pay you seventy-five dollars to tell me how to run relationships, and you just told me you haven't had one longer than six months, and you haven't even got a child. Who's nuts here?" He looked at me, and he went over and ripped up my check. He didn't say a word. I was shocked. That was it for counselors.

Rick and I were constantly sitting down trying to figure out what to do. One day I'd be boosting his ego and the next day he'd be boosting mine. Or one day I'd be blaming him--he never really blamed me. I have to say, Rick is kinder than I am in a lot of ways.

My mother kept saying, "Stop talking to people. Look to yourself. Look to Rick. You fix it. This is your child. No one knows this child like you know her. You're a good mother. You're a good wife. Stop acting like a victim. You stop this. Fix it. Daddy and I will be here if you want to talk to us. If you want to talk to people, talk to people in the family who love her."

I stopped talking to friends. I went to the library and got out all these books on difficult teenagers. I got the book Tough Love. I sat in bed one night reading it to Rick. We both just cried. It was like someone had written a book about us.

We found a Tough Love group and joined it, found out there were people who had far more difficult problems with their children, which we didn't even think was possible. We found out that it wasn't our fault. Betsy was out of control. How were we going to stop that?

The youth officer from the police department was there. If you had ever told me I would talk to the youth officer about my child's problems, I would have said you were crazy. I couldn't imagine talking to the police department about something like that, but he was wonderful. He knew we loved Betsy. He knew what we wanted wasn't unreasonable. We wanted our child to go to school, to be loving toward us, and not to date drug dealers and have sex with every boy in town.

He asked if he could come to the house and talk to us and just visit. We were like these little shattered people. Betsy was off somewhere.

He said, "You have a younger daughter, don't you?"

"Yes."

"Where is she?"

"Well, she's in her bedroom."

"Why? Is it her bedtime?" This was at about four in the afternoon.

"I don't want her to hear all this bad stuff that Betsy is doing. I don't want her to be upset and be part of this terribleness."

"But she is, and she knows everything that's going on. Is she doing badly in school, by any chance?"

Well, she was.

"She knows everything that's going on, and what you're really doing is excluding her. You need to bring her in and make her part of this solution."

I went to the bedroom and asked Jill to join us. She threw in little ideas that were just great, not a lot, but I looked at her and realized, "She really does know everything." I WAS excluding her. I was doing it out of love, but it was the wrong thing to do.

I was covered in hives and constantly crying for three years. My mother said, "Look, you and I are going to Europe."

Rick said, "Absolutely, you're going." We had our tickets three days later. Betsy ran away from home the day before we were supposed to leave.

Of course, I said, "I can't go to Europe."

The youth officer came in and said, "Rick tells me you're not going to Europe."

"No, I'm not."

"Oh, yes you are. This is a control thing. She is doing this to stop you from going to Europe. You're getting on that plane. I'll bring my sleeping bag over and help things go here."

I went off to Europe not knowing where my daughter was, weeping and crying. I had a fine time in Europe, but I kept thinking, "What is going on?" Jill had an overnight camp that week, so Rick was home all alone handling this whole wild event. I called him every night.

Rick just was great. This was really the turning point. He called Tough Love people, and they all formulated this plan. Their thing is to keep throwing the ball in the kid's court and making the child react. We had been reacting to her all the time. Tough Love said, "She needs to react to you. You're the parents. This is your home. What you're asking is not unreasonable."

Rick changed the locks on the door. Locked the windows. She had been just coming and going, getting what she needed. He left a note on the door saying that if she needed to talk to him, to call the number of another mother in Tough Love. After about two days she called this other mother in Tough Love. Betsy, for the first time, was floored.

"Why can't I talk to my father?"

"Well, you give me a message, and I'll be glad to give it to your father." Suddenly, since she couldn't get into the house, nothing was hers.

It was good I wasn't there.

Rick told her through this other woman that he wanted her to come home to live, that he loved her, but that there were three things she had to do. She had to stop seeing Randy, the drug dealer; go to school every day; and be cheerful around the house. The bottom line in Tough Love is to come up with two or three things--keep it simple--that you just have to have from your child. Let all the little stuff go. Those were the three things we had decided we had to have from her.

It switched the tables on her. "You mean I just can't come and go and watch Mom cry and Dad throw a fit? Now I have to do something?" For a couple of days she said she wasn't going to do that. On about the fifth day, through this other woman, she said she would do those three things. She wanted to come home.

Rick said, "Fabulous. Where are you? I'll come pick you up. I can't wait to see you."

113

He picked her up, took her out to dinner. They had a wonderful dinner and came home. Then Betsy said, "I'm going to see Randy Saturday night." This was her final try.

Rick said, "Well, you know the rules. If you do that, you can't live here."

She just stared at him.

"But," he said, "I can't just let you run the streets either, because I love you so much. We're going to put you in foster care." Can you imagine saying that to your child? Can you imagine anything worse? He said, "I have to have someone responsible for you. You cannot run the streets. You are too young. You are not an adult. You are a very intelligent child, but you are a child, and you cannot be on your own."

She was sixteen. She just stared at him and said, "You'd do that, wouldn't you?"

He said, "I love you that much. I would."

She turned around and went into her room. She stayed the night. Stayed in her room all morning. Rick stayed home from work, puttered around the house, waiting to see what would happen. She walked out of her room, and that was the end of our trouble.

It was a test of wills. She is a very strong-willed child. After that disastrous party we told her that she had to stack seven cords of wood that we were going to heat with that winter. We felt she should have stopped the party or come to us for help stopping it. Rick said, "You stack an hour a day, until it is all put up."

She stacked it all in one day. She started early in the morning and didn't quit for lunch. It was dark, and she was still stacking. She still is that way, but she has put it toward positive things now. She's in a master's program and is getting a tuition waiver, because she is one of the top two students in her department.

Rick and I had a hard time forgetting those years. If she would get even a little out of line, we'd say, "We're not going to go through all that again." We were instantly back there. That was unfair on our part, but it took us a long time to put it behind us.

She is very hesitant to talk about those years. Years later I asked her, "What was wrong?"

"I was just really angry."

"Were you angry at us?"

"No, I was angry at me." I don't know what that means. She <u>was</u> angry at us, but she was unhappy. She says that she tried to keep in this group and that it was very hard work. She never quite felt that she could hang in there with this little top echelon, and it really bothered her.

When she was in the first grade she would put her pencil down and fold her hands. I asked her, "Why won't you do your math?"

"I don't understand it. I'm not going to get it right, so I'm not going to do it." All or nothing.

I think we could have ended this whole thing a lot sooner if we had gotten clear that she needed limits, but I felt that was too hard on her. I didn't want her to not like us. Of course, she didn't like us anyway. She told Rick once, "Mom is just a <u>wimp</u>." She saw it as a weakness, that we didn't give her limits. It was only when we got very tough that she responded. Then I think it was a relief for her. All she had to do was go to school and be a kid. It was hard for her, because she had such a reputation at that point. She had to beat that down.

She has turned out, but it was hard work. I'd die if I had to do it again. I feel angry at myself that I didn't trust myself more, sooner. The whole thing made me very unsure of myself at the time. Now, I don't question my own beliefs as much as I did.

The whole thing also made my relationship with Rick a lot stronger. It made me respect him a lot. I wasn't giving him enough credit. I no longer feel that I have to be responsible for everything. I can let some things go to him.

But, you know, I'm sure there have been instances where parents got the opposite result, that their child just left.

DEBORAH GOHN
Age: 37

"If they will be good Christians, the rest of their life don't matter, because they'll make something of their life. That's very much my concern."

Deborah is Amish. The center of her life is her family and her Christian faith. She has four boys and one girl: Samuel, fourteen; Adam, thirteen; Reuben, eight; Esther, four; and Hosea, two.

I remember with the first children I thought, "I'm just not fit to do this. How can I take care of these little ones?" It just kind of grows in you, I guess. You get more mature, too. I was only twenty-one, twenty-two, too immature to be a mom, I guess. It was scarey just to think, "I will be the mom." To think that they all grow up, and they depend on me. They come to you about every little ache and pain and scratch.

If they come and ask me a real special question, "May I do this?" or "I mayn't do this?" --that's special to me as a mom. I kind of think, "Hmm, maybe I did teach them."

Samuel, the oldest one, is out of school. We just go to school until eighth grade. Then the children work. My brother has a farm. My oldest, Samuel, is out there every day. Our people, this is the way we do it. We have to go to school until we're fifteen.

My oldest couldn't wait to get out of school. I would have loved to go to high school. I always loved school. But there was just no question. I didn't really want to keep going, because none of my friends would have been there. One of ours loves school, and he'd be real good too, but you just don't even ask-- the child doesn't ask.

116

In our own schools we have our own teachers. They don't become teachers until they're around eighteen. They step in the classroom, and they have children in all eight grades.

Our children have to work. They have no choice. They've been going on out to the farm since they were seven. Now they get up at quarter after five, and they go out. They'll be out there all day, until seven o'clock. In the summertime, it'll be 'til nine or ten.

I guess they do kind of what we tell them to do, especially until they're sixteen. My husband has a business. When next year the other one is out of school, he'll probably go out there to the farm, and the older one will stay with my husband. Something like that. We haven't really discussed yet how it's going to be. It's kind of what they like to do, too.

We like to have them be with Christian people, because that has a lot to do with it. Not just even with our people, but with Christian people. You know they don't always listen. They're not always gems. They're not always these little jewels. We have some of our people that don't stay with the Amish.

I hope and pray the children won't be that way, but children can be a challenge. I think something like that humbles a parent. They're not rebellious, you know, but they kind of put you in your place. I used to think I was going to have these children that were going to listen on me, and they don't always. I think it kind of humbles me. Keeps me down where I belong!

Once they get to sixteen, it's a little bit different. They have a little bit more say in what they're going to do. My husband and I feel that before they're sixteen, we really have the say.

The older they get the more of a challenge they are. They kind of want to do it more the way they want to do and not always listen to Mum and Dad. But you have to let go--and hope and pray that they'll be a good Christian.

They work with their Dad a lot. That means a lot to me. They go hunting with their Dad. They say, "Mum, we need something to put on the table," but it's really more of a sport for them.

The first time Samuel shot a rabbit, I was very upset. I didn't want to be bothered with butchering it. I just didn't want to be bothered with it, but, I declare, I will never do that again. He was so hurt. He wanted me to make his rabbit. He likes me to make his pheasants. He butchers everything himself, but he likes me to make them. He was hurt. I could see it at him. I'll make them, but I won't eat them. The rest of the family will.

As long as they're good Christians, I don't care what else they do. If they will be good Christians, the rest of their life don't matter, because they'll make something of their life. That's very much my concern. I'm praying for that now already, that they'll be that way. We have families and their children aren't that way. You just have to hope and pray.

Every other Sunday we have church. I think we have a hundred churches just around here, and we can still go to them, but our church has church twice a month. If we don't go to another church on the in-between Sunday, we have Sunday School at home. The children aren't allowed to go out until twelve or twelve-thirty. I just love it! It is so much fun! Just as a family, just to be together. We read to the children from the Bible and ask them questions about it, and we sing. And, then, we read as a family. Even the two youngest ones can answer questions. It depends what it is. They just kind of get brought up with it.

Some just don't live a Christian life. I'm not the judge. I don't want to judge, but, hey, you can see it. Once they get older. We're not supposed to divorce or have anything like that, but there's some that went out and did divorce, once or twice, from Amish families. They have left being Amish. If they're running with one woman and two women and three women, I don't call that Christian. I feel like if you want to live a Christian life, you wouldn't want nothing like that.

Our families are really close by. You don't live from one state to the next. There are some that live out a couple hours. You take my family and my husband's family, we just love to be together. There's gobs of children. My husband was one of nine. A lot of our people have seven, eight, nine, even ten children. We don't often <u>all</u> get together. But we're used to being together a lot. In the summertime it's no big deal for us to have fifty people for a meal. The children are thrilled when any one of

118

their aunts or uncles come. They go running and hollering. Very special. That's how our people are, very much.

We have rebellious children among our people. That's what's scarey to me. Parents have to let go sometime. The children have to go their own path. Did I teach them enough? I'm sure a lot of these mothers whose children left our people, they taught them and they prayed. That's what's scarey to me, because they did. I know the moms. I know they're Christian women. I'm sure there's children out there that you just can't tell them nothing.

I'm sure there are people that left our church, you know, and got married and got out and got really out and then wished they wouldn't have. They talk about coming back. It's really hard. Can you imagine? They have a car and electric and everything. They'd have to give all that up. It's not very often done. Very seldom, because it's too hard. They often don't have an Amish wife. She could become Amish, but I don't know of anybody that ever did. It would be too hard for her. She wasn't brought up that way.

We have a lot of in-the-home work. We're used to being at home. But it's starting to change. Women go to the market. They sell crafts and really anything that you can imagine. My husband is used to coming home and supper will be ready. We're just used to sitting around the table every night and talking.

I make quilts now. I don't always want to do that. I might go to market. I'll work for somebody--that way I can come home, and I won't have the headache. I don't want to do it myself. But as long as the children are at home and in school, I feel my place is at home, the Lord willing.

RACHEL MUELLER
Age: 40

"No one else is going to care about their self-image and show them how life works."

Rachel is Chilean, Jewish, and the mother of sixteen-year-old and twelve-year-old boys. She lives in San Diego. Rachel discusses the role of the family in producing children who will contribute to society. She has just decided to stay home for her children rather than continuing to work outside the home. Although she wishes she had made this decision sooner for them, she is still ambivalent about the impact the decision may have on her personally.

The goal of motherhood, for me, is to eventually have children that are beneficial to society--and happy. I would like them to be productive in society in whatever path they choose.

I would like them to preserve a little bit of the importance of the family. For us, coming from another country, family is very important. You meet and you have tea time, or you have dinners. You keep the family going together, together, even if you don't like the people that much. You keep the family always going together. The small family and the extended family.

As a teenager I grew up in a family where everybody was incorporated into the parties, to social events, to talking. Here it seems once the kids reach adolescence, they don't want to talk to their parents. They don't go to the movies together. It's like they are a different species, a different race. That is very strange. I have tried to tell my children that although I understand that here it is not always cool to be with your parents, that we should not forget that in other countries it is okay to interact with your parents and to go places together, and no one thinks any less of you for that.

If you are together socially, or if you are together not just for dinner-time, you interact in a way that is a lot less stressful. You get to talk about different things that maybe at home you wouldn't talk about. You get to hear different opinions. You get to hear how your children react. You can try to maybe effect a little bit their thinking to how you would see things. It is communication in a non-stressed environment. They have visited Chile enough that they know there is a different country out there and not all what we do in America is the right way or the only way.

Also, they should not forget that they are Jewish, even if they intermarry to someone of a different religion, which they probably will. They should never, never, ever forget that they are Jewish, even if their children would not be Jewish. They should always remember. Most of my family was totally slaughtered for their beliefs. My family was all lost in Europe. We observe the traditions with our children. Chances are they will not marry into the faith, but so they will not forget the tradition. The tradition lets them know where they come from, where they got their thinking.

Sometimes you don't know what is right or wrong when you grow up. I came to this country very young. I did not belong to the Latin community or the American community. I had the values of the Jewish community and could ask, "Is this acceptable or not acceptable to my community?" You don't have to be kosher, and you don't have to be that religious. They should always be introspective and think, "Is this something that would be acceptable to the Jewish community?"

I learned my mothering from my father. My mother worked a lot. I had these fantastic conversations with my mother when I was a teenager. I think my intellectual side is from her. But I got mothered mostly by my older sister and my father. My mother said, "You feed the child only every four hours." From my father I learned the other thing, "You don't let the babies cry. You just go and massage them and play with them. You throw them in the air!" He would wash our hair and do our bows. He

121

had a very warm mother. Someone that everyone loved and that he loved dearly, dearly. She didn't make it out of Europe.

Now in my family we are back to the traditional way. I am the person who takes care of the children. They have a frequently absent father.

It is like a constant war within myself to be a mother and have most people say, "Oh you don't work?" A lot of my energy goes into improving myself and trying to find a job, when I think I should be giving more time to my kids. Those years with them are gone and who the heck cares if I worked or not? I am always bombarded with highly educated people, women, men, with PhD's, because of my husband. I always feel like I have to keep up with some kind of something, so I always opted to work part-time, but I don't know. I think that what I can give them nobody else would. No one is going to give them that unconditional love and the patience that I give them. No one else is going to care about their self-image and show them how life works.

I wish I had been stronger, to resist the pressure. I would have liked to have been home full-time for at least the first five years. Now, the sixteen-year-old needs me more than the twelve-year-old, because the twelve-year-old is still under my influence. I still can tell him, "If I'm not here by four o'clock, your homework has to be done ... ," and it all works.

But the sixteen year old ... last year I worked in the afternoon. The little one would have all his things done. The other one would tell me he would be going swimming, and he was really out in the neighborhood smoking. He needed that checking-in, that "who's really your friend there?" So, I decided I was not going to work.

It's a decision I made. I will pay dearly probably. When they are gone, here I will be dangling in the air and no profession. But, last year while I was working I thought, "What for? I'm always going to be very bitter that things are not as they should be at home." To me the motherhood business is more important. It is better not to have a profession and a career, but you know that you have put two people in society that will help society and not be a liability to society.

LIZBETH PETERS
Age: 45

"When we were talking about having children we both knew that we had to decide what we were going to do about the religion before we had them. A lot of people don't do that, and they end up doing nothing, because it is too hard, too complicated."

Lizbeth is Jewish. Her husband Dirk is an ordained Christian clergyman, who works as the executive director of a social service agency in California. Their children are Ben, thirteen, and Edward, nine. Lizbeth talks about her and Dirk's decision to raise the children to celebrate their place in the history of the Jewish people.

You can't deny where you came from. You can't erase your history. Your history informs you. I'm lucky that I come from a history that I celebrate. Dirk, my husband, does too. I want our kids to feel that.

I think it's really hard to be Jewish, to really be Jewish, in a society that totally assimilates Jews, where you no longer are forced to hold yourself separate. When Jews were forced to hold themselves separate, it was very easy to be Jewish. They had no choice. But today it is easy to let it slide.

I feel that I have an obligation. I think the religion is wonderful. Because of its sense of peoplehood, because of its sense of infinite history, it deserves to last. I have a responsibility in that regard. That is why I am actively Jewish.

Judaism is a religion and a people, too. It's a religious civilization. As Jews we live in two civilizations, in the dominant civilization, wherever that may be, but we also have our own civilization that we carry with us. I feel an obligation to a chain that goes back to Abraham of Ur. I feel that all over the world I have relatives.

So many times in history events have conspired to destroy that civilization, and the most dangerous of all, I think, is assimilation, because it's painless. If anything, it's comforting. It's wonderful to be mainstreamed. The rabbis today are in an uproar, because they see assimilation as a terrible, terrible threat to the people. They are scared that this is going to wipe us out. More and more people are intermarrying. (No one in my parents' generation intermarried.) That next generation, my children's generation, is not going to feel that power, that imprinting that says, "This is important. You carry this. You remember this. You are a keeper of tales, a link in that chain. You don't break it."

Some of Ben's religious school classmates were given the choice of whether or not to bar mitzvah. I did not give Ben that choice. I told him that is part of being a Jew.

We're tough parents in that regard. There are oughts and shoulds in their lives that they have to abide by. I worry sometimes that they will rebel. I don't ever want them to be angry that they had a strong religious education. I don't want them to feel, "I should have been Christian."

I would be the last person to say that Ben and Ed must marry Jews, but I want Ben and Ed to have Jewish homes, to raise Jewish children.

When I first met Dirk, he asked me whether I would rather marry a religious Christian or an irreligious Jew.

Off the top of my head I said, "A religious Christian."

"Why?"

"Because we'd be talking about the same stuff."

In a home where one person is irreligious, the effort to make a religious home, to talk about God, and to use religious language would be much harder.

When we were talking about having children we both knew that we had to decide what we were going to do about the religion before we had them. A lot of people don't do that, and they end up doing nothing, because it is too hard, too complicated.

It was a painful discussion, because both us of really care about our faith. I probably had the edge, because it really mattered to me viscerally. I felt that it was bad enough in the eyes of my ancestors that I was married to a non-Jew, but to bring children into the world and not have them join that line, would be a terrible thing in terms of my sense of history and of my responsibility to my people.

For Dirk, it wasn't the same, but he would be giving up tremendous things, which he has. Dirk is the one who has lost in this. He has given up the opportunity to share his holidays, truly, with his children. Christmas morning with his kids, Good Friday solemnity, Easter morning joy. There was a tremendous giving on his part with the agreement.

Then he said something that has driven me ever since, which was, "They can be Jewish, but they better be Jewish, or else they're mine." And so, they're Jewish. Basically what he meant was that if I didn't do it well, if we didn't raise children who could take their place as religious people, then I had failed. At Ben's bar mitzvah, during Dirk's talk to Ben in front of the congregation, Dirk turned to me and said, "You did it."

I've raised them differently than I was raised. It was much easier to raise a child in a totally Jewish home. There was no dilemma in December. When I was a kid we just kind of battened down the hatches. We didn't participate at all in Christmas, even though it was everywhere. There was a real sense of, "Let's just get through December, and we'll be okay." You just know you're Jewish. Mom is Jewish. Dad is Jewish. Both sets of grandparents are Jewish. So, you are, too. You don't have the "Why?" questions that both Ben and Edward have.

When Edward was born, Ben asked in the hospital whether Ed was going to be Jewish or Christian. We said, "Jewish." He said that he thought Ed should be Christian, so Dirk "could have one too." He just thought that was fair. That would have been real complicated!

When Ben was three he came home one day from religious school and asked why we didn't celebrate Shabbat. We've been doing it ever since. So, we've learned from the children, as well.

We sit right here in the living-room and push the h'ors d'oeuvres aside, and everybody who's here joins in. We light the candles and do the prayers and go on with whatever we're doing. We take candles with us when we go on vacation, for wherever we are. We've had to find our own way of doing it.

I don't want the kids to think of Christians as something less. Part of our family, <u>Dirk</u>, is Christian. Ben errs wonderfully in the other direction. He gets really indignant if people ever say that their faith is right. He says, "It doesn't matter. I just happen to be Jewish, but I'm not saying that Jewish is right. I'm just saying that's what I am." He has kind of gotten what we intended him to get.

Both kids have asked me if I wished that Dirk were Jewish. Or that I had married a Jew. My response is, "Sure, I would much rather that Dirk were Jewish. It would make it much easier. As long as he had everything that made Dirk Dirk." There are always things for both of us that we wish we could both share more wholeheartedly--and can't.

We've tried to be real clear that God lives here. We have chosen to have the children speak with a specific language to God. We agree that in order to be engaged in religious stuff, you have to have a framework to do it in. You can't come randomly at God. That doesn't work. We have told the children that a Jewish framework is our choice. They are obligated to stay within that framework until they're adults. To try and give them both a Christian and a Jewish perspective would have left them with nothing, because the language is different. The approach is different.

We want to give the kids a way to address their bottom-line "why?" issues. We want them to be able to struggle with the big picture and not be nothing.

3

Challenge

Every mother is an individual woman before she is a mother. Her first challenge, when she becomes a mother, is to give up her autonomy without losing herself. Some mothers feel this transition acutely:

All of a sudden I had this baby that needed my attention twenty-four hours a day. He was all my responsibility. I just felt so trapped. I was very depressed. I couldn't understand why, because I had this beautiful baby, and I was so happy about having this child, but I felt my life was never going to be the same. I wasn't me anymore. The person that I was was gone. Now I was this mother, and all this was expected of me. I couldn't just leave the house and go out. I had to think about this other person. I was just swallowed up.

Other mothers do not seem to notice this passage and slide through it gracefully.

Mothers struggle to raise their children. One deals with a toddler who is rarely in a good mood, who will not cooperate, and who is attracted to life-threatening situations. Another has triplet babies, with a fourth baby on the way. A third has children of all ages, eleven of them, ages one to nineteen.

A teen mother tries to balance her need for a social life and for autonomy with her child's need for an attentive mother. A mother who is a doctor tries to balance the long hours she wants to give her career with her desire to be involved in her children's lives. A stepmother tries to balance the past with the present -- to balance the inherited failures of another mother and a father with her own desire to make her stepchildren whole. Guilt is a close companion who steps in quickly.

Sometimes when the challenge is more than a mother can manage at the moment, she says to her child, "I'll make it all up to you later." What does this mean? "I dug a small hole in your life. I gave your time-with-me to your brother. I gave your time-with-me to myself. But I will fill the hole before you feel the emptiness." Maybe. Be quick.

As children get older, there is very little that a mother can absolutely control. Teenagers offer a particular sort of challenge. Mothers must help them to navigate the swiftly moving currents of their own emotions, to find positive ways to assert their independence, and to avoid going down the very available roads which lead to pregnancy, AIDS, alcoholism, drug addiction, or death on the highway. The communication skills of the parents of teenagers are put to the test almost every time anyone in the house opens his or her mouth. It is not easy for parents to figure out when to stop trying to control their children. They have to learn how to manage their own fear about what may happen when their children leave in the car, for a changing destination with an undisclosed agenda.

The worst problems that any couple faces with their children are faced by a single mother alone. There is no second person to make contributions or to pick up the slack. No one else to help set the limits. No one to be a sounding-board for a difficult decision. No one to step in and do it differently and better when you feel you aren't doing it well. It is always you. You're on, all the time. Still, many single mothers triumph.

Single mothers of sons and lesbian mothers of sons carry an extra burden. The main agenda of adolescent boys is to learn how to be men in society. Mothers cannot teach boys how to be men. Only men can. These mothers want to know: how do fatherless boys become adults?

Mothers develop different strategies for meeting challenges. They constantly reach for more information, new perspectives, a fuller understanding. They evolve new attitudes and habits. "It could be worse." "You have to let some things go." "Don't wait until the work is done to make a cup of coffee and take a break."

"Some issues the children will have to deal with later." Leftovers. A mother may see herself with new eyes: "I always got through because I had no choice. You do what you have to do. You do wonders sometimes." You are lucky if you have a grandmother who comes to you in your dreams.

Sometimes faith in a larger reality helps a mother meet a challenge. She is curious about God's purpose for the child, or she sees God working in her life. The conviction that she is doing the right thing is a source of strength. Perhaps she believes that she is the only person in the world who will provide the kind of patience and care this child needs.

Sometimes the challenge is too great. Mothers cannot fix everything. Problems can come out of nowhere and change everything. Mental illness. A debilitating accident. Problems which put the child beyond the mother's reach. You are doing all you can, and it is not enough. You exist in sadness. Hope is elusive. Some friends will leave you, terrified by their vulnerability, which you have unmasked. Others may try to stand beside you, but you, like your child, are hard to touch, separated by your pain from those who laugh freely. You go on. That's all.

Managing money and having enough is a challenge that complicates child-raising. At the extreme end of financial problems is homelessness. Home is the place that has your things in it. And your cat. It is the place that you and those you love made the way it is, for yourselves. Your path at the end of the day leads there, and you belong when you arrive. You left shoes under the couch, a bracelet by the sink, an open book by a favorite chair. They're still there. You know where the tea bags live and what is in the refrigerator. Perhaps you chose the potted geranium for its perfect shade of red. You may go home and speak or keep silence, nap, choose your music, take off your clothes. If you are homeless, you do not have a place like this. But you may have a family. And you may want, more than anything else, to make a home for your family to return to now, and, in memories, forever.

DAWN MORRIS
Age:18

"To be honest with you, I don't like being a mother." . . .
"My daughter probably was the only thing that saved me."

Dawn gave birth to Aimee when she was seventeen. Dawn's challenge is to balance being a teenager and a mother. Aimee is now nine months old. Dawn is currently living in her parents' home for the first time since she was twelve. She is enrolled in a program which will help her to earn her G.E.D., teach her how to manage her life, and help her get into college.

There is tension in Dawn's statements and in her life as a mother:

I put my mother through so much. When I think about it, it really depresses me. My mother loved me so much, but she just wasn't around enough. She was on welfare and was going to work at the factory, so my grandparents took care of me most of the time. My mother did the best she could. My dad was never around. I didn't live at home from the age of twelve until I had Aimee. I went home maybe three days a week. My parents never knew where I was. I was with friends, drinking, partying. I never slept. I maybe got about three hours of sleep a week. I was constantly spaced out. Zonked. I didn't know anything. If it wasn't for my parents putting me in a placement, then I would never ever have been able to straighten my head out. They put me in group homes, drug rehabilitation, lock-ups. I've been in a lot of those.

When I got pregnant, I pretty much mellowed out. I didn't do drugs. I was totally straight the whole nine months. The day I had Aimee, I moved home to live with my parents.

To be honest with you, I don't like being a mother. I had so many years to be locked up and not free, and now that I'm free, I want to explore. I want to travel. I want to do school. I want to do so many things. I'm really limited in what I can do, because I have a baby.

I love my daughter. She is my main influence, my first concern. My daughter probably was the only thing that saved me. I realized I had to take responsibility for someone else. I had to start taking care of myself because of her.

There are so many good things about being a mom and so many bad things about it. All the love I put in, I get back. I like how if someone else is holding her and I walk up, she reaches for me. Or I walk through the door--she smiles! I know that she'd rather be with me than anybody else. I hate taking her everywhere I go.

I'm trying to get things together. It seems like there's one obstacle in front of another. I don't even have my license yet. Then I'm going to buy a car. I want a nice sports car, where people are going to look at me. Plus, I want to go to college. Basically my main inspiration is to prove everybody wrong. I want to prove that I can be a good mother and a successful career person. I'm not going to stay home with my kid and depend on a man. I don't understand how anyone can do that. I'd go absolutely nuts.

Sometimes I feel really guilty. If I had waited until I was settled down and married . . . blah, blah, blah . . . then, I would have been a much better mother. My attention span, to sit down and try and teach her something, isn't very long. I don't have much time to sit there and play with her and talk to her and love her, and I feel really guilty about it. Really guilty. But I am going to make it all up to her.

After I had her, I went through a depression. My boyfriend was in jail. "I am all by myself. What am I doing? How am I going to do this? Oh, my God!" When I finally sit down and think, that's when I get depressed. So that's why I'm always busy and don't like to be alone, so that I don't have to think.

When I finally do sit down and play with her, I just think of how much I love her. When she was little sometimes I'd watch her sleep.   I'd just cry, because it's like the biggest accomplishment I'll ever, ever achieve. I'm bringing up another life. I'm doing everything for her that I wished I had.

Some girls in the G.E.D. program say they love being a mom, and they want another kid. I'm like, "Are you <u>crazy</u>?!" They don't ever go out. Their high part of life is bingo. Come on! These are people who are eighteen, nineteen, who haven't even experienced life. Some of us probably don't even know what love is, or having a really good time.

I have a very poor self image, but I'm starting to look at myself in a different way. I've always hated myself. I'm starting to enjoy things like giving Aimee a bath. Before, I felt, "I have to do this; I have to do that." Everything just <u>sucked</u>, because I didn't want to do it. Now I feel, "This is my responsibility." I kind of like it.

Aimee was like a God-send: "Dawn, get your life back on track." I didn't care. "I'm going to do drugs and die. Who cares?" But now I have something to stay alive for. And I have a lot more things, not just Aimee. I have social status to work for. School. It gives me structure in life, and I like structure. I have things I want to accomplish.

It's so emotional. So many feelings. Some anger. Some happiness. Some guilt. I'd like to change all those feelings into just feeling happy.

SUSAN REHNER
Age: 40

"When we made the decision to adopt a black child, I knew that we were going to have to change."

Susan is white, a lesbian, living in Massachusetts. She has been with her partner Catherine for sixteen years. Catherine is also white. She is twelve years older than Susan and had already raised three children into their twenties when she and Susan decided to adopt a black baby. The baby, a little girl named Kiyarna, is now two.

It's like having a little pal. I know it'll get a lot more complicated when she's older, and we're dealing with the adoption and sexual preference and race.

The adoption agency treated us wonderfully. I told my social worker I was a lesbian, because I wasn't going to through this thing as a lie. She met with Catherine and me. I'm the identified mother. Catherine didn't need to be a mother again. I called the agency on a Wednesday and said I wanted to work with them in a few months. They called back with Kiyarna two days later.

I've had what has felt like two tasks since Kiyarna has come. One is to just in a general basic way be a good mother. The other is to be a mother of an African-American child. I'm learning more and more what that means: opening up our world, extending our world, not being just a white family any more, not doing things that just white people do.

Being involved in the black church is part of that. I work at the housing authority. That's put me in touch with a lot of Latino, Asian, and black families, too. We've been going to the church for about a year. I usher, and tithe, and work on a lot of suppers. We have been very graciously received there. That church is going to be a key for our lives. It doesn't feel right to me when Kiyarna is the only black person around. I feel better when there are all kinds of kids around, and not just kids, all kinds of adults.

When we made the decision to adopt a black child, I knew that we were going to have to change. You just have to change. You can't raise them white. I can't say, "It's fine to be black," and have no black friends, no black contacts, or knowledge of black culture..

I would like to know Kiyarna's parents. My preference would be for this to be an open adoption. We got a fifteen-page social history of Kiyarna, without the names, going back to great, great grandparents. That was exciting. I would like to be connected to those people, and I would like Kiyarna to be connected to those people. When she's eighteen that's an option for her. I wrote to the mother, through the agency. I couldn't use my name, and I couldn't use Kiyarna's name. I was saying, "If you'd like to have contact, I would."

I knew I would be transformed by Kiyarna, but I didn't know how much. Just being a mother is transforming. When we go to church, I dress up now. I wear heels. I'm not denying that I'm a lesbian, but I have to be in the world in a different way than I was. I have more at stake. Some of that is just plain appearances, keeping her dressed, dressing a little bit better myself.

The racism is a constant surprise. The assumptions that I have grown up with are being moved around all the time. It's every-day stuff, like one of the guys in church said that he was with the math department at the college. My assumption was that he was an assistant of some kind. I found out that he's a world-renowned math professor. I felt so ashamed.

This church is really split along class lines. I was approaching the church as if it were a homogeneous kind of thing: they're black, and they all like each other, and I'm white, and they don't like me much, or they're suspicious. When we went to a church social, we could see the academics were over here, the welfare mothers were over here, the working people were here, and Catherine and I were just sort of in the middle, complete anomalies.

I don't know what I thought it would be like having a little person around. I don't think I was prepared for the physical exhaustion of having the new baby, and how whacked out your schedule is for a whole year. I'd sit down, and I'd close my eyes, and I'd be almost hallucinating I was so tired. You have the physical reality of someone else in your presence all the time.

With a two-year-old you begin to have to draw some lines and make some limits and not be just a pal to your kid. Some of my instincts aren't very good, and if I don't use my instincts, what else is there? I can see ahead that it just gets more and more complicated.

Last night Catherine, whom Kiyarna calls "Oma," Other Mother, could hear from another room that Kiyarna and her little friend were jumping on the couch. I was going to just let it go. Catherine came in and said, "You can't jump on the couch." It's those kinds of things where Catherine will firm me up and show me that you can say "no," and there will be a storm, but it will pass. I'm learning a lot. It's wonderful that she's been through raising kids before.

I didn't know about the effect on the parents' relationship. After two years, I feel as if Catherine and I are finally getting stabilized with each other again. Not that it's been horrible, but we are being clear about taking time together and getting close again. It was hard for me to keep part of myself available to Catherine, when I had this child, this love of my life, that I was totally involved with. At the worst times I think Catherine felt she lost me and didn't get the baby, either.

Another feature of this is the complication of having an adopted child. I know there will be continuing developmental crises. At three and four when you're talking to the child about adoption, it's all about gain: "We've all gained this wonderful experience; you're part of our family." But in reality, adoption for the child is based on devastating loss. Whether it happens as a baby or as an older kid, it's a devastating experience. It's gain for you as a parent, and it's loss for the child. There's no getting around that. It means for her, "Who do I belong to?," "Who am

I?" I have never dealt with those questions, because I've always seen who I belonged to and looked like my parents.

They say that you start dealing with those questions around age six or seven, when the child can go backwards as well as forwards in time in her mind, when she starts to say, "Well, what did happen to me when I was little?," "Why was I given away?," "Why did they leave me?" A child may talk about being adopted when he or she is four or five, but it's just a word. I have information from the family that we will share with her.

I think about losing Kiyarna. When my mother died, it was an enormous loss for me. It felt like the bottom fell out of my world. It did. It took a year to get through it. I thought a lot about death and felt like I had sort of wrapped it up again. Then adopting Kiyarna just ripped off the cover again. The idea of my dying or her dying or Catherine's dying just kills me.

One of the things that came out of my mother's death was my trying to be a kinder person. That's all there was. If I were in her position I would just want the people I loved to be near me. What else is there? I'm trying to extend that into the life that I have now, and to be kind in the face of all the fragility and vulnerability.

Catherine says that in the teenage years with all the race, sexual stuff, sexual preference stuff, adoption stuff rolled together, she's going to go hiking in Nepal! I know that the com-plications are just beginning. On the other hand, if I think of it as a series of challenges, I like it.

KAREN LECLAIRE
Age: 40

"I took each of my girls down to the health clinic for an educational visit . . . 'I have a fourteen-year-old daughter, and I would like you to show her everything. I would like you to put it in her hand and explain every piece of birth control.'"

With Ann, Janice, and Sue now ages twenty, nineteen, and fifteen, Karen has survived most of the years in which she will be a parent of teenagers.

Teenagers are tough. They are so hard. So hard. Even good kids. They want so much to do what they want to do! Some of that's all right, but some of that's not safe. When the three girls were all home, and they were all in junior high school and high school, they were driving and were never where they said they were going to be. There were calls at midnight, parties. It disrupts your life.

One night we heard the rumble of a motor out in the yard. Two kids picked a third one up off the ground and carried her-- our Ann--to the door. One was under one of her arms; one, under the other, carrying the crutches that she was supposed to be using, from a sports accident. They said, "Hi, this is Ann."

"Yeah, we <u>know</u> this is Ann."

They were from Students against Drunk Driving. Ann got drunk, called them, and had them bring her home. There she was, stone-drunk, saying, "I'm not drunk," and standing up, and falling down, and getting sick, and still denying it. And the whole thing is, you can't get mad, because she did what you told her to do. The emotional check that you have to stay in . . . and this is just normal stuff. This is <u>good</u> <u>normal</u> <u>stuff</u>! They didn't drink and drive. They didn't steal. They weren't on drugs, and they didn't get pregnant.

I took each of my girls down to the health clinic for an educational visit. I swallowed it. It wasn't pride, it was my upbringing, my background. I was never told anything. "You shouldn't know anything, because you're not going to do anything." I had to get by that, and make the phone call, to say, "I have a fourteen-year-old daughter, and I would like you to show her everything. I would like you to put it in her hand and explain every piece of birth control."

Once they got to that first visit, I knew they would be given a business card and would know it was confidential. I wanted to set them up with somebody outside the family. At the same time, we were talking about intimacy and how to make decisions about whether you want to have sex. We talked about really loving somebody and what that means.

I remember when Ann told me that she was going to go to the clinic. She wanted fifty dollars for birth control pills. It was hard to accept that I was going to be paying for something that I didn't fully approve of. But I was glad she asked me, because I wouldn't have wanted not having the money to have stopped her. It's easier than abortion. I wouldn't want to ever have to sit down and talk about that decision. I've thought a lot about it.

Now she's in love with a fellow at college. She called me six weeks ago and said, "Mom, I'm going to run out of birth control pills before I get home from school. What do I do?"

"I don't know what you do! Why can't the guys do something?"-- that's what I was thinking. But you can't let them count on the guys. So, I said, "I guess you'll have to call the clinic, because they're not going to give me anything for you. You'll have to try to figure it out, but <u>don't</u> take <u>any</u> <u>chances</u>."

I told them, "If you ever need any help, just come and ask." If they asked, I had to say, "Yes." That's what's hard. You open your big mouth, then you've got to shut up and not preach. That's what drains you. It's like your insides say, "No, no, no," but intellectually you know you have to try to stretch.

Like, you know, they're never going to drink--right? Teenagers are <u>going</u> <u>to</u> <u>drink</u>. Parents who say, "Don't drink, don't drink, don't drink" are going to have conflict. You're telling them not to, and you find out that they do, and it's a big blow up, or the kids start sneaking. Kids can be very good at sneaking.

So, we started off by saying, "We know you're going to drink. For God's sakes, don't drive if you've been drinking, because we don't want you to get killed." The rule was: "If you need to stay overnight, you call us, and tell us you're staying overnight."

I remember sitting in the bathroom with one of them, while she was being sick, and smiling and thinking, "Good, experience this, and it will be good for six months." Now they don't even like to drink.

Kids are an emotional roller-coaster. Sue just finished the freshman year. She was very volatile, explosive. She'd go in the bathroom mad and slam the door. Ten minutes later I'd say, "All right, now, why don't you come out, and we'll discuss it?" No answer. She wasn't there. She had crawled out the window. She'd be out walking the streets. We have a friendly police officer who brought her home many times. We'd know to call and say, "Okay, Bob, she's gone."

My little Honda was in mint condition before they got licenses. Now it looks like death warmed over. The day before we left for vacation we got a call at eleven at night. They were in an accident. "Nothing serious, but we can't drive the car." All kinds of little stuff like this just constantly complicates your life.

They've all been to counseling, and it was because, last resort, we didn't know what to do. We do whatever works. With Jan, as a freshman, she'd come home after basketball games, crying.

"What's the matter?"

"I wish I were dead."

That's a red flag signal that you're told to pay attention to! So we picked her up from school one day, didn't tell her where we were going, and practically had to grab her arm when she realized we were going into a counseling session, to talk to somebody. She went to counseling for two, three months. Just to get through it.

We did it with Ann about her boyfriend. He was an only child and spoiled and controlling. Ann was so in love with him she didn't see any of this. She was bummed out all the time, didn't know, didn't know, cried.

I would not change the fact that I had them starting at nineteen, because I like being forty and being on the other side. I'm going to have the next forty years to do my own thing, and I'll be young enough to do it and enjoy it. Also, I loved being young enough to enjoy them as teenagers. We went running together yesterday. I can do those things.

I can't wait for them all to leave! Sometimes I feel bad saying this. It's like, "Great." Louis and I are so looking forward to just enjoying the time. I have had babies since I was nineteen! I want them all out of the house at least twelve months before I see a grandchild. I want to see what it's like not to have anything. I don't know if it's selfish. I don't even care! I just need to see what it's like.

LOIE STANIFORD
Age: 47

"A lot of humor. A lot of warmth. A lot of talking."

Loie is a free-lance designer, a single parent with a fifteen-year-old daughter, Anna. Loie's husband, a painter, left Loie when Anna was a year old. Loie's work has enabled her to come close to being a full-time mother as well as a full-time professional.

She articulates that she and Anna cannot replace what her husband Larry would have given the family if he had been an active husband and father over the years. His marvelous paintings hang in many rooms of the house.

Anna is steady, strong. She came to me that way, I think, but people say, "No, you had a lot to do with it." She's always had a good head on her shoulders. For the most part my job let me stay at home. I really enjoy her. She is sort of wise, in her own way. Anna was five when my mother died. She said to me, "Yoyo may be dead, but she'll always live on, because I'll always remember her." Just the right thing to say.

Her father was so mixed up, I guess that was why he could leave his child. To this day I wonder, "How could he have left this kid?" She was so cute. She was so innocent and healthy, and half-him. She looked like him, still does. She has some of his mannerisms. She's never known her father, and yet every once in a while, I see something in her that is <u>him</u>.

He had a bad mental breakdown when Anna was six months old. He left six months later. Maybe that was his gift--to leave, rather than making me deal with a man that was crazy. Fortunately, I had a career. I worked for other people for most of the first five years of Anna's life. Then the ad agency died. I decided that having a husband have a mental breakdown on me, and losing my mother that year, and losing my job was too much.

To break this chain of bad things, I took my little station wagon and filled it with camping equipment, and Anna and I went on a cross-country trip. It was wonderful! To me five years old was so much more mature than two. Now I look at five-year-old children, and I think, "How did I do that?"

Up until then, Anna had been raised mostly by babysitters. I didn't even know what she had for lunch. It didn't take too long before she was taking me for granted. It was almost as if she had been respecting me more than she should, because I wasn't always there. I know the relationship changed when I had her full-time. It was an important change, more normalizing. I wish it were possible for every woman to have a career <u>and</u> be a full-time mother, because it's so wonderful to have a career, and it's equally wonderful to be a full-time mother.

Anna began to take me for granted. There was less respect, more slapping Mummy on the fanny. There was more warmth, more familiarity, intimacy. A stronger bond.

She kept asking me all across country, "Are we lost? Are we ever going to find our way back? Are you going to take me with you, back?" I guess she had gotten so used to being dropped off at babysitters.

Finally, I said, "If I left you here, who would I have to tease all the way back? I need you around. I love you."

After that trip, I started working for myself. It's been tenuous. I'm a good designer, but I don't sell myself as well as I should. Some months I'll have a lot of work, and others it will just drop off. There were months when I didn't have any income. That's been the major stress factor in my life--finances. But just when you think you have it rough, you hear about someone who really has problems. I worry about money? Give it a rest.

I feel so lucky to have had this wonderful career where I could practically be a regular mom. When she came home from school, I was there. If she was sick at school, she knew she could call me up, and I'd come get her.

My sister has helped me out a couple of times financially. What do women do who are completely alone, without any help, no careers, and no financial backing from relatives? It's frightening.

After a few years, Larry's parents started sending a little money. I banked it for Anna, for the most part, but then I spent some on luxuries for her. I fixed her room up. Every once in a while I'd buy her some clothes that I couldn't afford. She wanted a big radio. She knows that these things have come from her grandparents.

It would have been really nice to have someone to discuss things with. When Anna was having temper tantrums, without another person right there, it was hard to know how to react. Was what this kid was doing normal? You talk with your friends a little. I did have some friends, whom I swapped child-care for a weekend with. I'd say, "Criticize my child, or compliment my child. Tell me what's good about her and what's not so good." I always welcomed that kind of input. There was nowhere else to get it.

Our relationship is wonderful. There's just a really good friendship. I love teasing her. She loves teasing me back. We laugh a lot. We hug a lot. A lot of warmth, a lot of talking back and forth. There's anger too. We get mad at each other. But it's always good. We always get somewhere with it. We always understand each other a little bit more.

I hear of people who aren't close to their kids. They're surprised if they find out their kids are on drugs. They think they're close. I don't know. How do you get that far from your kids? My mother and I were always close.

It's really hard to be the only disciplinarian. I just mean the discipline of getting her to do things, not punishment. That whole argument that ensues when you tell a child to do something, all the reasons they have for not doing it, or for not doing it now, which of course means they'll never remember to . . . that's the hardest part, the pushing. You have to do that. If you don't do that their little brains turn into mush.

I think it's good to have chores to do. Sometimes she'll get into it and do a really good job. Other times she'll do a lousy job, and I'll get mad at her, and then she'll explain that she didn't know how to do it--like vacuuming. She would just do the middle of the room. So I had to teach her how to do it--not just tell her to do it again.

I think that being a mother is the nicest thing you can do in your life. It connects you with everything important. It gives you a really good feeling about life that you would miss completely if you weren't a mother. You don't have to search for meaning in life. It's right there.

I wish that she could have had her father help bring her up. He was a really good artist. The thing that bothers me the most is I miss his not being able to spend the years and years with her that would have trained her to be an artist. I don't know how to do that. He had a lot of really good personal characteristics that I would have liked to have him develop in her. A lot of the ways that he was were passed through in her genes. Basically, he had a very uncomplaining way about him. Very pleasant. She's like that. I respect that.

It would have been really good to have his input, because I respected him as a person. He was very sensitive and very caring. It would have been really nice to have another person with as much at stake as I have.

I used to wonder if he'd just show up, but I don't think about it anymore. It was twelve years ago. After a while you wear yourself out wondering. You have to get the paperwork done to be divorced. I've never bothered to do that. I would if I met someone that I wanted to marry.

People don't talk about insanity. I don't think that's right. It's very common. What they think was wrong with Larry was a chemical imbalance. There's a chemical that stops triggering the chemical that keeps your brain on an even keel. That's what they think causes the mania. When people become manic they feel power. Apparently they can almost feel the blood pumping through their veins. When he was admitted to the hospital, he gave his name. The doctor asked, "Who do you think you are?" Larry said, "Well, I'm God, I'm Jesus Christ, and I'm a monarch butterfly." He was dead serious.

It's kind of funny, unless it happens to someone you know who is a great part of your life. Then it's not funny, because you know that the person you knew and loved is now dead. That's how I had to accept it. That man, Larry, never came back. There were parts of him that came back. Lucid times when he was right there, but he was always confused, and he cried a lot. Men don't cry unless they're really confused. His parents didn't help. They kept telling him he was okay. He wasn't. He needed to be told he was off-kilter, and he needed to be taking medication. I guess all they had was lithium twelve years ago. They understand better now what happened to him.

I don't know. Sometimes I wish I had had the strength to deal with a full-time job, and a child, and rehabilitating a crazy man. I think that if I had done it all I would not have done any of it very well. I think that I've raised my child real well. She's wonderful. If you have to make hard choices, that was one that was successful. It wasn't really my choice. He left.

I have really taught Anna to be a good communicator. A kid this age will say, "Mom, you just don't understand."

A mother has to say, "You're right, I don't understand this particular situation. You've got to explain it to me. Talk to me. Help me understand."

It's going to be hard when she goes to college. I don't know what a long period away from her will be like. The abyss. I tease her about sending her to the college down the street, but she'll go farther away. You teach them to fly, and then you have to let them do it.

JULIA CADEAU
Age: 43

"There have been times when the prospect of a new life was just devastating," but . . . "This is what God wants. He might not ask someone else. Whatever we've got, whatever this family is, that's what He wants for this new life."

Julia is Catholic and has eleven children, ages one to nineteen: four boys, followed by two girls, followed by five boys. The children are an expression of her and her husband's faith in God. Julia's husband Roger works for the government. Julia sells baskets four evenings a week, while Roger is home with the children. Julia's philosophy of raising children weaves in and out of the anecdotes she tells. Having so many children has profoundly transformed her.

When I had my first child, I remember Roger's coming home from work, and my saying, "I have spent my entire day caring for this child. If I'm not doing formula and sterilizing bottles, I'm changing his diaper, or I'm burping him." Of course, on the first one everything takes so long. It seemed like that was all I did.

Then, when the second one came along, I felt overwhelmed. People say to me now, "I have only two. What do you do with eleven?" I remember when I had just the two, and they were fifteen months apart, just to go anyplace was such a major undertaking.

I did get more overwhelmed up to a point, and then it leveled off. Three made a big difference. I noticed that my husband was not quite as willing to have me go out in the evening. Then with four, I just thought that was the end of my life. On a rainy day, or in the middle of winter, you do not take four little boys and go

146

see people or walk around the mall. Now four seems very manageable, but I've grown a long way.

It was a moral conviction that we had and part of our Catholic faith. We felt that part of being married was being receptive to the children that God sent to you. You just went from there and made it work. I certainly never thought I'd end up with eleven children. They just kind of kept coming along. I realized that this was just the way it was going to be for me. I always kind of thought, "Four, maybe five," and then, at that point I would think, "This is going to be the last, I'm sure. God will realize that I can't handle any more."

You begin to hear this SuperMom syndrome. People assume that you have "extra patience." You _love_ children. You don't need anything else in life. You really just have boundless energy. For twenty years now I've been parenting and taking care of a home. You get more efficient, and with some things you say, "That's not important," and you let it go. I resent it when people act like things just don't bother me. Just because I can do it, doesn't mean it's easy. So, when I'm struggling along, I'm not receptive to that stuff. If I'm different at all, it's only because I've left myself open to growing, and because life has stepped on me once in a while. You just keep going.

I'd always have two afternoons a week no matter how little money there was, when I could get off just to have some time alone. I'd go to the mall or something. Sometimes I'd get there and realize I was too tired to go in, and I'd just sleep in the car all afternoon.

I had no preparation for all these boys. When we had the first four boys, they were all under five. I was saying, "What am I doing wrong here? These kids are wild. They're fighting. They're breaking things all the time." My husband said, "This is the way little boys are." I was a wreck.

I feel very lucky to have the two girls. I had begun to despair. Before I had a family I always used to think I'd have just two girls, and I'd put ribbons in their hair, and on rainy days they'd go through my jewelry box.

We can't afford to have eleven kids. I don't know how much you'd have to make to really do it. There are a lot of bills on the desk that we pay twenty-five dollars on each month. There are probably eight medical people that we pay to each month. From February through March: one son sprained his foot and was on crutches; another one broke his arm; somebody else broke their finger; my daughter also broke her arm, and one of the little ones fell and got stitches in his forehead. Then, the baby fell out the window.

These bills are a reality. You just chip away at them. Eventually a bill gets taken care of, and then there's something else. There's never going to be a point where it's all taken care of. I used to think there was going to be an extra fifty dollars when we got the refrigerator paid off. Then we needed a new transmission.

Children come with such varied baggage. Having a lot of children has freed me from feeling responsible for how each child behaves or the way each child is. With one or two children I think there's more temptation to ask yourself what you've done wrong. "Why haven't I made him more civilized?," or "Why is he so self-centered?" I have some children who are really very easy. They basically like to please. Others could care less what I think about them, and, in fact, if they can annoy me, all the better. There's just something in them that's not so attuned to approval! I could say, "I am so upset with you that I'm going to put you in your room for the rest of your life." "So? Is this supposed to be a big deal to me?" That's the kind of thing that sends steam out your ears. You wonder, "What's going on here?" But after seeing many variations on a theme, I realize that they come that way.

As a parent you have to work with what you're given. If a child's basic tendency is to be lazy, for example, you have to help the child work against it. Some kids in the summer want to go out and earn money and have it in the bank. Some want to buy things. Our situation is not affluent. We have food and clothes and everything we need, but when somebody else is getting a mountain bike for his birthday that costs $450, my sixteen-year-old is not. Some kids will say, "Oh, I can use the old bike," or "I can borrow someone's bike." Others will be like, "I don't think my life is going to be worth living, because I don't have the stuff that other kids have." Kids just come that way -- some of them like <u>stuff</u> more than others!

You can't let yourself think, "This child is going to be so materialistic. That's all that's ever going to matter. There's not going to be that balance in his life, or real integrity, or character." That's not true. It's just something that they have to work with.

I probably had five or six kids before I figured that out. I started seeing the positive aspects of having many children. I always felt that morally this was the way to go, but I began to see that my kids could handle things better. Life was not so comfortable for them that they were easily thrown by something. The sharing was positive. You had to wait your turn. There were not unlimited resources. I could see that they got to be a little more self-reliant.

I started to look at things differently. When the kids are little, people say to you, "Oh, these are the best days." You're like a dishrag on the floor! You can't even go to the bathroom by yourself. It's so overwhelming. Then some well-meaning person will say, "Oh, honey, enjoy this." You're thinking, "If this is as good as it gets, let me out now. Forget it!"

I can understand now what people meant. The concerns are different as they get older. When they're little, you may have a child who won't stay in his car seat, or won't hold your hand in the parking lot. But that's not like when they have their driver's license, and they GO. They're on the road with a million other nuts, maybe a third of them drunk. Friends in the car. Who knows? Those kinds of things are much more draining and upsetting.

On my first son's fifteenth birthday he said, "Since I'm going to be driving soon, why don't you let me try it out in the parking lot?" I thought, "What is he talking about? He's got a whole year." But in his mind he was almost there. I was thinking, "They don't give babies licenses in the first place!"

This Tuesday was the day for my third son to get his license. There was great anticipation for this day. I understand now. The license represents freedom. It is such a milestone. I had two different boys to drop off at lessons first.

A friend happened to mention to Ethan that morning that he needed his birth certificate to get his license. He couldn't find it. He was in an absolute panic. He was just this side of tears. I said I'd come back after I dropped the others off, and if he had found it, we could still go get the license. I felt so bad for him, but he has to learn to be motivated to do things, or they won't get done.

An hour and a half later I came back. He had called Motor Vehicles to see if there was anything else he could use. They said something like medical records that had his date of birth on it would be fine. He called the hospital from when he had broken something, an arm, I think. They had a bill with his birthdate on it. He called back to Motor Vehicles to see if that would do. He called the hospital again. They would make a copy, and it would be in the billing office. By the time I came home he had it all in place. I was so proud of him. I wouldn't have thought of doing that. We got the license, and he was thrilled.

I can't let myself protect my children from experiencing their own lives, even when it's painful. You want to be there to help them to get through the pain, to experience it, and grow from it. But not to make it go away. You never grow when it's easy. I don't want my kids to be wimpy. I don't want them to be beaten down by the first thing that comes along. Life deals you what it will. You have to realize that it could be worse. The bill collector isn't pounding on the door. (He may be on the phone . . .!)

A couple of weeks ago, when I was in the hospital for a miscarriage, Roger was there for me. Whenever we have a new baby in the house, it's a very wonderful time. You kind of pull back. You don't go out as much. There is this ambiance, this new life in the midst of the family. It pulls us together. When I had this miscarriage . . . it was such a disappointment.

I had to be induced, to go through labor and delivery. I thought, "This is the absolute cruelest . . ." I kept thinking how lucky I am to have Roger.

Our youngest fell out the second-floor window in March. He was seventeen months old. It was a warm Saturday. The eight-year-old had lifted him up in the window, to wave to his father outside. I don't know, somehow, the baby leaned against the screen. It must have been loose. He went right down on the driveway and landed on his head. We rushed him to the hospital. There were no injuries. It was a miracle. I can't look at him without thinking, "We are so lucky." I think we appreciate the value of these lives more because of those kinds of experiences and because of the loss of this new life.

Sometimes when the laundry is up to here, it's easy to not count my blessings, to say, "Oh my God, I have no life here." This one is beating that one on the head, or whatever. It feels crazy. "I'm not doing a good job, and who'd want to be a mother anyway?" But no, this is really a privilege, to be in charge of other lives. There are wonderful joys every day. Somebody sitting on your lap. Just experiencing how wonderful they are. Or they come home with a funny joke, and you see how their mind is growing. Usually they get the joke wrong!

I've been working for about five years. I started selling baskets right after our ninth child was born. I was ready to have something else to focus on. I still needed and wanted to be home with the kids, but I thought something else would give a balance to my life. Knowing that I was going out in the evening gave me a little bit of perspective on what I was doing. If the day was lousy, I didn't magnify it. Life wasn't just this endless series of days and nights.

After a while with the kids you're looking for something that isn't there: I don't get a whole lot of appreciation. The kids aren't saying, "Oh Mom, this laundry smells so good!," or "Great meal!" You hear, "Why don't we ever have anything good to eat in this house?" Appreciation is a learned thing, and it only comes very slowly, and it comes late. It comes when they've left the house and know what they've lost.

When I was home, usually by eight-thirty, I was done. I'd be sitting on the couch, not able to keep my eyes open, thinking, "I should be folding the laundry." When I started working, I wondered how I was going to stay awake. Instead, I discovered there was a lot of energy that I just hadn't been tapping into. I just needed a change. The work fulfilled me on a different level.

151

It was tangible. It was a little money in the hand. I was always rejuvenated when I came home.

I began accomplishing more during the day, because I couldn't leave anything for the evening. I had to deal with dinner by ten o'clock in the morning. It gave me more motivation to be more professional in what I was doing with the home and the kids. I had to plan menus and be sure I had the stuff. You couldn't delay dinner forty-five minutes because someone had to run out and get a can of tomato sauce.

My husband was there with the kids. I think it helped him to have a different depth in his relationships with them. Also, I think it's good for the kids' perception. They knew mothers worked and women had jobs, but it was always other mothers. They couldn't believe that I was going out and doing something that earned money. Talk about a crushing blow to the ego! It was like, "You mean you think you can really do this?" Here I thought I had this aura of, "I've got all these kids. I can do anything." Obviously that didn't transfer to them. "Outside the house?" It was sort of a revelation to me that they assumed that I couldn't do anything else.

My husband would always say on Friday mornings, "The weekend is almost here," and I'd think, "Big deal, the weekend." It was the same as every other day for me. There were actually more people in and out of the house. More mess, more confusion, and less structure. But when I started working during the week, the weekend represented time that I didn't have to go out away from my family, and I looked forward to it, too. Also, on Saturday nights my husband was much more eager to go out, because he was spending more time with the kids. He wanted to have some time just with me.

There have been times when the prospect of a new life was just devastating. Particularly once I started working, because I saw how helpful my work was financially. There were times, frankly, when I just didn't want to do it again. I could see how wonderful my children were. But initially, it would be unsettling: "Oh, I'm being asked to do more here." But this is what God wants. He might not ask someone else. Whatever we've got and whatever this family is, that's what He wants for this new life. Which doesn't mean that I don't blow it at times. It only means that I'm willing to try, to give it my best.

I'm conscious of the fact that that can seem very irresponsible to some people. They think, "They can't even pay their bills, and they're having more kids," or "How can they possibly do all the nurturing that they need to do?" People will say, with great charity, and sometimes not, "How can you keep track of what everybody is doing, and their friends, and their needs, and give them quality time?" Sometimes what they're saying is, "You obviously don't realize that these kids need things."

I pray a lot. I pray, "Take care of these children. Help me to see what I need to do for them. Let me show them a mother who has confidence in God, so that they will have that confidence that they're meant for great things." I pray very hard that if someone needs something, that I'll see it. That if a kid needs to talk to me, that we'll be going somewhere in the car, just the two of us, and there will be the chance. If we need shoes, I'll pray, "Help me find a pair of shoes that will fit this kid that doesn't cost sixty dollars."

Little things happen. Roger's secretary happened to bring in a suit when my son needed one for a summer job. It fit him. Or someone is going on vacation, and they take one of the kids to be a companion to their kid. I couldn't orchestrate that. God is really very good to me. He lets me see that it's working.

Our son, Jason, who's eight, was the seventh child. When he was born, he had no muscle tone. His head seemed large in proportion to his body. He wouldn't suck. He just lay there and didn't move, didn't cry. He was in the hospital for about five weeks, and they didn't figure out what was wrong. When he was a year old, he couldn't even hold his head up. He was almost totally passive. He was very thin. He would never cry to eat. You had to wake him up and feed him through a tube. I was so depressed by this. I had these six other children to care for, and I was supposed to do physical therapy with the baby.

At this point I got pregnant again. I had thought, "I won't have any more children, because now I have this child with all these special needs, plus the other kids." I felt like I was down

153

to the bare bones, and here I was being asked to do something else. I thought, "This is it." I wished I would just die and not have to deal with it anymore.

If you accept that you're not asked to accept anything more than you can handle, then obviously, anything that comes your way, you can somehow handle. But it was hard. I was unhappy. Tired. I was sad for this child. I felt that I wasn't doing justice to anything. And here I was going to have this other baby. "What if something was wrong with this next baby?" It was a hard pregnancy.

They were saying Jason would probably have hearing impairment and be in a wheelchair. That he might start having seizures. It was a bleak picture. I saw the little boy in the wheelchair at the baseball field knowing he can never do it, and I thought, "I cannot live seeing my child go through that."

Then one day, right before the baby came, Jason seemed to be holding himself up in his little seat. He started making progress. Sean was born, and he was lusty from day one. A big, healthy, perfect child, who was a source of great joy immediately.

Very soon I saw that Jason was not the baby of the family anymore. A lot of the preoccupation with him was taken off of him. I had to be taking care of this new baby, so I couldn't be orchestrating Jason's world as much. Also I could see that the new baby wasn't going to defer to Jason the way all the rest of us had been doing. He would yank stuff back. He had to make it on his own. Nobody but a younger sibling could have done that for him.

That was a big turning point for me. What I had perceived to be the most awful thing happening, a handicapped child and then another baby, was the very best thing. I thought, "I'm not going to question anymore. All I have to do is cooperate with God's will."

It wasn't until Jason was about four that we got a correct diagnosis. He has Prader Willi Syndrome. That gives him a tendency for compulsive eating. The brain doesn't give the message, "You've had enough." There are horror stories of people chaining refrigerators shut and coming home to find the child gnawing on the chain.

He's eight, and he doesn't have access to food on his own. He doesn't have money in his pocket and can't go to the store. He's reasonably agreeable about it: usually he will accept that he's had all he can. You can't leave him home alone. We can't lock up the refrigerator--there are too many people eating out of it. We'll have to see how it works out. There are other symptoms that he'll be dealing with. He has learning disabilities. His intelligence is low average. He'll always need extra support.

Having Jason changed my life immeasurably. It made me really ask myself, "What do I want for these children? Do I want to make life easy for these kids, so that nothing touches them?" What do I care what kind of car we drive? What is important here?

That's the great thing about being a parent, it makes you better than you are. You've got a newborn baby, there's no way that kid is going to survive unless you get on your feet whether you feel like it or not. When they get older, you do so many things for them that you wouldn't do for yourself. That makes you better. You do things that you didn't think you could do. You have to do it, and you do.

Every year on our anniversary my husband says something like, "Now, tell me, twenty years ago when we got married, if you'd known that you were going to be pregnant with your twelfth child at this point, would you have married me?" I just laugh.

GAIL AMES
Age: 54

"What I would tell you about step-parenting is that it really can't be done. You can be there. You can go through the motions. You can be grateful for all the good that comes from it, but you <u>cannot</u> correct the damage that's been done. You can stem the tide. You can avoid doing any more damage."

Gail and her husband Phil live in Hartford, Connecticut, where he is a physician. When she was thirty, Gail married Phil and acquired four troubled stepchildren in the bargain. Within a very short time it became clear that Gail would be up against impossible expectations and would have primary responsibility for the children. Only the birth of a fifth child, Matt, kept her from leaving this family.

The children were thirteen, eleven, seven and five. Their mother had walked out on them two years before. When she left, Phil hired a housekeeper who moved in, did the cooking and the laundry, got the kids on the schoolbus, and was there during the night when he was called out.

At six o'clock on the morning of the first day I lived in the house with them, I had four children wanting to know where their clothes were. Their clothes were in the hamper. That's when I learned that the housekeeper had done the wash <u>every day</u>. The first thing I did as a mother was to buy everyone enough socks and underwear to get through a week, so that I would never again have four children looking to me for clothes at six in the morning. It was like waking up in a foreign country and not even knowing what country it was.

156

I had never cooked for six people in my life. I had for all practical purposes lived alone for years. I was an urban, apartment dweller.

The woman who introduced me to Phil said, "I think you're going to marry this man, but there's one reason you might not." She had already told me that he had four children. The one reason was one of the four children, Mark, who was the second oldest, and very prone to bouts of rage. He would go from rage to tears. He sobbed so loud through our wedding ceremony that people couldn't hear our vows. He is very bright, sensitive, and fragile. He is by far the most intelligent, but the most impaired of the four, and has a strong tendency to depression.

Elizabeth, the youngest, had unbelievable temper tantrums. Tom, the oldest, went through the early seventies drug stuff. He's the one we had to bail out of jail. He's the one we later learned was dealing marijuana from our house. He's the only one who ran away from home and stayed gone for several years. He got a lot of rebellion out of his system and is, oddly enough, the one with whom I am the most comfortable now. He's a lovely guy. Clear and warm, and content in his own way. He never talks about those days.

Paul seemed a breeze. He was seven and adorable and snuggly. Sailed through high school, national honor society, first trumpet in the band, varsity sports. He got to the end of high school and didn't have any ideas about what to do with his life. Didn't want to go to college or work. He went to work for his uncle, who had a printing business in Mississippi. He clearly got messed up with the wrong people. Lived in a pig sty. We never found out what happened, but his uncle fired him. He came home sick. I suspect he fried part of his brain. He functions, but he had a total personality change. He is not athletic, he is not musical, and he is not interesting now. He is remote, a stranger.

What I would tell you about step-parenting is that it really can't be done. You can be there. You can go through the motions. You can be grateful for all the good that comes from it, but you cannot correct the damage that's been done.

I really truly believed that I could turn these kids' lives around. I believed that we could be the perfect family. I saw

157

everything that happened that was disappointing or upsetting as my failure. I kept thinking, "There's something I haven't figured out yet." It wasn't until I went through therapy late in my forties that I was able to truly let go of the feeling that whatever didn't work was my fault.

I wouldn't have stayed if I hadn't given birth to Matt. He is golden. I couldn't have endured the situation if I hadn't had a child of my own. If I had not been so committed to Matt's having a stable life, with people who truly cared about him, I wouldn't have stayed.

I really had had no idea what I was getting into, but I had never shied away from something because it was hard. I certainly was in love with Phil, and I wanted to be married to him. I did not long to be the mother of his children.

I saw that Phil was a very present, loving, open parent-- which I had never had. I saw him as a great father who did things with his kids, played with his kids, picked out great presents for his kids, had good ideas about how to entertain them, seemed to be really thoughtful and concerned for their welfare, on a day-to-day basis and for the long-term.

However, after we were married, he kind of disappeared from that role. Work became his primary focus again. I was disappointed, because I saw that the children didn't have the sustained attention and interest that I thought they had.

It was as if he felt with relief, "Now I don't have to do that anymore." It was a removal of himself, a stepping-aside, from being an active parent, except when I said, "I need you to do this." Then he would re-engage. I definitely had to let him know that I needed him to take part, to be home for dinner whether it was convenient or not, to speak to a specific child about a specific issue, to attend a conference with a teacher who had called me that day. But there was no leading up to it and no following through. He would do just what I had asked him to do.

I just never expected him to remove himself. I could not have anticipated that in my wildest dreams. The way he was functioning as a father to those kids was part of what I was attracted to in him.

The other thing was financial. Phil was flat-broke when I married him. His ex-wife had taken the furniture from the house, because it was mostly hers. She had charged everything she wanted and had drained the bank accounts. I walked into a financial disaster.

I know now that, as step-parents, it is essential that you put your primary energy into the relationship with your partner. We didn't. We made the assumption that our relationship was okay, and I put my primary energy into parenting, and he put his into his work. I see now that a step-family comes out of that relationship, by definition, and if you don't put your primary energy into the relationship, then you're asking for a bad relationship, and when the problems come you don't have a firm base.

I was the primary decision-maker for the kids. Phil never disagreed with me, but he didn't participate. The kids surely felt on some level that it was not my right to make the decisions for them. Phil was always the straight-faced, ponderous one, or he wasn't home.

I should have been enraged at him. Instead, I felt even more that I was doing a bad job. He left me high and dry. Not maliciously, but he did leave me high and dry. That is his personality, and his work lets him get away with it. It took me a long time to figure that out.

I realized just recently that I have never felt truly secure in my role as their parent. I am tense and unnatural with them. I still, to this day, only feel truly comfortable in the presence of one of them. When they're around I still don't feel like part of the family. I think that goes back to never having talked about what happened. The kids never asked questions. "Why did Mommy leave?" Never. There was just a great absence of information. No lies were told. I longed for someone to say, "Can we sit down together and talk about this?" I've never felt that I should be the one to initiate it.

Those twenty years leave me feeling very sad. I did think about grabbing Matt and leaving. My way of staying was to go back to graduate school and to create a life of my own that gave me some of the benefits I wasn't getting at home.

I did want to have a second child, but five children was too much for me to take care of--too much for us to support. We just said, "We can't do this again." I really wanted another.

I would not do this again. If the truth be known, I would like to have twenty years of my life back.

BONNIE GRIFFIN-CASTLE
Age: 41

"Every motion for me is doing something. I literally run through the halls at the hospital. I'm always racing the clock, because I pick the kids up from school. The culmination of my day is getting there on time."

Bonnie has struggled to balance a high-powered medical career with raising two children. Bill is thirteen; Susan, ten. The Griffin-Castles are Jewish. Both parents are medical doctors. The family lives in a very large house with a live-in cook and housekeeper, a gym, a computer room, a fax machine, and a xerox machine. The children attend private school.

Bonnie discusses the differences in her relationships with her daughter and her son.

Women's Lib doesn't work. Gloria Steinem lied to us. She's a big shot. Of course, she's not married, and she doesn't have kids. The reality is that I have sacrificed myself to have a full-time career and a family. You can't really do both. I do nothing for myself. I have no hobbies. I have very few girlfriends. We spend all our time with our children on the weekends. I <u>had</u> a life. I used to play the piano. I played the guitar. Scott is an equal partner in this. The same is true for him.

Twice I've gone in to quit my job. Once was right after Sue was born. I was supposed to go to England and then Hawaii to lecture for major symposia. I pulled out of both of those. She was sick and in the hospital. I just couldn't go. That hurt my career terribly. For years the men who ran those courses didn't want to talk to me. I've turned down lots of great opportunities to lecture.

161

The other time I went in to quit was when Bill was in first grade. He developed a stutter. I was told by the school that it was because I worked. I just decided I couldn't carry the guilt. Luckily for me, the man I work under told me to take time off and not quit. I took off six weeks. Of course, I hadn't had a vacation in seven years, including no maternity leave. During that time, Bill's stutter sort of faded. It comes back when he's tired or stressed. I think it's something that's just part of him, that hopefully he'll outgrow.

Children are a full-time job. It's not the cooking, because I'm willing to give the cooking away. Nor is it the cleaning or the ironing, because I'm willing to give that away, but the child-rearing can't be given away. So, I pick my children up from school every day and always have. I'll bring the children home and settle them in and often go back to work. The kids can always reach me. My secretaries know that no matter where I am, if the kids call, they get me.

I worked while I was in labor with Bill. I went into labor around noon. I stayed and worked until eight o'clock that night. I fed my husband dinner, and then I went to the hospital and had a baby a few hours later. The same thing happened with Sue. I had her at two a.m. I signed out slides and saw patients the next morning at seven. I was a working woman. I was a division chief at twenty-nine.

When the alarm would go off at four in the morning--I mean, I'm human--who wants to get up, especially if you have a good-looking, warm man lying next to you?! He looks so enticing. It's winter and cold. Fear got me out of bed. I had work to do. I had a job to do, but it was horrible. I wouldn't want my daughter to do it.

When Bill was born I was working literally fourteen and sixteen-hour days. I would be at work between six and seven. I wouldn't get home to the house until seven or eight. Then I would meet my boss at four in the morning to work on the book we were writing. Plus, I was studying for my national board exam.

I pride myself on having surrounded myself with very bright people. That's the key to success. I know that as their boss I need to stay one step ahead of them. I am forever paranoid. They will say something, and I will say "yes" to them, and then I'll write it down and go home and look it up! I come in the next day, and I'm the world expert on it. These kids are younger than me, and they're sharp. I have this terrible fear of slipping. I bind one set of medical journals, and I highlight and rip up a second set and file it. Within seconds I have all the current information on any disease.

When my kids are in college, then all stops are out. I don't know what I'll do, but look what I've done with both hands tied behind my back. I'm a workaholic. I have endless energy. I love medicine. I'll do something.

I look at the men, and they do such nothing, and they have these women who feed them dinner and clean for them and take care of the kids. The men have no responsibility. They putter around the hospital being very unproductive. They stand around and bullshit. Every motion for me is doing something. I literally run through the halls at the hospital. I'm always racing the clock, because I pick the kids up from school. The culmination of my day is getting there on time. The few times that Scott has done it, he can't believe how horrible it is to have that pressure on him all day. Two children are waiting for you.

Let me tell you about my daughter. I adore my son. I'm forever amazed that out of me came a boy. But to have a daughter is to have a soul-mate. A best friend. When my mother is sick, my son, who adores my mother, can deny it and put it out of his mind. Typical man. But Sue is sensitive to every inflection of my voice. She'll know if I'm down.

You see yourself so much in a little girl. And I worry about her in a whole way I don't worry about him.

She's like an alter ego, an extension of myself. She promises me she won't rebel--I want her to put it in writing! We talk about this all the time. I'm not going to just let her slip into this rebellious phase. . . it must be very painful for mothers.

{Sue comes in. "Can I report how my mother is? My mother is wonderful and beautiful and loveable and friendly and athletic and intelligent--she's perfect."}

With Bill I allow it to be discussed that he might go away to boarding school. With Sue it's not even discussed. Over my dead body would I let her go away. I would like Bill to be stronger. He goes away to sleep-away camp, and he's quite homesick. There are lots of phone calls. Sometimes I think maybe sending him away will make a man of him, which he has to be. He has to grow up and be tough and strong. Although I feel Sue also has to grow up and be tough and strong, she doesn't have to be a man. There is a difference.

She will be bat mitzvahed. She will not have the big function that Bill had. First of all, it was outrageously expensive. It was the happiest day of our lives as a family, but it was an insane amount of money for one day. Traditionally, it's entrance into manhood, and my daughter is not going to become a man. It's entrance into adulthood in the religion. Her education in the religion is as important to me as his.

She has made her choice. We're going to buy her a horse, instead. For the amount the bar mitzvah cost us we can buy a horse and keep it for ten years. She rides every week. We'll have a kids' party at night and a luncheon for twenty or so family members and that will be it. She will do the same thing in the temple. Absolutely. That's all that really matters. The rest of it is all nonsense.

The development of her mind is as important as Bill's-- maybe more important.

JOSEPHINE SMITH
Age: 39

"If your partner's another woman, all the sensitivity in the world doesn't help this male kid."

Josephine is the lesbian mother of an eleven-year-old boy. Years ago she moved across the country to put some distance between herself and her family, who do not know she is a lesbian. Josephine teaches at the college level.

Here I was the mother, the bread-winner, the <u>everything</u> to this child, and his perception was quite different than what I'd hoped it would be--even at four years old. The team I coached and another were tied for first in a tight tennis match. The winner of this match would be first going into the conference tournament. Lots of pressure. We were tied when the last singles match began. I was pacing back and forth. Stuart asked me something like, "What's the matter?" I explained to him that I was very nervous, because I really wanted to win the championship. He said, "Well, their team is going to win, because they have a man coach." I was absolutely shocked.

I had been holding things together and had something of a career and was spending time with this child. I'll never forget how clearly it came to me: no matter what I am doing, his socialization is coming to him faster.

It's going to get even harder. Stuart is eleven now. He's very connected to me, but it's kind of a love-hate thing. I need to find a balance where I keep my sanity. I can't sacrifice my life. I can't live my life through him. In a lesbian relationship, we compromise all the time for him. We can't put up things in the house that we otherwise would. Artwork or pictures of us. We sort of hide our sleeping arrangements--not from him--I've

165

always been very open with him--but to protect him when friends of his come to the house.

It's very hard on him also. He's not very open about his feelings. He and I were talking recently about the step-parent thing of him and Sandy. He said,

"Well, none of the kids I know like their parent's partner either."

"Are you talking about straight people and step-parents, or two moms or dads?"

"Two moms."

"Oh, you know some other kids that have two moms?"

"Yeah."

"And they know about you, about us?"

"Yeah."

"That's interesting. Is this just the guys at school, or do all the guys in the neighborhood know?"

"They all know."

I wonder if he has been teased by the neighborhood kids. I'm intensely curious about it, but probably won't be able to get at it directly with him.

It's so awfully guilt-producing to be a single, working parent. Add to that that you have what's considered an abnormal or strange life-style. That makes it tremendously hard for a kid. I know I'm not spending enough time with my kid. And, I love this woman. That makes it hard for him.

Sandy and I have been together for three years. I've told him that doesn't mean that I hate men. I feel more comfortable being with a woman. My explaining it doesn't make him really understand it.

It's really not easy. Things get too intense. I feel torn in the middle, because Stuart and Sandy sometimes hate each other. Sometimes I resent that Sandy has the freedom to walk away from Stuart, and I cannot. I've thought of telling his father, "You take him, or I'll send him to a foster home." That lasts about thirty seconds, but it's there. Stuart would not survive with his dad, and the trauma of separation from me at this time in his life would not be workable. The best times are when I just

166

drop what I feel I should be doing, and he and I take off and go do something. He's a wonderful child, but not an easy child.

For me to do a good job teaching at the college, I have to bring mounds of things home at night. I drive home an hour; I do my home duties for a while, which includes getting Stuart to bed; then, about nine, I go back to my work. Daily. Splitting time. There is not enough time for both my job and him. Now that I'm up for tenure I have a reminder that I have not written anything. Where would I find time to do that?

I was divorced when Stuart was a baby, so he's never lived with his dad. He sees him sporadically, but in his mind his dad has become this big mystical figure that can do anything. It went from that to the notion that if his dad and I were together, his life would be so much better. Finally he said, "I don't want two moms." He feels ganged up on.

Stuart doesn't have much connection with his father. Stuart would like more contact with him. Not only does his father live far away, but he doesn't want to be in a position where Stuart can make any demands on him. Kevin seems to have trouble really talking to people at any sort of depth. He was always afraid of Stuart, even when he was an infant. Kevin's wife doesn't want to have anything to do with Stuart. Last Christmas Kevin just sent money to Stuart. He didn't even pick something out for him. He neglects Stuart. What Stuart needs is some reassurance that Kevin is proud of him, or loves him. Kevin won't even call him.

If your partner's another woman, all the sensitivity in the world doesn't help this male kid.

If I'd had physical distance from my family, I would have worked through a lot of issues sooner, and I probably would not have had a child. It's hard growing up gay in our society. Since I was tiny, I've felt different. That's difficult in a rigid family. Trying to conform and be a good little girl meant denying a lot of myself. My getting divorced was the first time I did something for my real self. My dad called me the L-word the other day on the phone, and that was "Liberal." I am so far beyond what would be acceptable to my father. I don't think he would even speak to me if he knew I'm gay.

Part of me says, "You've got seven more years, and Stuart'll be out of the house, doing what he's going to do, and then you can do the research you want and get to be known in your field." Part of me says, "Things are going by me all the time."

Stuart and I will have this big fight about something, and an hour later or so, when we get back to our uneasy peace, I'll say, "Are we still mad? How long do you think we'll be mad...." I'll start to tease him out of it. He's just such a cute kid. Sometimes. And he's funny. He'll say some things that just break me up. To see those little glimpses of who he's going to be, who he IS. Even when he's working through the stuff, there are times when he's just terrific. There are times even when we've had a horrible day, and he has gone to sleep, I'll go in to sneak a peek at him! What can I do? I love this kid.

But I've got to keep my sanity some way. We don't have any other lesbian mother friends. How do you meet them, find them? Having Stuart could cost me my relationship with Sandy, which is so stable and fulfilling. I don't want to lose her.

LYNN KRETZ
Age: 40

"I never knew if I'd see him again, or if he'd live his life in a mental institution. I never knew if he was coming back."

Lynn was a divorced mother on welfare with two baby sons at age twenty-two. She worked her way through college and eventually earned a master's degree in social work. She discovered that she is a lesbian.

Lynn's greatest difficulty was in dealing with the behavior of her second son, beginning with his adolescence. After years of problems which no one could explain adequately, Scott was diagnosed as having bipolar illness.

I met Scott and instantly liked him. He is now eighteen. He seemed guileless, vulnerable. He said that it has been difficult having his mother be a lesbian. He would have liked to have a father, "someone to teach me to shave."

I sat at Lynn's kitchen table, drinking orange Kool-aid and eating cheese popcorn while I listened to her story. When I left, Lynn asked, "You mean people just let you in?" "Yes," I answered and thought, "and you have more than most."

I was married for three years to a guy I went out with all through my adolescence. He went to Vietnam and came home addicted to alcohol, marijuana, cocaine. I decided that I'd better get out of there before he killed us, because he had started getting crazy. Mark was two, and Scott was three months old.

At that time I worked as a secretary. I would have made more if I quit my job and went on welfare. So that's what I did. I was in the pits. I had to live in welfare housing, all single mothers with children, living in the slums with cockroaches and not having enough money. We couldn't afford to live. We ate

169

macaroni and beans. People beating up their kids and being drunk. A man three doors down shot a woman.

A man got me out of there and into a better apartment. He got me to go to college. I started that, and got grants for older women, when Mark was five and Scott was three. I went to college for six years and got my bachelor's degree. I was still on welfare.

Mark and Scott were probably ten and twelve when I went back to get my master's degree in social work. They didn't understand why I was going back to school. They would do guilt trips: "We're the only kids in the neighborhood that have no parents. No parents. We don't have a father. You never spend any time with us. We're the only kids in the neighborhood who don't have a mother."

When the boys were eleven and thirteen, I found a house that was really cheap and bought it. I started having these really strange dreams--about being with women. Every time I would go out with a guy I would start fantasizing that he was a woman. I didn't know why that was happening. Prior to college I was brought up lower class, so we really didn't believe that lesbians existed.

I started feeling more and more that I was probably gay, but I had been a welfare mother, a divorced woman at age twenty-two, and I didn't want another negative status. I tried really hard not to act on this, because I was tired of always being in some deviant sub-culture.

I started a relationship with a woman. I had to tell my kids, because they lived with me. I was really frightened, because I didn't want to hurt them in any way. They are real important to me. Being a mother is very important to me. I feel it's such an important job. In a way you're responsible for somebody else's life. It's not fair to screw them over.

So I had tried really hard not to let any kind of my shit affect them. I never let them know I was on welfare. I never would take my kids to the welfare department when I had to be certified, and I never let them know the welfare check was coming. They thought I got money to go to college. I let them think that.

So to tell them I was a lesbian was very difficult for me, because I knew they were going to struggle with that. I had to tell them, because it was so much a part of my life. On the day that I decided I was going to tell them, my blood pressure went up to 200 over 110 and I passed out at work.

That night I said, "I need to talk to you guys. You know I really love you, and it's important that we're really open."

They asked, "Is it about Marie?"

"Yes."

"Are you going to die, and she's going to take care of us?" (That's how scared I looked.)

I thought, "Oh, thank God, now it will be less than that."

I didn't want to use the word "gay," because of the negative stigma. I wasn't gay from what they heard gay was. I didn't want to use the word "lesbian."

"You know how men and women love each other, and they share this special relationship. Well, I don't feel like that towards men. I feel like that towards women."

Mark said, "Some people call that 'gay,' Mommy, but that's not what you are, is it?" He was thirteen.

"No, I'm not what people call 'gay.' It's a totally different thing that I am." They had never heard about homosexual lifestyles. They had heard "lesie" and "dyke." So, I said, "no," that I wasn't what they'd heard. Then they said that they didn't care what I was as long as I was happy.

Mark was okay. Scott had a harder time with it. He was bummed. Scared about what people would think. He told his best friend, and his friend said, "So is Johnny's mother." He got to know more people. We started a gay fathers and gay mothers group where we'd bring the kids. So the kids would get to know other kids with gay parents. That helped.

Mark has continued to be pretty okay with my lesbianism. He was an easy kid to raise. He'll be in his senior year of college next year. He wants to be a financial planner. He loves money. He's always worked three jobs, and he's someone I could always depend on.

Scott was a different story. When he went to school, it was awful for him. They called him "lazy" and complained that he was nothing like his brother. He started getting punished for not doing his math lessons. They'd take his lunch away. In the fifth grade he was coded "Learning Disabled." He had a low I.Q. They wanted to put him in the mentally-retarded class. I had to fight like crazy to keep him out of that class. They decided he was probably emotionally disturbed, because he would cry when he went to the class. So they put him in the emotionally disturbed class. He was in that class for a couple of years, and then they decided that he wasn't behaviorally disturbed, so they put him in the learning disabled class. This was in New York.

He did things like set a fire in the urinal, set the woods on fire. He was okay for a while, and then he started stealing candy bars at the store. He was about ten. He'd steal things like change out of my room. He would go into Mark's room and take whatever he wanted. He didn't have any boundaries.

I would do all the things a good mother should do: take him back to the store and make him apologize and pay for the candy. Then, he started stealing things out of cars. Then, he would get up in the middle of the night and dress in black clothes and go out. He was about thirteen, fourteen. I don't know what he was doing. Then, he started stealing cars. This was at about fifteen, sixteen.

The psychologist said that Scott had an impulsivity problem, due to his learning disability and his lower I.Q. He said Scott couldn't help himself, because he couldn't put together that there would be consequences for the behavior, so he would just do the behavior at the moment. The police department didn't understand this. He was stealing cars. He was coming home and crying and saying, "I stole a car. I can't stop."

He was doing this kind of criminal behavior, and he is too innocent. He wouldn't have made it in prison, especially in New York. He would have been raped. It's not like Vermont. You don't get thrown in jail for not paying your speeding ticket. These are criminals.

He was out of control. He got arrested, and was in jail. They wouldn't let me get him out. I took all the money I had in the world and got a lawyer for Scott. They put Scott on probation, and he kept on stealing cars. One time he stole the car three houses from where we lived, kept it for a week, washed it at the carwash, like it was his car. He must have stolen fifteen cars, and he got caught with three.

I sold everything I owned and moved rather quickly to Vermont to save Scott's ass. I thought, "They're going to put him in prison. That will be the end of him. He will be a dead kid. He'll never be okay." He was so young and so out of control, but he was not like a criminal.

Scott was doing okay in Vermont. He was in a smaller, country atmosphere. Then, he started drinking. He started hanging out with the lowest class of kids. Drinking and drugging and not coming home, being out of control again. He was seventeen.

He started getting depressed. He missed his friends in New York. He was sleeping all the time, and he didn't have any friends here. I had given him an ultimatum that he had to sober up. So, he had to go to A.A. every day for thirty days, and he did. Then, I let him go to New York on a bus. He was staying at his best friend's house. He was supposed to call me and let me know when he was coming back on the bus. He didn't call.

I called him and said, "Scott, you were supposed to call me and let me know when the bus is coming, so I can pick you up."

He said, "Mom, the strangest thing happened. There's all these people outside, and it's raining, and they're all washing their cars, and the whole place is bugged, and somebody came in here and moved all the stuff around, and everybody is an undercover cop, and they're all after me, Mom. They put a bug in my tooth, and it's poison."

I was at work. I was working in an out-patient psychiatric unit. I was listening to my son, and he was psychotic--in New York. I couldn't even get to him.

I had his friend's father put Scott on the bus to Boston, but Scott only went from Schenectedy to Albany, which is a half an hour. In Albany he got off the bus, because he thought everybody on the bus was undercover cops, and that they were trying to get him. He called me collect. Thank God. He told me that they weren't going to let him out of New York, and that all the undercover cops were laughing at him. He was crying.

I called my ex-lover, who lives in Albany, and said, "Scott is psychotic. Go to the bus station and get him." She went to get him, but she doesn't work in mental health. She thought he was a little nervous, gave him some money, and put him on the bus to Boston.

Lisa and I went to Boston to pick up Scott. We found the bus, and he wasn't on it. I was scared to death. Finally I found him walking around the bus station saying, "Go ahead, go ahead, search me, search me." He was talking a mile a minute, crazy as a loon.

The hospital decided that he was probably schizophrenic. They put him on haldol, and he was there five weeks. I took him on a picnic, and he was talking to the radio. He thought the radio was talking to him.

I did finally agree to take him home. He couldn't dress himself. He would stand in the middle of a room and tremble all over and cry to me, pleading, "Mom." The doctor told me that he was acting. I felt that I couldn't take care of him. I'd go in his room, and he'd be lying on the floor, naked.

We went to a therapist who saw us for three hours. He was convincing me that if I took Scott to the hospital it was going to make him more chronic, and that I shouldn't do it. We went home and Scott was kind of seizuring. I called the psychiatrist and said, "I can't take care of him. I'm sorry if I'm going to make him more chronic, but I can't take care of him."

I got him admitted to a different hospital. I kept telling them that he had been really depressed before he went to New York and all this started. I didn't think he was schizophrenic. They took him off all of the medication the other hospital had him on. This was in November now, from July 5th to the middle of November. They took him off all his meds, and there he was: my kid, again!

Then, he started being depressed. They put him on an anti-depressant. Three days later he was crazy, threatening to kill people. The sheriffs came and handcuffed him, and they took him to the state hospital. But, at least now they knew what was wrong with him. He's not schizophrenic; he has bi-polar illness, which means he gets real depressed, or he gets manic, and when he gets manic, he's dangerous. He thinks he can do anything.

The state hospital was terrible. They didn't take care of him. He lost all of his clothes, and he didn't take a bath for five days. I'd go in, and the door would be locked. Scott would be lying on the other side of the door, crying. I'd say, "Scott, go get somebody to let me in."

He'd be crying in this little sad voice, "No, help me, help me."

I'd say, "Okay, I'm leaving now," and then he'd get up and run to get somebody. It was awful.

Finally, he went back to the hospital that he'd been in before the state hospital. They put him on lithium, and he wouldn't stabilize. They put him on tegretol, and he was on lithium and tegretol, and he started to stabilize. He was there for a while and then was in a day treatment program. He got stabilized, and that's him--the same kid that you met. He's been sober for over a year now. Nothing to drink. No drugs. He hasn't been in any trouble.

He was in so much trouble, and no one knew what was the matter with him. That must have been what was wrong with him all those years, from the time he was thirteen. He was out of control. He would cry and tell me he was out of control. It wasn't like somebody that would say, "I got away with it." He would say, "Mom, I can't stop, please help me."

But everybody thought it was me, the mother. The mother doesn't set limits. She doesn't this; she doesn't that. It's enough to drive you crazy: being a mother. I don't know any other profession where you're totally responsible for somebody else's behavior. They don't take into consideration any of the other variables: genetics, peer support, financial stability, where you live, what happens in school, how the person is treated, what their self-esteem is... it's just... THE MOTHER.

Scott's been through hell. Psychosis is like living in a nightmare. It's like somebody putting you in one of those thriller movies and leaving you there. He thought they were changing him into a girl. He'd call me in the middle of the night saying, "They're trying to put me in the air-conditioner, and it's poison in there."

I kept on thinking, "I don't think I can live through this anymore." I never knew if I'd see him again, or if he'd live his life in a mental institution. I never knew if he was ever coming back.

He gradually went back to school full-time, had tutoring two days a week, and passed his G.E.D. He gets Social Security disability. He's looking for a job.

I hope he finds his place.

ELINOR McILVAINE
Age: 55

"I didn't think there could be anything worse than having a gay kid."

Elinor has five children, two of whom, Keith and Carolyn, are gay. For a few years Alice, also, thought that she was gay. Keith is thirty-two; Alice, thirty-one; Marc, twenty-nine; Carolyn, twenty-six; and Clyde is twenty-three. Now Elinor works zealously for gay rights, but she did not start out as an advocate. When she first found out that one of her children was gay, she said to a friend that it would be better if her daughter were dead.

God, I was busy. I was really busy. I really loved them. My kids are great kids. They are nice to have around. Interesting. Lively. I have nothing but very good memories of all those years of bringing them up. Christopher was a great father. He loved being home on the weekends. We took them camping. We did a lot of that nice, simple stuff. I didn't enroll them in zillions of lessons. I guess I was slightly competitive--feeling that my kids are really better than anybody else's kids. They didn't get into trouble. They got A's. So, suddenly, when Alice told us she thought she was a lesbian, I was brought right up short. It shook me. Was it because I was a strong mother? You remember all those things that you heard, "Homosexual people come from the wrong kind of parenting." There was tremendous guilt.

When Alice told us she thought she was a lesbian, we went flying to Cambridge to talk her out of it! I could see her through the window of her house when we got out of the car. She had had beautiful, long, brown hair, and she had cut it all off short.

177

"Oh, my God!," I said, "a whole new person." Actually, she looked adorable with her short hair. She looked wonderful, and she was so happy.

Alice has always been a daughter that was older than I. She is a wise person. She was able to handle all the things we said: "Oh, you'll outgrow it," "How do you know?," "You'll be so miserable." I said some hurtful things: "You come home, but don't bring your friends with you." I said it to hurt her. She had hurt me. I said, "I think you shouldn't be too close to Carolyn." Meaning, "You might infect your sister." She just looked at me.

She had a relationship with a woman. It lasted two years. Then she fell in love with Dave. We were delighted. She has told me, "The older I get, the more heterosexual I feel, but I can't deny that I did have this relationship."

Alice gave me books to read. I could barely read them. I could barely read that word "homosexual"--"lesbian"--! I couldn't even say it. It was so awful to think this was in my family. I didn't think there could be anything worse than having a gay kid. There are many worse things!

This has made me an activist. I often don't want to be. It horrifies me to see my name in the paper. I want to put a paper bag over my head and hide. The newspaper came and interviewed us. There was a whole article on why we couldn't be foster parents, because we had two gay children. If the children would promise not to come home, to stay away, maybe they'd let us be foster parents. When I saw the article in the paper I almost died. I went to a meeting where I volunteer. I couldn't even look up. The director called me into his office and gave me a big hug, "That was the best thing you ever did!" Whenever I think, "Oh, why did I speak up?," someone will come up to me and thank me for doing it.

I am braver now, and more open about personal things. I still find it hard to do. I do it when I get mad enough or feel it's important enough, and, then, I go back into my shell for a while --lick my wounds.

When Keith was about twenty-four he wrote me a long letter saying he was gay and that he felt very guilty, because he wouldn't be able to have children, for me. He is a dear person.

178

A great, big, six-foot-four-inch, handsome man.   Keith is charming and brilliant and fun and loveable--<u>normal</u>. To be gay is normal for him.

You know we all tell our kids, "We just want you to be the best, whatever makes you happy. If you want to be a garbage man, be the best garbage man you can be." We don't really mean it! When Alice told me she was gay I thought, "She found the one thing I would mind; she found my real tender button." I didn't even know I had this prejudice. I never thought about it. Alice helped me get over it, and so, three years later, it was okay for Keith to tell me.

I remember going to bed at night and crying. I'd wake up in the morning and think, "Oh, nice day!" and, then, I'd remember. It's like a death in the family. It is like a death. I remember thinking, "Death would be so much easier to explain to everybody." Everyone would feel real sorry for you for this terrible tragedy in your family. As it was, I couldn't tell anybody.

My husband, Christopher, was very upset, but not quite as upset as I was. I think he took it a lot better than I did, but he felt guilty, too. He didn't read all the books that I read. He accepted it. It hurt him to see how much it was hurting me. He has begun to tell people and be much more open about it. We did, of course, ask our children before we told people about it. It was embarrassing to us, at first.

I remember saying to the first friend that I told about Alice, "We'd be better off if she would just die. It's so awful."

"Elinor, how can you say such a thing?! That's the most terrible thing I ever heard! Grow up!"

Then I began thinking about all the people I had always admired who happened to be gay. Margaret Mead. Willa Cather. I began to feel differently. I could see that some of the really neat, creative, bright people are gay. My daughter fit right in there. Then Alice told us she <u>wasn't</u> a lesbian, after all.

Then I met another mother who has a gay child. We happened to room together on a tour. We talked all night. It was wonderful. She told me about a nation-wide organization for parents of gay children: Parents and Friends of Lesbians and

Gays. I wouldn't go for years. Then, I found out that Carolyn is gay! I went through the whole thing all over again. You expect to share certain things with a daughter. I finally went to a meeting of PFLAG. I sat there on the edge of tears the whole time.

My son Marc is the strong, silent type. He loves Keith. I was so pleased when he got married--he chose Keith as his best man. I was so glad that he did that. There is nothing nicer than knowing your kids love each other. It is sort of a final reward as a parent. I don't think all this bothered Marc. Before his wedding I went through all this nervousness, "What if somebody says something? What if Keith's partner comes? What do I say when people ask, 'Who is that?'" I decided I could just say, " He's a good friend of the family."

Sometimes I do presentations to college students. You see the kids in the audience just leaning forward with their eyes shining, because they have never heard a parent talk about their gay kid in an accepting way. One time one kid waited until all the others had left. She said, "Thank you. I can't dare to talk to my parents. I'm the only child. I have all their hopes on me."

There is a responsibility of parents to accept and love their kids unconditionally and not try to mold them after our pattern. They don't have to be just like us. But, the child also has a responsibility. So many kids come out to their parents and then never mention it again. "My parents haven't said a word, and it's been a year now"-- or, five years.

The child has to push them. The child has to teach the parent. Say, "Look, it really hurts me that you never talk about my life. You're my mother, and I'm not going to let you treat me this way. I love you." Maybe the mother needs to hear that. The child should ask, "How are you dealing with this?"

"Oh, it's okay. We don't want to talk about it."

"Well, we've got to talk about it. I am still the same person that you always loved. It is just your perception of me that is changed. I haven't changed."

Children have to keep working on their parents and be very patient. I'm lucky, because I had Alice to break me in.

I am really proud of every one of our kids. After Alice came to visit the other day, Christopher and I were saying, "Oh, aren't we lucky?! We have the neatest kids."

And there was a time when we were saying, "Oh, God! What have we done?"

CHRISTINE TRUE
Age: 37

"Alison looks in the mirror. She knows she's pretty, but everybody looks at her and laughs."

Barbara and her boyfriend run a grooming kennel in rural New York. She volunteered that they "hope to be middle class someday." Barbara's seventeen-year-old daughter Alison is retarded. After the interview I thanked Barbara for talking with me. "Thank <u>you</u>," she said, "No one ever asked before."

As you can see, Alison's very normal-looking. Until you sit down and talk to her you don't realize she's retarded. She passes for normal quite a bit. When teenage boys realize she's retarded they feel they can take advantage. Your normal girls can say "no," and they can push the boys away. She doesn't know what to do.

We've talked about sex. She understands it. She doesn't know how to handle the attention. She's flattered by it. The idea of her being kidnapped or raped is a very strong possibility. It's always on my mind that this could happen, knowing there's people loose in the area doing this.

There's the idea, what would we do if she became pregnant? She could never understand or handle a pregnancy. She could never raise a child. These are very real problems that you have to face every day.

We keep a very close eye on her. In this rural area there's not that much to do. Most of the children here are a lot younger than her. She has friends her own age, and they go to the movies or to the fairs. They kind of keep an eye on her, but when they're with their boyfriends they're not keeping as good an eye on her.

We tried to put her on birth control pills. That didn't work, because she didn't understand. She skipped them. She hid them. It was like she was embarrassed by them. We don't know how much she understands.

If you want to sterilize a child like her, it takes a court order. I don't have the money to go and get a lawyer and get a court order. They have advocates that would present her side, why they think she would be capable of having a child. I know very well she shouldn't have a child.

Two of my boyfriend's children live with us. They're seven and eleven, and I'm raising them. I just . . . I don't want another child, a grandchild to have to raise. What if she has a child that is more severely retarded than herself? Because we don't know why she was mentally retarded. She was born that way. Her father and I are both farm people. We've handled dangerous pesticides and chemicals from the time we were children.

From the time Alison was born I knew there was something wrong with her. Then I had to spend two years proving to others that there was. "This is your first child. You're a nervous mother. You don't know anything." First there's frustration, and then there's anger. I never went through denial. A lot of people deny there's something wrong. They'll take the kid from doctor to doctor to doctor, hoping somebody is going to have a miracle cure. I knew. My child's nine months old, and she doesn't sit up. Don't tell me I'm a nervous mother. My child is a year and a half; she doesn't walk. Don't tell me I'm a nervous mother. "Oh they'll come around when it's their time." Sure, their time is when they're three years old. I can see my friend's child does this, mine doesn't. Why? And there are no answers. You have to cope with it. You can either look at it as the greatest tragedy of your life, or you can just pick yourself up and say, "Okay, this is what I've got to do, and let's make the best of it."

Alison's father could not accept imperfection. He thought she should be hidden away- not institutionalized, but "We won't take her out to the movies. We don't want people to see her." This kind of thing. He would never say, "I'm going to the store for bread and milk. Come on, Alison." He was good to her at home, inside the house, where nobody could see her.

He told me, "You do too much with her." Well, she needed more. I'd look at him and say, "Well, you're an adult, you don't need me for this." We drifted apart. I couldn't take any more of it. It was frustrating enough being with her, but to be frustrated by this other adult that was supposed to be helping . . .

So, Alison and I lived alone until she was thirteen. I didn't go to work until Alison went to school. I've worked different jobs, but I've always gotten jobs where I worked hours she was in school. If I had to work a night or a Saturday, I always set it up that she was with a relative. She was never with someone that didn't care.

Also, knowing there was something wrong with her, I began babysitting for other people with handicapped kids. I always took in kids that were her mental level at the time. Maybe she was nine, and I was babysitting four-year-olds, so that they would not be so far ahead of her, and she would learn from them. Someone that's eleven would not have the patience to throw a ball a hundred times for her to catch, but a seven-year-old that can't catch any better than her . . . they can play all day long, no problem!

People said, "Alison will never learn numbers. She'll never learn to read. She'll never ..." I always said, "Why not?" I don't know what they thought they knew. They were all professionals.

It made me angry when they told me not to bother trying to teach her how to read. If they don't bother and I don't bother, nobody is going to teach her. It's been a lot of frustration. I could sit there and -- seven plus three is ten -- she got that right off. But if you said, "How much is three plus seven?", she could not understand it was the same numbers in reverse.

I stuck with it to the point that I would get frustrated, because I just couldn't say those numbers one more time without screaming or ripping my hair out. Then we'd take a play break and do it again tomorrow. It's being able to go back and do the same thing tomorrow and tomorrow, and it may take two years, but one day the light comes on, and it's been worth it, because you can see the change. She's grasped something. Retarded children, when they've grasped something new, their whole being lights up. It's a beautiful thing to watch.

She knows her numbers. She knows how to write out a deposit slip. She reads on probably a third- or fourth-grade level. She can appreciate simple books and stories. She's just beginning to do addition where you have to do carrying. Multiplication doesn't make any sense to her, but as long as she can do her basic addition and subtraction and counting, she can get by.

She's in a school where she's learning a vocation and life skills. What we want is an independent life for her, as independent as possible. She's not capable of abstract thinking and decision-making, but she can do things with her hands. She loves to work in the school kitchen, cooking and serving the other students. She understands that she's doing a job. She understands getting paid for it. They don't care if she says "ain't" and "I don't not do this." What they care about is that she can put eighteen snaps in a package and seal it, and she can do a hundred packages a day, and that's an improvement from ninety-five yesterday. They have efficiency ratings, and when they do really good they get a bonus. They get raises. The kids understand this.

When you have a retarded child you have a tendency to do too much for them. The school is great because they make the kids do it themselves. If something happens to me tomorrow, who's going to look after her? She'll be semi-capable of some independence.

She takes pride in the Special Olympics medals she's won. This is something she can do that none of the other kids can do. They can't win a gold medal. She gets tormented by people, "Look at the dummy," "Gee, you're stupid, you can't do this or that." She can feel, "You're stupid, because you can't win a gold medal. I can be on TV--you've never been on TV." They get their feelings hurt, and you've just got to be there to help pick them up. You can't step in every single time and say, "Don't you talk to her like that." They have to learn how to deal with it, because all their life people are going to be like that.

185

She's learned to cope with it, and she turns everybody around into being her friend. She had a little boy in her class who used to pick on her. The teacher told me, "I don't know why she doesn't hit him." I said, "She's not allowed to." The teacher said, "He hit her. I turned around and looked, and she was sitting on the floor saying, 'Come here, Ralph, I want you to share my crayons.'" Alison told the teacher, "If I make him my friend, he won't hit me anymore." This is what she figured out herself.

Going through the teenage years is the most difficult, because she has all of the feelings and emotions of a seventeen-year-old girl. She looks in the mirror. She knows she's pretty, but everybody looks at her and laughs. When she was going to the junior high, she liked the normal boys, the handsome ones. She'd say "hi" to them, and they'd make fun of her. Most retarded kids are not nice-looking. She doesn't want to be seen with a boy that looks retarded. In her own way, she's just as prejudiced as the rest.

I don't know. We just go on, day by day. There isn't anything else we can do. When she does something wrong we point it out but we try to minimize it. One of her big things is to say, "I'm stupid." We say, "No, you're not stupid, you just don't know how to do it. Now you know how to do it. You can do it right." When she does something good we build it up so big. When she's having a hard day you can go and rub her on the back and say, "Let's go and pick strawberries, then we can come back to this." You have to help them deal with their frustration. I can see it building inside her. When that happens I try to divert her into something she can do and accomplish very well.

I fought the school system for years. They felt sorry for the kids, and instead of helping them achieve their fullest potential, they babysat them. They were not looking ahead. They would let her throw things if she was frustrated. She can't do that on a job. You can expect as much out of them as a normal person. It just takes more time to get there. That's basically it. You wouldn't let a normal child throw a book across the room. Why would you let one of them? They didn't treat them like human beings. You have to treat them <u>more</u> like human beings than normal people.

Now my boyfriend and I have been together about five years. He has been a terrific help. She gets no special treatment. Just like the other kids, if she messes up, she gets yelled at. If a seven-year-old can feed the pigs and not spill the grain, so can she.

The more normal we treat her, the more normal she acts.

You have to realize she's seventeen only on the outside. On the inside she's somewhere between four and nine.

JEAN HILLYER
Age: 31

"I used to feel like I was Mike's sister or his aunt, just somebody there trying to help this kid along. We did nothin' but argue. It was like we were enemies. I never felt like I was Mikey's mother, the person who's supposed to help him get through all things. Now I feel like I am in control. I am the mother, and I am the one that takes care of his needs."

Jean cleans houses and offices for people in Baltimore, Maryland. She is a single parent with one child, Michael, who is just eleven. Jean has had a lot of difficulty with Mikey, who is coded as having Attention Deficit Disorder and having a chemical deficiency in his brain. When we first talked, Mikey had spent the last year in a residential program. He had been back at home for three weeks and was still attending the program's school. Through this program he was being taught a different way to live, and Jean was learning how to be a more effective mother.

When Mikey got into first grade the teacher was telling me about some problems. She wrote me a note saying, "From now on whenever we have field-trips, if you can't come with us, we ask that you keep Mikey home." That was the first sign to me that he must really be a handful.

He was a handful at home, too. If Mikey sat idle, he was sure to be in trouble. If I said he was punished for something, he would punch a hole in the wall or hit me. He doesn't do that now. He'll take his time-outs now and accept responsibility instead of lying and saying, "I didn't do it."

He was in trouble with the law, busting windows, shoplifting. It took me a year to get him into this program. All kinds of psychologists and doctors came to the conclusion that he's got a chemical deficiency that affects the reasoning part of the brain. If he'd done something wrong and the consequence would be something he knew about, he wouldn't even stop to think about it; he'd just immediately go do right what he wants. He's a follower and a leader. I've seen him persuade kids to do things, and I've seen kids persuade him, which doesn't take much.

It was so bad that nobody in my family would even babysit him, even for an hour. They just did not want to deal with him. I, honestly, did not want to deal with him. If you knew Mikey when he was nine, ten years old, you would not have wanted this child living in your home. I got nothing in return but a hard time. For a long time I wanted to have another child. Then I would think, "Oh, God, what if I have another one like Mikey?"

I've been with Ralph, my boyfriend, for almost seven years now. It really put a strain on our relationship. Five and a half of those years were just crazy. Ralph endured a lot. It's hard enough to have a relationship with someone else's child, but especially a child with a problem like this. The minute Mikey came through that door, I immediately put Ralph on the back burner and had to watch Mikey.

It was horrible. Every day was a nightmare. Just to get him up and try to get him dressed was a real chore. Like I said, he was in trouble with the law. I have a thick folder upstairs of things that Mikey had to go to court for. Age ten and younger. He took a bat one day and hit the back of a man's car. Mikey just wore himself out with everybody.

Mikey kept on getting suspended from school. I would call the school every day at noon to see how he was doing. That tells you something right there. Parents of normal kids don't call the school every day. I had to quit with the cleaning agency I was with and go on my own, because two, three times a week I had to go to the school.

One day the teacher told Mike she was going to call the principal. The principal arrived, and Mikey kicked her in the leg. Then they called the assistant principal, a man, and he told Mikey he could either walk to his office, or he would drag him.

Well, that set up a power struggle right there. He had to drag Mikey down to the office. Mikey completely destroyed all the plants and turned furniture over in there. He carved nasty words in the principal's desk. That was the day they told me he was more severe than what a public school could do.

So, then he had just a home tutor. I don't know how many days I had to take off a week while Mikey had the home tutor. The tutor only came twice a week for an hour and a half. My mother had to watch Mikey. Plus he was losing all that education. The tutor said he was glad when each day would end, because Mikey was so oppositional with him. Mike would think of any excuse not to do his work. His pencil needed sharpening. The eraser broke. The chair is not in enough. A math page would take him an hour and a half.

Now, homework is the first thing Mike does when he comes home, because he wants his playtime. Playtime is any time up to five-thirty after his homework is done. We've worked out a schedule. He follows this religiously now. It has consequences, and he is rewarded when he does well. Each day he comes home from school with a point sheet, one to four. For ones and twos all week we get to go out on Friday and get pizza or a candied apple. If he comes home with threes and fours, he loses some of his playtime. I can't take it all away from him. That would drive me crazy too, keeping him in the house when he wants to go out.

So far this plan is working. He has to be within reach of my voice when he's outside. That gives him a little free play with the kids in the neighborhood. If he can't hear my voice, we'll have to knock some time off, or he'll have to stay in the yard. I still have to peek my head out every now and then just to make sure he's still on the street. Every time he goes out I yell for him and within a minute or two, he's at the door. If I have to go look for him, he gets a consequence.

He has between eight and nine o'clock to take his bath. The school will notice if he's not doing it and will call him down to the nurse and make an issue out of it. They tell me not to get in a power struggle over it. Let him come to school, and they'll deal with it. The same thing with homework. If he didn't do it, I used to go crazy. If I helped him, he would say, "I'm a real dummy." If I didn't help him, he would say, "You don't even care." I was losing either way.

I think he thinks I'm trying to make him into this perfect child. I'm not. I'm just trying to prepare him. It's rough out there. People aren't going to keep catering to him. He has to respond.

I don't think I wanted to admit it, but I needed outside help badly.

People who don't have this problem look at you funny, like, "You can't control your child?" You feel like you're the only parent with that problem. I felt that way. Look at all these parents in this neighborhood, how lucky they are to be able to let their kids go out, and they don't have to keep peeking their heads out the window! They can go to the store and tell their kids, "You can look at the toys. I'll be in the next aisle." I couldn't do that. He wouldn't be in that aisle. I don't know where he would have been.

Sometimes I just feel like this drill sergeant, this bully. Do this. Do that. But there are times when we sit down, and we play, and we get along really good.

Every morning I try to get up and fix him a hot breakfast. Bacon and eggs or french toast. He loves that. I feel better sending him to school that way. I do a lot of extras for him.

I used to look at it like, "Why me?" I was really mad that I have a kid like this, but I guess in the last year with me learning more about myself, I see things that I would do that would trigger him to do the things he did.

I used to really resent him. I did not like having him around at all. He was driving me nuts. Everything was an effort. Even if he just went to the bathroom. If he was in there too long, I would have to go in and check and see what he was getting into. I was a screamer. I would scream right in front of his face, and he wouldn't even flinch. Now I get real calm, and he'll stop and look at me and absorb what I'm saying. He might not do what I say, but I know he's heard it.

I used to feel like I was Mike's sister or his aunt, just somebody there trying to help this kid along. We did nothing

191

but argue. It was like we were enemies. I never felt like I was Mikey's mother, the person who's supposed to help him get through all things. Now I feel like I am in control. I am the mother, and I am the one that takes care of his needs.

Hopefully I can help him to be a good person. If I just kinda keep getting him off of that bad track that he was on and keep him going straight, I feel like that I've done my best. This may sound a little harsh, but I also keep in mind that once he's on his own, if he decides to go the wrong way, the only way that I'm going to be able to live with myself is to know that I did do everything that I could. I had to give him the chance to do this program and turn things around. Everything is better. Nobody's got hit here in three weeks. Nobody has had to scream.

Last night we sat down and talked before he went to bed, and I told him how much I had been waiting for this time to come, for him to be home. I told him how glad I was that he was home.

The scariest time in my life with him was one night I had to discipline him for something he had done. He was in the living room, and I went in the bedroom to sleep. I dreamt that night that he came into my room, which he didn't. The next night, when I was in bed asleep, I could feel a presence. I woke up, and Mikey was just standing there. I said, "What do you want Mike?" He wouldn't answer me. I said, "Mike, what do you want?" He just turned and walked right out of the room, like he wasn't even there. His body was, but it seemed like his mind wasn't. I told Ralph that from then on I wanted a lock on the bedroom door. That's how scared I was of Mikey. So many people have told me that they were afraid for me--that he was going to kill me. He was that off. He was so hurtful to me. He almost enjoyed seeing me hurt. He would hit me so hard, or if I cried about something, he would mock it. He could be cruel. But it's so different now. He's a kinder person, and thinking more before he talks.

My expectations are really limited. I used to really hope that Mikey would graduate from high school, because he's my only child. That was my big goal for Mikey. If I set my goals too high, I'm going to be let down. I want him to know that people were behind him and not saying, "Forget you, kid, you aren't worth it," because he definitely is. He has so much potential. If he would graduate, that would be great. I almost cry thinking about it.

[Jean called me a year later, because she thought someone might have read this who would know of something that would help:]

Mikey did all right for about four months. Then there was a lot of trouble. He was in a psychiatric institution for a while. He is diagnosed manic depressive and is on lithium.

I was scared being in the house with him alone. He's bigger than I am now. He would get up in the morning and leave the house before we were up. I couldn't get him to go to school at all. He's been stealing money, matches, knives out of the house. I called juvenile services, but they can't do anything unless he commits a crime.

Then, last weekend he stole a truck. In one week they got him on charges of assault and battery and grand theft. I recommended that they detain him for the month before his hearing. It was horrible. He was in shackles in the courtroom. It tore me up. I am burnt out. I am not giving up.

Finally, someone said to me that his being manic depressive and hyper is something he was born with. It's nothing I did. That lifted a little weight off.

He needs a year-long residence program some distance away, so he can't run away to home. He needs a much more structured environment.

When they said he would be in a detention facility for a month, he said to me, "What's going to happen to me?"

I said, "I don't know, Mikey. It's like I have been telling you--some time you're going to get yourself into so much trouble that I can't get you out. This might be the time." He blames me for all of this. He's making bad choices, but at least he didn't hurt himself or anyone else. I think he is crying out for help. We're running out of time here. We don't have much more time to break him out of the mold he's in.

RUTHIE CHELSEA
Age: 56

"Don't worry. You can have them all back once you get
back under control."

*Ruthie lives in the projects now in Boston, Massachusetts.
She began having children when she was sixteen. She had five of
her own and five of her husband's to raise from his previous
marriage. When her husband died in 1969, Ruthie was thirty-
two, the youngest child was two, and the oldest about seventeen.*

*Soon after her husband's death, Ruthie fell apart
emotionally, and her children were taken from her. It is not
clear from her story how long they were gone--perhaps until the
blizzard of 1978, for nine years. Or, perhaps, for only four
years. Ruthie worked in a hospital for about four years at one
point. About a year or two after the blizzard, Ruthie became
homeless. She lived on the streets for nine years, until she got
into the projects five years ago. It is not clear where all of her
children were all of this time.*

*Listening to Ruthie is like watching traffic in a city: the
traffic is all flowing roughly in the same direction, but some cars
are changing lanes unaccountably, some are turning off, some
appear out of nowhere, some appear to be going somewhere that
others could never get to from here. It is difficult to keep track
of any one car, but the traffic flows along.*

I have ten kids. So I got all them and seventeen
grandchildren.

My husband died of a heart attack in 1969. I raised up all
ten. I was living in Maine. I met my husband up in an apple
tree. It was autumn time, you know how they have it. It was
picking time. He was from Boston. Once I came here to Boston,

I lived here. I've been here in Boston maybe about twenty-eight years. Maybe more now. I'm just guessing.

When my husband died, we had a little problem. I went into state of shock. So all my kids were taken away. From me. Because there was no one there to care for the little ones. The only one that got adopted was Martin. He's my favorite, him and his wife Alice. Him and Leroy, my oldest. If I'm out of food or something, they help me out. Alice says, "Ma, there's the frigerator, take whatever you want."

I'll always take care of my kids. They'll come to me and say, "Ma, can I stay a couple nights?"

"Sure." I never throw my kids out like a lot of parents do.

My kids were taken away. They were put into private schools. I had one went to the state hospital. I had one put down in Fall River. Then I had one put into the Springfield place. He was only two at the time. So, the youngest, he got adopted. They told him a lot of stories, "Your mother died. I'm going to be your new mother," and all this, but my son never gave up. He looked, and he looked.

Then, finally, he met my girlfriend Sherrie, my best friend for years. He knew who she was, and he said, "Is my mother dead?"

Sherrie says, "No, I know where your mother is."

"You give me the address?"

All of a sudden, he come knocking on my door. "You're my mother, right?" He says, "I've never forgotten ya. I've been looking for years and years for you. They told me you were dead."

I said, "Do I look dead?" I never forgot him. I always had presents under the tree. I knew some day he would come home.

He said, "Oh, you still got presents?"

I said, "Those are all yours." When he came back to me he must have been nine to ten years old.

He says, "I can't come home until I'm eighteen." He wanted to come home so bad.

He turned sixteen, and he ran away from his foster mother and came home to stay. He changed his name back.

All the rest of the kids came back as they got older. I've raised them. My family needs help, I'll help 'em. Even if I don't have it, I'll try.

About a month after their father died, I had this ice cream in the frig. They wanted to melt the ice cream; it was so cold. They went and lighted a fire in the closet to melt the ice cream. The knitted things got on fire. Leroy was sleeping. They had to carry Leroy out through the window. Here I'm crawling through the smoke. They're all yelling, "Where's my mother? Where's my mother?"

The whole house was full of smoke. I'm trying to put the fire out. I got burns. I got a big hole in there, and I'm all loaded with smoke. I got burnt on my whole chest. They took me to the hospital. My niece took all the kids until I recovered. They told the kids, "Your mother is dead." Because they gave me gas, and they weren't supposed to because I'm an asthma victim. I was out for eight hours--they thought I was dead. They told the kids I'm dead.

They had the rabbis; they had the priests; they had the minister. They said mass over me and everything else. They called the guys to come in and pick up my body. As they were coming in, I woke up. The doctor said, "You all right? We thought you were dead. You had no heartbeat. No nothin'."

Every one of them said, "You were dead. We felt you. You were cold as ice."

Then they saw there was a sacred heart on my chest. "Good Lord, how did that get there? She must have been to heaven, otherwise she wouldn't have got it." So, all the time I was healing that mark never left me. It was a heart with a little heart inside of it with a sword goin' up through the heart. It stayed there until the day that I got ready to go home. It was protecting me.

They did everything they could to save my arm, from the fire. They didn't think they could. Finally, three weeks later, it was healed, and the heart was gone. The priests all came to see me in my house. They said, "You're a miracle woman." That's what they all call me. Ever since that day I've had good luck. Maybe not luck to have an apartment, but luck, otherwise.

People ask me, "Was heaven like they say it was?"

I said, "It was more beautiful than whatever they said it was."

It was very strange. That story really happened. God said, "I'm keeping you cause you got the kids to look after."

The kids stayed with me for a while, 'til I took the nervous breakdown and went into a mental hospital. After the funeral was over and everything else, I just couldn't handle myself. I wanted to die, because he wasn't there.

They said, "Well we're going to have to take the kids, because you're not under any control to take care of any of the kids."

I said, "You're not taking my God damn kids."

They said, "Lady, you can't even handle them. Don't worry. We're not putting 'em in any foster homes, only maybe the youngest might have to go. Don't worry. You can have 'em all back once you get back under control." So they went away for about a couple of years. They told me, "You show us what you can do, and we'll give ya back your kids. We don't think you can." They put me on welfare, but they said they couldn't put all my kids on it.

That's when I got the job and told welfare that I was going to work. I did job training in a hospital. They kept me on the job all those years. My kids all started coming home during the blizzard, sometimes around 1980. That's how all my kids came home. They kept telling me Leroy can start coming home on weekends and see how it works out. Then he came home for good in the blizzard, in 1978. He said, "Ma, are you going to have a Christmas?"

I said, "I don't think so. We don't have no tree. We don't have the money." All the months I was sick I didn't even look in the closet. There were three big boxes of Christmas presents. Must have been their father knew he was dying. But the kids were too big for the toys.

I was on my fourth year when the accident happened. I got hit by one of those big garbage tanks. I went crippled. For life.

After the blizzard I started looking for my own apartment. I found one on Leonard Street. I lived there two or three years with my son Leroy and my son Martin. I kept getting new landlords all of the time. Finally, he come over with no warning. He wasn't supposed to move us until the court told us we had to move. Saturday morning there he is, moving us out.

I said, "What the hell you think you're doing?"

He says, "You've been evicted from the court."

I says, "I didn't receive no letter from no court."

"You must have got the letter." Very sassy.

"I didn't get nothin'."

"I'm sorry. I'm moving you out." It was pouring rain, and I had no coat, no nothin'. He threw everything into boxes.

The lady on the third floor came out and gave me a pink raincoat. She said, "This will keep you dry."

He never gave me a paper saying anything about storage. Where my furniture was going. I kept trying to find out where it was. He said, "You don't need 'em now. You ain't got apartment."

That's when I started being homeless. I used to see my children. I used to help my son Martin. Martin went to Springfield. He had a place to go. Leroy started living in the armory, different shelters. If I got a couple of bucks and I saw him, I used to give it to him, 'cause I had plenty of food shelters I could go to. But him--you don't eat at the armory. Then they started giving meals at night time, because it was getting colder. We couldn't get no money. I used to collect bottles, cans and bottles to live on. That would be my car fare to get around.

We couldn't even get food stamps. Finally, St. Francis house said to my son, "We can get you temporary food stamps." All he used to do was buy a sandwich, buy a loaf of bread, "Come on, Ma, we're going to eat tonight." Store 24 you can buy anything with food stamps. I used to bring food to him when he didn't have the food stamps. A nun gave me a fifty-dollar bill once. I went out and gave my son twenty dollars and told him to go get a meal. Then I saved the rest, and when we needed it, we'd have a hot meal. If he needed to buy cigarettes or something, it was always there.

I get disability now. I can never work again. The only thing I can do now is babysitting. My daughter pays me. I told her I didn't want it, but she says, "Ma, you need it as well as I do." She's a welfare recipient, too.

I get around pretty good. As long as I have my two legs and my two arms and I can do things, I'll do it. Plus I have a hernia. A nice big hernia. From carrying all those bags around. You know when you're homeless you carry all your bags, 'cause you can't leave 'em in the shelters. They steal them.

I was scared 'cause I used to sleep on benches, park benches. One time I was up by Jordan Marsh. I was so tired 'cause they get you up at 5 a.m. in the morning. Any of the shelters get you up at 5 a.m. in the morning. You gotta wash. Some of the shelters have breakfast; some of them don't. You go in for breakfast; then you help around the kitchen, and you're out by 7:00, sometimes 6:30. One afternoon about two-thirty, three o'clock, I was so tired I couldn't stay awake. I laid down on the bench, and I fell asleep. This guy come up behind me, clonked me on the back of the head, "Hey, you God damn bum, get the hell up outa here." The nail went through the back of my head. Where he had this timber thing. I didn't know it. I got up. I'm walking. This woman says, "You know your head's bleeding." I started feeling dizzy after while. One of the train drivers asked me if I was all right. I says, "No, I got hit in the back of the head." He called an ambulance. I had to have seventeen stitches.

Then, six weeks later, this same guy came up and stabbed me in the chest with a knife. I landed up in the hospital again. The knife didn't go all the way through. I was lucky. He was holding me down. This other woman yelled and the cops came. They set up a date, and he got fifteen years to twenty years in prison, attempted murder. He yelled out in court, "I'll kill that b" --(see, I don't swear, so I'll say "b").

The judge says, "You go ahead, I'm going to make sure she's armed. If you come after her after your fifteen, twenty years, we'll get you."

They took me from one place and put me in the shelter on the island in Quincy, so he would never know where I was. I was put on the island permanently, until I got the place in the projects. I lived there for quite a while, five years, until my time was up. It was like I was in prison. I wasn't free. In case sometimes the prisons are overloaded, they let them go. The judge wanted to make sure I was safe, and the guy wouldn't come after me again. It was horrible out there. It was cold on that island. You got to go through hell out there. The only kind of food out there was spaghetti.

I got in about five years ago in the projects. It took me a long time to get in. I went down every day. I was homeless for about nine years. I stayed in shelters and with my daughter some.

DOT GILMAN
Age: 30

"I had to go out and turn tricks to get money to feed them."

Dot is black. She was homeless when we talked. She and her five children are staying in a family shelter in Boston, while she tries to find an apartment. Myeisha is thirteen; Charlene, eleven; Anthony, nine; Bryant, seven; and Joseph, four. Dot has held a number of jobs--as a records clerk and as a sales person. She has had a cocaine problem.

Despite a life full of awful events, Dot persists in trying to put a life together for herself and her children. If she can keep off the cocaine and doesn't get pregnant again, she has a fighting chance. Dot's smile is as magnificent as any saint's or any child's. It made me want to change the world for her.

I had my first baby when I was sixteen, Myeisha. She's like my friend now. That's my buddy! Yeah. When I need advice or something bothers me, I'm crying, she's always there for me. "It's okay , Mommy." When I used to be sick or depressed, she'd tell the other kids, "Be quiet, Mommy's sick. Don't bother Mommy. What do you want?" She would do it for me.

When Joseph was born--his father had been arrested and was incarcerated--she would hear the baby crying and jump up. She made the formula. "Mommy, you can rest. I'll get the baby." She's an A-B student. Very bright in school. She's something else. She's so sweet.

I went back to school after I had my fourth child. I had gone to eleventh grade and dropped out. I walked across the stage seven months pregnant with Joseph. I still have the rose that the mayor gave me. I pressed it in my Bible. It was a struggle for me. It was hard. I went back to school, because I don't want my kids to say to me, "Well, you dropped out, so why should we finish?" They'll not say that to me. No, they won't. I appreciate the system. They helped me get the kids into day-care. It was rough. I had homework and was running back and forth to clinics when one got sick. I worked my behind off to get that diploma, and I'm really proud of myself.

I went to college for a year at Roxbury Community College. My goal really is to go the aerotech school--to rebuild jet and helicopter engines. It's a nine-month course. I'm really thinking about it, once I get myself stable. I have to have a place to live. I want to go back to school. I can do it. I just want to get a roof over our heads, first.

When I was nine months pregnant with my second child, I would go out every day looking for an apartment. They would tell me, "Come back tomorrow. Come back tomorrow." It was cold. Snow and ice on the ground. I think they wanted to see if I was really determined. Every time, I would go back. My husband, he wouldn't help me. I finally got the apartment after Charlene was born. I cried the first night I got in my apartment. I finally realized that I had a big responsibility. Paying my bills, seeing that my kids eat, seeing that they go to bed on time. It was a lot to think about, and I was scared. It was totally different being on my own.

It's still hard, but I've proven to myself that I'm a pretty strong person. I have faith. I was raised in church, and I believe in God. I know that there is nothing that I can't accomplish with a little help and a little prayer. I've slipped. I got into drugs. It's a fighting battle, and I'm still fighting. I try to tell myself that I deserve so much better, and I have more potential than that.

I've done a lot. I put my apartment together. I got my kids into school. These are things that I did without anybody's help. I don't have anybody to back me. I don't have any family that's willing to help me. I was always the one helping other people. I don't think there's really anything I can't do. It's just sometimes you need a little encouragement.

My grandmother raised me. I was a state ward. My mother was never around when I was a kid. Then she came, took us from my grandmother in Florida, and brought us to Massachusetts. I was six.

She married this man. He started abusing us. He'd beat my brothers. They were three or four. If they couldn't bathe themselves, he'd punch them and bust their eyes open. Blood would be all in the bath water. He would beat me and my sister and have us stand up in corners, butt-naked, all night and dare us to go to sleep.

He and my mother would feed us one meal a day. The teachers used to sneak and feed us lunch at school. They started seeing us being bruised and stuff. They used to tell us, "Eat your lunch. Don't take nothing home." When we'd go home, we'd have to go to bed straight from school. We never could go outside. I grew up with a complex. I was scared to go places, because we couldn't even go outside. We never played with other children. We couldn't watch TV. We just stayed in bed all the time. On weekends. All the time.

I want to give my kids better, treat them better than the way I was treated. When kids are bad, you spank them, but I talk to mine. I punish them. I take things from them that they want. They ask me can they go somewhere, I say, "You have to do such-and-such work." I tell them, "If you want something from me, earn it." I tell them what I've been through. They all know that I had a drug problem. I told them I don't want them to hear that from nobody on the street. I ask them to bear with me, because I'm trying to do better. "If you feel that I've said something to hurt your feelings, or I did something or forgot something, tell me." I don't ever let them talk back to me, but if something is wrong, then we'll sit down and talk about it. I love my kids.

I try to give them what they need, and some of the things that they want. These are things that I was lacking when I was a child. I try to tell them that I love them. I never had anybody tell me that. A man, yeah, because he wants something from ya, but a relative or a friend, or my Mom. I seek that from my Mom so much. That's why I went to be with her.

Two years ago, I went to California, because my Mom had a stroke out there, and she asked me to come out. She had been trying to get me to come out there for years. I packed up my stuff. I sold my furniture. I gave up my apartment. I gave up my kids' being in school. I gave up a job I had, paying me under the table. I left in the middle of February.

Just so we could go out there and she could treat my kids like she treated me when I was a child. My mother was abusive to me. She fed Bryant food out of the trash can while I was at work. When I asked her why did she do that, she said, "Pack up your stuff and get your kids and get out of my house."

I went back to doing drugs. I gave up. I took a bunch of pills and tried to commit suicide. I was in a coma for four days. I was on probation. My probation officer said to me, "You are really bright and intelligent. What's the matter with you?" I said, "You know, it's not really what's wrong with me, you just really don't know what I've been through all my life to make me the kind of person that I am. I've given my heart to people, and I've helped people. Everything, and they've walked over me."

I ran into this guy. His name was Willy. I talked to him about my kids. He was forty-four. He put my kids and me in an apartment. He got to know me for real. We fell in love. He spoiled me. I never had to cook or clean. He used to tell me, "All you have to do is keep yourself looking good. Stay pretty. You are a beautiful, young lady. You don't have to be out on the street." He didn't want me doing drugs no more.

I almost lost my kids. I was really bad off, on drugs. I was worried, and I was scared, and at the same time, at that point, I didn't care. I thought maybe it was better for them. "I can't take care of them any more. They deserve better. I'm not doing what I'm supposed to do." But you know, God is good. He changed my mind. He didn't let that happen to me.

Willy was my knight in shining armor. He always rescued me when I got in trouble. Then he'd get on me about it, and tell me off, and make me cry. "You know better than that, and you can do better." I started looking at that.

Even though I did drugs, I always tried to find someone responsible enough to hold some of my money and not give it back to me. I gave my mother a hundred dollars for groceries, and the money for the light and gas bills. She took my money and went to Long Beach with her boyfriend for the weekend. Left my kids. They woke up, and the door was open. Anybody could have went in there and killed them.

I had to go out and turn tricks to get money to feed them. The state lady came and said, "We're going to take the kids and find some place to place them." I was on the verge of going back to jail. I had been in jail for selling drugs, crack cocaine, and using at the time. Then, because I tried to commit suicide, that's a crime too. She was going to take the kids, because I was still using.

Willy moved me. When they were looking for me to take the kids, he moved me. He put me in an apartment with two refrigerators and cabinets full of food. The kids had clean clothes. He cut the boys' hair, permed ours. He was really special. He always kept me out of trouble. He was always saving Dottie. He was right there for me. He helped me keep the kids together, until I got them into school. We were going to get married. I had been with him for a year.

Even after what my mother did, when I heard she got sick again, I went looking for her. I took her into my home. She brought her boyfriend. He was younger than her. He tried to molest my oldest daughter and my oldest son. Willy didn't like that. He moved us again.

Willy reminded me of myself. He never really had love, and he was always looking for it. I used to say to him, "What's wrong with you? You're watching TV." I like to cuddle, or hug, or kiss, or just talk. When you're in a relationship, you should always have something to talk about. I don't care if it's, "The refrigerator broke down," or "Was you outside today? Did you see the moon that was up there? What about that star?" Always. There should always be something to talk about. It's like building a house. You have to start with the foundation and build it up. I think I showed him what love was, and he showed me a lot, too. He'd say, "Your personality is nice. You could get a job anywhere you want." I've never had that confidence in myself.

We had just got back together. He said, "I can rest now. My family is home." We were going to get married this month, and he ended up getting killed. I had asked him to go to the store for me. On his way back, right in the backyard. I heard some shots. My daughter's little friend came up, "Dot, someone is laying in the backyard!" I went out there. I freaked out. It was him. They shot him twice in the head and once in the chest. Blew his brains out.

My kids had to see it. Myeisha went up to him, trying to help him get up. Even now, she still cries. We all do. I miss him. He helped me get myself together. You know? I loved him. That's all the kids talk about sometimes. They used to call him Cincinnati. "I miss Cincinnati," they all say. They loved him. I see them doing things that they didn't do normally, "Cincinnati would have liked us to do this," they say. He marked our hearts.

I was staying with my sister when I came back from California. She is just like my mother, mean and hateful. The reason I'm here now is because she pulled a machete in front of my kids and had them crying, "Someone needs to kill you. I'm tired of you."

My two little boys' father, Alan, was in and out of jail. One time I bailed him out, two hundred dollars. He went back and did the same thing again. The bail was five hundred dollars. I got up the money again. He went to court for three months every week, and I was there. Got my kids off to school and went. I wrote the judge a letter and told him that I would stick by Alan no matter what his ruling was going to be and help him out. I told him I had his children. Alan was a good provider. He just went about it the wrong way. If I did not have food, he would go out and do what he had to do to make sure me and my kids ate. I explained that to the judge. He called me up to the bench. He said, "Every time he's been in this court room, you've been here. You know he's facing five to ten years. I reviewed your letter. I'm going to give him two years. One in the house of correction, one probation." He only did six months.

You know what Alan said to me after that, "You didn't do any more for me than any other bitch would have did." I would make sure the kids had and he had. As long as they was happy, I said, "I can always wait." He showed no appreciation for nothing I did. None whatsoever. He has regrets now, but I don't. I try when I'm in a relationship, just like with my kids, to put one hundred percent in. I still care about him, but I also cared enough to let him go, because he's no good for me. I try to do better for my kids.

Myeisha and Anthony both got twenty-five dollar checks from the Treasury Department for being outstanding students. I feel bad because I did cause them to lose a year and a half of school when we went to California. I hope and pray that they can still make it up. The teachers say they're so far behind. I feel like if they don't want to pass them, don't, and let them repeat this year over again. They missed a year, and there is <u>nothing</u> I can do about that now, but they're here. I can't make that up now. I can just go forward.

After I get an apartment and get my kids to the clinic, and get things squared away, then I can go back to school and look for a job. I've got that potential. Everywhere I've worked people have offered to hire me back. I try to be nice to people. Everybody wants someone to care about them. Even a dog deserves the time of day.

My goal is to get into something that is going to pay me good money. And that I'll enjoy. My dream is to get a home to leave to my kids, which is something I've never had. I want to buy a house and leave it to my kids, so they'll always have a place to call "home," because I've never, ever had that.

I'm not going to sit back and wait on the shelter to find me a place to live. I want to break a record. I'm only going to be here a month. This is ridiculous. I didn't come here to live and for them to pry into my business. I came here to get housing, and that's all I want from them. They told me to give my kids up and go into a rehab. I told them I'll go into a motel if I have to. I'm not giving my kids to nobody. They've been through too much. I'm not that strung out that I don't know what I'm doing. My kids are not that bad. I had no help for them to learn manners and all that stuff.

This is the second week I've been here. I told them I'll go two more weeks. I know they can work faster. What's wrong? All these people say if you're in a shelter you have first priority to get an apartment. So what's the problem? Why are all these people still in this shelter? I've been sending letters out. Something's going to come. I'm working on leads of my own.

I used to say, "People have been so mean to me all my life, I'm just going to turn mean and hateful." Somebody told me, "Don't do that, because that's not you." God didn't give me that hard heart.

I remember when my grandmother passed away. I had been mad at her. I didn't talk to her for six months. She was delirious. She had had a heart attack. I don't think she knew I was there. It hurt me. I cried and cried and cried. I never got the chance to say I was sorry, and I miss her. I used to be able to call her when I was crying, and she'd say, "What's the matter? I was thinking about you today." She always knew when something was bothering me. She raised us well, with morals and principals. I appreciate that. It helps me in life now. You know? It helped me to raise my kids. At my lowest lows, when I'm hurting inside, I think about her, and I cry, and sometimes she comes to me in my dreams.

Before Bryant and Joseph were born, I was going with this guy. He started off all right, and then he started changing on me. He didn't want me to go places and talk to people. I had gotten pregnant by him. I was almost five months. This was during the time that my grandmother was in the hospital. I really wanted to keep my baby. I'd never, ever had an abortion. He wanted me to have an abortion. If I didn't have one, he was going to knock the baby out of me. I was scared. He was a big guy, two hundred and fifty pounds, six feet three. He was huge.

I went on, and I had the abortion. If I hadn't had that abortion, he would have kicked it out of me, and I would have lost it anyway. I wanted to keep the baby, because I thought that was part of my grandmother. You know how they say, "A life is taken, so a life can be given." They had to induce my labor. I was in labor nine hours, and I had that baby. It was as big as my hand. I wanted to see it. Fully developed hands. That hurt me so bad. I never wanted to go through anything like that. I cried.

He said to me when I got home, "What are you crying for? It wasn't nothing but a blood clot. If you want to cry, then you cry by yourself, because I don't want to be around no sad-ass bitch." And he left me, just like that. He would still come around though and bother me. He jumped on me one time, so bad, the only thing kept me alive was hearing my kids cry in the next room.

When I was fifteen years old, I was a virgin. I was raped. Why would a person take advantage of a child? It bothers me.

I'm going to try my best.

4

Violence

Violence lurks in a corner inside each of us. Perhaps you banished it there yourself after you raked your fingernails down your brother's back and saw the lines of bright, red blood leap out of his skin. He would not hear your words. He would <u>not</u> leave you alone that day.

With enough provocation anyone's violence will explode out of its corner. Provocation may be a child who will not cooperate. A child who takes more than he gives. Provocation may be a chance word, which scratches like a claw on an old wound that still aches for the kind of touch that would heal it. Sometimes only a constant struggle keeps violence in its corner, out of the midst of the family. Sometimes it is as if violence is safely caged there until alcohol lifts the latch.

When violence runs free, it becomes a law unto itself. It lashes out. It tries to smother pain, to fill emptiness. Or it sneaks off with a little child and draws blood from her soul. It seeks the ecstasy of power, at any price.

Violence may be a way of life that knows nothing else, that pretends no offense. It is like drunks playing with a knife. Careless, stupid. But violence damages everyone in the house, at the most basic levels. Pain, confusion, and loss take the places of nourishment, kindness, and trust.

Violence persists like poison in the family well. Far below ground, the poison continues to dissolve into the water for generations. Once the well is poisoned, how can you get the water clean again? Sometimes the only way to free yourself is to seal off the well, move away, and deal only with the poison you've already taken in.

In this chapter, Lucy Willets struggles to keep violence in its corner. At the other extreme is Marion Salyards, who poisoned her new family's well, blindly and thoroughly. She is now in prison for the murder of her four-year-old daughter. She was surprised when they charged her. Deficits beyond measure.

How does a mother defend herself and her children when her husband is violent? When one mother takes her broken child to the hospital, the child is taken from her. She fights for months to get her back. Another mother leaves her husband, takes her children to a shelter, and begins a new life as a single parent. A third mother, living in terror, does not see a way out. She uses her husband's own weapon against him. Their violence kills him, puts her in jail, and will probably take her children from her forever.

How does a mother face herself and her children if she is violent with them? She chooses either to continue to take life from her children or to begin the process of banishing violence to its corner. Perhaps there will be gentle surprises if she makes the harder choice. Forgiveness where she could not have expected it.

LUCY WILLETS
Age: 40

"I say to Martin, 'I HATE this child.' He'll just shake his head and say, 'I hate him, too.'"

Lucy, a North Carolinian, was a tennis professional before she had children. She is a delight--positive, full of life, but hurt by her experience of mothering. Her daughter Sally is nine. Her son Timothy is six. From birth, her daughter has been easy; her son has been intensely difficult.

Lucy speaks about the depths of rage Tim has stirred up in her and in her husband Martin. She voices the temptation to be violent to release her hostility and pain. Lucy's voice is a voice of endurance and restraint.

Hopefully Tim will grow out of his difficulties in time to give his mother a second wind.

It was so easy for Martin and me to have Sally. She enhanced our own good friendship. She was our little treasure. Everything we did was for each other and that child. It was how it is supposed to be! There was the difficulty of being up at night--but it was still wonderful. You know, everything is so monumental, the child's first step. It was just a real good time for the family. Then Tim came along, and everything just went to pieces.

I call Tim "the child from hell." Not <u>to</u> him, of course, but Martin and I try to keep as much of a sense of humor about Tim as possible. Tim never, ever stopped crying. For two or three years he cried <u>all</u> the time. The only time he would stop screaming was when he was konked out. It was awful. The three of us, Martin, Sally and I were so excited about this little baby. This baby was going to stop crying soon, and everything

213

was going to be fine. It never stopped, and it never stopped. All day long and all night long, until he would just pass out. You couldn't hold him. He would fight away. He was just pissed off at the world.

When he was born they handed me this child and, I swear, I looked down into these little black beady eyes, like Charles Manson's. He just looked up at me, and I looked at him, and I looked at Martin and said, "Whoa! Serious baby!" Now, knowing how angry he is, I remember that.

Several months after he was born I went through a terrible depression. I talked to our physician. I was just not doing well with this baby. I lost all my patience. I was not sure how I felt about this child at all. After I got through the depression I thought, "I need to get out of here. I need to go back to work. This is just not healthy for any of us."

If someone told Tim to put on his shoes, he'd shout, "You hate me," and he'd go into this full tirade, screaming, ranting, raving tantrum. "You never put on my shoes. You hate me. You don't ever let me play Nintendo." He would just blow up. We got so we just wouldn't go anywhere, because everything was such an effort.

When he was three or four, Tim talked a lot about his past life, "You know when I was a baby before, Mommy . . ."

"What do you mean 'before'?"

"Before I was born here. I used to like . . ." I can't remember specifics. I wish I could.

On many occasions, he'd talk like this. I thought that was real interesting. I didn't make a big deal about it. I just would say, "Oh." That would be that, but then he would mention it again, a month later, six months later. He'd say something about "before, when I was alive."

Over the years it's been some real, true, serious hate. I say to Martin, "I HATE this child." He'll just shake his head and say, "I hate him, too." Tim has brought out a fury in Martin, too, that he never knew he had, either.

One day I picked Tim up at school. "Hi, Tim, how was your day?"

"It was terrible, and you're never going to let me play Nintendo, and you don't even like to come pick me up, and nobody likes me at school . . ."

It went on and on, yelling and screaming. <u>Real</u> angry. I was driving and listening and thinking, "I wish somebody else could be in the car and hear this."

He worked himself into saying, "And I just want to die. I just want to kill myself." He had talked about that before. He has actually run out into the street and stood in the middle of the street, screaming, "I want to kill myself. I want a car to hit me." Awful. This is a five-year-old.

He said, "I'm just going to jump out of this car and die." As he said that, he opened the car door. As he did it, he looked at me. He actually opened the door. I could see the fear in his face. He closed it right away.

I pulled the car over. I clenched my fists on the wheel. We sat in dead silence for about two minutes. I was so angry and so upset, I couldn't even speak to him. It was just so scarey. Once I could breathe again, I said, "You cannot do that."

So, we went to Children's Hospital with him. They did a lot of tests. A therapist found that Tim was severely depressed and very, very bright. They don't know where the anger comes from. They said they can usually tell, but that they can't figure this one. The therapist said they are only just beginning to understand what children's depression is about.

A therapist worked with Tim for a while, helping him to talk through things. Then, the therapist ended up leaving the area, but Tim was doing much better. Once Tim could speak and express himself, he improved some. Now that he's able to read, he's improved more.

He's got a real self-esteem problem. He thinks everybody hates him. He's real serious about a whole lot of things. But, now he's playing soccer and liking it and doing well. The other kids are liking him. He's got friends. He's feeling good about himself. But he still gets back into some of that stuff.

He's burned us all so badly on him. When he falls into some real natural behavior for a six-year-old, I can't even stand it. I've had it.

I used to teach lots and lots of children tennis. I was always real patient, and kids were great and fun. I had never ever hollered or screamed at anybody, until I had this child. When I scream now, I think they can hear me two towns over. This voice -- I don't know where it comes from. It's coming from some deep place. I hear myself, and I don't like it.

I have been out of control, to the point where all I want to do is hit him. I think how good it would feel. I have actually fantasized about my hand going across his face and how good that would feel, to hit him as hard as I could. That is a terrible feeling. This is a whole lot to deal with.

I've actually--this is awful--I've stood in Tim's room, so mad at him that I took his shelf of books, and I just turned it over. That's an awful thing for a four-year-old to see--his mother turning over a piece of furniture in anger. I could not physically remove myself and be mature about this. I <u>had</u> to lash out at something. Why is that? I can be so objective and a lot smarter about it when I'm not in that rage. It was like I could look at myself and say, "You're not making a good decision here." But then I'd feel, "I don't have a choice."

Then you feel like a terrible person. You understand murder. I don't really understand it, but I understand a piece of it, because I have felt that anger that I have, that desire to hurt something to vent my anger. This child is hurting me.

It has changed, because now he is becoming more of a normal kid. There are rewards. To see happiness on his face after a soccer game, and to see that happiness last for a couple of hours, and, then, for a whole afternoon. We've actually had good <u>days</u>, a day that we haven't had a major knock-down, drag-out argument and screaming fit from him. It used to be that we would cherish five minutes of that fit not happening. Martin and I are sitting on the edge of our seats, going, "Will it hold? Will it last?" That good energy is getting to happen on a more regular basis, so the four of us can sort of get better.

I think he's going to be a real neat, hopefully real happy, kid. He's just wearing us out on the path. One part of me is very optimistic; the other part of me says, "I don't care. Let me be done with it." I'm just so burned out on this motherhood business. I hate that. I've found myself going, "They'll be off to college pretty soon." I'm not enjoying it. I'm constantly angry at the mess, or Tim will go into one of his tantrums, and my anger is just instant, and then I can't deal with any of them.

Yesterday Sally and I went to the city, just the two of us, for her birthday, just to have a fun day. It was neat. We don't do enough of that. We giggled again. But it's sort of like a dead marriage that you don't feel like reviving. She's not having any fun with me. She's acting like a teenager. When we have the energy, when we're not both burned out, then we can enjoy each other. When Tim is there, he has to have Sally's attention or my attention.

It has been awful. It's been quite a test. I don't want to be tested anymore! I just want to go to the Bahamas! I don't want to be at work. I don't want to be raising these children. I don't do anything at home. Martin cleans. Martin cooks. I'm not even helping him. I don't want to be doing any of this. Just get me away.

MARION SALYARDS
Age: 34

"The abuse got worse. That made their behavior worse. They were just stiffening up and not showing any emotion when I hit them. That made me even madder. It got bad all over."

Marion has been in prison for ten years, guilty of the second-degree murder of her third child, Maribeth, at the age of two. Isolation and ignorance play a role here, and Marion had precious little to draw on from her own childhood as she became a young mother. However, other girls-turned-mothers have met hardships without such disastrous results.

Marion married at age sixteen, after being sexually molested by her father throughout her childhood. She had difficulty managing her first baby, Theresa, who was born within the first year of her marriage. Theresa died. Marion had difficulty managing her next two children, Luke and Maribeth, and abused them when they didn't mind her. A fourth baby was born, Lisa. She was a happy baby, and Marion enjoyed her. Marion did not abuse Lisa, although she was abusing the other two children increasingly. Then, Maribeth died.

Marion now has no parental rights to her two remaining children and has not seen them in nine years.

I was sexually molested by my father. From when I was little up until the time I was engaged: "No more, because I'm getting married." I grew up with no hugs or kisses. There was a lot of fighting, arguing. My parents, my brothers and sisters. There were ten of us. There were four younger than me. I was very withdrawn.

My mother always told me that I would amount to nothing. She was always in a bad mood. I can never remember her in a good mood. I was always afraid of her. My father was mean. That's all I can remember. I was always afraid of him. He was tall and mean. He had a bad temper.

When I met my husband, I was sixteen. We dated for a little while. Then got married. Within a month after we got married, I got pregnant. I was still going to high school. I graduated right before Theresa was born in April. I had to learn everything on my own. It was a difficult time. She was a colicky baby, too. Crying all the time. It was difficult. I didn't have anybody to turn to, either. I didn't have any friends at the time. I kept to myself in school.

Then the baby passed away the following October. I was home at the time. She was laying down for a nap. I went in to check on her. She was crying. I picked her up, and her eyes started rolling to the back of her head. Vomiting. By the time the ambulance got there, she was gone. They said it was pneumonia, but the death certificate said "crib death."

I was seventeen. It was a shock. My first child. It was just bad. Bad. I was even more lonely and empty-feeling. And I had lost a brother and a sister just prior to that. My sister was twelve years old when she was hit by a car. Walking home. Then, a year later, my brother was twelve, and he died of a rare disease. Then, after I lost my daughter, my brother lost one of his daughters the following year from crib death. It was just like there was no end.

It was a bad time for me and for my husband. We had trouble between us. During that time we were just mourning. I didn't have anyone to talk to about it. I just passed my time.

Two years later I had Luke. I had problems with him, but it was nothing out of the ordinary. I guess I got bored a lot. I felt like he was intruding into my pattern that I was used to. I abused him. I got angry, and I used to hit him. When he didn't mind me, I got angry and hit him. I would feel sorry for him because he was getting the brunt of my anger. I felt like, "Why should he be punished because I'm angry?" It always made me feel bad to hit him.

I had no one to turn to. We had moved out of town to where there were distances between the houses. I didn't work. I didn't drive a car. So, it was hard being there all day long with him. I never saw anyone during the day but him. Then, my husband would come home, and it was like everything was all right. It was like nothing happened. Luke would be all happy at night. Then, the next morning would come, and he was cranky, crying all the time. I used to get angry at my husband, because he didn't see what I had to go through during the day.

I think I didn't know how to love Luke. The way a mother should. I didn't know that the things he did was normal for a child his age. I've learned that from classes I've taken in here. Like the "terrible twos." That's what they do. I didn't have any idea of how to raise a child. I guess my image was of a robot-- you tell them what to do, and they mind. I had no one to tell me it's normal for a child to cry for attention, to cry to get changed, to cry because he's hungry. I just thought that he was crying to irritate me.

And, three months after Luke was born, I was pregnant again. All I was hoping was that the next baby would be better behaved. When I had Maribeth, I was twenty. Maribeth was a very crying baby, right from the day she was born. She cried all the time. In the night feeding she would only take a little bit of milk. Then I would put her down. She would sleep for two hours and then wake up hungry again. This went on and on all the time.

My doctor told me, "Don't feed her except for every four hours."

So when she'd wake up two hours later, crying, I didn't know what to do. I brought this up to my doctor, "She takes a little, goes to sleep for two hours and wakes up."

"Let her cry. Let her cry for the next two hours."

I wanted to follow the doctor's orders. I didn't know any different. So, we tried doing that. It gets on your nerves after a while.

Luke cried because he was jealous of not getting any of the attention. So, I had two babies crying all the time. Just . . . well, it's nerve-wracking. Maribeth was a very picky eater, too.

We had some good times. We used to sit Luke out in the playpen in the yard and just sit and watch him. He'd play this game where he'd pick up one of his toys and throw it outside the playpen. You go over and put it back in, and he throws it out again. He used to play that game a lot.

They were taken away for a short while when they were toddlers. Maribeth had fallen out of her highchair and apparently broke her arm. When we took her in for a check-up, the doctor wanted to put her into the hospital, because she was underweight. He said she was malnourished. I tried to explain to him how picky-eater she was. They took them away saying that we neglected them. There were signs of abuse, too. I had been hitting them a lot. I was hitting them with either my hand or a leather strap.

They were gone about nine months. It was very sad. It was very lonely. Here I was without anybody again. We had visits with them, but for only an hour or so. Then, I got pregnant. Before they would give Luke and Maribeth back, they wanted to know how I was handling the new baby.

It was different with Lisa. I don't know how to explain it. I was happy. She was happy. Easy-going. It was just different. When she was six months old, she got very sick. There's a muscle in the stomach that wouldn't let the food pass through. I had to feed her constantly to see if some food would get past. They told me to do that. I think during that time I felt really sorry for her, because she couldn't hold anything down. She was just constantly sick and crying. I felt sympathy toward her. That surprised me. I <u>knew</u> why she was crying. She was hungry. She was hungry all the time, and I had to feed her constantly. But, it got to the point where she was dehydrated, and they had to operate, to open that muscle up.

Things with me and my husband were getting better. Because there wasn't the stress of the kids with the two at the foster home. And me and Lisa were getting along great. It felt good. Lisa was such a happy baby. I didn't abuse her at all.

A few months after Lisa was born, we got the other two back. They were still in diapers. I had all three in diapers. The foster parents didn't want to potty-train the other two. So, I had to try to potty-train them. It was hard having them all in diapers.

It was hard trying to potty-train them. I didn't know exactly what to do.

Things got worse. Things just went downhill from there. I had more problems with Luke and Maribeth. It just got worse. I was staying home all the time. The abuse got worse. That made their behavior worse. They were just stiffening up and not showing any emotion when I hit them. That made me even madder. It got bad all over.

We ran out of heating fuel that winter. In the middle of the night the temperature dropped. The next day I called all around to see if we could get any heating fuel. We were denied everywhere I turned to. We just had no place to go. I called the town hall. I called fuel assistance. Fuel assistance said it would take days, maybe weeks to get approval. I called the fuel company, and they wouldn't give us fuel on credit.

We borrowed some electric heating lamps, and we bought a couple of heating lamps. Maribeth became sick. I called my doctor's office to get a prescription for her, and he said he wouldn't do it over the phone. I had to bring her in. There was no way that I could bring her in, because I had the three of them. Plus, she had marks on her from being abused. She just got worse.

One night she just got really bad, and by the time we got her to the hospital, she died.

She had pneumonia, but we didn't know until after she died. She had frostbite on her toes.

They said that she died of pneumonia that was brought on by her immune system being so low from the abuse. That's why I'm here, today. They brought charges against me for her death, because I abused her.

The night before she passed away I was really, really scared, because she was so sick. I didn't know what to do for her. I didn't know what was wrong. If I had known that she had pneumonia, I would have taken her to the hospital, not even thinking of the consequences, just thinking of getting her better.

They wanted us for questioning. After we were questioned, I was arrested and brought right to jail. I was charged with second-degree murder. I was surprised that they were charging me. I was scared. At the time I felt that I didn't do anything wrong to cause her death. That I didn't kill her.

It was hard to believe she was gone. But then a part of me was relieved, because she didn't have to put up with any more abuse.

I regret everything that has happened. The night that she died, they took the other two kids away. I didn't get to say good-bye to them.

I went through a trial and was found guilty. I didn't see the two kids for two years. Finally, the judge agreed to a one-time-only visit. I didn't recognize Lisa. She was so changed. That was the last time I saw them. Luke was five and Lisa was almost three. Now they're fourteen and twelve.

I try not to think about not seeing them. They're adopted now by the same family. We signed away our parental rights. The parents agreed to send us pictures once a year along with a letter of progress, so that keeps me going. Other than that I just try not to think about it. It's just too depressing.

It's difficult around holidays and their birthdays. I have a book I write in, like a diary. I write to my children on special occasions. Telling them that I'm thinking about them and that I miss them. So when they get older, they can read it.

When they get older, it's up to them to come search for me. I can't look for them.

I was sentenced with thirty years to life. That means I will be in for twenty.

JUDITH HARDY
Age: 28

"Melanie asks sometimes, 'Did he get punished?'"

Judy is tiny. She does not look large enough to bear a child. She has two daughters: Melanie is seven; Susan, four. Judy's ex-husband, the girls' stepfather, was violent with Susan. Judy is a different person as a result of fighting for her daughter. She spoke in a quiet, even voice.

After I got a divorce from Paul, I met Tom. When Susan was a year old, he and I got married. About four months later he came home drunk one night. All of a sudden I heard a scream. I ran into the bedroom. Melanie was sitting on the top bunk. She said, "Susan hit the wall." There was blood all over Susan's shirt. I didn't see how I could make it stop. I grabbed her from Tom and took her to the hospital. He had broken her wrist in two places, her arm in three places and ruptured her stomach. The doctor said it was like when a football was drop-kicked. Also, he said there were injuries that had happened before. They took Susan away and put her in a foster home.

My husband was from a prominent family. The chief of police in charge of the investigation was his uncle. I was told things like, "If she had died, you'd have a case." "You should have known that he was going to hurt her." I was told that it was my fault: I didn't protect her. Finally, I got tired of being told that I had done things wrong, like not keeping her bloody shirt for evidence, and I decided to fight.

I did get a grand jury indictment on him. It took a year and a half to get it into trial. Melanie saw everything that night, but she was only three and a half. They told me I'd have a better case if I put her on the stand. I didn't, and we lost.

224

Then Susan took a fall down the stairs at the second foster home. She had bruises all over her. I said, "What happened?"

"She fell down the stairs."

"Why didn't somebody call me?"

"Well, we didn't know that she had been hurt."

"Why didn't you realize it?"

"Because she didn't cry."

Bingo. I'd been telling people that she didn't cry when she was hurt. They saw that, and how frazzled I was getting: "Give me back my daughter." I had had Melanie all this time. It didn't make sense that I could have one and not the other. I got her back.

She still doesn't trust people easily. She has scars. One of her breasts will be deformed. Melanie asks sometimes, "Did he get punished?"

I have to say, "No, he didn't."

"Why?"

I just say, "We did it the best that we could." Those are the hard things.

But it really changed me.

After five years of no contact the girls' father wants to get involved. We're going to go to court first, because I know it's not the kids' interest he's after. Paul just wants someone to wait on him. After we got divorced I took him back so many times. "I don't drink anymore. I've changed. I don't gamble anymore. I want to be a family." Then, it would start all over again. It was terrible. I wasn't interested in him. It wasn't love. It was pity. He wasn't going to change. He still thinks I'll take him back, but he doesn't realize I've changed now.

I know I can do it on my own because I've been doing it. I work a steady job as an office manager during the day, and then when I get home the kids are number one. I do a lot of bookkeeping for people late at night. Then, I also do cosmetics consulting. I take in typing for people. I don't have insurance. I worry a lot. But I make it. The kids have what they need. Up until a year ago I was going to college at night, too. I'm half-way to my associate's degree, but it got to be too much. I'm proud of what I've done.

SAMANTHA DION
Age: 32

"How could I stand by and let those kids be raised in an environment like that? Natalie would do the same thing I did, and Michael would be an abuser."

After eight years of a second marriage, Samantha left her abusive husband, Daniel, and went to a battered women's shelter. After almost eight weeks in the shelter, she and her two children, Natalie (age five) and Michael (age three) moved, with the help of the state, into an apartment. Samantha had been in her apartment for three months when she and I talked. She had long bright blue and foil acrylic fingernails and a smile which seemed to come from far away.

Samantha's story is full of ambivalence and contradictions.

Natalie saw a lot. She was little, and Daniel would come after me. The blood-curdling cry out of this little, little baby . . . she knew. It was awful. As she got older, she was defiant and withdrawn. She had these big, red circles under her eyes. She wasn't growing or progressing in any way. I couldn't see nothing changing in her. She would not pay attention. She'd be talking to me, and she'd turn around and walk--smack!--right into the wall. She was real hyper, into everything. And cry, cry, cry, all the time.

Now, day-care is helping tremendously. She has settled down a lot. She still can't sit still, but her attention span and her ability to play with other kids have improved dramatically. She wasn't even willing to bother with anyone else before. If she played before, it was abusive. She would treat me abusively. When she was little she used to always hit me in the face. That bothered my parents.

Now, her days are very structured. She knows what's acceptable and what is not. She knows when I speak that she should respect what I'm saying. She's eating me out of house and home. Now she's doing something new every week, like tying her shoes. I can see progress. She plays with Michael real good, and she's real sympathetic to me. It's sweet.

Michael didn't see the fighting as much as Natalie. It won't be in him as much.

If it wasn't for the kids, I probably would have stayed with Daniel. It was very scarey to pack up and leave. But the love for my children is far greater than the love of having male companionship in my life.

I've never thought very much of myself. I was married at nineteen. I wasn't growing up to be an old maid--no way. Someone found me attractive enough to want to marry me--my God! Let's go for it! It will be my only chance. He left me four times, and I took him back. Then, finally, I said, "Get the hell out of my life." That was devastating.

I went back home. And it was a good home. So why would I get myself into such dysfunctional relationships? It took me a long time to even half-way get over that first marriage. I was a failure, and all I ever wanted to do was make Daddy proud of me. I grew up fat. That, I think, is my major problem. I was never asked to the junior prom, because who would want to ask a fat girl? I still get mad about that.

Then I met Daniel, who was an absolute dreamboat. Daniel was eighteen, and I was twenty-four. We lived together for three years before I married him. When I married Daniel, he was abusive. He was an alcoholic. He was a drug addict. He broke my nose prior to the marriage.

When we got married, I was pregnant with Natalie. I loved Daniel. If we had not gotten married, I would have had to name Natalie my maiden name. I could not give her the Dion name. Therefore, I was kind of trapped, because I wanted that wedding band on my finger. It made my father happy. And I thought that I could fix things. Change him. I thought that it was just a matter of time that he would realize what he had, and he'd have to straighten out.

227

It took me eight years to get out of it. If it hadn't been for the drinking, we could have done anything together. When he was drinking was when he was most abusive. At the very end he would hit me when he was sober. But I don't blame him. There was a lot of trauma in his life. I know there's a lot of good in Daniel. He had a horrible upbringing. I blame his mother.

I think the children should know both sides of the coin. Of course, they're too young to know the truth now. I don't think they should be left to make assumptions, because they're going to make wrong ones. Right now Natalie needs to know why we're here, why we went to the shelter, that her Daddy loves her, Daddy is sick, and Mummy loves her. We're going to be okay. Mummy's always going to be here to take care of her. She's very secure with me. I've never left those children.

Daniel was out of work. He went into a deep depression. It was a big thing because I went to cosmetology school, and he was out of work. It took a tremendous fight for me to be able to go to school. Well, his mother came over and was getting on me about school. Daniel heard the commotion and thought I was going to go after her. He came up to me and picked me up by the throat. I passed out. His father had to take his hand off my neck, "Daniel, she's passed out."

I knew something was coming. It was either him killing me, or I was going to kill him. I would have killed him. All I wanted to do was go out and buy a gun. I would have killed him. My mother knew it too. She said, "You were capable."

When he took the car I used to pray, "Get in an accident and kill yourself." I was so mad and so angry and so full of hate. I was so sick of being hurt and hurt and hurt. I wanted him blown off the face of the earth. It was either me doing it or hiring a hit person to do it.

If I had ended up in prison, if it had been just me, myself, and I, it would have been worth it. I meant what I said, that I was not putting up with any more of that. I said that, but it meant nothing to him. Nothing. I'm nothing.

Natalie misses Daniel. She talks about him a lot, but she said to me last week, out of the clear blue, "I don't want Daddy to hurt you anymore." It's amazing . . . her mind is working.

She don't speak about him as much as she did. I answer her with the truth for any question she asks me, for what her little brain can stand. If she needs to know more she'll ask me. I can't lie to her, and I do not talk bad about Daniel to her. She can form her own opinion, and it will be the right one: he abandoned her.

Daniel lost his license. Every day I had to pick Daniel up at five-thirty. From six to seven Star Trek was on, and he was this Star Trek fan. The kids were expected to sit down and shut up for that hour. Well, they're starving, okay? I'm racing around, trying to cook supper. I could never beat twenty-five past six. Do you think he could get up and move from the TV to eat supper with us? By that time I am so frustrated. I'm right off the wall. I couldn't handle nothing. Every day. Every day. By the end of the day, I was wiped. Nothing would go right, and the kids would walk all over me. What good was I? Go to school, run all the errands, blah, blah, blah. I hated it. I hated myself. I hated everybody.

I resented those kids for a long time. I don't anymore, but I did, except for Michael. I did in a way. I had the same feelings, but Michael is so special. Even my mother told me that it is noticeable that Michael is my favorite. I love Natalie, but I didn't like her, from birth, and she picked up on it. Every day we fight like cat and dog. She will argue; she has to have the last word. We clash.

When Natalie was a baby, she was colicky, so Daniel'd leave the house and go down to the river. She'd start at four-thirty in the afternoon and go to nine-thirty. Daniel was never around. She was cranky. She didn't like me, and I didn't like her.

Whereas Michael is cute. He's not whiney. He's funny. Natalie is very special, too. Don't get me wrong. I love her dearly. There's nothing I wouldn't do for her. I'd lay down my life for her. Which essentially, you might as well say, I've done. I've given up my whole world to make sure those two kids have what they need, so that they can be happy.

But Michael's special in many ways. He's the spit and image of Daniel. Looks like him. Acts like him. He's even got a temper where he will get mad and go right into a brawl. He'll

229

either bite or hit or scream and then--snap!--he's out of it. That's something I've got to break. Not by hitting back, but with time-outs, strict structure. Keeping reinforcing it, being patient. Being firm. I have to be firm with both of these kids, or they'll walk all over me. They still do it, but I don't take as much.

When I was pregnant with Michael, Daniel got another DWI charge. He is a habitual offender. We're talking some substantial jail time for driving drunk. I think he got six months that time. He come home right before the baby was due.

Giving birth to Michael was the greatest thrill of my life, and Daniel shared that with me. Then, he went home. One of his friends told me Daniel's car was in the yard, and the shades were down, but he didn't come to the door. I won't tell you who he was with. It would blow your mind. When I got home the next day, he was sleeping. The house wasn't picked up. Nothing. My parents brought me home. It was humiliating. That's why Michael is so special. So special.

I left Michael, a brand new baby, and Natalie, when Michael was a week old. It was always me leaving, because Daniel couldn't find a place to stay. I was gone probably three weeks.

I yell and holler and get mad. I wish I could be the perfect mother. My expectations have not been met yet for myself. There's just so much work that I've got to do. I want to be able to provide for myself and the children. I want the kids raised properly. They may get what they want from their father, but they're going to get what they need from me. I might as well be by myself. I wasn't getting any help from Daniel. All I was getting was more aggravation.

I've lost the love of my life. There's a lot of bondage between us two. But the abuse is unacceptable, and I just can't take it anymore. The children have a chance now.

That day I dropped Daniel off at work and, then, I got the car packed. I was driving down the highway, crying my eyes out. I had the two kids and was going to the shelter. It was frightening. It was scarey. I was closing the door, turning my back and walking. It tore my heart--to think that I had to walk away, and there was nothing more that I could do.

I had warned him. I had been back and forth, back and forth, the whole eight years. But the last time I had warned him that if he decided to go out drinking, and come home drunk, that the law was going to get involved.

I knew I couldn't go back, because of the kids. How could I stand by and let those kids be raised in an environment like that? Natalie would do the same thing I did, and Michael would be an abuser. How can I let that happen? I can't. That's not why I had children.

I just got to make sure they grow up decent.

RHIANNON LYONS
Age: 27

"In my mind I had no other choice. I shot him."

Rhiannon killed her abusive husband Billy four years ago and has been in prison since then. Her two daughters, Kari and Sheri, are eleven and eight.

I grew up with my grandparents, who were very old. The house that I grew up in holds everything. There was drug abuse, alcoholism, incest, sexual abuse. You name it, it was happening, but nobody talked about it. My childhood was like night of the living dead.

My real mother would pop in once a year, usually with a new husband. I knew who she was. I don't have any bad memories of her. She comes up here every now and then to see me. Because of the help I'm getting in here, I can talk now. But she grew up in the same house I did, and she's still walking around like a zombie.

My grandparents let me get married when I was thirteen to a man who was thirty-eight. I was just starting to get into trouble. I was starting to get into drugs. I had ran away. That marriage lasted until I was sixteen. It was abusive, mostly sexual abuse. I got a divorce and immediately met up with Billy. Billy was a biker-type. He had a very bad reputation. It was a mess from the start. He was an alcoholic and a drug addict.

My first daughter, Kari, is actually my step-daughter. I got her when she was a year and a half old. I had been living with Billy, her father, for six months, and Kari was living with his ex-girlfriend. She just kind of dropped Kari off in a parking lot and said, "Here you go." I was seventeen.

Billy sat me down and said, "You have a choice here that you have to make."

I said, "We'll try it." Kari instantly took to me, and I instantly took to her, but it was rough. She had diaper rash from the middle of her back to the back of her legs. She hadn't been fed. She was sleeping about an hour a night. She'd wake up screaming. I knew that there were problems, but, being seventeen, I didn't know exactly what they were.

I had Sheri when I was eighteen. I wanted to get pregnant. I thought life would be wonderful if I had a little sister for this other child of mine. I loved staying home for the six weeks that I could stay out of work. I worked in an electronics plant until Sheri was about two, and, then, I got hurt at work. I stayed home after that.

I'm in prison for second-degree murder of their father.

Mostly my oldest felt the wrath of the father--as I did. My youngest was in the midst of the violence, but it wasn't directed at her. He never did her. We were living in a one-bedroom, second-floor apartment. Kari was barely sleeping, screaming and crying. My husband was doing a lot of speed at the time. One night Kari was tapping her foot on the side of the crib. She wasn't even crying. He jumped up, grabbed her by her t-shirt, and hung her out the window. He said if I didn't make her shut up he would drop her. I finally got them both back inside. I took her and ran down the street and just walked around for a while.

When other people were around Billy would always say, real proud, "I got a girl, but look at this," and he would hit her on the arm. Not like you would hit an adult, but certainly not like you would hit a child. He'd be playing with her, tickling her, and he'd just snap, and it wasn't a game anymore. I'd end up pulling him off of her. By the time Kari was three years old she was so shut down from this man that she didn't cry.

The longer we stayed together, the angrier he became. Not just at me, but at everybody. The drinking got worse. He was doing cocaine. I had a drug problem, prescription drugs, from when I got hurt at work. What a wonderful thing to have when you're getting hit in the head. The painkillers just dulled everything out.

It wasn't even so much the beatings--the pain eventually stops. It was pure terror--twenty-four hours a day. What was going to happen? When was it going to happen? Why was it going to happen? Scrambling around the house trying to make everything perfect, knowing it never would be.

When he was gone, it became a normal household, with normal children, who made noise and ran and laughed and broke things. Even in the midst of a drug problem I was functioning well. Everything was normal. Then he would come in, and everybody had to shut down.

It was all very gradual. He would say, "I don't want you going out," and when I opened the door to take out the trash two hours later, there he would be, saying, "I told you not to go out."

Then he started saying things like, "I could take you out right now, and nobody would even notice." He had already separated me from my family. I had no friends. That wasn't allowed. Going out wasn't allowed. Literally the only places I ever went was the supermarket, the drug store, and the post office.

He would play little games with me like, "Where did you go today?" I would say, "The drug store and the supermarket." He'd say, "And the post office, too." I still don't know if he was following me. He worked right across the street from our apartment building. He would stand out there and watch the house. He would just stand there and stare.

He'd hold a gun up to my head, and say, "It would be really easy."

My whole world was Billy. He was bigger than life. Nobody could ever conquer him. He had a record. He described different battles that he had gotten into. He said, "There is no cop that can ever take me down." He always ended up in jail, but he planted it in my mind somehow that he was always the hero in all of this. He would leave for two or three days at a time and tell me, "Don't leave the house." I would not leave the house. I don't care if I needed milk, bread, whatever, I was not leaving the house.

For two months I had started putting away money in the bathroom. Something in the back of my mind. I don't ever remember consciously deciding to leave.

That night he had come in real drunk. He didn't say anything. He ate and went to bed. Then he called me into the bedroom and grabbed me and said, "I know what you're doing and don't think you're going to get away with it." He was always predictable. If he started screaming and yelling, he grabbed me and hit. This time he just grabbed me and then let me go. That wasn't normal: it wasn't settled yet. Something in me said, "This is not just a threat tonight. This is it." If he had beat me, I probably wouldn't have done it. In my mind I had no other choice. I shot him.

I remember shooting the gun and running down the stairs and thinking, "He's going to be on me any second." The police were there, the ambulance was there, his family. I still was just staring at the stairs, waiting for him to come down. He was that big.

Earlier that day somebody was calling the house and threatening him, through me. They would say, "Tell Billy we're going to get him tonight . . . " When he came home from work, I told him, and he said, "Get the pistol loaded. Keep it under the couch in case anything happens." That's what I went for that night.

By twelve the next afternoon my kids were picked up by welfare workers and taken off to a foster home. I was here in prison. I had no way to contact them. I didn't know where they were. Nobody was willing to give me any answers. The girls came to the prison about a week later. I tried to explain to them what had happened, but because of my case, I was shut off by lawyers about what I could tell them. I didn't want to see them sitting in the middle of a witness stand.

My kids have been through four or five foster homes. They have been separated. My oldest daughter, about a year into foster homes, flipped out. They put her in a girls' home for emotionally disturbed kids for a year.

The judge feels that because of the crime that I committed there is no way that I could be a good parent. My kids have been thrown into a whirlpool. When the judge found out that my oldest daughter's mother was back in the picture, he thought, "Great, blood is definitely stronger than water," and I'm not her real blood, so he terminated my visits with no explanation.

Finally, I got back into court with a good attorney, and the judge said, "Okay, she can have her visits back." By then Kari refused. In the meantime, the judge had introduced her to her biological mother and had moved her and Sheri in with my in-laws.

My youngest one visits about every other month. Not only is she living in a household that talks bad about me, but she's living in a household with her sister, who is now very angry with me because of everything that she has heard. Kari's biological mother visits there. So Sheri's sister has a mom, and Sheri doesn't. "Why can't I have my mother?" She's only eight.

The bottom line is: I killed somebody. My sentence is fifteen to life. Everybody has decided I can't be a twenty-four hour a day mother at this point, so they're not going to keep paying for all the trips up here for the kids to visit. Welfare is tired of paying for these kids. It's been four years. The direction they're moving in is just closing me out of the picture. They always say, ". . . in the best interests of the child."

I don't understand how they can with a clear conscience look at Sheri and say they're doing it for her best interests. Her desire is to come up here and see me. If I was eight and something I was doing was hurting me, I'd stop doing it, but she's not stopping. There is that bond. She wants to see me. There's nothing I can do about Kari. Legally she wasn't mine from the start.

Three weeks ago the therapist came up here again with Sheri and said, "You need to get the message across to Sheri that what you did was not right."

I said, "Okay." We started talking. I was crying. I told her that I was very, very sorry for what happened to Daddy and that at the time I just didn't know any other way out.

She immediately started telling me things that she remembered from different fights. She has her memories. I am her memories. I represent home. I represent those times. No one else can do that for her. I told her that what I did was wrong, and that sometimes people make the wrong choices.

Kari is surrounded by people who have made her father into some kind of hero. They think that they're somehow hurting me, but what they're doing is messing up Kari more. She needs to have a full circle of information before she can even begin to heal. When I try to explain that to them, I think they think that I'm trying to defend what I did. These children are going to be women some day. They need to have all the information about what happened in their childhood.

Four years ago when I walked into this place, the only thing I had looked at for the last ten years of my life was the toes on my shoes. I never looked at people. I talked to nobody. I weighed about ninety pounds because of the stress and the drug abuse. I was here about a week, and my defense attorney sent a woman to evaluate me. I was just reciting my life from the time I was little to the time I killed him. I was saying it like it was no big deal, like, "isn't this how everybody lives?"

The therapist said to me, "What you're describing is horrible stuff. You're acting like this is just okay."

I remember saying to her, "Well, isn't it?"

I believe in my heart it was just a matter of time. He would have killed me. I didn't have anybody to reach out to, to avoid what I was in. I wouldn't be in that situation now.

I have no idea what will happen with my children. I may never see Kari again. It would be wonderful if she and Sheri came to me one day and said, "Mom, we understand what happened, and we forgive you."

CARLA MacPHEE
Age: 44

"When I get depressed the only one that thinks about it or worries about it is Linda, because she's afraid I'm going to die. She's terrified of all change. She says, 'If you die, who's going to take care of me?' That makes me feel worse."

Carla says she has been an alcoholic from the first drink she took at age eighteen. Alcohol and violence have been large realities in Carla's adult life and in the lives of her three children: Gail, twenty-one; Matt, eighteen; and Linda, twelve.

There is a child here, Linda, in desperate need of a mother. Linda's messages are not getting through.

I love my kids, but I don't have one good thing to say about mothering. It's been really hard work. You feel that someone is always judging how you are taking care of your kids. I felt really drained. I raised my kids by myself. Linda's father died when she was a year and a half old. I get social security for her support, but I've never gotten anything for the other two.

That kind of resentment that you feel about doing it by yourself comes off on the kids. I really did resent it. All along. There's no break. There's no relief. In the beginning I was on welfare, so there was nothing. It was just surviving. I was young enough then. I just got caught up in surviving. I think I feel more resentful now. I feel my kids have been gypped. I've been angry. I could have been a better parent to them if I had more support. If there had at least been someone to take an interest in the kids. I took on their pain of no father, no birthday cards, no nothing.

I didn't love their father. When I graduated from college I didn't know what I wanted to do. Marriage was the next thing I felt I was supposed to do. I was actively alcoholic. I knew I better do something, so I immediately got married, just for a solution. I thought, "Well, I'll have kids and do what I'm supposed to do here." It was just random, the whole thing.

It was crazy here; it was. I was an alcoholic. My children's father was crazy. He just never drank.

My son Matt has had quite a struggle. It's been difficult for him. He's had no role model at all. My older daughter, Gail, says to me, "I don't know why you keep saying that. It was just as hard for me not having a father." But I think boys, after the age of twelve, should be with men. I don't think women should raise them. Things get real screwed up when a boy doesn't have a man around. It's a terrible loss. If you talk to my son, he would say, "That's not important."

Actually the drinking probably got me through when the kids were little. I had a regular routine. I'd get up in the morning. I'd take them for walks, take them to the playground. I was doing a good job! The reward, of course, was the booze at the end of the day. I think I was more in control then. I drank only in the house, never in bars. I knew I would be drunk. Lots of times I would be sick the next day. I'd ask my mother to take the kids. When they were very little, I could manage it.

But, when I was divorced, I had a little bit of a problem. I worked for welfare. I was paying for a babysitter, so I could work. I thought, "These women are better off than I am. What am I doing? I'd rather be drinking than doing this." I couldn't work and drink and take care of kids. So, I figured, "I'll quit this job, and I'll drink." That's exactly what I did. I went on welfare, and I drank. I fooled myself, saying that if I went on welfare I could be home taking care of my kids.

At that point, I was not available to my kids. The only time I was available was that first couple of years before I was divorced. After that, I was either drinking, or I was working. I was emotionally not interested. I didn't want to hear it, because I didn't want to feel any pain. I remember being in a therapy session with my son one time, and he said, "My mother only wants to hear the good things." He's right. I don't like to hear bad news, because I don't know what to do about it.

239

Linda's father, Ethan, was killed in the house by a neighbor. That was a tremendous trauma. I met him at AA, and I started right into drinking again. We had a relationship for a couple of years. After Linda was born, he got very concerned about the level of drinking that I was doing. He kept trying to get me to stop. I kept drinking, because it gave me power over him. He was going to contact the other two kids' father to see if he would take them, because he thought I was incapable of caring for the three of them. And he was right. I was drinking daily. I had two small children and a baby.

But to cope with the situation, instead, he picked up a drink himself and started in again. He had been sober for five years. I was happy when he started drinking, because I thought, "Oh great, now I have somebody. We'll just drink ourselves into unconsciousness around this whole mess."

Ethan was drinking beer by the case. Drinking it all day. Drinking it all. Drinking fast. One night he was here and left to go home. When he left, he asked me if I wanted to go next door to this woman Kathy's house and drink. I had three kids in the house, but I didn't even think about that. I said, "Sure." I checked on the kids and then went over and started drinking with her. Then he came back. I started yelling at him. I was drinking with somebody else now. He hit me. I was mad. He knocked me right off my feet. I was bullshit. I told him to get out and then went back to continue drinking.

I went out at two to get cigarettes. I took the baby. I was putting Linda back to bed when he came in the house again. This time he was bullshit, hitting me. I started yelling and screaming. The next thing I know this woman from next door, Kathy, is at my bedroom door, saying, "Should I call the police?"

When she said that he went right for her and started banging her head against the wall. I ran down to call the police. While I was on the phone he came down. His shirt was covered with blood. He sat down at the table. I thought he had smashed her head open or something. I was still screaming at him. I ran upstairs to see if she was all right. She was standing there--okay.

240

My oldest daughter was downstairs with Ethan when I got back down. I was looking at the blood, trying to figure out where it was coming from, when he just keeled over. By then the cops were coming in the back door. Kathy had come over from her house with a knife and had stabbed him. It was really not necessary to do that.

The cops tried to bring charges, but she got off on self-defense, because he was violent. He was very violent with her. There was bad history between those two.

It traumatized everybody. My son said, "I didn't like Ethan anyway." Linda didn't have him to hold her. If your father is stabbed, it sort of says you're a bad person. It's not like having your father die of a heart attack. I was sober from the time he was killed to last summer, and I drank last summer.

You don't know what little kids will do with a trauma like that. My older daughter is extremely successful. She's an over-achiever. I'm sure she has a ton of things to deal with on the inside, but on the outside, she functions. Then, my son has been in and out of trouble with the police, spent time at the Youth Detention Center, has been in therapy since who knows when.

Then Linda. She had been sexually abused by a neighbor, a kid down the street. I didn't find out about that until three or four years later. This kid was mean, but he was always very nice to Linda. I was suspicious about that. She had a lot of trouble in school at that time. The police told me that the sexual abuse was more of a secondary trauma to her, after the murder.

She always says, "I never knew my father," but she doesn't express many of her feelings to me anyhow, because, well, all of my kids know how I react if they have a problem. It's not, "Let's discuss this rationally." It's, "Oh, really?" and, the next thing they know, they're down to see the psychiatrist. So, they don't talk. I don't know too much about what's going on.

The twelve years that I was sober after Ethan was killed, I never went to many AA meetings. I got involved in the church. I pulled myself together, got to work. I thought the alcohol problem was taken care of, because the surface of things looked good. Meanwhile there was utter chaos going on in the house. I was always verbally abusive to my kids. A lot of screaming. "What are you asking a stupid question like that for?"

The kids think I'm pretty crazy. I can still get really depressed. When I get depressed the only one that thinks about it or worries about it is Linda, because she's afraid I'm going to die. She's terrified of all change. She says, "If you die, who's going to take care of me?" That makes me feel worse.

Last summer I was so depressed. I was just going down and down. I was feeling basically <u>stuck</u> in my life. When I thought, "I'm going to drink," that was it. When I started, I thought, "This is great. I feel such a relief."

But when it's four-thirty in the morning, and you drank two six-packs, and you're throwing up on yourself, it's not great. I don't think I went to bed. I went to the store first thing in the morning and got going again. I knew after the first two beers of the next six-pack that I would not stop. I literally could not drink anymore, but I was trying to figure out a way to get the alcohol. Could I get it intravenously somehow? I knew I was going to be dead. So I called the hospital for de-tox.

I'm <u>semi</u>-available to the kids now. I don't have conversations with my kids. Really. I'm sober. Just the other day my older daughter was home, and she was telling me something, and she said,

"You didn't hear a word I said, did you?"

I said, "Yeah, I did." I was trying to think, "What did she say?"

Then I said to her, "I don't know what you said."

"Yeah, I know." That's been one of her biggest complaints about me. I have not listened. I have not heard. My son has had the focus of my attention, because he has had obvious problems that have needed my attention. My daughters just kind of do their own thing. Luckily for me, they have done the right thing.

It hasn't been easy for them living here with me. But, on the other hand, I think it's the basis of what's going to make them strong. I don't like a lot of things about myself, but I've managed. I've coped. My kids have seen that I coped. I can admit now that I make mistakes.

My mother was always angry. I think when a parent is resentful, it rubs right off on the kids, and they get an attitude. My mother was always pissed off about something, so I come by that naturally.

Things are coming together. I've been in therapy a long time. I'm taking my disease a little more seriously than I was. I don't want to feel like shit for the next twelve years. I stay out of situations that are not going to make me feel good. I'm starting to like myself a little. It's hard to like yourself after those events.

I want my kids to be independent of me. I want them to feel that they don't owe me. I would like them to lead lives that they want to lead, regardless of what my opinion of that is. And I would like to live in a little one-room cottage. And I don't care if I ever have grandchildren. They can come and visit me once in a while, or they don't have to. I just want my kids to be okay and not hurt anybody.

I would like to at least once or twice a month take Linda away from the house and be with her. Even if it's just out to a restaurant. I was really surprised--I took her out one day recently. I bought her a new pair of shoes, and we went out to lunch. I had never, ever done this with Linda alone. I was so surprised at the conversation. She's a young girl--not a baby. She's got thoughts, and she's got ideas. I was shocked. Her routine is to come home from school. She'll be watching TV. There's no communication here in the house until it's time for bed. We don't eat together. We used to. We don't anymore.

At bedtime she'll come in sometimes and sit down and talk. It's kind of goofy talk. It's not serious talk. It's nighttime, and Linda gets real worried at night about who's going to die. But this day when we had lunch, I was so struck by the fact that there was a person here. This is a person. There is something that's frightening to me about that. I can't put my finger on it, yet. I don't get too close. I keep it real superficial. I guess it's because I'm not sure what a relationship is supposed to be with the kids. I don't know what that's all about. I don't have a clue.

When I think about my own mother now all I can feel is criticism. I remember a lot of fighting with her when I was a teenager, and I remember I always ended up apologizing for those fights, because she never spoke to me until I did. I don't think I had a relationship with my mother, so I don't know what that means.

My daughters have been fortunate enough to have friends whose mothers have been very much involved with the girls. They have taken them on trips, and my girls have always been invited. Just recently Linda said to me, "Can't we ever go on a vacation? I'm tired of going on vacations with my friends. When are you going to take me?"

I thought, "Darn it. I thought I was getting off the hook." I'd rather spend money on a new patio or something for the house than for a vacation. I don't know why she wants to go on a vacation with me. I should ask her. I think she'd say, "Because my friends do it."

I do appreciate Linda a lot. I would like to go out with her a couple of times a month. I like her the best to be alone with. I think of my older daughter as kind of critical, like my mother. Gail is smarter than I am. I feel kind of stupid when I'm around her.

Linda is a lot like I am. She's a very likeable kid. There's not a mean bone in her body. She cares too much about other people. She's very sensitive. It's a nice way to be, but I don't know if that's going to be healthy for her in the long run. I think we'll see Linda in a Twelve Step Program down the line.

BRENDA CARROLL
Age: 43

"I wanted to find a different way than how I was brought up."

Brenda is from Oregon. She is a survivor of incest. She still works to fully free herself from this part of her history. She is the mother of one daughter, who is sixteen.

My mother was a drinker. So, she was absent, somewhat.

The incest started when my mother was in the hospital with my sister, who was four years younger than me. My father. It was very intermittent but, nonetheless, traumatic. I remember being on top of him. It wasn't violent violent. I didn't know what it was. It hurt. But there wasn't a lot of movement. He was just big enough so it hurt.

I remember trying to make conversation, because it was so awkward. I remember not wanting to ask anything too directly, because I just had a feeling about it. I remember answering the phone once and seeing the sperm going down my leg. Of course, I didn't know what it was until years later.

I got the classic "this is our little secret." I didn't tell my mother. I instinctually knew there was something bad about it, so I didn't tell. It separated me from the whole rest of the family, because I had a secret.

And my mother drank.

I remember years and years and years of being in bed at night and listening for him. When I was close to puberty I told him, "That's it." He didn't approach me after that. I think he knew I knew what it was.

I knew my parents were miserable. I knew my mother was having an affair. I was babysitting across the street. I heard the tinkle of glasses and her laugh. That was okay with me, because she was happy.

I was the great looker-through-drawers. I found poetry that she had written and drawings she had done. This wasn't the person I knew. Frustrated, stuck in a miserable marriage, she wanted to divorce, and her father would not allow it. My mother died when I was fifteen. She was thirty-nine. Choked on a piece of meat.

I had an abortion when I was sixteen. My first boyfriend. I went to my father and told him I was pregnant. He asked me what I wanted to do. I told him I didn't want to have a child--I had great plans. His father, my grandfather, gave me the abortion.

Actually, I had a second abortion before college. Same guy.

The turning point was that I went over to see my grandparents, and we got into a fight. My grandfather, my <u>mother</u>'s father, stood up and said, "And how many abortions have you had?" My father had <u>told</u> him!

I walked out of that house and over to my house and said to my father, "I have kept your secret all of these years." There was no reason for him to tell them, unless he was kissing up to them for money. That was the big break with my father. He broke the trust that I had kept.

I put my thumb out, and went out on the road, and started my hippie life. I left college. I was probably eighteen. I had been in college a couple of months.

That was the time of free love. I had a number of relationships, never had an orgasm, and that started worrying me. I called my father and told him I needed money to see a therapist. I thought I was dysfunctional, because of what had happened. He admitted to me that he was sick when that happened. He admitted it to me, but he said he wouldn't give me any money. At least he took responsibility for the incest.

I remember in high school telling myself that I was going to accept responsibility for this happening. Not meaning that I was at fault. I didn't cause it. If I thought of myself as a victim of my father, I would not have been able to handle it emotionally. I did not want to be a victim. I was trying to find a comfortable philosophy that would enable me to live with all of it. My philosophy was that in the universe we're all responsible for the positions we are in, because we have something to learn. That was my way of not being a victim, to put it on another level.

If you change one thing, it changes everything. I've always been one of these people who takes whatever is positive out of anything I can. I had this vision of life passing before my mother's eyes before she died: "All the time I wasted. Trying to do what other people expect."

So, I had this list of all the things I wanted to do before I died. I wanted to go out and build my own life. Find the life that I could lead that didn't have to be this dark secret thing that I grew up in. In the late sixties and early seventies was a great time to do that. I didn't spend long in any place, because when something would happen on my picture show that I didn't like, I just split. I always worked, mostly secretarial jobs. I spent several years not making commitments, did a lot of acid, loved it.

Then, I lost a friend. My lover, actually, lost his mind on a trip. He was completely spaced after that. I quit drugs. I decided to do something else with my life. I was twenty-five.

I was working with children, and I found that I wanted to have a child. It was shortly after that that I met my husband. We got married, and I got pregnant, although that was not in his plans. It hurt me that he didn't want the child. He left.

I decided to leave the area. I didn't know where to go. I didn't want to have anything to do with my father. My mother was dead. My brother and two sisters lived a completely different life-style than I did. There wasn't any place where I wanted to go. I had money from a trust fund that had been left me. That probably gave me more courage.

I sold everything I owned and traded my car for a van with cupboards inside. I was seven months pregnant. I started doing all the right things. I really never had been at peace enough before. I had always been a smoker. I cut down to two cigarettes a day. Ate fruit. Ate grains. Started walking. I needed something in order to get away from feeling sorry for myself that my husband left. I had to do this "the way out is the way through" kind of challenge. I was going to do the courageous thing. Instead of whimpering and being afraid of what was ahead, I was going to go ripping and screaming ahead.

I drove to Mexico all by myself. I wanted to handle this birth experience with the courage of a goddess. I was more afraid of being a victim than I was of any danger of going to a foreign country and doing whatever I had to do to have a baby there.

It was wonderful. It was the right thing to do. I got a place to live. I met all kinds of people right away. People were always fascinated with what this pregnant woman was doing down there. I would talk to anybody. I didn't really know the language, but I learned more every day. I found a wonderful doctor who was educated in the States. He was willing to do the birth naturally. All these people just sort of adopted me; we adopted each other.

I believe that there's magic. I want to believe that there's magic. I had remained friends with my husband's mother. I never broke that connection. I thought my daughter needed to have grandparents. I figured out the due date. When I called and told her, she flipped. That was her birthday. I just knew that my child was going to be born on that day. And she was. She is named after her Cherokee grandmother: Shanoahee. The moon was full at her birth.

After she was born, she was in bed with me. I wanted that child with me. I just remember waking up after my first dozing. She was <u>looking</u> at me. We were <u>looking</u> at each other. I remember just talking to her.

I had been very down on my body. It was just in the way. I was interested in spiritual things. That whole birth experience gave me great respect for my body and how the physical plane works. During labor I sort of got about four feet above myself and watched my body work. I didn't make a sound. I'm not saying it didn't hurt like hell. I chose to look at the birth experience a certain way, which made it a certain way.

My father was a beater. We were beaten with belts until we bled. We'd go to school, and we'd lie about the welts, because we didn't want anybody to think that we had been so bad to

248

deserve that. As a child I remember thinking that I was from another planet. It was a mistake that I was here. Even as a very young child I knew that this was not the way things were done. I knew this was not the way it had to be. I remember sort of, more or less, saying, "I would never do this."

I was one of those people, and I still am, who never passes anyone who is hurting. Always take the runt of the litter. I wanted to prove to myself that what I had lived wasn't the way life is. Life is full of the good guys and the bad guys. I didn't want to let the bad guys win. I didn't want the bad things to win over my spirit.

It's kind of a delicate thing. There's one level of taking responsibility, and there are other levels. I can remember being punished for things I didn't do. I saw things that were unfair and that dropped my father in my credence. I have always had a strong sense of what is fair. I didn't think that I must have been bad for those things to happen to me.

I was bright. I read a lot of philosophy and psychology. I tried to use everything I could. I just made decisions that I would get over these things through understanding. I would find all the truth in them that I could. Very early I found a way to understand my father and what he did, so that I could forgive him for it. I didn't want to be bitter. That would have put stops on me.

I learned a lot from my mother's death. It freed a lot of expectations. Her life taught me that doing what will make other people happy is not the point. You may have to disappoint people in the short run, so that you can be yourself. If they love you, they don't want you to be miserable.

I have had emotionally troubled times. I guess I have always thought enough of myself that I have sought help. I learned a long time ago that therapists don't solve the problems for you. What would be really wonderful would be to find someone to ask the right questions. That's almost impossible. I'm a loner in a lot of ways. I have never been able to go to my friends and pour out my heart. My opinions, but not my heart.

I changed my life when my daughter was born. I got off the road. I started building the life that I thought would be best for her. We moved to the country, had a little farm. I taught myself how to farm and can, this and that.

I got involved with a man whom I eventually married, whom I'm still very good friends with and whom my daughter considers her Dad. She is sixteen and there have probably only been three relationships in that time. The man that I married is the only one that I lived with. In other words, I don't bring it home.

I have never been able to spank my child. I was never able to do it. However, twice in my life I made her go out and get a switch off a tree, and I spanked her bottom with that. I wanted it to hurt. Those were two times when she lied to me, when she was four and six. It was one of the most difficult things I have ever done, but I felt that I had to, because I always told her that there was nothing that she could do that would be worse than lying. We could always talk about what she did, if she told me the truth.

I have always worked, but in the last five years it has probably been more desperate than it had ever been. Shanoa has seen me go through a lot of hardship, because rather than stay in an untenable position, I've left. I've always been argumentative and willing to confront and question anything I don't think is right. My daughter has seen that. Shanoa has never been afraid of adults. I didn't bring her up that way, because I didn't want her to be afraid to say, "No." Like I was. These things get translated into your kids in different ways.

When I was brought up, we were told what to do, and that was what we did. We were given no respect. We weren't allowed to discuss anything. I don't remember ever being given an opportunity to gain any self-esteem. We were less than people.

Shanoa and I have always talked. I'm not the best person at it. What I wanted her to know from me is that she is loved, and, more than that, she is worth being loved. I've never been afraid of apologizing, telling her I was wrong. I have to check and double-check myself, but when I lose it, I go back and talk to her about it.

250

Ninety-five percent of her teachers have said to me, "This is the most eloquent child I have ever met." She is one of the most out-spoken and direct people--tough in what she wants in life. Directed. She wants to be a zoologist. She's serious about the rain forest. My daughter is an exceptional person. Bright. Independent. She is a citizen of the world.

You have to decide if you're going to allow that experience of incest to run your life. Fight fire with fire. When a lot of trauma happens, a lot of doors get closed.

I've tried tearing them open, but oftentimes, feelings that I have or voices in my head are telling me that I'm stupid or I'm a failure. One time I was driving along singing happily to myself, and I hit a bad note, and this voice kicked in: "You can't sing worth shit." It was such a violent difference in attitude toward myself, I thought, "What is that?"

I stuck with it, and it taught me a great lesson. That negative voice is my parents, every Sister Superior I ever had, every bad thing that ever happened to me, every weak part of myself, every part with no self-esteem. It's there, and I'm going to acknowledge it, but I am going to listen for the positive voice and not pay much attention to the negative voice. The thing is to <u>not</u> think that negative voice is <u>me,</u> and that what it says is all true. Some fear, something, kicks that voice in at times. That voice is very powerful.

I know that being depressed and being scared is not where I want to be. I can enjoy wallowing around in it just a little bit! But when it hurts and gets uncomfortable, and I'm not getting out, I go find somebody I can talk to. I have gotten stuck. All I have to do is get the bad stuff <u>outside</u> of me. Then I can put it in perspective and walk away.

RUTH TAYLOR
Age: 46

"That was the way I grew up: you hit first. You don't even explain."

Ruth is stepping away from violence, her mother's, her ex-husband's, and her own. She raised three children alone, drank a lot, and worked as a bookkeeper. Four years ago, Ruth stopped drinking. Last year she began to study for her bachelor's degree. She is now working only part-time, so that she can attend college full-time. Her son is twenty-six. Her daughters are twenty-one and twenty.

I got married right out of high school at eighteen. I was a baby. I was nineteen when my son was born. When he was a year and a half old, I got divorced. I got married again quickly, about a year later, again to get out of my mother's house. Someone to rescue me. Then I had my daughters and got divorced after six years of that marriage. I never remarried. The kids were two, four, and nine when I got divorced the second time.

I didn't think I could take care of myself. I remember saying to my brother, "I can't take care of myself. How am I going to take care of three children?"

He said, "You're the only one who loves them enough to take care of them. You are the only one qualified."

That meant a lot to me. It was something I hung onto.

One thing that my mother did give me was the value that you don't abandon your children, no matter what. There was no option for me to give my children to my husband or foster care or another relative. I'm glad, because sometimes if you have too many choices, you go crazy. I'm glad I didn't have the choice. But, I was terrified.

I had divorced him. It was an abusive marriage. I knew I couldn't stay married. The thought of raising three children alone was less scarey than staying with him. I have never regretted the divorce.

My parents got divorced when I was seven, and my mother raised four children alone. I think in a way that was a model for me, because if she could do it, anybody could. She had a lot less to work with than I did. She was pretty crazy. We had a terrible childhood.

It seemed that no matter how set I was that I was not going to be like her, I couldn't help but be that way. I projected my own inadequacies on my children. I had a resentful attitude. I hated life. I was not going to be an alcoholic, because I was raised with it. Even when I was afraid I was, I kept saying, "I'm not one of the alcoholics." I didn't want to become the parent that my parents were. No matter how hard I tried not to, I did.

You can't live with an alcoholic and not be affected by it. I used to slam the kitchen cupboards saying, "I hate this life! I hate my life!" We never had any money. We were just poor all the time. I worked. I was tired all the time. I used to think I drank because I had such a hard life.

When I got sober my younger daughter was sixteen and still at home. I made amends to her. I told her that my whole life was so bad that I drank. But it just made it worse.

She said, "Remember when you used to say, 'I hate my life'? Was that because of me or the alcohol?" She cried.

I told her, "It had nothing to do with you."

So, I gave these children the same feelings that my mother gave me. Those are the kinds of things that I didn't want to pass on, but I did, unconsciously. In order to be a good parent you have to take care of yourself. I couldn't.

It's amazing how forgiving children are. When I made amends to my other daughter, I said, "I was all you had, and I was drunk."

She said, "Oh, Mom! Don't feel so bad. It's okay."

My mother's been sober for about fifteen years, but she never came to me or to my brothers to say, "I'm sorry." She used to call to ask me to forgive her. That's not the same thing as saying, "I'm sorry."

I'd say, "For what?" There were things that I couldn't forgive her for, that I haven't forgiven her for. It put the burden on me. Even if she had just said, "I know I hurt you, and I'm sorry," but "Please forgive me" was putting a demand on me, and it made me even angrier.

I had a blackout, and I came to in the middle of a conversation. All I could think was it was like being Sibyl, being a multiple personality. All of a sudden I was sitting in my girlfriend's kitchen, talking and drinking wine. I was far gone by then. I was in bad shape. My younger daughter, Carrie, was the only one living at home.

Carrie said, "Mom, your drinking is scaring me."

I said to myself, "Then I won't drink in front of her."

My last drunk was very frightening. When I came to, I was fighting with my boyfriend. He took off, and I wanted to go chase him. I went to get in the car, and my daughter grabbed the car keys. She and I got into a physical fight. She's a big girl, athletic, but I had a lot of adrenalin going. We got into a terrible wrestling on the floor. I was absolutely crazy. She wouldn't give me the keys. She locked herself in the car. By the time I came out, she had honked the horn. The neighbors came and took her in. (I'm sorry I'm crying.)

I got on the phone with my son. I was still crazy. All I wanted to do was chase after this guy. My son came over. He found my daughter next door and talked to her. He got me to bed. The next day I remembered what had happened. I wanted to commit myself to the state hospital or kill myself.

But, I called AA and found out where a meeting was. I told my son I was going to a meeting. When my daughter came home, I told her. She was happy. When she came over I thought, "She'll never forgive me." I thought I had lost her, but she was very forgiving.

That was two and a half years ago. My life has changed a lot since then.

254

Things come up over a period of time. About a year ago, my daughter and I were driving past a bar in town. They were putting up a Dunkin' Donuts next door.

I said, "They'll do a lot of business. I used to come out of there at midnight or one o'clock and go have breakfast."

She said, "Where was I? How old was I?"

"Probably fourteen, fifteen."

"Where was I?"

"I don't know."

She didn't say anything.

I said, "I'm sorry."

She said, "You know, I don't have any regrets. I'm happy with who I am. I figure I had to go through what I went through to get to be the person I am."

I figure I must have done something right.

My attitude toward my kids has been different from my mother's. My mother is very narcissistic. She didn't like women. She didn't like herself. She didn't like me. My mother used to tell me, "Don't feel bad that you're not as smart as your brothers, because you'll make some lucky guy a nice wife." She told me, "You're not college material." If you didn't have a penis in my family, you didn't count.

My two older brothers were over-achievers, and my younger brother died when he was seventeen. I raised him. He was three when my parents got divorced. My mother went to work, and he was my child. I was eight years old, taking care of him. It was like losing my child when he died. It was a train accident. He was hopping a freight to California. The train crashed, and they never found the body. It burned with the cars. So there is no grave. I'm still trying to get a death certificate. His death left me really alone.

If my brothers and I got in trouble, my mother would get mad at us for causing problems for her. I remember her saying, "I sacrifice for you and look at what you've done." Everything was directed back to her. I did have the attitude--because I was a mother from the time I was eight years old--that I had to take care of my children. I wasn't drunk all the time. Even if I was drinking and my kids were in trouble, I knew they were in trouble, and I tried to help them.

I cooked meals and went to their events at school. I did all that. I was the best mother I knew how to be. My drinking went through different stages. For a year after I got divorced, I worked at the police department nights, and I had a live-in housekeeper. I had to have someone there at night while I worked and during the day while I slept. Some of the policemen and I would go out after work and drink. I'd come home and go to bed.

I noticed my children starting to change. They didn't behave like my children. They had a different air about them, because another woman was raising them. That was a red flag, so I put temporary controls on my drinking. I would know things weren't right, so I would change something.

I felt I had been dealt a lousy hand. My children weren't raised with a lot of joy. I was functional, but I was angry. Very angry. I made some bad choices for husbands. I blamed them for my troubles, for not making me happy and giving me a good life. I didn't know that it had to come from within me. I lived my life inside out. The real problem was me, and I didn't know it.

AA helped me. I felt responsible for everything that had happened, but I blamed other people. After a while of being sober I began to clear out my thinking. It took a long time. I was in therapy for four years before I was in AA. Everything helped.

My mother did some very damaging things to me. I grew up with a lot of violence, at the hands of my mother. She was hysterical, a very unhappy person. She was pretty sick. Sick. I grew up in a real crazy house.

I hit my kids. I would never do it today, but I did then. I remember when my son was in first grade I went to Back to School Night. I was still married, and I wasn't drinking. This was just the way I was raised. He came running up to me to tell me something, and I was talking to his teacher. I flipped him in the mouth with the back of my hand. That was normal for me. The teacher took a deep breath and got this look of shock on her face. It had never dawned on me that that was no way to treat a kid. I didn't know I was doing anything wrong.

My mother used to hit me with belts, even when I was seventeen. That was the way I grew up: you hit first. You don't even explain. I'm the parent, and you're the kid. You have no rights. I did it to a lesser degree, because I hated its being done to me.

A friend of mine pays a lot more for child support of one kid than I got for three. I said to my son, "Your father pays me the minimum for child support."

He said, "You could have always taken him back to court."

It dawned on me that he was right, but he didn't understand how hard it was. I had no fight left in me. How hard it was to be a poor woman. It took all the energy I had to go to work and take care of the kids. I didn't have money for lawyers, so I would have had to go through the public defender to fight some guy out in California with money. That takes guts, and I didn't have it. I didn't have the confidence.

My kids have grown up to be nice people. They're compassionate, and they have good values. I gave them that. They do understand things. My son is a mental health counselor. My older daughter is a senior at the University, and the younger one is going to beauty school.

Sometimes I feel guilty and wish I could have given them a better life, but I couldn't help it. I did the best I could. I can't do anything about it now. All I can do is go from here. I've had to come face to face with myself and forgive myself. That has been the first step. I can face things I did now, instead of wanting to run and hide.

I feel like I did my job. I did a good job. I'm on my own. I can't believe how easy it is. I'm not tired all the time. Sometimes I used to go to bed and cry, because I was just bone-tired.

My daughter and her boyfriend both got laid off this fall. I don't have any money now. I told her, "Gee, I wish I could help you."

"Oh, no," she said, "I feel better about myself if I do it myself. I think about what you went through, and I think, 'If my Mom went through that, I can get through this.'"

"Oh, I'm glad I was a model for you."

"Oh, yes, I think about you all the time."

A lot of good came out of what I did. The only thing I knew how to do was struggle.

There was a time in my life when I said, "There is no reward." My kids were all teenagers. Now, it's absolutely worth it. I wouldn't not have children. One of my brothers felt the only way he could stop that circle of pain was to not have children.

I've tried every way I could think of to find a safe way to relate to my mother. I moved three thousand miles to get away from her, and she followed me. She is very controlling. When she moved back here I was very angry. I was thirty. I tried again, to build the relationship and put boundaries. It didn't work. She just knew which buttons to push. She finally pushed the last button. I wrote her and told her, "I want you out of my life." She can blow my self-esteem. Use me. She has no confidence in my ability. No respect for my wishes. I've worked too hard to come as far as I have. I just don't feel safe around her.

I think there were times when my children kept me alive. I was so depressed that I was suicidal. If it hadn't been for the fact that there was nobody to take care of the children . . . they kept me alive. I didn't love myself enough to keep going for me, but I loved my children.

5

Loss

When a conversation touches on the possibility of the loss of a child, one or more mothers will quickly say, "I don't know how I could live through that. It would kill me." The conversation stops. Then, it moves on in a different direction. Death of a child is the unimaginable, the most dreaded possibility in a mother's life. Though mothers talk endlessly about every aspect of raising children, they avoid this topic. It is as if by refusing to mention Death's name, they can keep death from their children.

For a young mother or a mother in her middle years, a child's death stands out against the rest of life's experience. For a mother in old age, death is no stranger. As life evolves, it is full of losses. When age starts doing little drawings around the edges of an old mother's mind, parts of the past slip away, like a child disappearing around the corner of the house. The sharpness of old pain is dulled, and old age delivers her to a gentler space, from which to make her exit.

Loss of a child is loss of the immediacy of that person, here and now. It is the loss of sunlight caught in a daughter's hair, the loss of a son's rowdy holler carrying in through a window.

Loss of a child is, also, loss of the future. Loss of all the hoped-for times together in the years ahead and of the special privilege of seeing your child's personality fully developed and busy in the world.

The sadness is so deep that no comfort can reach it.

After a death, a mother has to depend on memory, and memory is fickle. It steals details. It hides things, and loses them, and cannot always be persuaded to go find them, and give them back.

In the stories in this chapter, one mother is helped by knowing that others--a husband, her parents, little cousins of the baby who died--feel the pain, too. It helps her to talk to friends, to voice the pain. For another, a mother with no direction and a history of drug abuse, the loss of her son comes in the middle of so many other problems that it tips a precarious balance and sends her spinning. How can she endure the pain? She would rather die than feel what she feels. Where is there any help? Who could possibly understand? Guilt weighs heavily against her, also, but perhaps a new life can tip the balance back.

When another mother anticipates her own imminent death, she faces the loss of both of her children, and of everything else as well. As she tends to fewer and fewer of the ongoing details of daily life, she tries to prepare herself and her children for an end in the road ahead, but it is difficult to let even her imagination travel that way.

Death will have its impact, and then, so will grief. Grief will spill over everything that is near it. It will affect a mother's relationship with her husband and with her other children. One mother is brought up short when her daughter says, "You have to be dead to really matter in this family." Another mother whose first son committed suicide narrowly succeeds in preventing her second son from following him.

Sometimes the loss refuses to recede with time and stays fully alive in the present. It may stay alive as an unresolved chord, or as a creative force that transforms a life. A mother has little control over her response to her child's death. At that depth, her life will play out its strongest themes, which were written long ago.

MABEL SARDUCCI
Age: 87

"As long as I know they're okay, that's all I care. And now I got two of them gone, so I ain't got to worry about them either."

Mabel is from Maine. She is confined to a wheelchair and lives in the county home now. She raised three children alone. When we talked, she wasn't sure she wanted to bring up old memories. Two of Mabel's children have died, and she has no contact with the third. She does not dwell on what she's lost.

Marshall was the oldest. There's Ed and, then, Louise. Marshall died of injuries he got in the war. I was too upset. I don't remember what war it was.

Ed is married, and he lives near here. I haven't seen him in years and years and years. I haven't seen him in more than twenty years. His wife got mad at me, because I went to the son's wedding, so she don't want him to talk to me at all. And she's treacherous, so I just have to suffer without seeing my own son. I've been through hell in life, believe me I did. Plenty. She's the boss. She'll threaten him and let him have it. I know. So that's that. I'd rather him not talk to me than get squashed in the road.

I've been through hell all of my life. Now is the best time in my life. Yes. My other sisters and brothers used to do something, and they'd say, "Mabel did it, Ma," and I'd get the beating, with a good stick as big as my cane I used to walk with. Across the back. No wonder I have a bum back today.

So, that's life. Now is the best time in my life. Right now. I live in a beautiful place. You couldn't ask for anything better. They're so good to you. There's nothing you need that you don't get, or nothing they won't do for you. 'Course I don't feel

261

too good. I'm bad off with arthritis. I can't walk. But I'm living a nice life. Right now.

My daughter died of cancer. She was married. She didn't have any children.

When my kids were little, oh, they were so darling. I hugged them, and rocked them, and rocked them, half of the night. Oh, I loved them! Couldn't love anybody, anything, better than that. I loved my kids. Yes. And I did everything I could for 'em. Loving the kids, that's the best part.

I was raising them alone. This day that girl knocked at the door and said she was pregnant with him. I slammed the door in her face, and when he come home, I slammed the door in his face. "Get the hell out! Don't you come in here." I told him why. That was it.

I don't remember how I fed them. That was in the Depression. I must have had a way, but I don't remember. Like I say, I've been through so much my mind is going. I don't remember. I know I had them, and they went to school. They were good kids. I raised 'em very strict. I never beat 'em. The only punishment I did to 'em is if they done anything wrong, I'd put 'em to bed an hour or two earlier at night. I never beat 'em up. I wouldn't. I got enough beatings without beating my own.

This is my home 'til I kick the bucket.

I have grandchildren. Don't ask me how many. My grandson from Iowa was here last week. You want to see the nice thing he brought me? Binoculars! Look outside with them! Isn't that a beauty? I got the best view in the house. I can see the mountains. My grandchildren are good to me. Anything I want, they get it for me. They all live far away. Nothing you can do.

I got married young. I wanted to get out of my house. So, my sister was living down the street. She had a man living with her, a roomer. I got with him, and we got married. He was a barber. That got me the hell out of the house. I wasn't abused anymore. Now I'm alone, and I'm going to stay that way.

Raising kids, that's gone by, now. Thank goodness it's all over with. As long as I know they're okay, that's all I care. And now I got two of them gone, so I ain't got to worry about them, either. God love 'em.

When they were little, I wanted to give them enough food to feed 'em, that's what I wanted the most. I did. I used to work day and night. My landlady would help me. She would bring 'em up and put 'em in the house for supper. When it was time for bed, she'd put 'em to bed for me. I had to go to work. I had to go to work day and night to raise three kids. In them days, you didn't make much money. I worked in the laundry all day long, and then, at night, I'd go scrub floors in private offices. My landlady would look out for the kids. Oh, she was so good. I didn't have to worry that way.

I went through hell both times, when my mother was bringing me up and after I got married. But I brought up three good kids.

VIRGINIA WILLIAMS
Age: 84

"But the hardest thing, I think, is the death of a child."

Virginia is the mother of seven children, including Meleanna Williams whose story is in Chapter Six. As Virginia describes her experience of being a mother, loss emerges as one aspect of a full life lived to old age. Loss of the old ways, loss of all five siblings, loss of her partner, and of a grown child. Finally, loss averted by love.

We were brought up in a small town in New Hampshire, and there was no outside activity, so we were a group in itself. There were six children in my family. I'm the only one left. And one of my brothers' wives. That's all. It's sad. The end of an era. It has been very difficult to lose all those people.

We used to be taught respect at home and at school, and our mother would be inviting the teachers for dinner, and we would have to behave ourselves. Of course now, I don't know, I have a hard time accepting the youth. They have no respect for anything. And is that the mother's fault? Is it the upbringing? The conditions in the world? I'm not one for permissiveness. Sometimes I think there's too much permissiveness--doing what you want when you want to do it. There are other people in the world besides yourself.

I was always here. Of course, with seven children, you certainly couldn't go very far anyway! But I do think that makes a difference, the security of someone when they come home from school. Someone's there that cares about them.

My seven children are all entirely different. What one didn't try, another one did. If I'd had less, I could have given more to each one of them. I remember thinking, "Another baby. How am I ever going to cope with one more baby? How am I ever going to give that child what she or he should have?" But you do. You worry before it happens. But you do cope and <u>survive</u>, shall we say. Maybe I did well, and maybe I didn't. I don't know.

When Jim was born was during the war, and he was born with these feet... Of course all the young doctors were in the service. I had this old man who shook like a tree in the wind. Then, back in my room, you know how you look at the baby. I looked down at his feet. They were toed way in. I yelled for the nurse.

"Didn't the doctor tell you?"

"No, he didn't." He should have warned me. I was terribly upset. They immediately put casts on both feet. One responded, but one didn't.

I'm very short, and I thought that the way the feet were inside me, maybe, they didn't have room enough. But next time I went to the clinic I saw this woman that was over six feet tall, and her baby had the same problem, so throw that theory away! But it was during the war, and I've read since that it was lack of protein. Of course, being a mother you gave to your children and went without yourself. Eggs and meat were very difficult to get. What you got you gave to the children.

My daughter Meleanna and her son Sawyer live here in the house with me. In some ways I've been my grandson Sawyer's second mother. He's lived here from the beginning, like my own child. Nineteen years, from birth. I was the one who was here when he came home from school and took care of him, evenings, put him to bed and so forth. But maybe I'm just being proud of myself. I don't know that I'm proud, but I am pleased that Sawyer is what he is, and I'm willing to feel that I helped. Not that I did anything for him other than be here when he came home. I think that is important. Give him a cookie, a place to bring his friends. It wasn't any effort on my part. I just was here. I looked forward to his coming home. I think he and I are quite close now. He's very, very kind to me, too, which I appreciate. Very thoughtful. Most young kids don't want too much to do with an old lady! But he's very kind to me.

I liked mealtimes with all the kids--everybody talking at once about what they did and so forth! Bringing their friends in. One time one of my girls said to me, "Shirley is coming to supper tonight, and we're going to have a good giggly meal." Shirley didn't have any brothers, so, of course, she did all the more giggling for them. I wish I'd kept contact with all of their friends.

As a mother I found the hardest was teenage years. It's very difficult to know how much freedom to give. If you didn't give, if you held a rein too tight, they went "fhewt!" out behind your back and would not come back and tell you anything. Where to draw the line? I think many people thought I was a lot of times too lenient, but I didn't want them to do things behind my back. I don't know if I did right or wrong, but I didn't have too many repercussions.

There was one period that the older children all had scarlet fever, and that was the time when they put a sign on your door, and you didn't go in or out. I was upstairs with the children, and Samuel would go to work, but he couldn't go upstairs where the children lived. That was quite a series. I had a girl living with us that wanted to go to school and didn't have any home. 'Course she was quarantined, too. She and I would go out after dark when nobody could see us, just to get out and walk on the road.

But the hardest thing I think is the death of a child. Ned just died. Of course, he wasn't a child, but that was very difficult for me. It was difficult when the two boys went to war, too. I found that about the hardest as they were growing up. Norman went right after graduation from high school. It was the thing to do. He didn't know what he wanted. You don't know what is going to happen. It's hard losing one of your children. Even harder than . . . well, of course Samuel, my husband, was ill . . . it was even harder with Ned. It was sudden. He was my child. He was only fifty-nine.

This talk about gayness. That was hard for me to accept, too. Being of the old school, you know. I surmised, but I didn't officially know Ian is gay until three years ago. I blame myself. Ian was always . . . the way he was brought up, there were older

266

women upstairs, and he was always visiting them. Maybe if it had been different. But they tell me it's inborn anyway. But I did blame myself. I didn't know. I surmised maybe, but I didn't know.

Even when Ian told me I was upset, to feel that I failed. But everyone says it wasn't my fault. You see many mothers that don't accept it at all. But I accepted it. I didn't get really upset, thank goodness. That he knew of. It was all inside me. Because of course I was brought up when that was not... in fact there was a man that worked for us for years that was gay, and they wouldn't allow him to drive the bus because of the children. I went through that too--how it was a disgrace. I guess almost a disgrace is the word. It was hard for me to accept, as you can understand, but I thought I did well. I accept his partner, too. You have to accept these things as a mother, don't you? Or you lose the child. You lose the child entirely and you lose a part of yourself, too.

LAURA TOBIAS-HEATH
Age: 35

"We scattered his ashes on Mother's Day. I was a childless mother."

Laura has a double uterus and didn't know if she would ever be able to have children. She became pregnant after a year of trying and was considered "high-risk." She gave birth to that baby at twenty-five weeks, and the baby died within an hour of its birth. Laura talks about the birth and the death.

I had chronic pelvic pain and was seeing a doctor every two weeks. I kept pestering him about what the prognosis was. Finally, when I hit the second trimester he sort of reluctantly said that things "were hopeful." With that I let my guards down. At that time I was director of a women's health center. I made arrangements to work on a part-time basis and hired an assistant director.

At about twenty-four weeks I went into labor. The doctor admitted me to the hospital for the weekend, under the diagnosis "irritable uterus." On the way to the hospital, I started to bleed. They did an ultrasound. That evening the doctor told my husband Alan and me that the baby had birth defects. He said he thought that part of the baby's intestine was on the outside of its body. He would keep me on the medication to quiet the uterus. On Monday they would transfer me to a hospital that could do more sophisticated ultrasounds.

I remember saying to Alan, "I'm going to quit my job." The doctor said, "Just hold off for a few days and see what happens."

Over the weekend we talked with a number of people who knew something about this birth defect. My sense was that it was scarey, but correctible and wouldn't have any long-term effects.

On Sunday afternoon the labor broke through the medication. It was weird labor. I was bleeding while I was in labor. The doctor came in and said things were "ominous." On Monday they shipped me to the other hospital. The doctor examined me and said, "You're three centimeters dilated. This baby is coming imminently." He looked at my face and then said, "I'm sorry."

They did the ultrasound. The liver was involved and the defect was massive. There might be a chamber in the heart missing. They were telling me that the baby wouldn't survive. I asked all the questions that I had put off asking until I thought there was no hope: "How do you take care of the remains?" I knew I wanted to hold the baby and name him.

The next time, the doctor came in to examine me, I said, "I want to talk before you examine me. I need to be sure that there is no chance that the baby will survive. Can we do something to investigate whether the heart is involved?"

"Sure." He ordered one more test, that afternoon. It came back, and he said, "There's no chance, even if we were able to maintain the pregnancy until forty weeks."

Once the medication to quiet my uterus was ended, the labor proceeded. Someone finally said I could push. As soon as I felt a contraction start, I pushed. The pain overtook my whole body. My eyes were closed. I saw a streak of light as if the light was being torn away from me. I heard myself scream. Far off. And felt an explosion from my body. They were yelling at me to push again. Pain. I heard myself scream again.

A nurse was working on something bloody between my legs. I thought it was the placenta. Then I realized it was the baby-- his birth defects. I got my first real look as someone carried him out of the room. Bluish. Little arms and legs. A baby. Alan was whispering in my ear. I just lay there, numb.

Then they brought Bud to us, wrapped in a pink receiving blanket. He was tiny--one pound, nine ounces, twelve inches long. His head was the size of a tennis ball. His little face was perfect. Later I looked at his father as he slept to remember

Bud's face. Bud's eyes were closed, fused shut. He had a bit of fuzz-like hair. I realized he was alive, but dying.

I quickly removed the blanket. I wanted to take him all in. The birth defects didn't phase me at all. They were there, his organs on the outside, covering his entire chest and abdomen. It wasn't bloody. We could see a bit of his heart, moving slowly. I lifted his little fingers. They dropped ever so slowly, curling on my finger, as if he was in a deep sleep.

Bud's little body was just a handful, but lanky and floppy, so he took two hands to hold. Too little to cuddle. I propped him up on my knees. I wondered out loud to Alan how we would ever be able to hand Bud over to the nurses for the last time. Alan was crying. I was so full of love for him that the final parting with Bud was easier. We gave Bud a last, thorough look. He had become cold to our touch. We turned him over and saw his thin buttocks. We commented on his eentsy penis, like a grain of rice. I stroked his head with my finger.

Alan and I talked for a long time back in my room, and then he fell off to sleep. I put my hand on my belly. It was flat. There was no life in there. I wept.

When I had gone to the hospital it was a beautiful fall day, warm. When I came out, it was as if Mother Nature had completely changed her face on me. The color was gone. The whole world was dark and cold, damp. They wheeled me out of the hospital. I had seen mothers being wheeled out of a hospital, carrying their babies, the fathers all flushed as they helped the mothers into the car. I was holding a plant that someone had given me.

We had a memorial service for Bud a few days later. Throughout the service you could hear the coffee perking in the church kitchen: life goes on. My parents came. In thirty-five years my mother had never seen my father cry. He cried like a baby. As he left I saw his face distorted, trying to hold back the tears. It was comforting. The older of my nephews, a small philosopher, kept saying, "Why? Why?" The little one sat on my sister's lap in tears and said, "I want that baby back."

There was an incredible outpouring of love. Calls and cards, and people bringing food by. Many people called and didn't know what to say. Some people said they were sorry "about my baby." That was kind of nice. Some people said they were sorry "about my son." That was real nice. Some people said they were sorry "about Bud." That was the ultimate comfort, to hear people acknowledge him by name.

We scattered his ashes on Mother's Day. I was a childless mother.

I dealt with the loss partly by talking to my friends. To me it was really important that Bud was born alive. That meant that we had to deal with funeral rites, but it gave him an identity as a living person. I was clear that I was not mourning a full life of my son. I needed some assurances that it was okay to do some full-scale grieving for a baby who had only lived a few minutes.

I joined a support group. There was a woman there who had lost a baby at birth ten years before. She was still trying to cope with her feelings. At the hospital they had whisked him away. She did not know what had happened to the remains. She had kind of a waking nightmare that he was just thrown in the trash, and that in fact he wasn't dead at that time. All on her own she had named him.

Bud's legacy is the love that came pouring forth after he died. I had never appreciated how much I was loved. It was overwhelming, powerful. There was a woman at work who had a two-year-old daughter. I knew she was trying to get pregnant again. When Bud died she hugged me, and we cried together. Several months later I saw her in the hall. She had just gotten a positive pregnancy test. "I wish it were you," she said.

LYNN JONES
Age: 24

"That's when my life took a real downfall, when Aaron died.... People said to me, 'Lynn, it's going to get better. It's going to get better.' Do you know? It just got worse and worse."

Lynn was already addicted to cocaine, but her life fell apart after her oldest child was killed by a drunk motorcycle driver. She had two other children. She is in prison, now, on drug charges. Lynn had another child, Beth, six weeks ago, while she was in prison. Beth is living with a foster-mother, who brings her to the prison twice a week to see Lynn. Lynn is in danger of losing all of her children.

I had my first child, Aaron, at seventeen years old. I was living at home with my mother, and the baby's father was living with me. I wasn't ready to be a mother. I was in my teen life. I wanted to do everything else but be a mother. I wanted to do things for myself, and I didn't know how to take care of a baby. I basically counted on my mother to do that for me, which she ended up doing. Good old Grammie, she was there whenever I needed her. "Oh, Ma, I got to do this, I want to do that."

"Okay, okay."

After I had Aaron I had no patience. I used to stand over his crib sometimes at night and say, "PLEASE, Baby, PLEASE just go to sleep!"

I split up with Aaron's father when Aaron was a year and a half old. I got married to an older man and became pregnant with my second child, Marie. During that time I was in a rehab for drugs. My life became a lot better, because I stayed clean.

My husband was a homey-type person. For a year or two I tried to live his way. He wanted me to stay home, not go out with people my age or do things that people my age do. That's when the downfall came in. Kind of like straightaway. A lot of arguments. I wanted to go out and do things, even with the kids. He wanted to just stay home and stay home. Then we had my third child, Richard, just a year after Marie.

I had an active addiction from start. Before I even had my first child. In between these times of having children, I would relapse. I would get clean for a few months, and then I would end up relapsing again. I didn't drink much at all then. My alcohol addiction never stepped in until January of 1989. My first son passed away in 1988.

That's when my life took a real downfall, when Aaron died. I didn't want to live no more. Why couldn't it have been me? I'm the bad one. I'm the one that's doing something wrong. People said to me, "Lynn, it's going to get better. It's going to get better." Do you know? it just got worse and worse. My addiction became more and more and more.

There was a point in my life where my mother and father were pulling Aaron one way, my husband was pulling him another way, but yet that little boy always stood by me. "You leave my Mummy alone. My Mummy is sick." I had an active cocaine addiction then, but I was home, taking care of my kids, feeding them three meals a day, bathing them. Mummy was always around, and I did my addiction after they were already sleeping at night. It was affecting to them not at all. My son used to see me. He'd get up in the middle of the night. He'd say, "Mummy what are you doing?"

I'd say, "Aaron, you go potty and go back to bed."

I was faced with a lot of guilt when my son was killed. My family turned against me. They said, "It's all your fault."

That's why I left my husband and two kids. I thought, "What if something like this happens to one of my other kids?"

The night before my son was killed, I had a big argument with my husband. He said, "Just get out; just get out."

That was the last time I had actually seen my son. I tucked him in bed. He was wide awake. He said, "No, Mummy. Stay home, Mummy."

"Mummy's going to go out for a little while. I'll be back." I never went home that night. I was out doing what I knew how to do best--getting high.

Around noontime the next day my husband walked my kids to the store, bought them ice cream and stuff. They had just gotten back. Aaron was out in the yard playing. That's when the accident occurred. At this time, I was on my way home, walking up the same street. My husband saw me. He come running down to me. "Aaron's been hit by a motorcycle--a drunk driver." They held me back from the scene. It was one big thing. We got to the hospital, and they said my son was dead.

Then my husband and I had a lot of arguments. It was like I still wanted to drug, and it got even worse after my son was killed. I left my husband about six to eight weeks after Aaron was killed. I told him, "Look, I got to go. I can't stay here no more." I didn't want to put the other two kids through the hurt and pain I was going through. So, I left him.

He said, "If you walk out them doors, don't ever come back."

My husband wouldn't allow me to see my kids. I didn't see them at all. I used to call and cry. I was in like a depression state. I didn't even want to live. I was using drugs twenty-four hours a day. Staying up seven days a week. No food, no sleep. I was just constantly using the drugs to stay awake. I was selling the drugs for this man I was living with. I used to put my kids' pictures in front of me and cry. I felt like there was nobody to turn to, nobody to talk to that could really understand what I was going through.

I was arrested a few times in the year after that for possession of drugs. I did six months on them charges. When I got out last year I had expected to move in with my husband and two kids. Everything was going to be fine and dandy. It turned out very wrong. He had been living with his new girlfriend for a few months. I had no knowledge of this until the last month of my sentence. It was like, "Wow, I'm not going home to my kids and my husband." Very disappointing. I went downhill all over again.

But during the time I was out and not in prison, I had been seeing my kids. Off and on. I'd call my husband. I'd have him meet me at the laundromat. I didn't want him to know where I was living. Or he'd bring the kids to see me at my mother's. I'd see them for fifteen, twenty minutes, and he'd have to leave. His girlfriend don't want me to see my kids at all. She tells them to call her "Mommy." When I saw them it was very upsetting. My little girl would say, "Mummy, I don't want you to go in the alleys."

I saw my Marie and my Richard in December last year. It was the night before I got arrested again. I brought them out for pizza and had bought them birthday and Christmas gifts. I got them a card with some money. I had met my husband at the laundromat. I told the kids that I would come to the house in two days, to take some pictures. They wanted some pictures. Well, God only knows, I never made it. That was the last time I have seen my kids.

I really miss my kids. But he still hasn't brought my kids up to see me. My husband's girlfriend won't allow me to talk to them on the phone, either. I'm hoping the courts will allow me to have visitation rights to my kids. I don't know if I'll ever get to see them again.

I just recently had a little girl, Beth. She's being taken care of by a foster mother. I see her twice a week for an hour to two hours. Basically, that's it. I hold her almost the whole time when she comes to visit. I tell her "Mummy misses you. Mummy loves you a lot." I try to get her to smile and coo. I try to keep her focused on me the whole time she's here. I see the way when she hears her foster-mother's voice, she's kind of focusing that way. That's why I talk to her, as her mother, and try to keep her focused on me. What scares me is I don't know if this is going to do anything to her life, me not being there for her right now. The foster-mother says she's "a mother's dream." Just a happy baby.

I don't know when I'll be getting out of jail. I have a year and a half to three years, but I've done five months already. They want me to go into a one-year intensive drug rehab for the last year of my sentence, but, by the time I get sentenced, by the time I go through the sixty-day waiting period to get into that program, it could run over the eighteen-month time limit to get back on my feet. I could lose my parental rights to my baby daughter. That scares me.

There's no way I will ever give her up for adoption. Not on my worst day. I do not want to lose my daughter. She's a new beginning for me. She's my strength right now. My little girl.

My husband has no claim to Beth. Beth's father is one of my best friends. When I got out of prison last year it was sort of like a friend type deal. It just happened. It was just one of them things. I don't think I'll see him when I get out though. He's got an active addiction off and on with the alcohol and the drugs.

Beth has given me hope. To go on and better myself. I've learnt my lesson now all the way around. There's a lot of groups here--parenting, AA, domestic violence, drug and alcohol--I'm in all of them.

At AA meetings people say how they got these DWI's or how they almost killed someone. It's very hard for me. It hurts. I just want to stand up and say, "Why were you behind that wheel drinking?" I'm very angry toward them people on account of Aaron, but I don't say it. My eyes start to water, and I hang my head down, like I don't even want to look at them. I try to talk about it, because I feel it needs to be pulled out. It needs to get out in the open. I try to start talking, but I can feel the tears coming, and I feel like I'm going to burst. All of a sudden it just goes RIGHT back inside. I say nothing. I can't go no further.

My mother is more in my life now than she has ever been. There was a time after my son was killed that she wasn't a part of my life, because of the negative way my family was thinking. We started talking. Since I've been in jail this time, my mom comes and sees me every other week. She writes to me. She's where a lot of my strength is coming in now.

I need to make it out of jail and be in a family again. That's what I want most.

"You never know how it's affecting the kids."

Natalie has AIDS. She lives in New Hampshire with her husband and two children, Paul and Karen, who are fifteen and twelve. Natalie has difficulty bringing herself to think about the loss she is facing: the loss of everything, including her two children.

After this interview Natalie lived for one more year.

In 1986, I received a telephone call telling me that I had been infected with the AIDS virus in 1984, through a blood transfusion. It came absolutely out of the blue. I was always very healthy. I was a marathon runner. It changed everything.

I didn't tell the children right away. Over time Larry and I have become more open, but neither of the kids has told even their closest friend. Paul told me, "Mom, they tell AIDS jokes every day in school."

I told the kids about a year after I started to get sick. I deliberately did it when my husband wasn't there, because I felt that he was going to fall apart going through that process, and I didn't know if I could get through it. The kids were great. They were furious that other people knew and that I hadn't told them: "You told your <u>sister,</u> and I didn't know?"

Then I started to speak to groups of people about AIDS. I never speak around here. The kids worry, "What if somebody from one of those schools comes to our town?" It's a healing thing for me to speak. I feel that I can make some difference in it all. I wish that everybody who's walking around making AIDS jokes would <u>think</u>. They don't know who they're talking to or who might be listening--ever.

One of the first years that the kids knew I had AIDS, Paul was on a Little League team. His coach was standing there drinking a soda.

One of the kids came up to the coach and said, "Can I have a sip of that?"

He said, "Well, you can if you want to, but I have AIDS."

Paul was standing there while everyone laughed and laughed.

It's been so stressful to talk to people and not know what they know and have that pull about protecting the kids. I had a support group. It was all gay men except for me. They became sort of like family friends. But all those people have died, except for one. So many times I would go from a funeral to a soccer game. People would say to me at the game, "Are you still going to Boston?" I didn't know why they thought I was going to Boston. Who knew what? I just couldn't stand it.

You never know how it's affecting the kids. When my daughter was about eight, she was asking about why all these men from the support group were calling. She was teasing me. I said, "Well, you know Nathan is gay. Do you know what that means?" I gave her an explanation, and there was no reaction at all. Then she said, "Well, all I know is, he has an awesome car."

The kids are so focused on what's happening at the moment that they help me to do that. One day when I first found out that I was sick, I got a call from my doctor in Boston saying, "Your blood platelets are almost gone. This is really serious."

Paul was coming in the door from day camp. He didn't know it was AIDS then, but he knew I was sick. I told him I had just gotten awful news, that I have a pretty serious blood disorder.

"We'll get through it," I said, "but I want you to know that there is going to be a lot of tension here. Don't take it personally if we're real crabby."

He sort of looked at me and patted me on the shoulder, literally, and said, "Mom, I'm really sorry to hear that . . . I am absolutely famished. Could you make us something wonderful for dinner?" That has been a lot of my survival. I can't get preoccupied. I have to make dinner or take them somewhere.

I have what I call my "June Cleaver psychosis." If I had a little lull in all the medical stuff, I would invite every kid in the neighborhood over for lunch. Clinging to what's normal. Every time that I got a bad test result, I'd start chopping vegetables. A few years back, Paul was in this little rock group that would practice at the house, and I would be leaving for Boston, never knowing if they were going to hospitalize me or not, and he'd say, "Could my friends sleep over tonight?" Eight of these little pre-adolescent boys.

I've been very sick in the last few months. I was in the hospital for a month with pneumocystis. The doctor told my husband that she didn't think I was going to make it. My lungs filled with fluid. I had thought about AIDS as a slow process. Suddenly they were talking about my dying.

Karen is phobic about hospitals, and I had promised her before I left that she would never have to come to the hospital unless she wanted to. Then it was such a long hospitalization, and I missed her so much. I just felt I couldn't make her come in. She sent flowers that she made. She was trying to be involved.

Paul did come to the hospital eventually. He wanted to see how the bed worked and all that. When he left I said, "Thank you so much for coming."

"I had nothing else to do," he said. Typical fifteen-year-old. From the beginning he was joking around, saying things like, "You've just got to be real cool about this and not take it out on us."

I was told that I needed to be very clear about the prognosis. It's so hard, though. I would love to have denial like the kids have. They just put it out of their minds. I don't want to take that away from them. The doctor's saying, "It's a terminal situation," but we don't know if that's a month from now or two years from now.

I felt that Paul listened to me when I said, "You understand that it was a very close call? We don't know what's going to happen." He and Karen know what's going on. I tried to say a lot of the things that I love about them, and that I think they're going to be okay, because they're good kids. Karen put her hands over her ears.

I just feel so attached to them. It's almost unbearable. I may not have much time. I want to be doing stuff with them. I want to see them grow up.

Now I'm so tired all the time, I have to be more protective of myself. Karen is really into having sleepovers now--with ten people--and I've just had to say that we can't do that. There are ways that all the normal stuff is eroding.

I'm so weak. It's so hard just to brush my hair... I can't do the stuff that I did with them. Karen was having a hard time for the first couple of weeks of seventh grade, because it's a bigger school. Before I would have done things with her, little outings. I feel helpless.

The doctor doesn't like me to do stairs. Every night Karen still likes to be tucked in. Every night Larry would go up. I finally just decided I wanted to do those stairs once a day, so I can go up and tuck her in.

I actually like being here in the downstairs, because the kids flock in here. I'm glad that Karen brings her friends in. They just sit here on the bed and chat. I don't know what I would do if one of them asked me, "How come you're in bed all the time?" They just kind of come in and take it in stride, and there's no discussion of why I'm here like this.

Paul likes me being here. I am kind of a captive audience. He's a talker. I know everything there is to know about Guns and Roses. He'll say, "Will you watch just this one video? Mom, it'll be quality time." He's very funny. He's always had a flair.

My mother stayed here and did everything while I was in the hospital. Karen had some real battles with her: "This is my house." They had a fight about washing the curtains. My mother wanted to do it, and Karen said when they washed the other ones they ended up different lengths. "This is our house. You shouldn't be making these decisions."

My mother said to me, "She wants you. She doesn't want other people here."

I haven't done much cooking or things like that since I've been back. One day I decided I was going to cook dinner. It was a disaster. I was so weak that stuff was flying out of my hands. I ended up sobbing. I dropped this food processor full of grated onions all over the floor. I was just awful. Then I thought, "Maybe if I do littler things . . ." I made Luke breakfast one day last week. It felt so good.

Both kids have really great relationships with Larry, so that's another kind of security. He and I are pretty balanced in how we deal with the children. It's not as if one of us is the disciplinarian. There wouldn't have to be a big shift, if I'm gone. He would always try to get home from seeing me in the hospital to pick Karen up at her soccer practice, or whatever. He's held it together here in a lot of ways.

I'm anxious to have some strength back, so we can just do a few more normal things, like going out to eat. Larry tries to fill in the gaps, but it's not the same as doing it as a family.

A lot of the way that Larry and I deal with the sickness is by still hoping for a miracle. A new drug. Otherwise, it's just too painful. I can't really follow through on thinking about dying and not being here.

With Paul at fifteen, Larry is starting to give him driving lessons. I can see Paul sort of slowly turning into an adult. I'm going to miss that.

I find myself, with Karen especially, being very over-protective. I get right into being in seventh grade and being rejected by the girl that "used to be my best friend." I think it's because I feel vulnerable myself. I just want to wrap myself around her and shield her from all the things that are going to happen over the next few years.

Everybody has always teased us about Paul. Larry and I used to do workshops on non-sexist parenting. Now we have this real macho kid! We're involved in a lawsuit, for malpractice issues, and he says he wants to be a lawyer: "When I'm a lawyer, I'm going to be defending the companies that you're against." It's all joking, but I have a lot of curiosity about what he's going to be like.

Karen was a very shy, younger kid. She turns out to be a really good athlete. It has changed her attitude about everything. She's embarrassingly aggressive! It's so out of character, in a way. I like those changes. She does fine in school. I think that's important in terms of choices she'll have. I worry about safety things. Paul is much more cautious, even though he's more outrageous. Another thing about Karen is that she always includes people. She has that quality.

The kids can be so difficult. Karen now, one minute she's wonderful, and the next minute she's having a temper tantrum. Up and down. I'm real conscious about being glad to be here for all of it. I could get outrageous back at her, but I think about how I want them to remember me.

I think about dying, and I can't stand it.

NICOLE SCHROEDER
Age: 63

"You never have the same degree of trust and security again. Every time the phone rings in the middle of the night, it's the first thing that comes to my mind. Before that we felt we had a charmed existence."

Nicole had six children. Her second child, Ben, died in a mountain-climbing accident nineteen years ago, when he was eighteen. He would be thirty-seven now. Bert is thirty-eight; Hilary is thirty-four; Susan, thirty-three; Richard, twenty-nine; and Laurie, twenty-seven.

Nicole went back to school and completed a graduate degree in counseling when she was fifty and then worked full-time as a therapist.

Ben had earned his own money to buy his climbing boots and things to go West. Howard keeps saying we shouldn't have let him go, but he was eighteen years old, and he didn't require anything from us. He was, of course, right at the peak of his rebellious adolescence and had left home very angry with me, in particular. That made it hard. He wanted to take the truck. I was the one who told him, "No." We just barely had our goodbyes before he left.

He was staying in Oregon with a teacher from prep school. The teacher had climbed in this area where Ben and his friends were going to go camping on this weekend. The teacher said, "There's a rock climb there that is very inviting, but it's really not climbable." He had fallen on it and hurt his back the year before. "It's very dangerous stuff." That's all you need to say to Ben.

The next day Ben and another boy were climbing the place he'd been warned about. According to this other boy, Ben had reached the top and grabbed a bush, and it let go. He fell well over a hundred feet to the rocks. They were not able to retrieve his body for many hours.

We had been up at the lake. It was the last day of Howard's, my husband's, vacation. We had had a lovely day. We'd been on a picnic. I was playing "Clue" with the girls at about four o'clock. Howard said he thought he'd go upstairs and have a nap. He seemed very subdued. I thought, "Well, he's sorry his vacation is over." We had dinner, and then he went home with Hilary and Laurie. I stayed with Susan, because she had a babysitting job across the lake the next morning.

About ten o'clock Howard called and--this has been a thorn in our relationship--he said, "Nicole, come home. Ben's dead." I guess there's no easy way to do it. I would never call somebody and tell them this news. I would call someone else and have them go and be with them. Those words were just emblazoned in my depth for the longest time.

It took us forever to get back from the lake. I was trying to gather together things I might need--totally useless things. Everything felt as if I was walking through mud.

Ben was a real dare-devil. He was a second child, always seeking that number one spot. He was a superb athlete. Bert said, "I can't believe he could have fallen." It was so hard for us to accept. Our boy was so strong and such a good athlete--how could this have happened? Ben did take lots of chances.

We had a terrible time locating Bert in Australia. I got a letter from Bert before he heard. It had been written August 14th. Ben died on the 13th. Bert said they had gone to this waterfall in Australia. On the thirteenth at one o'clock, he had jumped from the top of the waterfall. He said, "Mom, that was the silliest thing I ever did. I really think I could have killed myself." I could have had two boys dead on the same day.

There was one mother who called and said, "I have this great need to call you. My boys liked Ben so much. It seems to me something more compelling . . . I don't know what it is, probably just one mother reaching out to another. I just had this need to call you. If I get clearer about what it is I need to say to you, I'll get in touch again."

Then she wrote, "I think I know now what it is I'm to tell you. I have this message for you from Ben. His death was indeed an accident, and his work is not done. He will be back with your family in the future, possibly as a grandchild."

Then, little Ben was born to Bert on that same date. He doesn't look a thing like Ben, but there's one thing that is so characteristic of Ben--he twiddles his hair in the exact same spot!

At first, this kind of thing was so important to me. I had to believe that Ben's spirit was living on. I became quite mystical. I've always been interested in Eastern religion and the idea of reincarnation. It doesn't seem to be that important now. I sort of feel that Ben's essence is around. I was quite concerned actually when Ben was born on the same day, and Bert, who wouldn't ever let me talk about any of this stuff, came home and said, "God, Mom, this is really eerie. There's something in this."

It feels as if it's a burden on anybody to have to be somebody else. I don't want little Ben to feel that he has an uncle that he has to measure up to. A Jewish friend of mine said, "In my religion this is a great honor, to name someone after somebody that's died that you loved and cared about." That was helpful to me. That we weren't trying to make this little baby into Ben, but we were honoring Ben's memory and that this would be a gift to him, to tell him about his uncle.

We've done some family therapy work in the last two years, and a lot of it still is about letting Ben go. You never ever get over it. Howard says there's not a day that goes by that he doesn't think about him. It's less painful than it was. But we miss him, and think about what it would have been like for him to have his own family.

I think we were so devastated that the other children really felt quite neglected during that time. I remember Hilary said once, "You have to be dead to really matter in this family." That was an eye-opener. She has pushed the family to have some kind of resolution about this. She said she would like to have some kind of ceremony to say "goodbye" to Ben.

I had had breast cancer and was in therapy dealing with that. The counselor asked, "Well, what <u>did</u> you do with Ben's ashes?"

"Nothing. They're sitting on the dresser in our bedroom."

He almost fell out of his chair. He said, "Yes. You need to do something."

At the tenth anniversary of Ben's death, we all got together and had a ceremony at the lake, where we'd had so much of our family time together. We shared some memories and scattered the ashes and planted some plants. Howard and I had a plaque made, which I'm not sure was necessary. It's fastened to a rock there. Susan had expressed a wish to have some place to go when she needed to feel connected with Ben.

We should be saying, "You're all adults now. We haven't been perfect parents, but whatever we've done, we've done with the best intentions. Now you need to make your own way." We need to get on with our own lives and maybe not be so child-centered.

I guess I've learned that there is a big plan that is going to continue and that I, as an individual, don't matter that much. Mothering has sort of prepared me to not be here forever.

MEREDITH JACKSON
Age: 44

"Tom's life was like a firecracker. It came up, bright, splendid. Then it slowly fizzled and went out. I could feel that downhill run."

Meredith is a single parent and a nurse. Her son, Tom, killed himself three years ago, at age eighteen. Her younger son, Kevin, is now eighteen. She almost lost him, as well, as he suffered over losing his brother. Meredith was also suicidal in her grief.

For the last year of his life Tom could not express any feelings except anger. He didn't express loving well, and I don't think he let much loving in. He felt people were angry at him, and a lot of his behavior made sure that they were. His expectations for himself were very high, and, repeatedly, he did not meet his expectations, so he had a tremendous sense of failure. An incredible sense of loss at his father's and my divorce, even though it was five years before. He needed his father a lot.

Certainly his brother was there, and I was, and his therapist was very good. But he was a loner. Even his brother said, "Tom was a funny person. He never really let you know what was going on." They were exceptionally close. Kevin learned how to drink with Tom. Tom taught him how to drive. They did a lot of not-good things, but they were together. They used to climb out the window at night and go trooping through the cemetery together. Normally in adolescence you see a kid wanting to leave this pesky little brother behind, but Tom never did. Yet, Kevin didn't feel he ever really knew Tom.

It was like a roller-coaster out of control, on pretty much a down-hill course. I had this feeling that I was losing him. People would tell me, "You have to let go of him. He's seventeen. He's trying to separate from you." All of that was happening, I know, now that I've been through it with another child, but there was something definitely more profound going on with Tom.

He needed to be hospitalized. I wish that I had done that. Even now I don't know if that would have ultimately prevented him from killing himself. In a hospital he could have been on anti-depressants. He needed to have been on those, but he was drinking so much that they didn't dare to put him on. He wouldn't agree to stop drinking. He could have easily killed himself that way. I can see that I could have regretted that decision. In a hospital he could have had anti-depressants and maybe changed his perception of things and made the corner.

I forget how brilliant he was. World-wise and street-smart. Aware of all levels of things. He read and read and read and whatever he read, he had permanently. As a small child he was effervescent. Well-behaved, bubbly, and quick. He had big, blue eyes, and they just sparkled. He wasn't cuddly, and I was an uptight mother, but he certainly seemed to be loving and outstandingly happy. He had a big grin, and he talked all the time.

Then, when he hit adolescence, it's like a dark side came in. He began to beat Kevin up. I know boys fight. I had no yardstick, because I had a little sister six years younger, and we weren't allowed to be angry. Nothing to draw on. Boys fight, but do they draw blood--frequently? I could see from time to time a look of rage in his eye--he wasn't crazy, he wasn't mentally ill, but that rage could almost make him crazy for a moment. He told me, toward the end, that he'd get so angry at school that he'd think about breaking people's necks. He read how they did it in Vietnam. I asked if it scared him to feel that way. "Yeah," he said,"it scares me a lot."

I felt that to let go when he was doing dangerous things, making bombs--I'd find the gunpowder, and he'd deny it--the therapist said we were in a power struggle.... I could see that we were, but Tom wouldn't let me back up, because he wouldn't stop doing those things. He couldn't stand to not have me angry at him. Now I've seen it with Kevin, with a normal kid. It's easy to get into a power struggle. They will push you to the limit. But I've also seen with Kevin that I can feel myself getting dug in over something, and I'll say, "Hey wait a minute..." and just let go of it. Kevin will let go of it, too. We'd kind of jostle around and say, "That was stupid, wasn't it?" Other times we'd still be pissed about it, but we wouldn't conceal it, and it would go away.

The only way Tom knew to connect was through anger. It's almost like he had that hook in me, and he wouldn't stop. It was as if we were both swinging fast, and then we sped up, and sped up, and then we hit the wall.

Tom made a tape as he drove to Springfield, to kill himself. The last entry was as he was coming over the hill into the town: "I'm really scared, and I'm tired. I don't know if I'm going to do it or not." His voice is flat. He was found two hours later, very dead. So, he acted fairly soon after that entry. He had changed into military garb, put black face paint on, cut twigs to stick in the exhaust, pulled the hose in, ran it in the car window, and fixed the tape, so he could talk. He went through all that preparation, and didn't change his mind.

He put a lot of pictures of himself, me, his father, and Kevin on the dashboard. He had a sense of drama. He was very occupied with dying. He was very frustrated with the frivolity of life, the surface stuff people talk about. He always wanted to be where the essence of life was. I felt that too--when I went into nursing, I wanted to do the most critical nursing. He and I used to talk about that. About the dugout fraternities in Vietnam and how intense that must have been.

He had flipped the tape over. It was blank on the second side. I think he intended to talk as he died. It would have been very like him. But I think he died faster than he thought he was going to.

Tom obviously had planned it for a long time. The letters he left were written in December, and this was in May. He was living with his father at the time. The day that he did it, he and I had had an appointment with his therapist, where he was very, very angry, because I wouldn't let him back into our house. I hadn't seen any behavior changes, and I didn't feel it was safe for me or for Kevin.

Then, he went to school and found out that he was flunking, not just one, but two, subjects. So, he was looking at summer school and not graduating with his class. He went to see the Navy recruiter after school. I think the recruiter told Tom that he wouldn't take him into the Seals, the best part, which is, of course, what he wanted, without a diploma. Tom wrote an essay in school that afternoon about how down he was about the divorce, how he was flunking, and, "Nobody will listen to me. Nobody loves me."

Kevin drank a lot all summer after Tom died. When school started, he deteriorated fast. He was refusing all psychiatric help. I remember him flopping down on the bed beside me with a book and saying, "Mom, this book is incredible." (He never reads.) "This guy is me." He read me a passage about a boy in a mental institution. He was part of his environment. He had no ego boundaries. He was worth nothing. He was a gust of wind. It made my hair stand on end.

The guidance counselor and psychiatrist felt that Kevin was suicidal and should be hospitalized immediately. My ex-husband, Anthony, and I met with the doctor. Then Anthony came to the house, so we could talk to Kevin. I was afraid Kevin would run away. We told him we were both getting help, and he needed help and had a right to help. He could go to the residential program or out-patient therapy, but he had to do one or the other.

Kevin listened, asked a few questions, and said, "Thank you, no. I'm not doing either one." He went into his room and got into his fatigues. Both of my boys always were into military stuff and had a full set of survival fatigues. He curled up in his closet in the fetal position, with an eight-inch Vietnam knife.

I had arranged with a friend that he would come over if we needed muscle. I ran next-door and got him. I called the doctor, who said he would meet us at the hospital. "Remember: he's a minor; you have a right to do this. You can call the police if you need to, and I will sign a release that he's a danger to himself."

Once we told Kevin that we were leaving in ten minutes, he was like a mouse. He changed back into his regular clothes. I was so afraid he was going to bolt out of the car. I told the doctor I wanted him checked every thirty minutes. He's smart, and he'd had a good teacher in his brother. If he escaped, we would never find him.

At the hospital the next day, Kevin showed me the sign-in sheet and said, "Look, I have to sign-in every thirty minutes." Kevin was so scared of what he was going to do. He was <u>mad</u> at us. He was bullshit. It took him weeks to get over that. But he never stopped talking to us. He would yell and scream at me when I went to visit, foul stuff. But he kept communicating, and he was safe.

After about a month, they started planning his discharge. We had family counseling at the hospital once a week, and the counselor was sure she could get Anthony, Kevin's father, to produce some emotions. She didn't succeed. Anthony and Kevin got a little closer, and Kevin was able to say to him, "I feel like you wish I'd died. Tom was your favorite. You preferred Tom."

Kevin did a lot of mental work in the hospital. He said to me: "I love my father, but I don't like him very much."

Now that Kevin's away at school, and Anthony is paying for part of the tuition, there's a symbol of his being invested in Kevin, for the first time. Anthony never paid child support. The boys could understand that love doesn't equate with money, but always resisting spending any money on your kids equates with not-loving. He would never be creative about doing things with them that don't cost money either, like going on picnics. They just sat and watched television.

I didn't realize it, but I had given myself a year to get better. The year anniversary was in May, and, then, Tom would have graduated in June. They were remembering him at graduation, so Kevin and I went. I didn't want Kevin there alone. And I knew a lot of the kids who were graduating. It was very hard, but I felt that it was something I needed to do. Then, I just headed down after that. For the next three weeks, I could stop crying at work, but that was about the only place I could keep it back.

I was totally preoccupied with death. It was almost like death was on my side. I had a boy on either side, and it seemed equal to me. Why was it any more important to be with one than the other? There were a lot of times when I wasn't thinking. I was just sitting. I felt this incredible yearning to be with Tom.

I was going to the cemetery two and three times a day. Crying. I couldn't stop crying. I couldn't sleep. I was losing more and more weight. It's not something you can just cheer up from. I was becoming suicidal. I would think, "What if something happens to Kevin?" Kevin was my only reason to draw my next breath. I'd think through what it would be like if something happened to him, and then that would give me permission to kill myself, because there would be no other reason to live. I knew that I was moving closer to suicide. I was scared. I didn't feel that I was going to do it, because Kevin was still alive.

Finally, in my therapy group I said, "I keep thinking about killing myself."

The therapist asked, "Have you thought about how you'd do it?"

I said, "Yeah, insulin. I'd steal it from work."

I'll never forget the look on his face. It was an incredible relief to have said the words and to have him take me seriously, that I hurt that much. I think he would have hospitalized me at that point except that I had Kevin to take care of. We made a contract that I would call him daily at a specific time. If he didn't hear from me, he would call me. That made me feel very safe.

I started on my second course of anti-depressants. I could sit for hours on my day off. Ruminating. Immobilized. I had a hard time walking and moving. Living in the past. Not sleeping. The pain felt so enormous. There were times when I could feel it coming, and it was like a tidal wave right over my shoulder. I'd try to put it off or hold on, and I'd get a stiff neck, and a backache, and a headache, and diarrhea.

All I could see was the negative. I felt like people didn't like me, people that I knew did like me. "Maybe I'm being hard to get along with. I know I'm not happy, I must be being hard to get along with." You know that awful circling--it chews away at you. Then, taking things wrong. Things that were meant to be jokes, the paranoid thread through them would be hurt. "Are they talking about me? Maybe they think I'm not taking good care of that patient because she had chest pain again." Crazy things, that normally wouldn't cross my mind.

I'm a positive person. I felt like I was going around the bend. I couldn't get rid of that heaviness. As the medication began to work, I didn't go down so far. I'd have moments when I would feel hopeful.

Gradually . . . it's as if someone turns on a light that has a dimmer switch on it. When I came back from that depression I really was on my way to being better.

Before Kevin went off to college this fall, he and I went to the safe deposit box, where Tom's letters are. He sat down and read the letters. When he read, "Nobody will listen to me, nobody loves me," Kevin looked at me.

He said, "You know, I'm sorry, Ma, that's bullshit." Then he said, "You did have people who loved you, Tom."

Coming from Kevin that was great forgiveness for me.

Then, he got further down in the letter. He had forgotten what this letter said... "I'll miss my brother most of all. I love you, Kevin." Kevin started to cry.

Kevin was saying "Goodbye" and moving on with his life. It was kind of a beautiful time, for the two of us to cry there together. Put the letter away and lock it up. "That's bullshit, Tom. Thank you for loving me."

I've always had a career and other interests, but I guess, first and foremost, I've been a mother. When mothers lose children there's that incredible yearning to be with the child, and that incredible sense that part of you has died. The green grows around that dead spot eventually, but the dead spot doesn't ever go away. I think Tom could have had a wonderful future.

When you stand back and look at your life as a continuum, everything kind of shifts in perspective. It doesn't make death fearsome at all, and it makes a lot of things in this life much less important. There's a legion of things I used to worry about and now I think, "So what if that happens?" It just doesn't matter.

I'll take it any way it falls now. There's a sense of power once you move away from it and realize you're doing better than surviving--you're actually living. If you can survive losing a child, they can throw anything at you.

Now, I'm just drinking in the peace and quiet. I feel good, but I feel exhausted. I feel like a dry sponge. Tom is safe. There is nothing I can do for him, except pray for him and have good memories. Having faith in God has helped. For someone who thought there was nothing there, no Being there, to care for that precious person you've lost ... that would be horrible. Kevin is launched, and happy. It's not what I ever thought it would be, and not what I would have hoped, but it's what I have. It's been four or five years of just coping every moment I'm awake.

The house is empty. It is hard to live alone. This chapter of my life is over. When I look ahead I do wonder what I'm going to be for the rest of my life. What course am I going to take? For the first time life feels orderly. There's a richness. It's so paradoxical to hurt that much and be that chaotic and to have this richness now. Anyway, you play the cards you're dealt. If you're lucky, you can find something good about the ones you've got. I do feel very fortunate.

The peace that comes is enormous when you finally reach it.

KATHRYN LONG
Age: 71

"Everything grew out of that grief experience. That was the watershed experience that made me start looking for what it was that I was meant to do."

Kathryn is married to Donald Long and is the mother of three children: Nancy, Marcia, and Eric. She was a full-time, at-home mother until her children were grown. Marcia died at age twenty-eight. Nancy is now forty-nine; Eric, forty-one.

At age fifty-two, in 1973, Kathryn earned her bachelor's degree. This was the same year that Eric earned his bachelor's degree, and Marcia earned a master's degree in sacred music. Kathryn says of Marcia, "I think she thought I was pretty stuffy." After Marcia died of cancer, in 1975, Kathryn began following her own path. She has become more like Marcia.

In 1981 Kathryn completed a Master of Divinity degree and was ordained. For the last several years, she has been directing the pastoral counseling center which she developed and serving on the pastoral staff of her church.

In 1992, at age seventy-one, Kathryn completed her doctorate in pastoral counseling. She recently resigned from her sixty-hour work weeks, to start a private practice.

My three children are all four years apart. I did that intentionally. I am the kind of person who can only handle so much chaos at once. I thought I would have the first one out of diapers and toilet-trained, feeding herself, and maybe even in kindergarten, by the time the second one came along. I wanted to enjoy each one to the fullest before the next one was born. That's about what happened. It was a good choice for me.

I was an only child, and I didn't understand the bedlam of siblings well enough to want to create that, although I was determined to have more than one. I never wanted to do that to anybody again. It was lonely. Every time my mother took to bed for anything I would think, "Please, this time, a little brother or sister," but it never happened.

There are a lot of goodies that happen for an only child, but it was lonely, and I was always in the company of adults. Our dining table was mother, father, grandmother, grandfather, and me. So, that was four big people. And I was a small child-- always at the end of the gym line. I had more things, more attention, as the only one. I also had to live out everybody's hopes and expectations of who I would be and what I would become.

Nancy, my oldest, was a World War II baby. Her father, Donald, was in Europe until she was almost three, so he didn't even know what it was like to have a child, nor she to have a father. There was some difficulty with both of them vying for my presence and my attention, until they got used to each other.

With Marcia, the second one, everything went more easily. Not so much anxiety about doing everything right as there had been with the first one. Marcia was, from the beginning, creative and independent, always thinking of something to do and be.

Then, our third one was a boy. Eric was very different from either of the girls in his male activity. Right from the beginning--running, climbing. The girls had never done that.

It's hard to learn things later and look back on what you would have done differently. I came into motherhood at the time that the behavior of new mothers was very directive. Rigid. I got a baby nurse to come in. She was of the school that you let the baby cry. Everything was on a schedule. The feedings came at ten, two, six, and ten. If they cried for three hours, you still waited for the clock. I would never let a baby cry like that again, waiting for a bottle.

I didn't have babysitters. When they were in school, I had to be home every day to feed them lunch. I went to the school once and said, "Wouldn't there be some way that some of these children could eat lunch at school?"

I got the tongue-lashing of my life from the principal: "You just don't want to do a responsible job with your children."

I remember going home thinking that I was a terrible person for even thinking such a thing. So, there were twelve years when I couldn't go very far away from the home.

The mothering of each of my children was very different, and each was important in its own way. Nancy has become my best friend as well as a daughter. Marcia helped bring about the most visible changes in my lifestyle and professional life. Eric is beginning to show his parents his heritage of love in the way he treats his wife and children, in his fathering, and in his work. I am so grateful for these two children who are still so active in Donald's and my life.

When Marcia came home in 1974 she and her husband Dennis lived here in our house, until she died a year later. She would not talk to me about death. It felt like protection, a protection that I accepted at the time. But, she would talk to her father. The first thing that she did was go out in the row-boat with her father and say, "Dad, I've come home to die. Can you take that?" They had, I guess, a wonderful conversation about the meaning of life and death. Getting real close to ultimate issues.

But, she never mentioned death to me. She and I would sit out on the deck side by side. She would nap. She wasn't able to do much that was active toward the last. I would sit there and knit. We would talk surface things, neither one of us knowing, apparently, how to deepen it, in the way that she could do that with Donald.

I regret that I didn't get to participate in that kind of sharing. There were times when she wanted to talk about death with the people she could do it with, and then there was me. I'm trying to remember now what she did with her sister and brother. I don't know if I was the only one left out.

That has a lot to do with what I do in my work, now. I do a lot of grief and loss work with people who are going to die soon or who have just lost a spouse or a child. There is no one that I work with now that I don't raise the point with. If there isn't open conversation at home, I will tell my little story.

Sometimes they will say, "That just isn't the way our family works," and there seems to be nothing you can do about that.

I ask them, "Will you be glad later that you stayed with the family rule, or will you wish that you had broken it?"

I think it all has to be dictated by the person that is dying. You really shouldn't force anything on them that they don't want.

Marcia died in October of 1975, seventeen years ago, very suddenly. Donald and I had gone out to an evening wedding, and when we got home, she was gone. We left her with Dennis, watching T.V. and eating dinner. Something just happened, just like that. When we got home at ten or eleven, Dennis had had the ambulance. She had gone to the hospital. She had died, and he was with her. He had stayed with her for quite some time and then had come home. He was here to greet us when we came in. It was a shock. A terrible shock, even though she had been sick.

I think I did a lot of denying at the beginning. That very initial numb stage lasted a longer time. It's like everything hits you and bounces off for a while. You actually live as if it didn't happen. Not that you don't believe that it happened, but there's some kind of protection. I think that's natural and God-given. That protection is necessary at the beginning. Without it I think people would just go down. Worse than ever.

I got so angry about all that stuff about God's will. People were writing things to me about "God wanted her for his little garden in heaven," or "God takes those that he loves best." The God I worship wouldn't do things like that. It really cemented my theology, along with the coursework I was doing. If you follow that line of reasoning, it gives you a pretty vengeful God-- that would decide to make us suffer. My theology includes a lot of chance accidents. Tumors are accidents of nature, I think. Something went wrong, but it wasn't God's doing.

People say that Grandma, Donald's mother, was getting senile. She didn't die until she was ninety-six, but she used to see Marcia standing at the foot of her bed. She would describe her in minute detail. "She came last night, and she talked to me. She had on the prettiest yellow nightgown." She'd tell us everything Marcia said. Well, maybe so. We're on this plane of reality, but there's another and another. Maybe Marcia is on one of those. How do we know?

Donald and I didn't talk about Marcia's death. Neither of us knows what the other went through. The stages of Elisabeth Kubler-Ross's grieving were very helpful to me. It's not orderly. But they all happened sooner or later: shock, denial, bargaining, anger, depression, and finally, resolution and acceptance. They were all mixed up together.

I guess it was all the way to the next year in June that I was kind of floundering around, trying to come out of my own grief. I decided to do chaplaincy training at the hospital, as a lay person. It was a little soon. It was very soon. I had nowhere near resolved my own grief. But it was like I was propelled. I felt this great need to go out and do something. I don't know if that came just from the grief, or from the guilt feelings that I had from not being able to do the sharing. I was propelled to enter that program, not knowing what in the world I was doing. I knew that I was following some direction.

That training was a very intensive time. It felt right. It was right, but it was exhausting. When I came out of it, I knew that I would do something in ministry.

Everything grew out of that grief experience. That was the water-shed experience that made me start looking for what it was that I was meant to do now. I had an empty nest by that time. I always knew that I was going to get more education, but I didn't know in what.

The path got clearer. In 1977, the new minister took me to lunch one day and said, "I'd like you to come to work for me."

I said, "Me? Doing what?"

He outlined the parish care program that he wanted developed.

I said, "How could I be the one to do this? Who says so?"

"Everyone who knows you says so."

In the same year the pastoral counseling rector offered to give me some training. Dennis, Marcia's husband, had already taken me to the center when he was counseling couples. He had introduced me to these couples as his "co-counselor." He'd tell me just to say whatever came into my mind. "You'll say the right thing," he said.

I said, "I don't think I can do this." But, I did.

Four years later, after completing the master's degree of divinity, in 1981, I was ordained. The parish care and the counseling developed side by side. Then, there were eleven years of actually doing ordained ministry, in parish work, and, finally, I ended up running the counseling center, becoming a pastoral counselor, and moving away from parish work.

Once one of my religion professors said, "I'll tell you how it is with me. I am walking on a path. It is like flagstones. I am stepping one to the next. About five or six flagstones down the way, they go off into the fog. I can't see where they're going. But I have never been misled yet, when I consult my own deepest spiritual core." I can look back now and tell you what the steps were, but nothing was clear really until it had almost happened.

I look at those stepping stones that were going off into the fog. Now I know where they were all going. I am amazed. It's kind of incredible to think that it was all leading somewhere, very logically. When I was getting my bachelor's degree, I thought I was going to major in English and be a teacher. A professor said to me, "Do, now, what you like." When I took a philosophy of religion course, I knew that that was what I wanted to study. I got the bachelor's degree in 1973. That was such a big moment. It's all a big marvel to me that it happened. All the right people in the right places. It's always been little miracles fitting together.

You asked me about Marcia's death. I'll say a few more things about Marcia's life.

She was an inspiration. When she first went to graduate school and found Dennis, I was suddenly aware, from the things they were doing around the Vietnam War, of how stultified my culture was here in Connecticut. There was a group of women in the church who were all about my age. All of them had it figured out that they knew exactly how to do everything, and everybody better do it that same way.

301

When my daughter called to tell me she was going to go to Washington to protest and take bandages to the wounded, I was terrified. "Oh, you're not, please."

My so-called best friend said, "How could you let her do such a thing? You should have stopped her." These women were hitting me from all sides that this was a very unconventional daughter I had.

While she was planning her wedding, I was at a dinner party one night. They asked me to talk a little bit about her wedding. I said it was going to be in Seattle.

"Not here in your own church?!"

"No."

"Well, you should have insisted."

Then, I told them it was going to be a pot-luck reception. I thought they would flip out! Which is what it was, you know, everybody brought a pot of food. Luckily, they had sunshine. They forgot to have any forks, but we had all these pots of food. I don't remember how that one was solved!

When Marcia called, she said, "Dad, will you please bring the wine, but you can buy that here, and Mom, will you please bring eight loaves of banana bread? That's all you have to bring." I said, "Boy, this is the best reception yet!" Nancy had had the traditional works.

Marcia was really something else. I was challenged on every side with that child. I cherish that. That's made me the nut that I am now. I am more like her . . . I think she lives on a little bit in me.

Her one bow to tradition was that she wore my wedding gown. She came home, and we fitted it. In the meantime, Dennis was making leather pants . . . I can see them. The morning of the wedding he was sewing on the fly buttons. "Do you think these will look okay?"

"I hope they hold throughout the wedding." Everything was just so unconventional.

Everything was always different with her. Everything that I ever objected to that she did turned out to be right. Like protesting the Vietnam War. I didn't know then, but I know now, that that was right on. Marcia and Dennis chained themselves to the draft-board doors, protesting the draft. She got locked up in jail for that. It appeared in the paper, with her picture. She sent me that publicity. It was wild. I don't think she did anything really destructive, where you could say it wasn't right to do.

The unconventional side of life suddenly became okay. I saw the rightness of so many of the principles that they were protesting for or against. Absolutely on target. She taught me that.

Marcia did a lot of living in twenty-eight years. She was a great teacher.

6

Mothers and Fathers

Before two people become parents, they are partners. When they become parents, each is tacitly agreeing to share their partner with a child. The energy that has gone back and forth between the mother and father is suddenly drawn in the direction of the child. A lot of the mother's energy heads for that baby. Will she still be sending a lot over to the father? Where will he be sending his energy--to the mother, to the baby, to both mother and baby, or somewhere else? Somehow, he often seems to have more choice about where his energy goes than the mother does.

The arrival of a child requires each parent to reveal herself or himself more fully. Styles and preferences, assumptions and expectations, conflicts and uncertainties appear. The temporary, initial stress of a new baby has the effect of a drought on a lake: everyone gets to see what has been under the surface all along.

One father has been assuming that rather than their hiring a babysitter, he will watch the baby, himself, while his wife finishes graduate school. Another father, a lawyer, brings work home, in a pinch, and works at the kitchen table while he holds the baby. A third father finds being a father and a husband is more than he'd bargained for, so he leaves, permanently.

One mother finds she is responsible for everything, especially the feeding, bathing, and dirty diapers, unless her husband chooses to do something. Another mother finds that she must constantly evaluate and adjust her expectations and her husband's, so that he--and she--do not somehow end up valuing her less as a person, now that she is primarily a mother.

Not least of what is revealed by the low level of the lake is a fuller picture of each partner's personality. For better or for worse, each partner sees the other interacting with the child. Each parent sees the other's capacities for patience, self-discipline, wonder, and frustration.

The arrival of the first child has a significant impact on the parents' social life. If they are to go out together, they must either take the child or make arrangements to leave the child with someone. The need for good baby-sitters can become as chronic as the need to have peanut butter in the cupboard. Then, if the parents stay out late, with or without the child, they will probably pay dearly for the hours of lost sleep, for sleep has become a precious commodity which at least one partner may now value more than dinner out, new clothes, or sex.

New parents have less time together than they used to, because of the baby's demands, but in some ways they may also have time at home, together, that they didn't used to choose to have. "Let's not bother with a sitter. Let's just get a movie and stay home."

The initial stress passes. The lake fills again. Negotiations between mother and father continue. Changes are made and are followed by more changes. One child may be joined by another.

Supper time is often a barometer of a family's style--or their stage in life. When children are little and tired and their blood sugar level has just crashed, whoever is getting supper may feel like giving away the fussy little appendages that hang on any available arm or leg. This can easily be the worst part of a long day. When children are older--but before they are old enough to be working and socializing elsewhere--supper can more easily be a civilized occasion.

Does each person fend for himself and catch calories on the run? Or, is this a family that tries to make supper a time to come together, to get caught up? Is someone missing? Why? Is this a family where everyone's voice can be heard? Is it a family where children from other families are comfortable visiting, or even a family to which they're drawn? Is this a family where everyone is nourished as they all sit down together?

At best, over time, parenting with a partner becomes like dancing, or paddling a canoe. You have to work out the leading and the following, the right and the left. You make more headway when you work together, whether you're on the open lake or in the rapids. Pulling together. Teamwork. Grace.

KARINA LOPEZ
Age: 24

"With my schedule, I was planning to have a baby-sitter. Ray said, 'No. I don't think the baby should be taken care of by a baby-sitter. I will take care of the baby.'"

Karina is Mexican-American. Her father and mother immigrated to this country when Karina was eleven. Karina and her husband Ray, who is Irish, are the parents of Connor, who is five months old. Karina and Ray's relationship has improved since they became parents. Karina resists a lot of pressure from her father to raise her son in traditional "Spanish ways."

I like having a baby. It's really beautiful. Babies get so attached to their mother. He always wants to be with me. He knows that I am his mother, you know?

I go full-time to school--for pharmacy. This is my last year, the fifth year. Most of the time my husband is taking care of the baby. When I graduate, he will go back to work as an accountant. He likes to take care of the baby. I tell him, "You take better care of him than I do."

Before I had the baby, Ray would never help. Most of the time, he would never be at home. When I got pregnant, he still wasn't with me. I used to go to my appointments alone. He wasn't paying attention. When the baby was born, he got totally devoted to the family. Everywhere we go, he always is saying now, "This is my family." When Ray said, "I will take care of the baby." I was glad. It's much better for the baby than with a babysitter.

My parents restricted my sister and me to a Spanish background. They always had the last word on our decisions. Even when I got married, my father decided for my reception.

Ray and I gave Connor a little doll. The doll is a little boy. Connor loves that doll.

My father said, "Take that away from him. He shouldn't be having that doll."

"He likes it."

"I don't care what he likes. You have to make him . . . don't give him dolls. Give him rifles and trucks."

Right there I noticed he is already trying to impose on the baby. I told my father, "No. Connor enjoys that little doll. He is going to have it."

Mexicans tell little boys, "You are a little man. Behave like one." That's the way it is. Little girls are allowed to cry and go to Mommy, but little boys don't do that.

My mother wants me to be very Spanish-like, but I told her, "Connor cannot just go one way. He has to share with his other grandparents." I like my in-laws a lot, and I spend a lot of time with them.

My father told me, "Don't let your in-laws impose on the baby. You have to do it your way." Even Connor's clothes, my father wants him to wear all blue and very rough clothes.

I dress the baby in baby clothes! Very gentle. Very soft. Pastel colors. My father thinks my mother-in-law is so close to me, she is trying to tell me what to do. But it's not that. It's just that's the way we like it! I was telling him, "Why can't Connor be just a regular baby?"

I've become more independent. My parents don't bother me as much as before! I never was scared of my parents, but I was always watching. I was very careful not to offend them. Now, if I have something to say, I just say it very clearly. When it comes to my baby, I don't want them telling me what to do. I told them their duty was me, and now my duty is him.

Ray adores his mother. His mother is all the way to the top for him. She is a very nice lady, but she can be stubborn. He knows that, but he adores her. I was thinking, "I wonder if the baby is going to adore me like that?"

In my culture, unfortunately, I haven't met a man who adores his mother as much as my husband does. In my culture, when boys are thirteen, fourteen, the mother gets detached.

When the sons spend a lot of time with their father, right there, the father is telling the son, "You have to spend more time doing your own things. Don't do housework. Don't help your mother." Once they are that age, they get a totally different view of women, and that changes their views about the mother. They don't want to be with the mother. They don't like to show their feelings, be affectionate.

If I had married a man in my own culture, I would be expecting to lose my son.

MARYANN TROCHEK
Age: 32

"It could get more stressed for Jim and me later. I'll be going back to work when Gina's six months old."

Maryann is savoring her maternity leave from full-time work for a utility company. Her return to work will change both her and her husband Jim's interaction with their two-month-old daughter Gina.

When Gina's sleeping I have to go see what she looks like. I have this person now that I want to see forever.

I've sort of fallen in love with my husband Jim again. I love seeing him with her. He was ambivalent about having her. I was the one that was gung-ho. If I had any ambivalent feelings, he got freaked out: "You're the one who's supposed to be really ready. I'm the one that's scared, and I don't know how to deal with you being scared, too." He still feels some ambivalence about the changes in our lives and the fact that we don't have a lot of time for each other, but with her he's just like a puppy. I knew he would be, but he didn't.

Right now, I basically do most of the child-care. He doesn't feed her, and he doesn't feel comfortable bathing her. He won't do dirty diapers. When I go back to work, that's going to have to change. He's just not going to come home to this smiling, clean, smell-free baby. Suddenly, he's going to have to pick her up from day-care. One of us will do one end of the day, and the other will do the other.

She is already exhibiting a preference for me, and that's hard for him. It's hard for me, because every time I leave the house I'm wondering if she's going to be screaming, because I'm not there. I don't want to be totally responsible for her.

I'm really not thinking about getting ready to go back to work. I know I should start looking for a baby-sitter. I'm putting it off. I will miss a lot. I'll miss her best times of each day. She's not going to coo at ten o'clock at night just because I'm home then. But, I also choose to work. I've had my own money for a long time, and I don't want to have Jim giving me money to pay my bills.

I think it will be important for Gina to see that her mother is more than her mother. My mother worked, and I never resented it, although her job was very flexible, which helped. She was there when she could be, but we were independent, too. I'd like that for my kids.

Also, I've been divorced, and I feel that you have to have a way to take care of yourself, in the event of divorce or death.

ELLEN DANIELS
Age: 35

"I am trying to figure out what I can have. How much can I be a mother, and how much can I still be a professional? How do I deal with the change in status and income? It makes a difference in my relationship with Julius."

Ellen was adopted from Korea as a one and a half-year-old baby. She has no baby pictures of herself.

Fourteen months ago, Ellen gave birth to Martin. Being a mother herself has given Ellen connections with her birth mother which she never had, and she can now give to her son in ways that her mother did not give to her.

Ellen is juggling home and work. She struggles not to feel diminished as she reduces her professional work hours. She and her husband Julius are constantly renegotiating power issues, as he continues to make good money and her life is disrupted by Martin's needs.

Julius and I got married in the midst of my thesis for graduate school. He was in a bigger hurry to have children than I was. It had taken me a long time to figure out what I was supposed to do in life. I had finally earned something, a master's degree in social work, and wanted a chance to work in my profession, as he had been doing for a few years already. It was very hard for me to make the decision to have a child, knowing what I was giving up. In our relationship, because my husband is in finance and will always make four times what I do, I was the one who was going to be making most of the sacrifices around what having a baby meant for our life.

But, I wanted to get pregnant. For the first time in my life, I realized how important it would be to have somebody who was biologically connected to me. I used to fantasize vaguely about my birth mother. If people said, "Do you think about her?," mostly I would say, "Yeah, but I can't imagine her as a real person." Being pregnant made me think about what it might have been like for her to be pregnant with me.

Every day, at a certain time of the day, when I was pregnant, the baby would get hiccups! I talked to the baby even before he was born. I held him as an infant. I couldn't even begin to imagine things like these before they happened to me. Now, I have that connection with her.

I began really imagining what it would have been like for this woman to have an infant and to lose that infant. Incomprehensible. There's a part of me that I lock deep down inside myself, a part that gets terrified to think that anything could happen to my child.

But I feel very fortunate to have all this with Martin. It's wonderful. One little person can make such a difference in your life! Martin is such a mix of Julius and me. He definitely looks Asian, but he's a blend. It's really neat to see someone who looks something like me. I grew up in a family where no one looked like me. That was very painful. Here is this little guy, and he's part me.

Having a child is a mixed bag. It's a struggle, because I'm a mother with a career. I am trying to figure out what I can have. How much can I be a mother, and how much can I still be a professional? How do I deal with the change in status and income? It makes a difference in my relationship with Julius. It makes a difference in how I feel about what I'm doing.

I love being with Martin, playing, and watching him become a person. But after an hour and a half of playing, I'm bored. Right now, he's become more clingy. It's hard to even make dinner at the end of the day, when he's tired, and I'm tired. He needs to be picked up, and I'm frustrated, because I can't get anything done.

Or, when he's napping, do I get my clinical notes finished, or do I take a nap? If I decide to take the nap, I feel rested, but then I feel like I'm not on top of things. Even though I'm only seeing a very small number of clients right now, I'm trying to juggle.

The differences that my husband and I have worked through constantly come up and have to be renegotiated. I need to feel that I'm still a valuable person. What we say has to be what we really mean, in terms of how much power I have in the relationship. A lot of power in relationships comes from income. My husband and I have an agreement that our money is both of ours. Except when you come down to it, when he has to go out and spend five hundred dollars for a suit for work, he does. If I need to spend five hundred dollars ... I would never, ever spend five hundred dollars! Those undercurrents cause a lot of conflict.

When I lose my work identity, it's very difficult to feel valuable. Motherhood is wonderful, but even I sometimes think that it's second-rate, because it doesn't get priorities in places in the world. How do I get a little bit of what I want? I cut my job back to eliminate some of the stress, but it created stress in other ways: sometimes I'm going out of my mind at the end of the day. I would like to get my hours up to about fifteen a week.

There is irrational stuff that causes resentments and arguments. We're very rational when we sit down and talk about it, but when we're both tired at the end of the day, and he says, "Can I at least have five minutes to get dressed?," I am saying, "No, you can't. I couldn't get showered until eleven o'clock today."

Julius is actually a wonderful father. Martin adores Julius. Julius is the one who does the raucous playing. The joke is: here's Mom, the chopped liver, and Dad comes home, and Martin is beside himself. And I help set that up, too, because I want him to be excited when Dad gets home. Julius and I will both walk in the room, and Martin will walk right by me to his Dad.

We both want to have at least one more child, if we can hang in there! I'm thrilled about Martin, but I really want a daughter. I know what is going to happen with Martin. I'm the more serious parent. Martin will always adore Julius. Julius will always play with him. Julius will always probably be less tough on him than I will be.

Women and men have different worlds. I enjoy a woman's world. There is something about having a daughter, to have that bond, to share that world. I can't imagine, even in the closest relationship with a son, that you can have that same bond.

CHARLOTTE NEWMAN
Age: 41

Somehow Charlotte and her husband came apart as a couple when they became parents. He left nine months ago. Their daughter Trina is now three. Charlotte has Trina most of the time and finds mothering overwhelmingly difficult. She wasn't planning on doing this job alone.

I think that my marriage started to deteriorate right after my daughter was born. I was overwhelmed by being a mother. I was so exhausted physically, mentally, and emotionally that I didn't have the energy to give to my husband, for a good year and a half, two years. I just didn't have the energy, and I wasn't interested in sex.

When he came home at the end of the day from his job, I just . . . It was, "Here's the kid." From his perspective, he'd just gotten home from a long day at work. But I needed a break from what I had been doing.

He got angry at me. I think he felt rejected, and he withdrew. I got angry at his withdrawal. Unfortunately, he wouldn't talk about it. Either he was not in touch with his feelings, or his way of expressing his anger was, "I'm not going to talk about it." So, we just stopped communicating.

Before there was a child, I could lavish all of my excess attention on him. After the baby came, I couldn't give him the same amount of attention and affection. I wanted him to understand where I was coming from. I tried to tell him, "It's my problem. I'm not rejecting you. But it's our problem. It's a life situation problem."

Especially the sexual aspect of it. Being physically tired at the end of the day, but not just that. Having spent ten hours of the day with a baby in my arms, I didn't need or want any more physical affection. Nor did I want to give it anymore. That part of me was drained. After giving to this child all day long, I had nothing else to give, and I didn't want to give anything else. I wanted someone to give me something.

ALISSA RUTCLIFF
Age: 41

"Mothers are not sexy people."

Alissa and her husband Grant divide the family roles fairly traditionally, with Alissa doing most of the child-care. She is reasonably content with this, but is adamant that she will not have the third child that he wants. Alissa works only part-time now, as a counselor. Grant is a lawyer.

Their daughter Naomi is seven, and son Billy is four.

For the first year or two of having Naomi, things were so stressful that Nick and I went into very stereotypical roles. We had been trained for those roles, and while we had made an effort to share more, as soon as the going got tough, we went into those roles, because it was the easiest thing to do. I've somewhat come to peace with that.

My husband really wasn't committed to an egalitarian lifestyle. I think I knew that ahead of time. What I was looking for was not so much a man who would do it fifty-fifty, as a man who would be emotionally available to me, a man who's very verbal and willing to talk about his feelings, willing to sit down and talk about problems.

Also, my father was an entrepreneur; he had his own business. We were on the edge financially, and I knew I wanted someone who was more predictable. It wasn't that I wanted him to make a lot of money. I just didn't want fluctuations.

In the beginning I used to call Grant up and say, "Come home, because I'm going to go crazy! I don't care what you're doing, bring it home, and pick this baby up, and hold him." For six months Billy could not be put down. He had to be in

319

someone's arms--for six months. I can still see Grant sitting at our table, bent over, working, with the baby in his arms.

The physical drain of having a baby--I just could not go through that again. My husband is so upset. He wants another child so badly. He's grieving for this. There's not going to be another baby, unless it's by mistake. I can't tolerate another whole year of no privacy, watching my child's every move. Some women like that closeness and someone needing them that much. I don't. The more kids I have in a room, the more incapacitated and spaced out I become. I couldn't imagine not nursing. It just seems like, the baby comes, you put it on your breast. My mind and my body are so connected that I had to be obsessive about what I ate, what I drank. I had to sleep every afternoon, or there wasn't enough milk. I'm going to be forty-two years old--I can't go through that again.

I was astounded at how my life completely, totally, utterly changed, and how my husband's life looked very much the same every day. He would get up, and get dressed, and go to work, and I'd be in disarray--in the early years. My husband said, "There's nothing I can do about that. This is the reality. I'm a lawyer, and I need to work a certain number of hours a week." That's true.

As soon as I got pregnant I lost interest in sex. I wanted to relate to Grant. I think we're a lot closer today than ever. I wanted to talk with him, share with him, be with him, but I didn't want him to touch me. It's sort of hard to be sexual when you don't want to be touched!

He couldn't believe it, because I used to be the exact opposite. But when we go away for the weekend, we have <u>no</u> problem, which is very reassuring. We've just recently gotten into going away.

We've got the interest back, but there's the feeling that the kids are <u>right</u> <u>there</u>. When I'm in the home, I'm such a mother, and mothers are not sexy people. They just aren't. If we're in a hotel, it's like being on our honeymoon again.

There are a lot of things that are difficult, but I love having these other people in my life.

GRACE BENSON-JAMES
Age: 43

"I said, 'But I'm the biological Mom, and I should have more say.'

She said, 'That doesn't mean anything.'

I was floored."

Grace, a psychologist, and her partner Marcia, a teacher, are lesbians. They live outside Worcester, Massachusetts. Six years ago they decided to have a child together by artificial insemination. Their son Russell is now five. Grace is Russell's biological mother.

Grace and Marcia have been in a lot of conflict about how to parent Russell, and, within the last year, have split up.

This is a story of two mothers who are competing over their child.

We decided I would have the baby, because I was older and had a lot of "baby-hunger," I guess you'd call it. When it was time to actually do it, Marcia was more eager to go. I wanted to, but I began to feel how heavy it was, how important it was, and that we were not a traditional couple.

When I first got pregnant, we were sort of quiet about it. We told some of our friends. Some of them are lesbians. They were really shocked that we had done it. We began to realize that we are sort of pioneers.

We went out for Marcia's birthday the night before I had Russell. She said she didn't want anything to change in our relationship. I had this sort of sinking feeling that it was already too late, that things were changing pretty dramatically. I think that Marcia was feeling that I was going to cleave to the child, and we'd be a symbiotic unit, and she'd be left out.

That did begin to happen. I can remember feeling really sad and exhausted. We were excited about having Russell, but it was overwhelming, too. It was like being in a fog. It was so much more all-encompassing than we ever expected it to be.

Marcia was very focused on Russ. She didn't want to get a babysitter for him, so we could do things together as a couple. We both bonded with Russell as moms and sort of set up that primary dyad. The couple relationship began to evaporate.

We got into conflict about ways of dealing with Russell. Marcia is a very organic, natural foods sort of person: "You have to breast-feed. You <u>have</u> to breast-feed as long as you can." She was hung up on me doing everything just right. She would focus on things that I wasn't doing well. I wasn't being as attentive as she felt I should be. Marcia would do a lot of the care-giving things better than I did. I began to defer to her in some ways. For example, I was sort of phobic about giving him a bath. She still washes his hair, and I don't usually wash his hair. He got ear infections, and she really didn't like him to be on antibiotics. She began to explore homeopathic medicine and wanted to go with it all the way.

I wanted him to learn to sit at the table. We both didn't want him to watch a lot of TV, but then she'd wind up letting him eat in front of the TV. She doesn't want to make him do something he doesn't want to do.

There were some ways in which I was indulgent. Bed-time. She would want to put him to bed, give him a bottle, read him a story, and leave. I would go in, and read him a story, and just lay down with him until he went to sleep. Marcia felt he was going to get dependent on me, and, then, in the nights when she had him, she wouldn't be able to get him to go to sleep. She didn't want to lay down with him for a half-an-hour. I really enjoyed that time and didn't want to give it up.

I wanted him to do things when I expected him to. She felt, "He'll do it when he does it." Now he has a speech and language delay. I think he's delayed in several areas. I think some of it has to do with our conflict. Some of it has to do with the fact that in the last few years her forms of caring for him have prevailed over mine. If I began to get stern with him, and she came in and rescued him, then, I had to fight both of them. He's very oppositional towards me. Some of it is because I'm stricter. Some of it is the dynamic that he experienced until we separated, which was that he could fight back at me, and Marcia would come to his support, and he would win.

At times, I lost my temper. I began to yell at Russ and reprimand him. Marcia did modify some of my anger and impatience. Through seeing things that she did, I began to soften my way, although certainly not to her liking. She would accuse me of being abusive, when I would be trying to discipline him. She couldn't tolerate my getting angry at him.

I felt guilty that I had had the child. Marcia was sad that she didn't have the child, and she experienced a loss of me also. I wanted to compensate, or give her more of him or something, as a way of making it okay. I felt like I had to give in, in order for us to stay together. Early on, I couldn't risk her leaving.

Somehow there was an emotional turning in me when I had Russell. I said, "I am going to take charge of my life, and I'm going to start doing what I want, not what other people want." I began to feel, "This is really something big, and I want to be the best person I can be for him." That means living the kind of life that I can be proud of, instead of always trying to please people and not asserting myself. I think Marcia's and my relationship had been based on my being more acquiescent in certain ways. I started standing up for myself.

I began to feel worse and worse about the three of us. I thought I could just accept the situation the way it was, though, and that that would be better for Russell than if we split up.

Marcia couldn't accept that. She had turned thirty-five. Having another child was the key issue. I finally told her that it would not be my choice to have another child, but I would help her. She didn't want to do it on that basis. She began to think about getting into another relationship. I was supportive of that, because I felt that if she didn't have another relationship to go to, she wouldn't leave me and Russell. I was not going to let her leave with Russell.

We separated right after his fourth birthday.

When we decided to split up, she wanted Russell. He's very connected with Marcia. Over the years I sort of backed off in order to maintain my relationship with Marcia. I sort of lost him. She wanted to stay in our house and wanted the woman she had gotten involved with to move in. I was to get a place in town. She felt she was the primary parent, and she should have him, because he was more connected with her than with me. I was outraged!

I wanted to have Russell most of the time. I would stay in the house with him, or move out <u>with</u> <u>him</u>. We locked horns. Then, she said she would accept a fifty-fifty arrangement. I said the kid had to have a home-base with one parent or the other. It wasn't going to be her.

She wants to have equal power in deciding things for him. Whether it's right or wrong, as his biological Mom, I feel I have more privilege in this. I don't want him to bounce back and forth like a yo-yo between us. I want him to be <u>settled</u> with me and have time with her. She keeps acting as if she's as entitled as I am. Way back when he was six months old, we were trying to make a decision, and I said, "But I'm the biological Mom, and I should have more say."

She said, "That doesn't mean anything."

I was floored.

Our couples therapist told us she felt that Marcia was the primary parent and that I should concede. That was very painful for me. She said that I was the dad, and Marcia was the mom.

I finally told Marcia that I had had it. She wasn't going to have the kind of power over Russell that she had had, anymore. I conceded to give her equal time with him, if she would give me more power over decision-making. I'm beginning to reestablish myself in his life, because I have my own time with him now. There isn't any interference or competition from her.

Russell knows he has two mommies. He knows that most people have a mommy and a daddy. About a year and a half ago, Marcia's brother was visiting, and Russell really got into being with him. He told me that he wanted Ron to be his daddy. I said that Ron couldn't be his daddy, that he didn't have a daddy. I explained to him Ron was his uncle, that a daddy was someone who had a baby with a mommy, and Ron didn't have him with me, that Mommy Marcia and I had the baby.

Then he said, "Well, I don't really want a daddy."

I think that as he moves into kindergarten and first grade, he's going to hit the wall. I think he'll get very upset. He's going to miss having a daddy. I think he'll balance out about it. I suspect it will come up again in adolescence. I think Russ's pretty secure in his own identity, in his maleness. I think he'll be fine. I don't think it's a big problem. Lots of dads disappear and actually do a worse number by abandoning their kid. But I can't pretend it will be the same as having a dad around.

Right after he was born, I finally got it. I felt like I had really put a load on him. I felt terrible. I felt sad for him. But, by God, I'm going to be the best that I can be and do well by him.

THERESA LAZZARONI
Age: 42

"I remember showing up at the school once and realizing the teachers didn't even know who I was. The phantom mother."

Both Theresa and her husband are Italian and Roman Catholic. They live in the state of Washington, where they own a gourmet cooking store together. Three years ago, they adopted twin Korean daughters who were six months old. Theresa and Len are both fully involved in raising Kim and Jill.

You have to take risks. We were already playing Russian roulette with fertility drugs. I had a dream that I went into labor and bundles started coming out, one inside the other. Finally, there were four little bundles. I unwrapped the first one, and there was a roasting chicken. The second one was a chicken, and the third one was a chicken. The fourth one was a beautiful little Asian baby that was just like a two-year-old I knew.

I was afraid of birth-defects, multiple-births. You agree to run those risks when you become pregnant at my age. It wasn't too difficult a step to go from that to adoption. You take a risk no matter what you do. Adopting these girls has been the most perfect situation for us.

We flew to Korea to pick them up. The babies were with nice people, foster-mothers in private homes. The mothers would get together, and the babies would play together. I felt so inadequate when I met them! "Help! We need help. These women know my children better than I do." We were in Korea for a week, and it was a sixteen-hour flight home.

Our feeling of inadequacy was intense. We took a couple weeks off after we got back from Korea. We had company for about a month. Then the company left, and Rob had to go back to work. I remember the first afternoon when I had to feed them. I was trying to set them up in those little reclining chairs and feed them both at the same time. They weren't quite able to hold the bottles. It was horrible.

I was a teacher in a Montessori school when we got the girls. I had to continue with my job. Rob was able to work half-time. We were able to stagger our schedules, so that we had the babysitter a couple hours a day, at the most.

It was frustrating, because it was very difficult to give undivided attention to Kim or Jill. I did wonder what it would be like to have only one. I never wanted to have only one, because they are so dear and wonderful, and they have sort of a third personality when they're together. I did long to have periods of undivided attention with one child or the other. In a way, once in a while we would get that, because their sleeping was horrendous, and one or the other would be up in the middle of the night. We'd have a nice long period at three a.m. with just one.

Now, we own and operate this store. We have to be here at least six days a week. Not full-time necessarily. Rob might take the children, and I'm in the store. It's often both of them with one of us. Time alone as a couple is something we always have to work at.

It's been really hard always having to do outside work while I have children. When I'm at work, I'm distracted by thinking of the children. I have this feeling that I should be doing more with my kids. At home, I'm distracted by my work. First, as a teacher, I was used to doing a lot of preparation at home. After we got the girls, I always felt that I was giving short shrift to my career. Here, at the store, which can consume any amount of energy that you give it, I try not to resent that the business is taking time away from the girls.

On the other hand, the fact that we have children has probably kept me more grounded, and kept a perspective on what I'm doing in the store, because the children are my reality. The children have anchored me, so that I don't go totally nuts with the work in the store. It would be even harder for me if I were at home full-time. I really do need the contact and affirmation that I get from the outside work.

Rob and I didn't ever divide up the jobs with the kids. It's just been pretty fluid. Rob has ended up taking the kids to school every day, because I have to be in early to get the cooking started. I remember showing up at the school once and realizing the teachers didn't even know who I was. The phantom mother.

Rob does more of the business end of the store. He's there from about two o'clock until closing, and I'm home with the children. He often doesn't get home until the dinner-hour is over. That's a real trial, because the children are tired. They often need similar things at the same time, so they often have an arm of mine--or a leg--each! And I'm trying to get food put together.

After becoming a parent, you have the most incredible respect for all parents. How difficult, how exhausting it is! One thing about having twins is the husband is always involved. He's got to be involved. Rob would be involved anyway, but twins do force that to happen.

POLLY BOISVERT
Age: 49

"The role model of the same sex parent seems to be the strongest influence on the children."

Polly and her husband Ralph have five children. Kerri is twenty-eight; Carl, twenty-seven; David, twenty-five; Alice and Marcy are twenty. Both parents have always been involved with the kids. Polly was home until the little ones were in kindergarten. Then she began selling real estate. She always did jobs that let her be home by the time the kids were home.

Our fourth was twins. When the twins were born, the others were eight, six, and four. We didn't know we were having twins until they were being born. We had just moved to a new house, to have room for the new baby, and we were broke. The first three months were just horrid. We have a photo of us sitting in the living-room, with bare windows. Ralph and I have huge circles under our eyes, and David, the last one before the twins, looks as if he could kill the two babies. Three months of basic misery.

The toy box was in the kitchen. Where do the kids want to be? In the kitchen with Mom, of course. The toys would be littered all over the place. I can remember taking the babies to the big kids before dinner and saying, "Here, just hold the babies. You can do anything you want, but just play with the babies!" I'd plunk two babies on two laps. I figured we would never get dinner if I didn't do that. When Ralph came home, we'd eat, he and I each with a baby on our hip. It was better than having them cry.

When people came to visit, I'd say, "Here, would you like a baby?" They'd hold her or rock her, or whatever. Most people were delighted. My mother got us a cleaning lady for one morning a week. She'd do things like change all the beds. That was a real treat for me. We tried to keep doing stuff for the bigger kids, so they didn't feel like their lives had come to a screeching halt.

I remember being exhausted, but we really had fun with this gaggle of kids. We'd do it over again. The house was cluttered. We had a round table built that was five feet in diameter, and we bought eight rugged chairs. It was really hectic, but I enjoyed it. We say a meal is good when all eight chairs are full.

It was hard on Ralph. At times he worked two extra part-time jobs. It was expensive having them all. Just clothes and sneakers. You don't do a lot and have five kids, unless you have tons of money. Ralph was trying to keep up with the kids, too. He is the eternal optimist. That's very handy! It would have been really tough to be home with a bunch of little kids all day, especially when two of them were throwing up or something, and then have a crabby husband come home.

Our kids got total support from both Ralph and me. Ralph has taught us all how to laugh in desperate situations, like when Carl went through a glass door. I did very well getting Carl to the hospital. They had me holding his hands while they were taking glass out of his arms. I had to leave, or I was going to throw up. Ralph went in and said something light that eased the situation.

With teenagers I worried more. Ralph was better at not getting upset about things like picking the boys up at the police station, and making sure he gave them a chance to say what happened. As they got older, our feeling was, "If you carry on about the unimportant things, what are you going to do when something really happens?" So, if their hair is long, who is it going to hurt? Save the big guns for the big problems. We've been lucky.

Bringing up boys and girls is different. They all took piano lessons. They all had to make their beds, do dishes, and set the table. There were no boy-girl divisions. If we were doing something in the yard, everybody helped. They all got bikes. There was no saying, "Girls don't do that," or "Boys never. . ."

But the boys model after their father. I see that. We made all the efforts at providing non-sexist toys, options for the girls to play with traditional "boy" toys, and vice-versa, but the role model of the same-sex parent seems to be the strongest influence on the children. As they get older I'm closer to the girls, and Ralph is closer to the boys. Perhaps that's because of shared interests. The boys talk more with Ralph than they do with me. The guys all love cars. Ralph always worked on cars with them.

The girls talk to me about their boyfriends. They won't talk to Ralph about that, but he doesn't like to talk about that stuff. He'd probably make some remark like, "In a hundred years, what difference will it make, anyway?" If David was having trouble with a relationship, he probably wouldn't talk to anybody about it. Carl clams up, too. That's their choice.

Typically supper-time was fun. Ralph is very good at bringing home dumb jokes. It was laid back here, which is probably why a lot of kids used to love eating at our house. I didn't crab at Ralph, and he didn't crab at me. I think in a lot of homes people are at each other's throats over the table.

David had a best friend who would call up late in the afternoon. Pretty soon David would ask me, "What's for supper?" I'd tell him. He'd say, "Okay, just a minute . . . well, we think we'll eat here tonight." We all got along fine with this boy, so we just laughed about it. With a big family one more kid doesn't make any difference.

A friend of Carl's used to eat at our house all the time. His mother had left, and he lived with his father. He was basically ignored, the last of three kids. I never got the full story. One day he said, "We never have dinner like this in our family."

"What do you mean?"

"Well, you just sort of fix what you want to eat, and then eat it."

We had a rule that if you were really hungry and Ralph wasn't home yet, you could eat just your salad. That was great-- it got them to eat salads!

WENDY GOODWIN
Age: 43

"I'm still at the point of asking, 'Has this marriage become a healthy relationship yet?'"

Wendy is a native-American. She and her husband, Luke, live in the pueblo where they grew up, in New Mexico. Her daughters, Diane and Arlene, are twenty-one and sixteen. Her sons, Greg and Leonard, are eighteen and twelve. Diane is about to graduate from college.

Wendy has been married to Luke for twenty-one years. Alcohol and violence have been issues in their life together.

Wendy has a degree in elementary education and has been a teacher in her pueblo and in neighboring pueblos. Recently she has returned to her family tradition of making beautiful pottery.

As a young girl I thought fun was partying. Our family was not happy unless we were drinking and partying. My Mom and Dad drank a lot. I thought the way I could escape this was to really hit the books and make something of myself, but when I was living day to day on the reservation I didn't understand what oppression is. You have to move away from it and look back to understand it. I wanted to be loved. I was looking for an acceptance of myself. I thought that would come from outside. I wanted somebody that would give me all the shelter, the protection, the support. I was still scared of life.

I married a man that was very domineering, very forceful. Then, I could hide. I could read books and do all the educational stuff, but I was scared to even talk to people. I married a man who would do all the talking and make all the decisions.

But he and I were still in our drinking, partying stage. I started to feel trapped. I thought, "What if things get worse?

332

What if he starts beating me up more often?" I thought, "I have to prepare myself to be able to take care of myself and my kids."

Being in a closed, small community is like a double-edged sword. In one way your culture is good. It strengthens who you are. But, in a second sense, it doesn't let you live down what you've done in the past. Changes are very slow in a community. You have a smaller choice of people. It will be the same persons years down the road. People need to use the guidance the spirits give us, because if vindictive thoughts or intentions aren't dispersed to the spirits, there is a tension always lingering. Then mistrust becomes the rule.

You live with your aunts, your uncles, your brothers, your sisters, your grandparents. Everybody is there. That support base is good at times, but at times it is not, especially if you have a lot of hurt feelings. If you've been molested by your uncle, it's hard to get away and start to heal.

Learning about the traditional ways is a way to find healing. I'm finding out that tradition comes down to two principles. You believe that you have a spiritualness available all around you, and you believe that you have other centers of knowledge. The spirits will guide your thoughts and actions and you will have inner spirit, love of self and others. My grandfather says it simply, "Be good." Goodness will open things up for you. Because you're good, things will change. You have to decide how you will carry out the basic traditional values of supportive love, forgiveness, and sharing, which is reaching out to others.

I ask my grandmother and grandfather about things that are puzzling me. I am thankful that I have elders to ask. They don't answer me directly. They give examples. I have learned from them that we are not on this earth to judge people. The spirits are watching. Your ancestors are with you. The past, the present, and the future are together here now. You can always call on your ancestors for guidance and spiritual support. People that do bad things will meet their consequences in another sense. It's not up to us to punish them now. You don't get even. You still treat them the way you would want them to treat you or your kids. You let things go, to be resolved at another level. The spirits take that burden away from you and help you deal with it or show you a way to disperse that ugly feeling, and leave something positive in its place.

You start your day with a prayer or meditation. You end your day with a prayer--good thoughts. You have to be thankful and conscious of each breath you take in the day. Sometimes that've very hard when you get wrapped up in things. You are thankful. The spirits are there for you. You just don't forget them. The spirits would be missing if we moved away from the groundedness that we have in the earth, in the air that we breathe.

I'm part of a group of native women that have formed a women's support group and a domestic violence advocacy group. We're trying to get laws against domestic violence put into the tribal code. But with my own kids I still am lost. Diane and I can talk frankly now, but the others are teenagers. All the insights I have, the things I see, don't even make sense with them. Everything I stand for doesn't even phase them.

It scares me that our older son, Greg, has picked up the pattern of acting out violently. Not towards people, but destroying something, punching a big hole in the wall. He doesn't show any remorse. It's, "Oh well, it happened in a fit of anger. I'll fix it when I have time. I wanted a window there anyway."

I am confused by the craziness of his behavior. I try to go back to my children's past and find out what their perception is of violent events in our family history. Memory-wise they probably don't remember, but feeling-wise maybe they do. I carry these things as negative memories. I wonder: are those events shaping the choices my children are making now?

Most of the girls around here are pregnant by eighteen. Arlene is sixteen. She says, "I'm going to go to college and marry somebody that is up and coming." She doesn't want to be trapped in a low-income family. She sees her older sister being independent and making it and enjoying herself. They have discussions. I do hope Arlene is processing all the data! I think she'll be all right.

My husband is very caring and gentle when he's not on guard. But when things are going bad, he lets it out, no matter what. He thinks we're a safe airing-out place, and he doesn't see what damage he's doing to us. I get so angry and just think I should get out of the marriage, but then I think: if you don't stick it out in the ground where you grew up, how are you going to make changes? My husband is very good at envisioning positive changes for the pueblo. I see him as a very capable person who can actually make changes for the whole pueblo. When he talks, I can hear his heart.

Four years ago he and I both quit drinking and made a commitment to work towards a healthier relationship and family environment. There hasn't been any violence in four years, but the fear that maybe this might be the night that it does happen again is still, quite, very, scarey. Yet, when I talk to him about it, he gets angry that I haven't lost that fear. For me, four years is just recent history.

I still can't sleep comfortably at night. When he comes back upset about something, even though I'm lying next to him, I can't fall asleep until he falls asleep.

I think to him things aren't that bad. Things _were_ worse. This is nothing compared to how we started out. He sees himself making progress, but I'm still at the point of asking, "Has this marriage become a healthy relationship yet?"

After I quit my teaching I went back to my tradition of pottery. The pottery has helped me to see things differently. It is an outlet for feelings. As I work with the clay, digging it up, cleaning it, working it, I am reclaiming my connection to Mother Earth. I have involved my children, and they do it with me. I want them to be grounded. I want them to feel the reciprocity with the earth, the positive energy going out and coming back through the pottery.

SUSAN NIDOR
Age: 47

"I wanted a child that has a mix of all of the things that it means to be a part of the world, including things that have been traditionally only in the arena of girls and women. Caring about something, feeling sad, those things aren't weaknesses. I wanted a balanced child."

Susan is a black sculptor, a painter, and a bookkeeper. Her son Isaac is now twenty-two. Susan and her husband Paul divorced when Isaac was eight, four years after Paul told Susan he was gay. Paul died earlier this year of AIDS.

This is a story about respect that endures beyond intimacy, beyond the end of the marriage, beyond death.

Paul and I both wanted to have children.

Paul was seeing a psychiatrist, and I assumed that his problems were job-related. He came home one day and said, "I'm gay."

My response was, "Well, but what about me? What does that mean for us?" I just wanted to know where we were. I must say that I was in a state of shock for a while. When I asked, "What about me, are we okay here?" there was an assurance that we were, but as time went on, there was definitely a distancing. There was less and less physical intimacy between us, although we really liked and respected each other.

Even in all of that, we were both good parents. There is a wholeness about Isaac. Even when we ended up separating and divorcing, our relationship was not full of flak. There were problems for Isaac in that his parents were in different places, but he didn't have a lot of arguing and tugging to deal with.

I don't remember having a lot of anxiety about being a mother. Friends said, "Susan, I'm going to give you my kids for the first couple of years . . ." I guess I seemed to be a mellow mother. That's not to say that I didn't go through changes. When there was a crisis to be dealt with, I dealt with it. I just don't remember having problems raising him. It was a loving environment.

It has been a challenge to raise a male child. Maybe I felt some of the deficits in terms of my own relationship with Paul. I wanted a child that has a mix of all of the things that it means to be a part of the world, including things that have been traditionally only in the arena of girls and women. Caring about something, feeling sad, those things aren't weaknesses. I wanted a balanced child. Isaac is a giving young man.

When Paul and I split up, Isaac was with me. Then, after about a year and a half, he was with his dad. I thought this was an important arrangement, for a son to be with his father, but it was tough for me. I'm the mother. Maybe I shouldn't let him go. I felt guilty. There was no one that ever chastised me. There were little innuendos from people. Because I felt guilty, it took on a little larger proportion. But, I never doubted Paul's parenting, and he always trusted mine.

At that time, Isaac didn't know Paul was gay. Paul didn't talk about it with him until he was about fourteen or fifteen. I did not intercede. I told Paul, "I think it's important that you tell him. I hope you won't wait too long."

When Isaac was in high school, Paul got a transfer to California, and Isaac did not want to go to California. He could have come to live with me. He preferred to stay in his high school, with cousins in Maryland, where he had been the longest in his young life. It worked out great. The extended family was at work. It was a good thing for Isaac to live in a household where there were kids as close to being siblings as you can get.

Isaac and I now have a relationship that has a certain peer quality to it. We are friends. When I have to be Mom now it's usually like, "This is station WMOM coming at you, just so I can get this out." Then, he's sort of prepared. He might smile a little bit, or he'll hold his ground, hear me out, and then, I'm done.

About a year ago I blurted out to Isaac to not forget to make sure that there's a satisfaction for you and your partner is also satisfied. "Just make sure that you both have your pleasure and that it's not one-sided." That was sort of tough for me. I had not ever been that forthright. That was a big step for me--to talk to my son about sexual intimacy. Then I said, "That's it." I didn't want to embarrass him. I knew that he got it. He didn't just clam up. He heard me. He might know that I was coming from a place where there was some deprivation on my part in terms of my relationship with Paul. He knew where I was coming from.

Isaac's going to be getting married. I think he's young, but we've talked about that, too. There was a lot of love that was there, but his family split up. There may be a little bit of a hole in Isaac's heart. He wants his own family.

I still do these little checks. Just last year I asked Isaac about the period of time when he was in fourth grade, and I was working at the foundry. He had a key to let himself in after school. He had his duties, and I would get home about an hour and a half after he did. "Isaac, when you had the key and let yourself in, how did you feel about that? Was that tough for you?" I did feel an overriding guilt about it. He seemed to do fine at the time.

"That was fine for me, Ma. I liked the responsibility." He did not feel neglected. That made me feel good. I never really knew that. As time goes on, I'm able to ask stuff. There are probably still some other things. I'll be able to say, "Hey, tell me what you thought about that."

Paul just died this year. Isaac was at school, in Virginia. His grandmother, Paul's mother, and Isaac ended up going to California together when we heard that Paul was in the hospital. Paul was always his mother's favorite child, and I wondered if she would be able to help Isaac. She did later say to me, "Susan, I got myself together for Isaac."

It was scarey for me, not being there. I wanted to see my child's face.

Isaac and I went out a month later, to pack up the household. I saw some things from Paul's and my life together that were in places of reverence or everyday use. There was a sculpture that I had made and given Paul that he still had. It was very pleasing to see that our lives had never really fully separated and disintegrated. Isaac said, "It's a part of saying goodbye to Dad that we came in as a family and took care of this." It was a good feeling. Sad, but we did it right.

ELIZABETH THORNTON
Age: 41

"I just get so frustrated. I want so badly for Jack to crack down on Zach, to put it to him that this is the real world, and this plan doesn't make any sense. He won't."

Elizabeth's life has been complicated by being Jack's wife and stepmother to his four children. Their children are: two Marys, age twenty; Zach, eighteen; Nancy, fifteen; Lana, fourteen; and Josh, thirteen. Elizabeth and Jack have radically different parenting styles. Neither was present to build relationships with the other's children when they were small.

Lana and Mary are mine, biologically. The other four are my husband's. When I started raising them, the Marys were eleven; and the littlest, Josh, was four; the others were in-between. Psychologically it's more like the youngest three are mine, plus my Mary, of course.

My husband Jack is very easy-going. He's not a disciplinarian at all. Whatever happens happens. His expectations for the kids' behavior are much lower than mine: anything goes! He says, "Basically this is a good kid." I don't know what his definition of that is exactly! I figure it must be "no criminal record" ...! I think probably it will work out too, but it's been a rough five years.

I work full-time, teaching teachers. My younger kids tell me that I'm not available to do the picking up and dropping off the way other parents are. Apparently I have a reputation for being late. I'm definitely a below-average picker-upper!

At work, for the last couple of years, I've been able to really push ahead. I am ambitious. I do feel like I've lost some of my potential. Sometimes I think, "What I could have done if I didn't have kids!" I've been held back. I've done a lot, but I haven't satisfied myself.

If I had it to do again, I'd run the other way when I saw Jack coming. I really would, even though I love him dearly. I got into an unhappy marriage, was in it for ten years, broke out of that, was finishing my doctorate, my kids were getting older, and I felt like I could breathe and get on my feet again. Then, along came Jack. I got involved with him, and we lived together for a year. He didn't have his children. They visited on weekends, and I thought, "Well, that's okay, I can live with that."

Then, the situation for his kids got really bad, and it was becoming evident that something had to be done. He asked me if I would "mind" if they all came to live with us, and I told him, "They cannot come live with us. Absolutely not." I couldn't do it. I absolutely couldn't. I was still working on my dissertation and trying to work. I just knew in my heart of hearts that I couldn't do it and be what I wanted to be.

We coasted along for a while. It became clear that he was going to have to take the kids. Then, it was a decision point: either we go our separate ways, or we stay together with the kids. I just didn't have the heart to go separate ways. I couldn't have done it. He really had no choice. You can't watch your kids suffer. I didn't want to see the kids suffer, either. I knew I could certainly provide a good home for them.

I have a hard time with the way that they speak to me, or to Jack. Their tone of voice, their choice of words. All of a sudden, at fourteen or fifteen, they come at you from a position of more authority. They want to be on an equal plane. But also, the anger comes across. They're very critical of us. They'll even critique our parenting style! Swearing is not allowed, but even if they don't use the exact words, they can be very offensive.

Zach, at eighteen, wants no one to tell him anything about how he should live his life. Of course, we should give him all the resources we have, to do whatever he wants to do. If he wants to stay out until three in the morning in our vehicle, that should be all right. Jack has more of an attitude of, "Let him do his thing." I'm still of a mind that he's living with us, he doesn't have his own financial resources, so we are entitled to make demands of him.

This is where the problems creep in for a stepfamily. Zach doesn't want to claim me as any kind of mother. Jack is always running interference between Zach and me. Jack's answer to every problem is, "Let me deal with it." His "dealing" with Zach is to give him a stern talking-to, and that's the end of it.

Zach thinks he's going to Hollywood to be an actor. I just get so frustrated. I want so badly for Jack to crack down on him, to put it to him that this is the real world, and this plan doesn't make any sense. He won't.

Even right now, Zach is being very disrespectful to me. Living for free. He would come out from <u>our</u> house in town, where he's living alone this summer, to the lake house, at supper-time. He wouldn't see us all day. Then, he'd eat supper that I'd cooked and, then, go back into town. I finally put a stop to that. I said, "If you don't want to be a part of this family, don't get into the chow line." He was very huffy.

Jack was crushed: "How could you do that?"--to his poor baby. That's why he's such a poor baby. Now it's been a few weeks, and Jack is saying to me, "He really misses your potato salad. Boy, he'd love some of that potato salad."

"He doesn't miss me? He misses my potato salad?!"

There is some of this that works the other way, too. Jack says Lana gives him a hard time, when I'm not around. When I go away, the three younger ones go totally wild. He says they won't listen to him. But, he hasn't had the practice. He's the kind of parent where it will be midnight, and they'll all be watching TV, and he'll just go to bed and leave them. If he was tired and wanted them to go to bed at ten, he would just tell them to go to bed. It would never occur to him that there might be a <u>right</u> <u>time</u> for them to go to bed.

I'm always under pressure of time. I probably don't have the time, but maybe I don't have the inclination to have long, heart-to-heart discussions with my kids. I always marvel at this friend of mine who tells me about her kids' lives in detail. I'm not sure I want to know that much. I don't find out from each kid everything that happened that day. If I notice someone is upset, I ask them about it. If they went on a field trip that day, I don't need to know all the details of what happened. Some parents can tell you who was there, who said what to whom, who did this funny thing, etc. I don't know those things. I think it's actually good for kids to have some privacy.

When the kids were younger, we used to take up issues at dinner. All eight of us would sit down, and it would be chaotic, but everyone would pretty much get their chance to say what they had to say and bring up their issues.

Meal times are not like that anymore. That's another thing I gave up on. Jack doesn't come home at the same time anymore. The kids don't all come home at the same time. With older kids you start feeling like a short-order cook. I cook now at a time that's reasonable for me and the younger kids, and we eat together. Then, whoever shows up later can get their dinner. I'd cook for eight, and maybe four would show up. They'd forget to mention that they had drama tonight, or they were meeting a friend and picking up a bite with him, or so-and-so was working late. With the older kids that happened a lot. Not that the leftovers aren't going to get eaten. But it's aggravating to plan for that many. If you were going to cook for fewer, maybe you would have done something easier. I got so angry that I changed my style. I think that's what happens, you get kind of forced to change things.

You do your work early. By now, it's too late. They already feel the way they feel about you--whatever that is. You set the thing in motion when they're toddlers, and then you just ride it out. When you don't have a chance to do that, like with step-children, it really screws you up.

LEE ENGLE
Age: 42

"Ellis was watching the kids. He was taking them to drug dealers' homes. He was shooting up in the car, with them."

Lee is a working-class woman from Arkansas. Her children are Kathy, fifteen; Amelia, seven; and Earl, five. Lee gave up custody of her older daughter when Kathy was a baby. She had her other children by her second husband. Lee has fought to keep her second family together, despite her husband's drug problems and time in jail. Lee has been on welfare and lived in a homeless shelter with her two younger children. She works now as a full-time secretary for an eye doctor and still has subsidized day-care. Her second family is intact.

I was raised in a small little town in Arkansas.

My mother missed third grade because of the Depression. She picked cotton and strawberries and slept in potato sheds, which were dug-outs in the ground where they cured the potatoes. It was a very, very stern family. My mother got a spanking for saying, "Heavens to Betsy." Her family was exceptionally tight. They all relied on one another just to get through.

I went to college to the University of Arkansas. I met a dashing young man. We had a flirtation which ended up with me dropping out of school. Now I regret that I didn't finish college. Mark and I had a quiet marriage. Then, I had Kathy.

Kathy was about three when my mother died. My husband was traveling a lot. I was alone a lot. I met my current husband, Ellis, doing community theatre. Instead of trying to work on the problems that I had in my marriage, I opted to be kind of free and loose. I ran away with this guy.

I knew immediately that having Kathy with me wasn't right for Kathy. Ellis is far from stable now. He was even less so then. Prone to alcoholic binges. I didn't want to put Kathy in a position of not knowing if we were going to have a roof over our heads or where the food was going to come from.

Mark was always a very good father, and he was ambitious, so I knew that she would be better off with him. A year after Mark and I split up, he moved to Vermont with Kathy. It was over two years before I saw her again. I was waking up in the middle of the night crying. We didn't even have a telephone at the time, so I had to borrow a neighbor's phone to call her.

I did things like drive the school bus and work in the cannery. Then, I had Amelia. When she was two, Ellis got into cocaine. He wasn't telling me this, of course. Things were getting weird. He was not at home a lot. Then, there was the murder. A woman a few houses down from me was murdered one morning. Ellis became a material witness in the murder, and a lot of people felt like he was the murderer, although the police were pretty sure the woman's boyfriend had done it.

At the same time we were getting evicted from our apartment. We decided we'd move to New England. Ellis had to promise he'd come back for the trial. We were in an old van. We broke down every hundred and fifty miles. It took us two weeks to do a three-day trip. We had everything that we owned in the van, including the dog and the baby. Amelia's car seat was in the front, strapped in with a bungee cord. I was sitting in a rocking chair behind the driver's seat with the dog at my feet.

In Michigan the transmission blew. Dogs really complicate things, more than babies do. People are willing to take in a baby, but not a big dog. A farmer towed us to his farm and spent hours phoning people who might help us. A minister came and took us to his church, and we slept in a Sunday-school room.

It was hot. I was about five months pregnant. I was laying in this church in the heat of the afternoon, wondering, "What on earth is going to happen?," when I felt Earl kick for the first time. I was crying. It was so wonderful that the baby was all right. I wasn't eating. Any food we had I was giving to Amelia.

Somehow, we actually made it to Massachusetts. We stayed with Ellis's parents for two months. Then we moved in with an old friend of Ellis's. I thought things couldn't get any worse! The friend turned out to be a heroin addict. He didn't want the heat on, because he didn't want to pay for it. We were starting into winter. There's where I was when I started to go into labor for Earl.

Ellis had gotten work for a construction company. We moved into a different place. Ellis started not coming home from work until late. There never seemed to be enough money. Then, I caught Ellis shooting up in the bathroom. He told me he had been diagnosed with lung cancer, and this was black-market laetrile that he was getting. I guess I wanted to believe that. There were people hanging around all the time, and in and out of the bathroom. He quit work.

I had started working part-time. I would be home during the day with the kids, and, then, I would leave at six when he got in. So, I had to go to full-time, ten to six. Ellis was watching the kids. He was taking them to drug dealers' homes. He was shooting up in the car, with them. It was cocaine again.

I was desperate.

Ellis was killing himself. He wasn't eating at all. Not sleeping at all. He was gone all the time. One Saturday night, he didn't come home. On Sunday, he called. He was in jail. He had put up some kind of a fight when the police grabbed him. The bail was set at $500,000. I didn't have $500. Part of me felt it was just as well.

I had no money. At this point I couldn't even work anymore, because I had no one to take care of the kids. Earl was a year old. Amelia was three. Someone from a church helped me go through the process of getting evicted and making an application with a homeless shelter. It saved our lives.

There were five families in the shelter. Each family had one room. Each family cooked one night. We shared the bathroom and the kitchen. I actually was able to use the time in the shelter to pull together all the ends and reach a point where I could start fresh. The food was provided. I didn't have to worry about my children being hungry. I didn't have to worry about them not being in a safe place. They were going to day-care every day. I had time to deal with looking for an apartment and to work out what was going to be best in terms of going back to work. We were in the shelter about six weeks. Then, I became eligible for subsidized housing. It was a humbling experience, but it was actually a good one.

Ellis was in prison for fifteen months. He was in a drug treatment program there. All of this time I took the kids to visit every week. It was a two and a half-hour drive. It was crazy, but we did it every week. I was really afraid Earl wouldn't maintain a sense of who his father is.

Then, after a year, Ellis started coming home for weekend furloughs and, then, gradually came back into the house. Then, he started school at a community college. He got a perfect 4.0 average for two years, and now he is at UMass to get his bachelor's.

We are a family. There were times when I didn't think that was going to happen.

I thought about leaving, lots of times. But after leaving my first husband and Kathy, I didn't want to have the family break up again. I felt that it was the most important thing to keep the family together. That was my job. My family in Arkansas would have paid for me and the kids to fly back home, but that would have been destroying the family. We'd have never come together again after that. Keeping the family together is what I fought for. I won that victory.

Even since Ellis came back, there have been times when I've thought about leaving. He's been home two years. It's been an adjustment. I was making all of my own decisions. I started from scratch. I came to a place that I didn't know, a culture I wasn't used to. I used maps to find my way around. I had no friends or connections. I found the apartment, worked with the welfare system, worked with the legal system, the penal system. Got a job. Paid the bills. Everything was mine. There are still times when I don't want to let go--out of fear or mistrust. It's easy to throw it back at him: "I did this without you. I can do whatever without you." That sometimes comes easier than I'd like it to.

KAYLA CULBERTSON
Age: 31

"If they want to see him, they can. It lets them know that their Dad is their Dad. The time that they spend with him, that time is theirs.

Kayla is native-American. She has three sons: Wayne, fourteen; Dale, eight; and Francis, five. Kayla and her sons reaffirm their place in line behind their ancestors every time they dance.

Although Kayla had her first son when she was seventeen, she finished high school and graduated with her class. Once Wayne was three and in Head Start, Kayla enrolled in college and went on to graduate with a certificate in word-processing. Then she worked in a lawyer's office until Dale was born.

When Wayne was seven Kayla became, in effect, a single parent, due to her husband's alcoholism. She seems wise in the way she lets her children work out their own relationships with their father, while, by being separate from him, she provides for their safety and for everything else they need.

My step-father started a dance group in 1974. We started off with nothing. Artificial feathers. I remember the first trip was to Oklahoma. Then Toronto, Canada. Now this dance group has gone to Canada about fifteen times. We were invited to Washington and danced at Clinton's inauguration. All of my kids started dancing at the age of three. Once they started performing, they were welcome to go on trips, to dance. It is all about sharing. It's about what we appreciate from our ancestors, what they have taught us.

Their father is going through a religious time now and is becoming a medicine man. They do the ceremonies in the kiva.

348

I told him that I think the kids need to be involved in that. He wants them there with him, too. It is a very respected thing.

There are a lot of people who have a receptive mind towards their religion, because it provides for them. In the morning I speak in my native language to Mother Earth. The religion gives us help. We dance the Buffalo because it has given us shelter, clothing, and food. The Eagle is protecting us. I am the same as an eagle, protecting my children, feeding them. Dancing gives me a good feeling. To see my kids perform is a good feeling, to carry on that tradition. Then, when we come out and share our dances with the non-Indian, the outside world, it touches them inside, too.

They say that when you are an expectant mother, the baby inside can feel you dancing. It's true. I was dancing while I was expecting. It was like being in the song. When they were babies, my Dad would sing to them. That's how they pick up. At my Mom's house, the drum is there. When they were in their walkers, they would go over and start hitting the drum. You have to know the song, first, before you want to dance.

My youngest one is graduating from Head Start this year. Thank God!

Their father is never there. I was married for ten years. Now I'm divorced for four years. I've been raising them on my own since my oldest one was seven years old. It is hard raising three boys. It's hard. Financially. I never received welfare, but I was on food stamps for a while. Once I got back on my feet, I dropped the food stamps. I can't see myself staying home, just collecting welfare. I can't do that. I tell my kids, "Go to school and become something. You've got to be strong out there."

I try to explain to them the disease of alcoholism. The oldest one to this day will not go spend time with his father. I've always said, "He's still your father." Now Wayne is fourteen. He hasn't had guidance from his father. "Hi," and, "Bye," and that's it.

Before Christmas their father told me, "I'm going to take the kids and the house away from you." I said, "As far as the house is concerned, I don't care. As far as the kids are concerned, you'll be in for a good fight, because I'm not going to give them

349

up. You better be prepared." After that, I never heard from him until late in the Spring.

The courts have no jurisdiction over the house. I have to go through tribal council. They are all his relatives. I'm not from this pueblo. I figure, "Forget it. The house will be his." I've been paying all this time for the house. I'm just going to lose out.

First, he told me, "The kids and the house." Now, it's only the house he wants. I have stopped paying for the house. I'm putting the monthly payments in the bank, instead. Once the tribal council decides if I keep the house or not, the delinquent bills will be mine to catch up, or I'll have the money to put a down payment on a trailer.

Dale has always wanted to go live with his Dad. He was real close to his father. I had to decide if I wanted to let him go live with his Dad. At first I thought, "No," but then I thought, "Give him the chance to find out for himself. He'll find out how hard it is for him to live with his father." Finally, at one point, his father said Dale could move in, but when it came down to Dale's moving, his father decided not to have him there. That hurt.

Their Dad will disappear for a long time, and then he shows up. The kids are getting so they are forgetting about him, or they are adjusting better. As soon as they adjust, if he talks to them, he brings them down again. They want to see him. There's times when they ask, "Where's Dad? Can I go spend time with Dad?" I say, "Let's call your Grandma and see if she knows where he's at." I'll make every effort to get ahold of him. Why should I hurt the kids?

I won't push them to their Dad, though. I tell him, "Just be honest with them. The kids want to see you. If you don't want to see them, just let them know. Why hide things from them?" After a while they stop asking me.

Sometimes they'll see him down by the river. Sometimes they'll go up to him and talk to him. Sometimes they won't, but they'll come home and tell me, "Dad was drinking again." They see too much of it. They know what's happening. I still tell them, "If you want to see him, you can. Don't let anybody stop you." It's not for me or for their father. It's for the kids. If they want to see him, they can. It lets them know that their Dad is their Dad. The time that they spend with him, that time is theirs.

A lot of people tell me that I shouldn't let him see the kids, because he doesn't give me any support. I haven't received a dollar from him since the oldest one was seven years old. I wasn't sure I wanted a divorce. I used to see other ladies going through a lot with their husbands, and I used to think, "If that was me, I'd be out of there," but it's never easy. But I found my kids suffering even though we were with him. Living with an alcoholic, and then a drug-user... Then he started abusing. My kids were in danger. I was. I made the right choice.

A part of me was thinking, "Will I survive? Will I ever make it with my kids?" I looked back over the time since I conceived my first child, and I said, "Well, I am doing it right now. My husband's not working. He's just another mouth for me to feed."

I had a job with the commodities program. The first year I was always wondering about my boys at home. I had no phone at the time. I'd call to my Mom's and ask my sister to go check on the boys for me. "Just pick them up, and tell them that you're going for a ride, and you're inviting them." That was her excuse every day after school. To check on them.

Just the other day Francis, my baby, came running in, "Mom, Mom! Close your eyes." So, I closed my eyes, and he says, "Okay, open them!" He had two vases with weeds in them! He had water in there and everything. I enjoy receiving things from them. They don't have to spend money. But they get paid for performing. Now Wayne will say to his Grandma, "I need to dance, so I can get my Mom something for Mother's Day." The two little ones even pick up rocks and paint them. After work I get home, and they'll have something for me.

They have bought all their school clothes for the last two years. When Wayne was seven or eight years old he would tell me, "Mom, we're dancing. We'll be getting money. I'll help you pay the bills." He'd give me money for the gas bill, the electric bill. I never asked him for it, but he always put in his money. If I didn't want to take it, he would always tell me, "I make the bills, too."

It's my children that make me go for what I want to go for. I used to be a weak person. I put up with a lot. Raising them as a single parent has improved me. I don't let anything stand in my way, now. Some things will go wrong; some won't. Sometimes I want to leave, get away from here, and just start all over, but, yet, this is their home. I can't take them away. They would lose what they need to grow up with.

To this day they still have me, and they still have their Dad.

MELEANNA WILLIAMS
Age: 57

"At times, as Sawyer got older, I would tell him that if he wanted to find Mark, his father, to let me know, and I would help him. I know I can find him."

At age thirty-eight, Meleanna chose to have a child, knowing that she might raise that child alone. She has, with the support of a large extended family, including her mother, Virginia Williams, who appears in Chapter Five. Her son Sawyer is now nineteen. He does not know his father.

As a child I was very quiet. I couldn't stand school. I wanted to be out with the fairies and the gypsies! The only thing I liked to do was color, but then I had to color like everyone else. I didn't like that. When I was in sixth grade someone said to me, "Would you like a part in this play?" Then I bloomed, when everyone else unbloomed.

My grandmother had done a lot of traveling when she was very young. Her stories always meant a great deal to me. She gave me the feeling that there was so much in life that I needed to feel and touch. She died when I was twelve. I kept her inside me for quite some time.

When most women thought of getting married and having children, I knew I couldn't do that. I needed to meet a lot of people. I would teach a year and then travel, then teach another year. I still had so many things I needed to keep on doing, and it wasn't my time to have children. I lived in Europe. I had lovers, in and out. Freedom was--is still--the most important thing to me.

By the time I reached thirty-seven, I had had some very loving male energies, but no one I would say "yes" to. But, then,

I wanted a child. I wanted a child very much. So, I asked the man I was living with if he would give me a child. He agreed. But, he didn't want to stay around when I got pregnant. That was fine--to a certain extent--but there was some sadness in there, too. I wanted him to know Sawyer.

How should I tell my parents that I had decided to have a child? How should I do that so that they could understand and respect me? I walked down through the meadow in back of the house. My father was there. I said, "Daddy, I'm pregnant."

He said, "I know. I'm so glad. I've never known a woman that I think would be so wonderful to have a baby."

Then the next one was my Mom! My father was more of a dreamer, a quiet, gentle dreamer. My mother is a little more rigid. My mother said, "Well, let's sit down and have a cup of coffee." So, we sat at the kitchen table. She was open and delighted. My whole family, all my brothers and sisters, said things like, "Bring your baby and come and live with me."

I knew that this child-boy needed to have his roots. He wasn't going to have any from the other side. I come from a family that has very strong roots. I decided that I wanted to come home to have the baby. When I went shopping I wondered if the people were staring at me and gossiping behind my back. Of course they were! It's a small town. I had to ignore that. But then there were wonderful little old ladies in town that knit me tiny crocheted booties and sweaters.

My father died when Sawyer was four. I was standing and looking out the window about a week after the funeral. This voice in back of me, which was my father, said, "Please stay at home and take care of Nanna." So I did stay, rather than moving back to the city.

Years later, Sawyer came home one day and said, "They all want to know who my father is." I said, "Sawyer, you can take any one of the Williams brothers you want." He sort of grinned. But I didn't sleep well that night. He toughed it out.

You have to be tough in your heart. At those times when he was hurt, if I made a big thing out of that, it would have made it bigger to him. If I opened up too much to that--"Oh, my poor little boy"--what's that going to do? You open it up, and you throw love around it, and then you close it. He has to deal with it.

It's been fine to have stayed. Sometimes two women in the house has been off-balancing. We've learned how to balance each other. My mother adores Sawyer. He was a gift--not just to me. He was a gift to my father while he was alive, and a gift to my mother. To my brother who's gay and will never have a son, Sawyer is his son. He has given a lot of people a lot of joy.

Sawyer and I have always really listened to one another. Mothering to me is listening. Listening sometimes when I don't hear words. Knowing.

I love the intimacy of his friends, with him, the laughter, the silliness. I love hearing him and his buddies tell the pranks they've pulled on each other. And the pain of trying to be cool and being a little chubby, and growing into manhood and wanting a girlfriend, and for a while having only short-lived ones.

Teenagers are such a hoot! They are so vulnerable, too. It's a time for the truest listening by parents. We, as mothers, and fathers, need to search our own hearts in order to be close to their hearts. I learned that from Sawyer. It's a time of huge transformation.

From the very beginning, I wanted Sawyer to know his father. To know him through me, and to honor him. His father was a wonderful human being. We've always talked about who his father was. Sawyer looks just like him and has many of his ways.

At times, as Sawyer got older, I would tell him that if he wanted to find Mark, his father, to let me know, and I would help him. I know I can find him. About three months ago, Sawyer came to me, upset, "I don't understand you. Why the fuck do you think that Mark is such a good person? He's never even wanted to see me."

So, I thought, "Okay, play it quiet and gentle. Let him get rid of all this."

He was sobbing, "He doesn't even care...."

Sawyer's working hard to save money to go to school. I think he was feeling, "No one's here to help us. He should be helping us." Angry, angry. I think it had been building for some time.

Inside I was crying. I asked if he wanted me to try to find Michael.

"I don't want to see that fucking ass-hole."

So, now, I'm just leaving it a bit. I do think he needs to see Mark, but the time isn't right, yet. I don't like to see him in so much anguish. Feeling lonely. I think he felt that he was abandoned and that he wasn't good enough. I can't make that change. That's the future, dealing with his father and his feelings about that. Part of me immediately wanted to go find Mark, and not tell Sawyer.

I hope I wasn't selfish in having a child and bringing him up without a father. I don't think it ever would have been this way if it wasn't supposed to be. I want other women to know it is okay and being a single mother can be done well. I feel so honored about myself. I did it. No regrets. No not loving myself, as a single person.

Sawyer was fortunate in being in a home situation where he had a lot of male energies around him, and other female energies, all ages. Tons of aunts and uncles, cousins. A huge family and lots of activity going on. Of any single child coming in, probably the way he did it was ideal.

MAGGIE HELMSLEY
Age: 49

"We all kind of left the nest together. A few years early."

Maggie lives in New Mexico. Her sons, Mike and Nick, are twenty-two and eighteen. Maggie talks about her sons' efforts, a few years ago, to convince their parents that they should not divorce. She talks about the family's triumph in a serious medical crisis, and about possible connections between these two events.

When the kids were maybe fifteen and twelve, Bob and I had a meeting to tell them that we were going to separate in order to determine whether we had any interest in being together. It was extremely difficult. They were so articulate, and vehement, and passionate in their response. It was very clear to them that they did not want us to split up. They said, "We don't see any abuse going on. We don't see anybody hitting each other. We don't see any heavy drinking. We don't even hear screaming. So, why on earth would you split up?" Especially, "Why would you split up when we don't want you to?" They really tried to talk us out of it. They tried to argue. There was no doubt in their minds that it was a bad move for them.

Bob and I kind of rallied our battered selves to say, "Well, we feel there is a very important reason to do this, and that is that we are not happy with each other. We've tried many kinds of help to be happy together, and we're simply not able to keep trying. We're tired. We like each other. We care for each other. We feel that we deserve better than this level of happiness."

They felt that it was their right to prevail. When I said, "This is because we want to have something better in our lives," Mike said, "You and your pitiful lives." They stopped at

357

nothing. Over the space of three or four months, they fought for their position, just like in a war.

They said, "Let's get this straight, are we the most important thing in your life--as you have always maintained? We have ruled the roost here and feel we are loved more than anything else ... is this true or is this not true?"

I had to look into myself and say, "As a matter of fact, there is something that is at least equally important, and that is going to have priority right now. Yes, I love you and I will love you forever--that doesn't change at all--but I have discovered that I have a right, also, to leave the nest." We all kind of left the nest together. A few years early.

I don't think I flew off. I crawled over the edge! On my own behalf. And shinnied down the tree. And looked around. I don't think that either Bob or I left the kids without a nest. We maintained or reinvented nests for them. I did that, and they saw that I could still love them to pieces, and be making a very important step on my own.

The divorce happened, and they lived with it--and beyond it. It is now six years later, and they've sailed out and away from it, as Bob and I have. Four people that were all one unit are now four separate units out there, doing very separate things, quite successfully.

Our family went through a lot of stress with a major medical problem with Nick. When he was just barely three, he was diagnosed with a very serious kind of a brain tumor. Bob and I sent Mike to his grandmother's in California and rushed off straight to New York City to the hands of the neurosurgical world. A world opened up that was completely unknown to any of us and completely horrifying. A world in which we all became experts in our own way.

Nick went through that surgery under microscopes for twelve hours. It was just unspeakable. Lost his pituitary gland in the process, because it was a tumor that grew on the pituitary gland. The tumor recurred when he was eight, and he went through the same thing--we all went throught the same thing--all over again. All of us. Mike says that his brother's having this tumor is the biggest influence on his entire life. He can't imagine anything else in his life will ever surpass it for formativeness. For shaking him to the core.

Nick. Well, who can imagine when you're three and when you're eight what it's like to be the subject of invasion, of warfare into your body? I can't even imagine. What I can imagine is what it's like to be the Mom. And I have a feeling for what it's like to be the Dad, because I know what Bob was going through. And somewhat what Mike was going through.

Naturally and, I think, inevitably, Nick and I grew to be a team the likes of which you have never seen. I'd put the two of us up against Saddam Hussein, General Patton. I'd take them all on. Nick and I are invincible. We can go through anything together. We really did it right. There's incredible power in that. There's pride and power and success in having done that and having gotten through it. We did it the absolute best that it could possibly be done.

And it's a horrifying, horrible, unspeakable, unjust nightmare. It's just a nightmare. And there's no silver lining. I don't want to talk about silver linings. I don't want to talk about God's will. It's just a horror that is visited on you.

But given that, there was this performance and this relationship that was very, very successful and tight with me and Nick. Bob's role was to support me, while I supported Nick. I was the nurturer and the one that was right there sleeping with Nick in the hospital. Bob was making money, so that all that could happen. Although he was there right with us, too. Nick was the absolute warrior, fighting for his life. And doing a beautiful job of it. I was back-up in every respect. We were just fierce. And Bob was back-up to me, and he was wonderful at that, but there was a very big distinction between battlefield team and back-up.

It's hard on the marriage to have that kind of medical disaster go on, period, but then this kind of division where Nick and I kind of welded ourselves together, and Bob was somewhat on the outer circle .... Of course, Mike was on an outer circle too, but not responsible in the same way. The two of them were floating out there.

It led to a real imbalance and a terrible, poignant distance between Bob and Nick. I was so close to Nick that there wasn't room in the inner sanctum for anybody else. Nobody could come close to me as providing everything for that guy--spiritual, physical, mental needs, humor, everything. I needed help when I was away from Nick. Bob gave me that.

The more Bob was excluded, the more he got into that role, and the less he had to offer Nick. I began to feel, especially as time passed, "What are you doing way over there?" As the horror of the event receded, I'd look around, and I'd say, "Well, don't you care about Nick? Why are you out there playing soccer with Mike all the time, and you don't ever pay any attention to Nick?" That's a gross simplification, but it was like that. More and more I felt that Bob turned his back on Nick.

Bob was terrified that Nick was going to die--that he was going to be seriously impaired--that he wasn't going to be normal--that he's not normal right now--that something's wrong. The more he saw wrong, wrong, wrong with Nick, the more he wanted to be out of there and looking at Mike.

So, I had all the more to rally around Nick, the victim, the abandoned one. By God, I wasn't going to let Nick know that there was some absence there. But, of course, Nick did know.

If you saw Nick now, you'd say, "That's okay, Maggie, it worked out great! Because look at that guy. He's fabulous!" He is. He's a freshman in college. He's in the honors program, majoring in Mandarin Chinese. He calls home and says, "Mom, listen to this!" Then he speaks in Chinese. It's just neat beyond belief.

He is health-impaired in some serious ways. He's blind in one eye. He has hormone replacements all the time, for life, because he has no pituitary gland. I had to give him growth hormone shots daily. When he was about twelve, he started doing it himself. When he was about sixteen, he declared that he was the ideal height for himself! He made sure he was going to be a little taller than his brother, and then he quit the shots! So he has some impairments, but it's not visible to anyone. And mentally he is a perfectly sharp guy. Emotionally he is, I think, one of the healthiest people I know. He's got a sense of both how fragile life is, and of how not to be overwhelmed by that.

For a while because Nick and I were so welded together, it was very hard for me to not be the child as well as the mother. Where does the child end, and the mother begin? Or where should it end and begin? It was hard to separate my identity from his, but it was also absolutely clear to me that we were totally separate. The one whose body that happened to, whose life we were looking at, whose future would be determined by all this, that one was not me. He was the one whose life was on the line. Mine was not.

I had to realize that very clearly, or I think I would have gone insane. I was the mother. There was suffering, and strength, and weakness all tied up in being the mother in the situation. As the mother, what was it going to do to the rest of my life? What was it going to do to my relationships with my kids and to other people?

If he died, was I going to die? If he doesn't live through this operation ... I say "Good-bye." I don't know whether he's going to live through this or not. No one will tell me. No one will promise me. No one will give me odds on <u>nothing</u>. Will he come out of it a vegetable? I don't have any idea. Well, Maggie, then what happens? He dies. What happens? Do you die? Do you drop dead at the very moment he drops dead? Is that the way it works? I thought, "Maybe. Maybe, because we're so the same. I care so much. I care so much, surely I might just drop dead at the same moment." And then I thought, "Probably not, Maggie. Probably not."

And it was that same kind of realization at the kitchen table. "I do care about you more than anything in the world, and yup, I'm going to do something, anyway, that you don't like." I would still be alive even though I cared about you more than anything in the world. I would continue. That recognition of separateness when you care so desperately and are so close is profound. I think that separateness has allowed Nick to flourish on his own.

Bob and I have talked a lot about what the impact of the medical crisis was on the two of us. He thinks that crisis

361

derailed us. I think not. I think, in fact, it may have kept us together longer than we would have been otherwise. The teamwork that it brought out in all four of us forced us to remain a family. In a heroic way. We all rallied and stuck together for some very good reasons for a certain number of years. I think it was not a coincidence that Mike and Nick were the ages they were when Bob and I split up. There was a certain freedom to go ahead and let go of the marriage. But Bob would disagree.

I also pushed the separation before the kids left home, on purpose. My parents got divorced when I was in college. I'm an only child. It was a miserable marriage! They stuck together. I don't know why. I don't think it was for my sake. In those days you did, more than you do now. Then, having suffered all those years with the two of them, I went away, and they split.

I was glad that they broke up, because I could see that they needed to, but I felt that they did something important without me. To dissolve the family without me really pissed me off. I came back after college. There was no house anymore. I had to look on a map of Seattle to find out where each of them was living. I couldn't find them. I couldn't find anything. Everything was gone. I wasn't around for the dissolution and recreation of whatever this picture was going to look like. They did it behind my back. I was mad. I'm still mad.

I knew this marriage was going to end, and I wanted the kids to be a part of it. They had a right to be a part of splitting up. They didn't have the right to dictate whether or not it happened. That was Bob's and my right. But they did have a right to be there to take part in that readjusting of the family, and to get it all straight before they left home, so that when they came back for vacations and to visit, they were coming back to something that they had left.

CAROLINE WOLCOTT
Age: 71

"It's a very rewarding business, being a parent. You get your rewards as you go along."

Caroline has three grown children, two sons and a daughter; and four grandchildren. She feels that she was fortunate to be able to stay home to raise her children. Her husband, a doctor, was very interested in and involved with the children. Caroline feels he was a full partner in parenting.

So many of the people I've loved are gone. My grandmother. Both my parents and my one brother. My husband. From the point of view of a widow who's seventy-one, my children are what hold me together. When you're over seventy you worry about what will happen. The thing that keeps me going is my children. If you don't have children, you don't have grandchildren. They give me a stake in the future. I was fascinated hearing my grandson talk about starting high school. If you don't have children, what is life like at my age? I think it would be so bleak, even though I have a number of good friends. I'm more active in the community now than I ever was, but my children come first.

I was able to take out about nineteen years to just concentrate on raising children. When I did go back to work, it was as a medical secretary, but only part-time. My youngest was in junior high. Then, when the nest emptied, I started to work full-time.

I think that I was just meant to be a mother. I really enjoyed it. I don't think I was meant to be a career woman. It seems to me it's very worth doing. If your husband is out earning the bacon, and you're raising the children, that's a fairly good division of labor. Raising the next generation, that's going to run the country and rule the world--or at least deal with the world--that's pretty exciting stuff. Now, of course, on a day-to-day basis it doesn't seem so exciting. It seemed to take up my whole life as I look back on it.

There's no way to train for being a mother. It's on-the-job training, and you're teaching yourself. You have to have some savvy, and the only way to learn is by doing it. You can get tips from your friends. In some cases I learned what not to do by watching my friends. I had one friend who used to smack her kids, hard. I had another who used to belittle children in front of other people.

My husband always backed me up, so when we got into some kind of a difficult thing, we dealt with it together. Lots of fathers didn't seem to have much of a handle on what was going on with their kids. My husband wanted to be with his children when he could.

If I had some kind of a ruckus with the kids during the daytime, you can be sure I talked to him about it and told him what I'd done, and we discussed whether that was the right way to handle it or not. He had a great deal to do with my children's upbringing, if only in bolstering my confidence to allow me to do what I had to do, as things came up. "Is it all right for him to ride his bicycle to the drug store?," for example. This was my job. Charlie appreciated it, too. It was my part of the family effort.

Life was so unpredictable, because Charlie was on call all the time. We were at the mercy of the telephone. It was important for someone to be there in the home to provide security for the children. So if he got called out, nobody was going to panic because there was no one there. That felt like a contribution. In return, of course I was supported all those years by my husband.

I felt very strongly that we shouldn't make any promises unless we were sure we could carry them out. Because of Charlie's job, it was hard to promise that we'd take the children to the park on Saturday, or whatever. So we said, "We'll see" a lot. I think the kids resented being put on hold, but we thought it was wrong to promise something and then not deliver.

I think I had it fairly easy, because the children went off to boarding school. It was at a tender age. When the first one went off, I felt that it was breaking the family circle. I felt things would never be the same again, and, of course, they weren't. I got conned into this boarding school thing by my husband, who had been to boarding school and thought it was a wonderful experience. He wanted his children to have the same. I got kind of . . . it wasn't my idea. When the children all came home at holidays it was marvelous. We came to life again!

The things I remember most are things when my children were more grown-up. I got a tremendous kick out of watching my sons row. That was a great period of our life. We'd go all up and down the Eastern seaboard to see one of them row in a race.

We took two camping trips to the West which Charlie planned. Then, we were all interacting, closeted in a car together much of the time. We camped in tents. We wanted the children to get some sense of the diversity of this country and the excitement of what a fantastically beautiful and productive, varied place it is. We were inculcated with my husband's passion for the outdoors and for nature on those trips.

It's a very rewarding business, being a parent. My mother once said, "You get your rewards as you go along." It isn't something where you work for twenty years, and, then, finally, have something to show for it. There were wild moments, but I have no complaints. It's still fun now that they're all grown up. When we all get together I love to see them and their spouses all interacting. It's fascinating! And to see my children now with children, to see their children interacting with their uncles and aunts. That's very nice. Continuity. To quote my mother again, "Continuity is everything."

JANE LLOYD
Age: 60

"What's his is mine, and what's mine is his."

Jane and Al have raised six kids on their sixty-acre farm in Ohio. Adam is now thirty-seven; Kathy, thirty-four; Neil, thirty-two; Hank, thirty-one; Barton, twenty-seven, and Mary, twenty-three.

Jane and Al went to the same grade school. She grew up five miles from their farm, which belonged to his mother. They are Baptists. Al joined part of the interview. His and Jane's respect for each other and devotion to each other run like bright threads through the fabric of their conversation.

I find that your worries just go on, and they're a little more complicated than when the kids had the measles or the mumps or didn't have the clothes they wanted. You worry twice as much, because you can't do anything. They buy homes. Are they going to be able to make their payments? When one gets hurt, and they are having their second child, what are they going to do? When you have a child, it's always your child.

Al farmed the farm: everything, corn, soybeans, beets, oats, hay, small fields of each, and then found a job at a feed company, working nights, too. He'd be getting home as I was leaving to drive the school bus. The kids would go next-door to their grandmother's for breakfast.

Al came in and leaned against the kitchen counter, listening.

Jane : Always along the line we figured that if things didn't work one way, somehow, God had a plan that was better than what we knew. It's always worked. If you can't make something work, it's not supposed to be.

Being a mother gives you a purpose in life. I wanted to experience all those things. There are times when it isn't all that glorious. I never wanted six kids. It was very traumatic when our sixth was coming along. I think Al thought I was going to leave him.

It had been four years since my last child. I was finally to this place where nobody was going to be spitting up on me; I could get somewhere on time; the kids were getting older; all these childhood diseases were behind us. I was finally just about there, and, then, back to square one! I just about went nuts, thinking of it. Then, all the kids did things with this last one. They raised her, and she's been delightful.

I can remember thinking, "Will they ever quit arguing?" Two of them it seemed like I was always setting on the chair. Or when they'd get chicken pox, and you'd be up all night. 'Course you knew if you had one with it, there was going to be another one or two. Would I ever get through this? But, then, there comes a time when they enjoy being with each other, and it's so interesting to hear their conversation.

Al : She's probably modest. She probably hasn't told you really what she does. She is the best seamstress I ever saw. She has sewed for a lot of people.

Jane : I quit working as a secretary in an insurance company in town when Adam was born. It broke my heart. I liked working.

Al : She quit a better paying job than what I was making farming.

Jane : I never went to college or anything. I just took commercial in high school.

Al : I guess we've always been in agreement on most things. The mother ought to be at home. But she has always done something out of the home, sewing or selling something.

Jane : What's his is mine, and what's mine is his. We never had any money when we were kids, Al or I, either one. We ate well. But as far as having savings accounts or buying whatever you'd like, you just didn't have that. Now whenever Al's had money, he's always been able to tuck it away somewhere for something special or an emergency.

367

So, as the kids are married and need money, he always tries to have some in reserve, so that when they have rough spots, he can say, "Here, use this." Then, when they can, they pay it back. "You don't owe me, but if you can pay it back . . .," and there's no interest. The whole family is this way. Maybe five hundred dollars would go three different ways at Sunday dinner. Somebody would be paying back a debt, and it would go to pay somebody else something, so it went a long way. It's just an understanding. So much nicer. Better than insurance. A lot of families aren't that close.

Al and I had never taken a trip. Vacation on the farm? When do you leave? With kids, especially. A friend of ours was going to lead a trip to Australia to visit sheep farms. Al said, "That would be the ultimate." A couple of the kids were out of high school, and the rest of them were down the line from there, three or four teenagers. That Christmas our oldest daughter went up to the bank and asked if they could borrow the six thousand dollars. They borrowed the money from the hometown bank, four kids, to give us a trip to Australia. They had it paid off in a year. Each one had a share. We had the time of a lifetime.

I go out with him on his paper route on Saturday and do that night run with him. We'll lift how many ton of paper a night?

Al : We'll go out with seven ton on the truck. You load it, and, then, you unload it. We're used to work.

Jane : I can help him on this job. Or, any other member of the family can go.

Al : We've got six of the best kids in the world.

Jane : I don't know why the kids turned out so well. A lot of parents that you think have been good parents--you wonder why their kids are the way they are. The parents will say to us, "We really envy you. You have a really neat family. I wonder where we went wrong."

We've never had any problem with the drinking bit, or the drugs. They knew right where we stood. Al told the kids, "I don't believe in drinking. Don't ever come home drunk, because I won't let you in the house. We'll move your clothes out."

A neighbor questioned him, "Do you really mean that?" Al said, "I mean it with all my heart."

My dad was a drunkard. Al had a brother-in-law who was a drunkard. We've lived with it. You have the idea, "My home is not going to be that way." You set the example.

Al : There's a lot of reasons the kids turned out so well. One, she was always here. And in the second place, I was usually here, because when you're farming, it takes all your time. When they were younger, the two older boys stayed with me. They'd go to the field on the tractor and stay with me, indefinitely.

My mother played an important part, living next-door. She was alone, so when they came over for breakfast, this was the big time of day for her. She used to be a school teacher. She read to 'em. Our kids could count, tell time, do the alphabet, before they ever got near to a school.

Jane and I both were baptized in the same Baptist church. All our kids are Christians and belong to the same church. Which, I have to say, is a big factor.

We stayed in the same place, and were pretty stable people. The fact that Jane has been here--well, she's not always right, you know!--I have to say that, but I think it's the only way to raise a family. The kids are good to one another. They're concerned about each other. You're not supposed to brag on your kids. They really are good kids.

We were gone twenty-three days to Australia. They made things work. They looked after the chores. The oldest was twenty-five, and the youngest was eleven. They got everybody to school. They bitched a lot after we got back, but they made it work. They've been very generous.

Jane : The way farming has gone, it's nothing that you could sell kids on nowadays.

Al : Farming is a great way of life, for us and our kids. They like to be from the farm. They like to be on the farm. I never touched a bale of hay this year. But as far as wanting to farm, you have nothing to encourage them. I have so much money tied up in equipment. It's my choice. But to tell a kid you can do this and this and make a living--you can't. I wouldn't hope to sell farming to them. I love it, but farming is a hard life. You do it every day of the year. It's a great way of

369

life. It's a great place to raise a family. You have the opportunity to have the right kind of influence.

Jane : I think you need to be together on everything, or the kids will find they can play one parent against the other. Al and I acted as one.

Al : We don't always agree, but we've never really differed on basic things. I'm a little on the lenient side, I'll admit, but we never allowed that to surface. I never paddled them in my life.

Jane : But I have--with my hand.

Al : We've had a very satisfying life together.

Her two girls love to go somewhere with her, and the boys tease her mercilessly. That tells you something.

Did you tell her what you do on Sunday? Have dinner for them every Sunday, come back for supper--as many as twenty-two people. She does it so easy. Just makes it look like it's smooth as silk, you know. Goes to church and comes home and has dinner on the table in half an hour. They look forward to it.

Jane : When I got married my husband said to me, "Now when you die people aren't going to remember you for how clean you kept the house. They're going to remember you for how you treated them."

7

Affirmation

Each child pulls its mother into a future which now has greater significance.

A baby smiles and reaches for his mother as she enters the room. Little children ask their mother at bed-time, "Mama, will you read us a story?" They snuggle up close and listen to her voice. A young farm boy brings out the heifer to hose off the day's heat, as his mother watches from a distance. The boy knows just what to do. A teenage girl loves to make her mother laugh. A teenage boy rarely kisses his mother now, but he frequently asks for a backrub at ten p.m., and it is a time to talk. There is pleasure in knowing they count on you, even if the knowledge comes through the daily question, "What's for dinner?"

The mother-child relationship is a partnership in giving. The mother gives the child a steady dose of her variable best, day after day, year after year. The child carves out the mother's depths and gives her a full heart. The child may inspire, or provoke, the mother to rethink her positions, her values, and even her own identity. He or she may give the mother's life meaning, a sense of ultimate purpose. In return, mothers arrange their work lives around their children and spend hundreds of dollars on breakfast cereal and pasta. They play with their children, keep track of them, hold their heads, and encourage their dreams.

A mother and even a very small child may be friends-- people who like to be together. Pack a lunch, gather up the kids, find Dad in the fields, and picnic under a shade tree. The words exchanged are long gone. What was in the picnic basket no longer matters, but the memory of time together is sweet. A poor mother in the city, herself the child of a poor mother, makes a ritual of the evening meal around the table. At the core of the relationship of mother and child is the assumption: We will <u>be with</u> each other. At the table, by the hospital bed, and on the telephone across half a nation, we will be with each other.

In becoming a mother, a woman invites adventure and risk into her life. She cannot know what each child brings down the birth canal or what the future for the child will mean for her and the family. The mother's partnership, if she is in one, may reach new heights or break apart. There may be other children waiting to see how a new arrival affects their place in the family. The mother's relationship with her own parents may have to be renegotiated.

Children bring new people into a family's life. They introduce their mothers to their friends and to the parents of their friends. Children invite mothers to accept what they have to offer: a boy with Down's syndrome teaches his mother that he has this own contribution to make. Thank you very much.

Awesome responsibility goes along with being the one who takes a child's hand. A baby can pull even a delinquent teen into a new life of responsibility. A mother on welfare asks, "How could I look at my kids and smoke crack, or get drunk and not feed them or make sure that they do what they are supposed to do?" A mother with an autistic child turns the extra responsibility into a family strength when she appeals to her other three children to share in tending their brother. Bearing responsibility may make a mother wiser. It may make her feel older, or closer to and more appreciative of her own mother. It may make her aware that she has a chance to redeem a sore piece of her childhood by guiding her children to a better resolution.

A mother develops a working tolerance for things that do not change, a tolerance for endless repetitions of boring details that do not count for you when they are addressed, but that quickly count against you when they are overlooked. Dirty faces and shoes that are too tight. No milk in the refrigerator, no underwear in the drawer.

A mother also learns to affirm change, or, at least, to adjust to it. She learns to continually search for balance. A new baby can bring a precious time of intimacy and reflection. This time can also leave a mother weeping with exhaustion and feeling that she cannot do justice to both her work and her child. Babies make life less spontaneous. Old patterns and, often, old friendships have to give way. At the same time, babies, themselves, seem to be spontaneously changing all the time.

Children throw change at their parents, "Quick! Catch!" There are smaller, more frequent changes for smaller children and bigger changes for bigger children, as they go off to school, into adolescence, and out of the house.

Mothers have the choice to keep changing along with them. A mother gets to revisit her childhood through her children. To be silly with them. To see things for the first time, again. As she sees herself reacting to them, she has a better understanding of how she is put together. What are her strong inclinations? What are the tender spots she doesn't want poked? Where is the unfinished business taking her? She can redesign parts of herself.

Becoming a mother ties a woman at both ends into history. Becoming a mother breathes life into her connection with her own mother, even if she didn't like her, barely knew her, or never knew her at all. One mother says, "I remember so little from my childhood. I have tiny memories out of those vast stretches of time. All that time my mother was taking care of me.... My kids don't even know they're alive yet ..., and yet, I've been changing diapers, and wiping noses, and feeding them, and settling disputes, and strapping them in car seats for all these years. They won't even remember it when they're adults." Although the work of mothers <u>vanishes</u>, it serves the child and the child's children.

As mothers claim special ways they did things in their childhood, they keep the past alive in the present. They reach ahead with their children with these traditions and with new traditions they create together.

To choose to be a mother is to affirm one's own past. To be a mother is to say <u>yes</u> to life now, as it is, and to say <u>yes</u> to a relationship with a child who will, one day, be an adult. It is to say <u>yes</u> to a long partnership in giving. To be a mother is to affirm adventure, risk, responsibility, boring routine, change, and an unending search for balance. To be a mother is to affirm the future.

MARIE REEVES
Age: 39

"The minute she was on my belly I had feelings that I never knew I had. When they said, 'Here's your baby!' it was like I'd never seen one before."

Both of Marie's parents died when she was in her twenties. Marie has been married for two years and got pregnant by surprise, at age thirty-eight. She talks about memories and traditions. Her daughter, Betsy, nine months old, is both a link to Marie's mother and a beacon into the future. Marie is home with Betsy full-time. Marie's six-year-old stepdaughter, Lucy, spends two nights a week at Marie and Kevin's. Nothing is lost on Marie. I followed her from sink to changing table to porch swing as she told me her story in snatches.

I'm really captivated. Captivated. My favorite thing to do each day is to sit around and stare at her. When people call and say, "What are you doing?" and I say, "Staring at my baby," they laugh, but they know that I mean it. I think they really know. What could be better?

Betsy's always happy when she wakes up. Or if she cries it's just for a minute, and when I come into the room her tears just melt away, and she bursts into laughter.

Some days I get into this thing where I feel teary almost, because I'll be cleaning out her bureau, and I'll find things that she can't wear anymore, and I realize that she's getting bigger every week. Even though she's totally discombobbled my life, I hate losing the infancy stage. This is a wonderful stage. I'll really miss it when she's a toddler.

I won't miss the first three months. That was hell on earth. Betsy cried and cried and cried. She had to be held every

375

minute. Every time I put her down, she'd scream. It wasn't like she could offer me anything. She wasn't doing anything except eating and sleeping. And sort of sucking life out of me, it seemed like. It was nothing like now. Now I feel like I get as much as I give. Even when she bites my tit for twenty minutes! But that first three months... I remember saying to several people, "This is pure hell. I would never want to do this again."

Now my one complaint is about her sleeping. People always said to me, "You'll never get sleep. Sleep will take on a whole new meaning." I mean, when it's time to sleep, I want to sleep. I dream of the time when Kevin will take me away all by myself, and I can sleep in.

I love watching her learn things. I love seeing her feel comfortable with me. I love how she sits like a big person with her little arm on my shoulder. I love how I kind of look over, and she's so casually relaxed. She has her legs crossed, and she's just like a big person sitting there. I love making her comfortable. I love it all. I think it's a privilege. As hard as it is.

I hate it, too. It's passion. It's like when somebody dies. It's terrible to say, but there are wonderful things about someone dying. There were aspects of when my mother died that were the greatest feelings on earth. Just as there are aspects of raising Betsy that are the greatest things, and, at the same time, they're incredible pains in the ass, and I wonder if I'll ever make it through. I just think that's passion at its finest.

The first time we drove home from the hospital, I thought every car on the road was going to hit us. "God, why don't people use their turn signals? Why do people drive like this?" It seemed like that ride took forever. I'd go to the hospital a million times to give birth, but I'd never want to bring the baby home again! I wish I could have taken a helicopter--without her. We had to stop at the grocery store to get Kevin some Coke, and I remember thinking, "God, can't he get it later?" She started to cry, and I was completely freaked out. I almost ran into the store to get him, to tell him to get out of there, because the baby was crying.

I feel like if anybody came towards me to do anything to her, I could handle it. That's the other part of the passion. I could protect her. I know I could. All she'd have to do is give me one of those looks, and I'd do whatever needed to be done!

If I can just clear my head and let my instincts take over, nine times out of ten, they're right on. They're there. They told me that about labor: "Read the books and then put the books away. Go in there and be an animal. Let your body do it." It's one of the few things that we do these days that's not embellished. It's just what your body was made for, so go in there, and let it perform. That is one of my favorite things about mothering, finding out about my wonderful instincts. They're there, all intact. They may not have been used for many years, but they're intact. I'm very feminine. I love that.

I just don't feel that I'm the same as I was before I had Betsy. I feel older. If I hadn't waited so long I would have two. If Kevin encouraged me at all, I would have another right away. He has Lucy, from his first marriage, and he has Betsy. He really doesn't want to have another, so we'd have to fight it out. I just don't know if it's that important. If we had another, he or she would be basically my project. It would be fine in two years, but I don't know that our marriage would stand up under another kid. I imagine it would. Who knew if we could even reach these heights?

I worry about living a long life. Sometimes I cry, because I think I'm not going to get to meet Betsy's kids. I think about her maybe being left without parents at twenty. But that wouldn't be all bad. I'll be a better parent than my parents were when they left me in my twenties. My father died suddenly when I was twenty-one, and my mother when I was twenty-three. My two living grandparents died in between. The dog of my dreams was run over by my next-door neighbor and was left crippled. It seemed like everything I was counting on was not there.

Having Betsy has made me more in touch with my Mom. It's made me think about things we did when I was a little girl that I liked. I had a lot of excitement around me as a child. There were always people in and out, a lot of adults. A lot of parties and great food. When the weekend came, we were either going to be going out in the boat and meeting a bunch of people afterwards for dinner, or they were going to come to our house for a barbecue. A lot of parties and people, laughter and talk. Having Betsy brings all that back. Even though mealtimes were incredibly painful, because Mother was always drunk, we were always around the table.

It's traditions. Like I've started this tradition with Kevin and Lucy, and Lucy takes it very seriously. Every Friday night I say, "It's casual dinner night." That means that you very well might get just pasta, and you might not have a green vegetable. You may just get a plate of chicken, or you may just get popcorn. It may not be the night you're going to get all your nutrients. Lucy will come and look up at me and ask, "Is tonight Friday?" She's already come to look forward to it, and it was just sort of an idea I had one day, to name this night.

I'm starting to think more now in terms of establishing traditions, of naming things and making a big deal about them, even if they're absolutely nothing. When I was a kid, it wasn't so much the things we did, it was the way we did them. If we decided to eat in front of the TV, we had TV trays. We got them all out, and we washed them all off. Mother trucked the food all down, and we all helped. We all helped truck the food back up. It was a tradition. Now I want TV trays. So does my sister, because there's something a little more magical about putting your dinner on one of those little trays than holding it in your lap.

Also, it's made me think, if I die early, the two things that Betsy will have are her memories and her traditions. Nobody can ever take those things away. They can be carried on for ever and ever. You've given them this incredible thing.

I think of things I want for Betsy, but then I think that's so self-serving, because she may not want any of those things. The thing I want the most is for her to be her own person. I don't quite know how to, but I want to give her that confidence. I don't know that I could do it for a long time myself. It took years and years.

I was thinking one day that I want my daughter to be pretty, and then I thought, "I don't even care about that," but I do want her to have a magnetic personality.

Who knows, maybe she'll be such a raunchy brat that I won't want to have anything to do with her! I know I gave my parents an incredible run for their money. My mother always used to say, "You are without a doubt the hardest child I've ever raised." There were three of us. I was The One. I was always right there, talking, noticing. I was always smoothing over and shining up. I was always on and always ready. Always wanting more. Listen, if we went to the Fair and rode every ride in the place, on the way home I wanted to stop and have pizza. There was always just one more thing we could fit in. I'm difficult in that respect. I'm great. I've come to think I'm pretty incredible, but I'm not easy. I think I'm not the easy-going person that people are attracted to. I really get in there and go.

It's good that kids adjust to their parents. Kids are so resilient. I can really rinse Lucy out about something and five minutes later she's on my lap. The other day I said to her "Do I get crabby?"

She said, "Yes, but it doesn't scare me."

One of the most glorious things about children and being a mother is that every single kid is different. It's the absolutely one thing where you don't need to feel threatened. You try one thing and if it doesn't work, you don't need to feel like you've done something wrong. You try something else.

The other night I fell into bed and said, "Kevin, I have nothing left. I don't know how I'm going to get it back by the morning." So he gave me a backrub, which was nice. It was perfect. I think I was sort of also intimating that if he started to get any sex, that would have been it. There was absolutely nothing left of me, and the last thing I had room for was to offer something big like that up.

Kevin and I do a lot more things separately since we had a baby. It seems like we can't find a lot of time together. When Lucy is here too, she has activities, and he'll take her on her activities, or I'll take her, and he'll stay with the baby. It's like we just sort of pass each other.

Since I had the baby some of my friendships have changed. I can't keep all the ends up. One day a friend mentioned to me at a party that she was sort of mourning the loss of me. I can't just drop in the way I used to. I don't, because it squeezes things together more. But I'm not whining--I'd much rather have a baby than be able to drop in at my friend's any time.

The first time Betsy had a fever, a bunch of my friends happened to be at the house, and all I could do was sit by the baby monitor and listen to this little crying thing Betsy does. I'd start to go check on her, and they'd say, "Sit down. She's okay." Here my baby was sick, and I was so worried about her, and I thought everybody should be wearing black, and nobody should be having a drink!

My friend Mary will tell me things that I used to say to her that were just off the wall. I don't think she got the right amount of support from me when her kids were small, because I just had no idea what she was going through.

When I really feel frustrated what works for me the best is two things. I look right into Betsy's eyes, and stare at her for a little while, and get some eye contact going, and just enjoy her completely. The other thing is to just clear my head and think about when I gave birth, and when they pulled that baby out, plopped her on my stomach, and said, "Here's your baby!" I always laugh. I always just remember how thrilled I was. And that's pretty amazing from a woman who was never going to have kids and never thought she could get into it. The minute Betsy was on my belly, I had feelings that I never knew I had. When they said "Here's your baby!," it was like I'd never seen one before.

At night sometimes after I put Betsy to bed and I'm tired, all of a sudden I'll look over at Kevin and say, "Gee, I sure do miss Betsy!" She's probably been asleep for ten minutes.

LYNN KNAPP
Age: 18

"I do her whole world for her. I get to be a kid again."

Lynn's family is Chezkoslovakian, and she was born and raised in Texas. She was sixteen when she got pregnant, and her daughter Anne is now sixteen months old. Lynn says Anne has been "a big angel," who slept through the night the first night she was home from the hospital. Lynn is eager to be off welfare, but will be on it for two more years, until she can finish an associate's degree in a medical-office-assistant program. She and her daughter are a happy pair.

Anne is probably the best thing that ever happened to me. When I was young, I would go out, party, do whatever it was, drugs, alcohol, to have a good time. I would have gotten addicted to drugs. When I got pregnant with her, I knew that you just don't do that stuff when you're pregnant. "Okay, I have to straighten up and act normal now." I did.

Now I have this connection-for-life with Martin, Anne's father, that I don't want. I can't get rid of him, but at least he doesn't live with us anymore. He's nineteen. He does nothing. He is the only negative thing that ever hit me. I can't change the fact that he's her father. Thank God he calls, because that reminds me of how bad it was with him.

He was from an abusive family. I kind of knew what I was getting into. It was like there was a light flashing over his head, "Stay away. Stay away!" I just wasn't watching. He used to be a boxer. He punched me in the face. It cracked my cheekbone. My gums on that side are numb. He just hit me that one time. It freaked me out really bad, but I had to go through a long process of getting away. I don't think I could handle a relationship with a guy now. I'd think about him, not me.

Now I have Anne to think about. I do her whole world for her. I get to be a kid again. I watch her do everything. Two days ago I got her dressed, nice clothes. I opened the front door, and she went out and walked over to her wagon. It had rained the night before. She knew the wagon had water in it. I saw her patting it with her hand. I said, "You better not play in that." I pulled the wagon away and went inside to get my purse. I came out, and she was sitting in the wagon. I laughed. I would have done the same thing! She's so much fun.

I'm moving into a new apartment in a couple of weeks, and I'm going to start college to be a medical office assistant. That leaves open the possibility of becoming a nurse later. In two years I'll have grown a whole lot. I'll be an educated woman, not "Lynn Knapp, the girl who got her G.E.D." There's just one road I have to take for another two years. Then I'll get a job and be settled. I'll be earning my own living. I'll have my own place and my own car.

I shut my mind off at school in sixth grade. Around eighth grade, right after my mom passed away, I was like, "I can't be here anymore. I can't handle it." People were fighting and shooting each other at school. I thought, "It will be a million years before I graduate," so I dropped out at the beginning of ninth grade.

I didn't get a chance to have that real growing up time with my mother. We didn't really have a relationship yet. She died right before I hit my teenage years, and I went wild. I went crazy. I was gone all the time. Dad must have thought I was weird. There was nobody there to say, "Wake up!" I never got to have the long talks with my mother about, "This is what you should do, and this is what you shouldn't do," about grades, or boys, or going to college.

A month after I dropped out, I got pregnant with Anne. I didn't intend to get pregnant. Everyone in my family thought, "Oh, my God, she'll be the worst mother," but since I've had her, I've only been away from her about four days. She knows I have to go to school. The way I see it, I'm going to graduate a year earlier than everyone that was in my class and go to college a year earlier, so I have already caught up! I have a lot of things that I thought I never would have.

Sometimes I feel if I don't get out of the house, I'll go crazy. Then I just take Anne, and we go to the park or to Taco Bell. She has all kinds of things to say. She tells me about her day. I tell her about mine, and she laughs at me. She knows what I'm saying. People tell me she doesn't, but she does. She catches on quick.

I'll be doing my homework, and she'll come over and sit next to me. I'll be having a really hard time keeping my train of thought. She will just sigh and look at me like, "Are we going to do anything fun?" That pretty much lets me know I need a break, because I've been ignoring her for two hours. At that point I can't get anywhere with my studying, so I spend some time with her and go back to it later.

When she turns eighteen, I'll still be young. I'll still have a lot of time in my life left. I'll be able to share it with her, too. I see her as a really good friend. She's really good to me. It's unconditional love. I'm always going to love her. That's what I needed. Knowing Anne the way I do now, I would feel really horrible if I gave her up for adoption or if I had had an abortion.

Sometimes I feel, "I'm so lonely. I hate this," but then I think, "I have Anne. It's all right." I'm glad.

VATSANA SOUTHIDA
Age: 27

"Just talk to them. I think it's the best part. We talk."

Vatsana is from Laos and has been in this country for twelve years. Her daughter Janet is five and her son Chuck is three. She takes great delight in them. She is a teacher's aide. Vatsana graduated from high school nine years ago and takes one college course each semester. She is majoring in child development. Vatsana and her husband live with his parents. Her husband is within a year of completing an engineering degree.

I like to take care of the kids. I always dreamed that I would be a teacher. I've not reached that goal yet, but I'm in the field. I'm working on it. I enjoy playing with them, socializing with them. I like the way they talk. You try to teach them words, and they try to repeat what you say. They're so cute. I just love when they're babies, and they walk, and they get into everything! I just like children! When I go home, you won't believe it, both of them, they're just jumping up and down!

My husband, he didn't involve much. He goes to work, and then he goes to school. Right now he got laid off. We don't have any health benefit to protect the children when they're sick. I'm trying to get a health benefit, talk to my principal. He just tells me all the problems of the school. Since I'm bi-lingual, he can use me there. Anytime he needs me he just asks, "Vatsana, can you come translate?" I say, "Fine," but when I asked him about the health benefit, he just came up with all these excuses.

I leave my children with my sister. I trust her. Before that I left them with my auntie. Now, right now, this week my husband takes care of picking my daughter up from school. My father-in-law, he helps out a little bit. I don't know what's going to happen if my father-in-law goes back to work when my husband goes back to school. Picking Janet up at two o'clock conflicts with when I come to work, at two-thirty. I had to quit here three times, because I didn't have a babysitter. Mostly they have Lao students here, and they need me. This is my third time coming back. I translate a lot for the parents when they are having problems.

Having children changed my life. You get to be family. Mostly, you spend time with them, like helping my daughter with her homework. When I have time at home I just play with my son a little bit. Usually I don't have time at all to spend with him. When I come home he just keeps bothering me. He wants me to play with him!

Back there in my country, the moms don't have that much. It lacks of a lot of things over there, and we have everything here. It's just there in the store for you! In my country the mothers have to provide everything. We don't even have the diapers over there. They have to use baby blankets and just keep using it, even if they have five or six children. They just keep using it. Pass it on.

My Dad was working with Americans, and the Communists were coming in. If we didn't leave at that time, they were going to take him away somewhere. Far away. So we had to escape. We had to pretend we were going to visit someone in another town. We don't let anyone, even our friend, know where we are going. We were in a car all day until midnight. Eight of us. Then we had to get out of the car and walk across the forest and the jungle until well dark. Then these two men picked up two canoes under the river, and we got on them across to the Thailand.

You have to be careful. Thai people are tricky. But some people helped us. We stayed in a Thai camp for about three months. We were coming as immigrants, not refugees. We were lucky. My Dad had a sponsor in Washington, DC. We came to California, because the weather is exactly the same as my country.

Every day we try to teach the children, little by little, about Laos. This month is our New Year. I just take them to the temple and see what is going on, how they dress, how they dance, how they are doing the New Year. They just look. Of course, they go for American ways. It's easier. We talk in Lao, of course. My daughter wants to talk in English more, now that she goes to pre-school.

My husband said to me, "Talk to her in English."

I said, "No, because she might forget Lao."

I think the children are going to be more American style. I can see that. The kids that are growing up here go with the society. It's hard for them to learn back to their country. I will be teaching them what I learned, what my Mom has been teaching me.

For Lao children that grow up here, it is hard to follow the parents' rules. Where I work, all these parents come up to me and say, "I have a problem with my kids. They won't listen to me. They just listen to their friends." They tell me all these problems. I found out that Lao parents don't like to talk to their kids. They let things go. They don't keep after them, come to school, and ask the teachers, "What is going on?" They don't speak English--that's what happened. They don't know how to read and write. I encourage them to go to school and keep up with their children.

I know what happens, so I will be keeping up with my kids, telling them what I learn from my experiences. The time is now for us to start.

Some of the rules of the Lao family, I like to keep it, and some of the rules, I like to change it. What is the best for them? You kind of look around your society. It's okay I think for them to make some changes.

I will keep after the kids to keep going to school, to go to college. I will provide them all the best that I can to send them to school. Without education here, it's hard for you.

Just talk to them. I think it's the best part. We talk. If something isn't right, just sit down and talk! Right now my kids are so little, I don't have any problem with them yet. I enjoy being with my kids. They're so cute!

HANNAH DONALDSON
Age: 41

"I'm 'Mummy.' I never thought I'd get that chance."

Last year Hannah and her husband Mark adopted a baby boy, Moses. Hannah is a Southern Baptist and believes that Moses is the gift of her faith in God. Hannah used to do hair. Now, she is happy to stay home with Moses. Behind Hannah's story is another mother: a fifteen-year-old girl who decided to give up her child.

I've been waiting for Moses for nineteen years.

About three years ago, after surgery, they told me that I was able to conceive. Just about that time, one day, I was reading First Samuel, about Hannah having her baby. It was like the Lord was telling me I was going to have a child. Hannah made a vow when she got her child, so I made a vow that if he gave me a child, I'd raise him in a Christian home, and, hopefully, he'd grow up to serve the Lord.

Nothing happened. No pregnancy. Then, we moved to Maryland. One day a lady in our new neighborhood, Polly, told me about a girl who was pregnant and was going to put the baby up for adoption. Then the girl changed her mind. I told her, "If you ever know of another girl in that situation, let me know." A while later, out of the clear blue sky, I got a phone call from Polly. She knew a young girl who was pregnant and wanted to put her baby up for adoption. I was in tears. This might be it. One other time we thought we were going to have a baby, but the birth mother backed out.

There were many problems that had to be worked out. The birth father had threatened to beat the birth mother. He didn't want her to have the child. The girl wasn't sure what she wanted to do. Mark didn't want to get his hopes up and then have the birth mother change her mind again. One by one, the Lord knocked down every one of the obstacles. Five weeks from that phone call, I was a mom.

We got to go to the hospital and feed him. I got to change the first stinky! The nurse said, "Welcome to motherhood! You do it." All I could do was cry.

I was afraid that this mother would change her mind. Really that fear did not leave me until I got word from the lawyer a whole year later that the adoption was final. When that call came, I burst out crying. A friend's children were at my house, and the little girl started to cry when I did. I had to explain to her, "These are happy tears. Moses belongs to Mr. Mark and me now. Nobody can take him." She stopped crying and went back to her hamburger!

I've told everyone all along that Moses is mine. God gave him to me. The world just had to catch up and make him legal. My confirmation was when we took him back to our home church. We went to our Sunday School class. The scripture lesson was the same passage in First Samuel!

There's no way to describe how I feel when that little face looks up at me and smiles. I'm Number One. All those years of seeing other people with their kids, the kid running up, and hugging his mother's legs, and sticking his head down in her knees. I never had that. He's doing that now. I'm Number One in this little guy's life. I'm "Mommy." I never thought I'd get that chance.

Moses' birth mother came and lived with us for a week before Moses was born. I think my husband was expecting spiked hair, leather jacket, and a motorcycle. But she liked Country Western music. She could talk old Western movies with Mark. She just blended right in with us. She's never seen Moses. She didn't want to. I think she would just like for us to leave her alone. I'm hoping that somewhere down the line I can talk to her. If Moses is asking to meet her when he's older, I'd like permission to contact her.

ANN SEWALL
Age: 33

"Everyone is not a designer creation. Everybody does have a contribution."

Ann and her husband Bert have four children. Son Bert is seven and has Down's syndrome. Ann talks candidly about what Bert's disability has meant to her and to the family. Her other three children are Tommy (five), Katherine (three), and Gordon (one). Ann's attitudes toward her children enable her to be a graceful and effective mother.

Every parent's nightmare came true for me. I couldn't get any sadder than I got with Bert's being born with Down's syndrome. That was rock-bottom.

We knew when he was five days old that he had a heart defect, and we'd have to get through surgery. We were living on a base in Germany. We were sent from the base hospital to a cardiologist in a German hospital. It was like something out of an old movie. It was a large stone hospital. The hallways were cold. There were empty gurneys all over the place. We brought Bert into a cold office with an examining table and paperwork piled everywhere. The cardiologist was in his seventies. Then they called in a genetics doctor who began looking at Bert's tongue and ears and toes. I was thinking, "This kid has a heart problem. Why are they looking him over like this?"

The doctor turned to me and said something like, "Have you ever had an abortion?"

"No." I was a little bit offended.

What he meant was a miscarriage. In German the translation would be "spontaneous abortion"--which is the medical term for it. He thought I might have had problems with other babies.

389

Then they told us that they thought he was "mongoloid." Again, the translation was missing, and so they used that term.

The first doctor was talking about the heart. In the meantime, in the background, these other technicians were poking Bert, trying to get blood out of him to do the chromosome analysis. Then we had to leave this hospital and go back to the one on the base and tell them what we were told. I don't think they should ever have sent us there without a translator. There was too much confusion with the language barrier. Then it was hard for us to get hold of any literature that was up-to-date. You'd want to shoot yourself if you read what they had in the old encyclopedias on the base.

All I could see was a severely retarded child with multiple handicaps. I remember thinking, "I will never ever laugh again." I can see how parents who give birth to a child with a handicap want to give the child up for adoption. You have to work through that grief. It is similar to a death. You aren't getting that child that you thought you were getting. I couldn't see any future for any of us at that point.

Everyone on the base knew me, because I worked there, right up until the day before he was born. They were popping in the office every day to see if I had had the baby. We knew that we were leaving within a few months to come back to the States, and so, we decided not to tell a lot of people about Bert. We didn't want people feeling sorry for us. I really needed to talk about it. I was dying inside. I wish that we had shared it with people over there. We could have gotten a lot of support from people. Also, now, looking at video tapes of Bert as a baby, I wonder, "How could I have been so stupid--not to have seen it?" His features are fairly subdued, but I think a lot of people may have suspected and didn't want to ask.

They fixed Bert's heart condition when he was fourteen months old. He had to have a valve repaired, but they found enough tissue in there to work with, so they made a valve for him, which was good, because a lot of heart valves are getting recalled now, too. That's all you need is to get your child recalled!

I can talk to anyone now about Down's syndrome and tell some good jokes. We joke about how much Bert loves rice and has an Oriental look to him. Anywhere we go he seems to make friends with people who are Oriental. You do develop a sense of humor about it. With kids anyway, if you don't have a sense of humor, you might as well just hang it right up!

Bert is actually doing wonderfully. He behaves very normally. He is slow in a lot of areas. His receptive language is pretty much on an average with most kids his age. He understands a whole lot more than he can express. There are things he says which we would never expect to hear him say. One day my husband said to Bert, "What's that, Bert?," when Bert was trying to say something to me. Bert said to him, "I'm talking to Mum," with an air of "Don't interrupt me."

Sometimes he acts a little younger than his age, but he doesn't have off-the-wall behaviors. I don't expect him to have off-the-wall behaviors or to be able to get away with that, either. He is not hard to control. Last night he didn't want to get into his pajamas. He took his glasses off and threw them on the floor. I sent him to his room and said, "There's not going to be a story. Not if you do that." So, he went to bed. I'm not sure he made the connection between throwing the glasses and missing the story. But I'm not sure I always have that connection with my other kids, either!

He's fun. I think we're really lucky to have him. I shudder to think what it would have been like if he had been a severely handicapped child. I think there's going to be a lot of hard times down the road with him. There will be moments of sadness through his whole life. I think it gets more trying with kids with Down's syndrome as they get older, because the distance grows between an average child and one with Down's syndrome of the same age.

Having him has brought a lot of my own strengths out. I have to be strong. It's hard to tell people, "My child is not normal." How do you handle that? I don't find that I wish him to be any different. I did when he was young. I got past that. If I were wishing that he were normal, I feel like I would be wishing him away, because this is who he is.

391

Sometimes I feel sad about it. If God were to come down here tomorrow and say, "I can change Bert. Right now I'll change him, if you want, to a normal kid," I don't know what I'd choose. Selfishly I don't want to change him, because I like him the way he is, but, on the other hand, then he could achieve all those normal things, like graduating from high school.

The other kids are aware of Bert's having Down's syndrome. We talk about it every so often. I want them to understand that he is more <u>like</u> them than different. Tommy can now pick it up in other people. Sometimes he tells me they have it, and they don't! He comes and whispers, "She has Down's syndrome." I whisper back, "No, she doesn't." That's a little awkward!

I think my kids will be more tolerant. I expect them to be as responsible for Bert down the road as my husband and I are. I'm not going to feel guilty because we had him.

I think Bert's here as a teacher. He teaches people to accept him and that the world isn't perfect and isn't meant to be perfect. In the beginning I thought of him as a genetic fluke. He was not a mistake or a fluke. There's more to this than that something went wrong in the genetic structure. Bert has an impact. He has touched a lot of lives already. He puts things in perspective. You realize life is a balance. Everyone is not a designer creation. Everybody does have a contribution.

Bert really is a joy. I guess it's what you'd call a bittersweet situation.

TONI BARRAZA
Age: 31

"I found out that the more I gave them of structure, of my strength, I would get strength from them. Yeah, I would."

Toni is a black, Episcopalian mother on welfare. She lives in Boston, Massachusetts. "THE most important people" in her life are Opal (fourteen), Debbie (eleven), and Donald (nine).

My kids are my friends. They're <u>okay</u>. Opal helps me out a lot. She thinks she's the mother! At the same time, she wants to be the baby. She says to me, "Don't you think it would have been real cool if you had just stopped with me? You could have stopped, and we could have been like sisters. We would have a whole apartment and be partying!"

"Opal, you know I don't party."

She is my special one. And Don is my special one. And so is Debbie.

Opal got hit by a car in 1985. She was only five. They couldn't even take her to be x-rayed. They had to bring the x-ray machine to her. She was comatose, and she had seizures. If you just barely touched the bed, she would shake violently. She was hooked up to everything a person could be on. Tubes everywhere. They had to keep her eyes open, and they had to keep putting stuff in them to keep them moist. They had to give her this stuff to keep her still, because the seizures she was having were so bad that it would give her brain damage. She just couldn't do anything. Her eyes were awful. Then she got where she could move a little bit, and she would cry. She would grab my hand.

I don't know. God saved her. She was sitting up in the bed eating jello three days later, looking like nothing happened. You couldn't even tell that the bolt was in her head, a brain monitor. When the doctor was explaining it all to me, it was like the words were just kind of going into me, but they weren't staying there. Now I can say all this, but I couldn't say it then.

God got me through. That's all. I'm not even going to sugar-coat it. I'm not going to say, "I think that maybe God helped me." No. God did it. God is the only thing that saved her, because she should have been dead. This person is precious to me.

She was right behind my house. I heard somebody say that somebody got hit by a car. I seen my landlord come running up the street. He came up, and then the girl from downstairs said, "You got to come outside. Opal got hit by a car."

I'm like, "No. No, sir." I made it down to the first floor. The landlord was looking real funny. I wouldn't go any further. I said, "I can't go out," and I started crying.

All these people started pulling on me. They had to drag me out of the house. I couldn't go see her. I was scared to death. I would not go look at her. It wasn't that I couldn't go. I wouldn't go. I was embarrassed that they found me that way, but I just couldn't see her. I couldn't go and look. I was scared I would just see her splattered all over the place. I just couldn't look down at her for long. I saw her down there. She wasn't crying or nothing. She was on the ground. I don't know if she was conscious. I couldn't look at her. She just wasn't crying. She was just down there. Everybody was around. All I could see was her legs and her hands. I went and got in the ambulance and sat there. I couldn't stand over there. I couldn't look at her. I was scared that if I did, she would be dead.

Someone called my mother. She met me at the hospital. I saw her and just started crying. Everybody was crying. We just prayed. My mother and I just walked up and down the hall in the hospital just saying the rosary over and over. I saw it on a piece of paper that the church people from the hospital gave me.

I keep these records for when I stop counting my blessings. For when I forget that God has done things in my life, when things are bad, and there's nothing to eat in the house. I know there's always a way. My kids don't go hungry anymore.

394

There's always a way. I draw for people sometimes. I make signs and posters. It's like I can fall back on that. God gives everybody a talent. Something you can do. God is the only thing in my life that has been dependable. My mother helps me a lot. I take care of my kids.

My kids--they're the ones that keep me going. How could I look at my kids and walk out and not come back home? I know women that do that. Or how could I look at my kids and smoke crack or get drunk and not feed them or make sure that they do what they're supposed to do?

I made a poster, and I put up exactly what we do every day after school. My kids follow that perfectly, to the letter. I've been doing it for about three and a half years. When they come home, they do their chores. After that, if they have homework, do your homework. That's all I ask. After that, you're free. Do what you want. Go out. And then you come back in here just before we eat. Wash your hands, because I don't want you to come to the table with your dirty hands. You sit down at the table with me, and then we eat together. We pray over our food every night.

I found out that the more I gave them of structure, of my strength, I would get strength from them. Yeah, I would. They just don't worry about things. I know in my mind that we're going to run out of food in a couple of days. My son needs sneakers. My daughter needs a coat. I know these things, and they're just <u>happy</u>. I take that lesson from them, and I get that strength from them. They're good.

My mother is my inspiration. She loves her kids. My father left when I was three. She was in college when I was a kid. I never knew she was on welfare. She took care of us. She has worked for the department of welfare for seventeen years. She is kind of bossy! She is NICE. She is just the nicest person. She has a lot of friends. Her clients would come to our house on Saturday to talk to her, because they loved her. She is just wonderful. She never gave up. She didn't give us away. She didn't get tired. If she did, she didn't let me know it.

If I ever decided to get rid of my kids, I was tired, I don't want to do it no more, if I ever did that, I could never visit my

395

mother or talk to her again. She didn't make me that way. She didn't tell me to quit. She <u>showed</u> me, without saying to me, that anything that comes in my life, I have to face, and I can do it. I don't have to run from things. I would fail her miserably if I did. I love her too much to fail her that way. I don't want her to give up on me. My kids are the one thing I didn't quit on or get tired of. Them and graduating from high school.

When I kiss my son, it's like eating honey or something. It's so sweet. When I hold his face right there, he's so <u>beautiful</u> to me. I kiss his nose all the time. I say, "Where'd you get this nose?"

"From you."

Debbie likes to hold me and rub my belly, "Oh, Mummy, don't get skinny, don't get skinny."

Opal, she likes to tickle me and make me laugh! Oh, that girl! She makes me crack up!

LOUISE CALLAHAN
Age: 52

"I'll never say 'No' if I can say 'Yes.'"

Louise and her husband Chuck have always made decisions together. Their four children are all in their twenties. Louise remembers some highlights from when they were little.

I remember waking Pam up when our golden retriever started to have puppies. It was three o'clock in the morning. She was four, and I thought this would be a wonderful experience for her. She wandered out into the kitchen. She watched two of them be born, and I said, "Isn't this exciting?"

"Yes, but why are they in baggies?" Baggies had just come out on the market. Then she turned around and went back to bed.

I thought, "Well, so much for that."

One day in church the woman behind us wanted to keep Pam busy, so she gave her a string of rosary beads. Pam was flipping them around. I told her to stop. Things were quiet for a while. Then we heard, "Hang on, Jesus, you're going for a ride!" She was whirling the rosary around in a big circle.

The kids always said I had eyes in the back of my head and "eyes in my ears, too."

I have a poem Pam wrote for me about how I make her favorite kind of eggs and leave her night-light on.

On cold mornings, I'd put their clothes in the dryer. Extravagant, but when you heat with wood, your house isn't always that warm. Molly used to come down stark naked, from two years old on, grab the chain that was on the fireplace screen, and pretend it was a microphone. We were all freezing, and she was on stage, naked. It's hard to pat yourself on the back, but I've been a good mother. And Chuck's been a good helper.

When David was about five, he was angry one morning, and he decided he was going to run away from home. I made a hobo stick and packed him a lunch, full of all kinds of goodies, hoping that he wouldn't go too far. Of course, I could see him all morning--he was across the street in the front yard. At noon-time there was a knock at the back door.

"I've come home for lunch."

"I don't have a little boy, where do you live?"

He sat down on the porch step and said, "I'll never do that again."

"Well, what happened to the food I gave you earlier?"

"Oh, Billy and I ate that at ten o'clock."

The next day, he decided he was going to run away again. "Well that's fine, but I don't have any food for you this morning."

"Well, then, I guess I'll change my mind."

There was a Christmas when I was going to make jam for everyone, family and neighbors. I had put everything out the night before, the five pounds of sugar, the currants ... you name it, it was there. I came into the kitchen at six-thirty the next morning, and Pam had mixed everything together. She just looked up at me and said, "I can cook, too." My first thought was "the money I have spent on this." I couldn't retrieve anything. Then I thought, "Well, she's going to be a cook," and she is. She's a good cook. She meant well.

When the kids were little they'd have a weekend that was their weekend with either Chuck or me. So, if it was Pam's weekend with me, she could pick Saturday or Sunday, and she and I would do whatever she wanted, and Chuck would stay home with the other children. We'd go to the movies, or shopping. It might be just to go see Grandma, but it was on a one-to-one basis. Sometimes someone would ask to go watch the airplanes take off at the airport, to go to the Aquarium, ice-skating, or to sit in the library for half a day, and go out to lunch.

It's important to take the time to do the things your children ask you to do. I will never say "no," if I can say "yes." If one wants you to read her a story, and you were going to roll your hair, take the time to read the story. Sometimes you need your own time and space. There are days when I would love to come home to an empty house. But you don't want to look back and feel you didn't give them what you could.

We used to have family night every Monday night after dinner, and we all protected that evening for the meeting. You got to tell it like it is. We started this when our oldest was in the third grade. If you had gripes, didn't like the way someone was treating you in the house, if you thought something was unfair, this was your chance to air it at a round-table discussion. It cleared the air on a regular basis.

It's hard not to show favoritism, especially if one child is being a pain and the other is a peach. When I was a child and was in a grumpy mood my father used to say to me, "Why don't you go to the Post Office and buy two postcards and write to all of your friends?" My mother would say, "If you smile on the outside, it's impossible to feel bad on the inside."

We lost a child when she was eight months old. She developed a very bad cold, and then her kidneys shut down. She was in the hospital for two weeks. In the last three days she was having special care around the clock. She was so sick. They told me, "Be prepared," but still you're not prepared. It took me about a year--you never get over it, but for about a year, I was very low. I didn't want to go anywhere or do anything, except with my own immediate family.

Some days I would just feel a little hand rubbing me on the back of the neck. Even as little toddlers, the two I had helped me. And it was good for me to have them to care for.

JULIANNE WEATHERSBY
Age: 47

"When I introduce them I will say, 'This is my nice child,' meaning Paul, and then I will say, 'This is The Girl.' That's what we call her. They're a lot of fun!"

Julianne is black, a Baptist, and the mother of two children. Jennifer is twenty-two and, having graduated from Howard University, continues to live in Washington D.C. Paul is sixteen and stayed in St. Louis with his father this year, when Julianne moved East to take a job as associate principal of a large high school. Julianne has always worked, first as a teacher and then in educational administration. She has been divorced for six years. Julianne appreciates her children's different personalities and obviously enjoys her relationships with them.

I always worked. I always had a babysitter to come in. My husband was the vice-president of a bank. We always had income, but I always worked. I loved teaching. It would have been very difficult for me not to work, because I liked it. It was just what I did. There were always teenagers at my house. My kids got used to students calling the house, or kids coming by when they were home from college to let me know how they were doing. My kids have always shared me with my friends and my students.

Jennifer is a thin little child. She rides that subway all over D.C. She just walks like she knows where she's going. She's like the little mother, telling her friends not to walk alone. I said, "Jenn, what could you do? You are about as big as a minute. Somebody could grab you and beat the hell out of you. What could you do?"

She just said, "Oh, <u>ple-e-ease</u>."

She goes wherever she wants to go. Growing up in Chicago was part of it. She's not afraid. She can hang with the best of them. I can't worry about Jenn. She's doing what she wants to do.

She's diabetic. We found that out when she came home for Christmas her freshman year. I think that really aged me. They did a lot of tests and then told her, "You are a first class diabetic."

I began to cry, and Jenn began to ask questions. "What does this mean? Will my life be shorter?"

I couldn't deal with it at first. I cried and cried about it. As a mother, if you could protect your kids from anything, you would. At her age, in college, she should be just doing exciting, fun things. That's a lot to bear, to have to give yourself a shot four times a day and constantly watch what you eat. Then, all I could remember was when I was growing up, people who were diabetic didn't live long.

Jenn said to me when she went into the hospital, "Mummy, I'm glad it's me and not you. You are so prissy. You couldn't do it. You couldn't give yourself a shot." It's probably true. My mother says that Jenn has always had more sense than I have. When I divorced, my mother said, "Well, at least you have Jenn and Paul. They'll take care of you. I won't have to worry about you."

I talked to my son last night. He said, "What are you doing?"

I said, "Oh, I'm going to watch a movie on HBO."

He said, "I know, because you don't have the VCR hooked up, do you?"

"No, Paul, I'm waiting for you to come to do it."

"I just think that's so pitiful."

My kids laugh at me a lot. They sort of nudge each other all the time, "There she goes, trying to do something, and she doesn't know how." So, you know.

When I talked to my daughter recently she said, "I don't know why you had to go off and move all by yourself. You know that you need to live with somebody, and it's not safe. I don't know why you're trying to be so brave at your age."

I just said, "Well, Jenn . . . you worry about me, and I'll worry about you."

Jenn is overdue to have a check-up with the specialist. I told her last night on the phone that I would be in D.C. next month, and I would make the appointment, and she would go. She simply said, "Yes, Julianne," which is what she calls me when she wants to make a point, and she's being sassy.

Jenn is my even change. She always has been. She's my match. On major things she will respect my wishes, but as she told me last night, "Mommy, I am grown."

It's hard not to interfere. You want them to live up to your expectations. I'm not happy with what she's doing now, and I let her know it. She's doing retail part-time in a mall. When I express my unhappiness, she will listen, and then she will say, "Goodbye, Julianne." Like, "I have listened to you and given you the proper respect, and I'm going to do what I want to do."

I had peaked in St. Louis professionally, and I wanted to relocate. I talked to Paul about it. He is very quiet, not like Jenn. When I told Paul that I had been offered this position in the East, he initially didn't say anything. I left him alone for a couple of days. Then I told him that I had talked to his father, and we had decided that we would let Paul decide if he wanted to stay in St. Louis with his father or move with me.

The whole time that we were divorced, Paul spent every weekend with his father. When Paul made sixteen, I figured he was pretty much a done deal. He's a junior in high school, and he decided to stay. He and I talk usually twice a week. He tells me what he's doing and assures me that he is doing fine. He misses me.

I didn't realize how difficult it was going to be, because I was so excited about getting this new position. The first week I was here, I just really went through it. I missed Paul. When Jenn went away to school it was really hard, but with Paul--he's like my buddy. I feel sort of guilty about leaving him. Did I make the right decision? Was I being selfish?

I'm forty-seven. They just don't hire fifty-year-old women. If I had waited until Paul had graduated from high school, I thought I'd be missing my chance. But I still feel guilty about leaving Paul, although at this stage of his life, I think he needs to be more around his father.

At one point he did say, "I don't want you to leave." I felt, I can't let this kid dictate my life. If I think the move is best, and I think he'll be okay with his Dad, and he'll still be around his friends ... Once I see Paul, when he comes at Thanksgiving, I'll feel better.

Then, I asked his sister to call him. I said, "Jenn, he'll tell you. Jenn, call your child and see." She is six years older. When they were growing up, it was like she was his mother. Sometimes Paul could barely stand her, because she was so bossy. Then I would say, "Jenn, I am Paul's mother. Paul is <u>my</u> child. <u>Leave</u> Paul <u>alone</u>!"

When my friends would come and visit they would say, "Oh, Paul, don't you miss your sister?" He would say, "No," and he was sincere.

Then when she would come home, maybe the second day, she would start in on him. "Why don't you . . . "

One day Paul said, "How long is The Girl going to be here, Mommy?"

I pretty much felt the same way. Once when she came home from school I was fixing spaghetti. She came into the kitchen and said, "What are you doing, Julianne? That's not how you make the spaghetti. Move over. Let me do it."

I said, "Jenn, Paul and I have spaghetti all the time. We like my spaghetti. You are a guest. You no longer live here. You are walking on thin boards, child."

She took over and fixed the spaghetti. I looked over at Paul, and he looked at me. Jenn said, "I see you all looking at each other. I saw that!"

She would upset the whole house giving orders. "Why don't you do this? When did you buy that? You didn't tell me you bought a new coat. You didn't buy <u>me</u> anything. Paul has a new TV."

Jenn really is a classy little girl. She has a lot of class. She just does. She's interesting. She and Paul are altogether different. He sits back, and he observes.

Sometimes Jenn will get upset, and she'll say, "You think Paul is smarter than I am." She will try to say that I make a difference between them.

I don't let her get away with that. I say, "Jenn, you have more than the law allows. You have more than Paul will ever have."

I will say, "Paul, don't you think you need some shirts?"

"Why? What's wrong with what I've got on?"

Jenn will say, "I <u>need</u> some shoes, Mummy."

With Paul, I'll say, "Paul, don't you need some shoes?"

Then when we're in the store he'll say, "Are these too much?" Or, "Thank you, Mommy."

When I introduce them I will say, "This is my nice child," meaning Paul, and then I will say, "This is The Girl." They're a lot of fun!

You have expectations for your kids. You hope that they turn out to be good citizens, that they will be of service to others. I always tell them they are going to have to take care of me in my old age. I expect the same services from them as I gave them.

I told Jenn, "Whoever you marry, tell him about Julianne, because I will have a room. You will take me shopping every Saturday, as I did you." You know?

Jenn says, "We're going to put you in a nursing home. Do you think we're going to put up with you Mummy, as silly as you are? And you're going to be real silly when you get old."

"Well, I know Paul will let me live with him."

Paul looks at Jenn as if to say, "No way."

"Okay, I'm going to write you all out of my will. You don't want me to revise it, now do you?"

Jenn says, "Oh, <u>ple-e-ease</u>."

I have been able to realize my aspirations career-wise as well as being a mother, and I think my kids are better off, because I didn't just dote on them. Because I did not give them one hundred percent of my attention, they can do things for themselves. You raise them to be independent and to think for themselves. Like I told Jenn, "Jenn, I meant for you to be independent with everybody but <u>me</u>." I still want her to take my suggestions, to live up to my expectations, to do what I think she should do.

I have always been able to do things that were important me.

CORDELIA CORAZON
Age: 38

"They can just love Jimmy. To me it is like, 'How did this happen?' It did happen. Sometimes I marvel. How did I get so lucky?"

Cordelia is Mexican-American. She has been the single parent of four boys for the past seven years. Her boys are twenty, seventeen, fifteen, and fourteen: Wayne, Jimmy, Lloyd, and Clark. Jimmy is autistic.

Cordelia grew up in California, close to the Mexican border. She is employed full-time, running a family health clinic in the marginal areas of Tijuana, in coordination with a family planning agency in Mexico. She works to provide primary health care and birth control to all of the families who just came into California. The population she serves includes thousands and thousands of teenage girls. After devastating floods recently, her agency was delivering food and clothing as well as medication and was raising money for pampers and milk and formula and antibiotics. "It is a very different, interesting, rewarding job."

Cordelia approaches her work and her mothering with the same attitudes. Both are uncommonly difficult, and she is unusually successful in both arenas.

When we got to San Diego after my divorce, I told them, "We're on our own. I have to work. I don't want to be dependent on any public assistance. Your father is not giving us any money. I am going to have to go back to school. It is going to be really tough." Wayne was twelve at the time. He was doing paper routes and things like that. He was helping me by buying his own clothing for school.

I told the boys, "I don't have the money to pay someone to take care of Jimmy, and I don't have the trust to just take Jimmy to a stranger, when he can't communicate if anything goes wrong. All I've got is you guys. You guys have just got me." I told them what the dangers were, and I told them that I was just going to have to ask them to watch Jimmy and watch out for themselves. "There is no leaving the house. There is no telling strangers on the phone that you are there by yourselves." They were like third and fourth graders at the time. They didn't fight me at all. They would get home from school before Jimmy got home, so they would always be there at the bus stop to pick him up and take him home.

Now, they are all teenagers. They've done really well so far. Luckily they haven't gotten into any trouble or had any gang behavior. They are home-oriented, and they do a lot of sports. They are very caring and protective of their autistic brother. They have learned to accept, love, and look after him. My oldest is in college, on a scholarship. He's working full-time, too. The other ones are very much college-oriented. I haven't had to talk them into it or promote it. It has been a given.

I'm a very feminist woman. I was raised with three sisters and three brothers. I came from the typical Mexican family where the sisters do everything for the brothers, and the brothers--I would hear my mother say, "It wears me out more to just push 'em and push 'em than do it myself or have one of you girls do it."

I'd think, "How unfair can that be? They get away with murder, because all they do is neglect. We girls don't get that break." I picked up how important it was to have a son, how important it was to continue the last name, how unimportant it was to have a daughter born. I couldn't understand why it was, but I was determined that I wasn't going to do it that way. I felt the one born first doesn't have more rights than the one born last. I figured, if I have anything ever to leave my children, it is going to be for all of them, sons and daughters alike.

I am the breadwinner in the house. We all have our chores. I hate cooking, but I am determined to cook for them right. It keeps you away from the doctor. That is my full responsibility, after my job, to make sure that they eat right. No leaving for school without breakfast. No cold cereals. I cook a square meal every night. That is my responsibility, and the rest is theirs.

Washing. Ironing. Doing the dishes. Vacuuming. Cleaning the garage. Washing the cars. Taking care of Jimmy. They have those responsibilities. Every month we rotate chores in the house, except mine. Mine is standard. One month one will do inside the house; another one will do outside the house; and one of them will have Jimmy as a responsibility, to see him to school, to bathe him, to brush his teeth, make sure he's got clean clothes, pressed clothes. The bus picks him up at seven in the morning.

The oldest one, Wayne, works at a men's department store, so he gets all these good breaks and will let the others know. Since he's working full-time and going to college, he doesn't have the time to do his chores at home. So, he hires one of his brothers to do his share! He rotates them. So, there's always one of them that is earning a little money and saving it and buying clothing with it.

Their nature is very mellow. They are very close together. The two youngest ones were born when Jimmy was already part of the family. They didn't have to adjust. They were able to see how important Jimmy is to my family. Sometimes I see this huge kid that is being made over and loved and just pampered by his brothers that are just about his same height--and they are all men. They're all <u>men</u>. They are all a lot taller than I am. To see this tenderness--not to a little sister--but to somebody that is already growing a beard and has a mustache. They can just love him. To me it is like, "How did this happen?" It did happen. Sometimes I marvel. How did I get so lucky?

They are not those little machines that I wish they were--that pick up after themselves. They can get lazy. They have to be told a million times. They will do it. They do it so-so, but if I go and look, it's like, "How can you guys not see the things I'm seeing?" I have come to accept that that is the way they see it. To them it is no big deal. If they get into the shower and leave their clothes there, they can come back later--whenever--a day or two later, an hour. They will do it. I have learned to let go.

408

They have their own bathroom. I have said, "Don't you come in my bathroom! I don't want a bathroom like yours."

They just dread when I get angry. It is very few times when that happens. Then they'll get on the ball. I am a very firm person, but at the same time, I wanted to make a difference in being a friend to my children. They all like to be listened to. But I am not a friend to the point where they would lose respect and not see me as a disciplinarian, an authority above them. Somebody that has the last word. When it gets to the point of "Why? Why?," and there are no more whys to answer, it is, "You're going to do it, because I say so."

If I have a meeting after work, I fix their dinner before I come to work. If for some reason something unpredictable arises and I cannot be home by five-thirty, they might be a little lazy to fix themselves a sandwich, but they will never let Jimmy go past five-thirty without fixing him a real meal. It's in them: Jimmy can't help himself. Jimmy doesn't have the same ability that they have, so he needs to be taken care of. If they want to starve, it's their choice, but Jimmy doesn't have a choice.

Jimmy is part of Wayne and Lloyd and Clark. They have never resented Jimmy's condition or been embarrassed or ashamed of Jimmy. They always bring friends to the house. I see all these kids in my house that are just so used to Jimmy. Sometimes he has tantrums or is in a bad mood. Lloyd and Clark and Jimmy are all in the same school now. Lloyd and Clark walk up to Jimmy, and they have no problem telling anybody, "This is my brother." Sometimes Jimmy comes up to them. Someone will ask, "Who's that?"

"That's my brother."

"You're kidding me."

"No, that's my brother."

One time when I had just gotten separated, we were all eating dinner and Clark, the youngest, who at that time was about eight years old, said, "Mom, what's going to happen to Jimmy if something happens to you?"

This concern is in the back of my mind twenty-four hours a day. I said, "Well, Clark, I don't have the answer for that. I wish I did. I only hope that the way you have seen Jimmy be

409

such an important and special part in our lives carries on and you will be able to make a decision towards your brother when I'm no longer here to say what to do. I hope that is going to come out of your heart." There was dead silence.

Then Wayne said, "That's why I'm never going to get married, because I'm always going to take care of my brother."

It was good to know that even at that young age they realized already there is a potential. There's planning to do. Just the thought of Clark thinking, "What's going to happen to my brother?" What was going to happen to him if something happened to me? He was only eight!

They are all open with me, comfortable to talk about things in a respectful way. I tell them that they have a responsibility toward the girl they date. If there's anything I want to see them accomplish it is: Never walk away from a responsibility. If there is a child born, it is a responsibility for life. There is no such thing as it is just the girl's responsibility. So, to avoid those kinds of situations, you take the responsibility. Luckily I haven't had any scares.

They are very respectful of me, but they would never address to Grandmother the questions they would address to me. They revere their grandparents. They treat their grandmother and their grandfather like gold.

It has been a special situation. Over the years it has just worked that I have always been able to rely on family. It has been a very pleasant experience. I just don't know how it happened, but I am happy it did. I have to work, and I don't have to worry.

KAY SNYDER
Age: 39

"I packed up the whole family and a picnic lunch and took it to the field. The babies you pack up in a car seat. Find a shade tree. Tom would come down on the tractor or the combine. The kids would get a chance to see him. He'd get to talk to the kids. They always begged to ride with him. Delightful. The good old days."

Kay and her husband Tom raise both crops and cattle on their Ohio farm. She and I sat on her porch early in August. It was very quiet, very dry, and very hot. Her two youngest, Emily (twelve) and David (eleven), rode bareback, double, past our view again and again, around and around the house on their old horse. Easy rhythms.

Jacob (sixteen) and Matthew (fifteen) were out in the barns with their father.

Out of necessity Kay works full-time at a grain company, in addition to helping with the farming. She tells a story of farming and parenting happily wound together.

I grew up in a little town near here. Then, in 1970, when I got married, I moved out on the farm. I love it here. I adapted to it real quick. We started trying to have kids, and we couldn't. We adopted Jacob in '75. He was five months old. Then the others just came along. I can't hardly imagine what my life would have been like without kids. I can't imagine missing all those feelings you get in your stomach, and tears coming when you see them doing something.

Raising the kids up like this is so much different than when I was raised. We're forced to be more of a family unit. We're together. In town I got home from school and just walked down

411

the block to my girlfriend's. Here, the kids just end up playing with each other more. I like that.

Matthew is like a little carbon copy of his daddy--is what he is. He likes his basketball, but he's more interested in raising cattle. He likes the Hereford cattle and the showing. He wants to go to Colorado State, which has the best animal science in the country and their own herd of Hereford cattle.

I told Emily she can be any kind of doctor she wants to be! She can be rich and take care of us in our old age! She wants to be a lawyer. That's okay--they get rich too! I tease her about it.

Her husband Tom appears in the doorway.

Kay : You want me?

Tom : I could go put that loader on.

Kay : You're wondering about lunch. You want to put that loader on and come back and eat a hamburger after that?

Tom : I guess. Certain time, you have to eat.

Kay : I was just going to put hamburgers on the grill and get tomatoes out of the garden.

Tom : It don't make any difference to me.

Kay : When you get back here, I'll put the hamburgers on the grill.

The kids will go get McDougal, the horse, and saddle him up and ride double all day long around here, the farm, barn, out in the pastures. Laugh and giggle. Get off and on him. The older boys, and even the little ones, come with us to help, like if we have to get cattle in. Now that Matthew and Jake are older, it's just a big help. They drive the tractors. My youngest, David, he thinks he can drive anything. When he gets home from school, he gets a snack, and he waits for Daddy to pull in, so he can go to the field with him.

They need to learn it on the farm early, because farming is so dangerous. The children need to be out there when we're doing stuff, so they learn exactly how to do it right. They say farming is the number one most dangerous occupation now, even more than mining. All the equipment, the bins. Unloading grain. All the shafts on the tractor, when you're running augers. The augers themselves. The kids need to be out there when they're little to start learning. You can't keep farm kids away from the farming.

When school starts, they do things there. Emily is a cheerleader--she can still be a doctor! This summer three of them went to basketball camps. Tom doesn't get to come to all the games during the school year, because he's in the field. He hates that. I never miss them.

My oldest boy is real good for helping in the house too. 'Specially with me working an off-farm job. I come home: "Your dishes are done."

"That's wonderful."

Right now, we're praying for rain. We usually plant in April and May. You start cultivating--between the rows--and you spray to kill the weeds. Then you make hay, if you have cattle. You always have the calves to tend to. You always have the hay to make. We start calving in March. You have to tend to them. Right now, if it had rained, people would still be making hay. There shouldn't be anything else you can do to the crops now. The county fair's over with. People might be mowing pastures. A lot of maintenance work goes on now. Getting the combines ready for fall.

I can remember, way back when we had normal farming years, this time of year, we'd get a real nice rain. It'd start in the morning, and rain all day long. We'd stand on our little front porch, and Tom would say, "Boy, this is a money-maker." It'd be nice now to stand out on the front porch and have a money-maker. Today, it's so beautiful. Look at the sky! It's gorgeous. So blue! Except that it's so dry. You'd be more appreciative of a day like today if it had rained.

If I were to come home at nine o'clock, the kids'd still want to know, "What's for supper?" Sometimes if I know I'm going to go to the field and work, I'll pick up something running. Come home, feed the kids, tell them to get their homework done, whatever, take off, and wherever I know Tom's at, I'll usually get that tractor and start workin' ground with it. That enables him to go to wherever his dad's at and relieve him. We'll do that until evening, or until I just get so tired I come on home.

Now I can leave the kids like that. When they were younger, I couldn't do that. I'd have to get my mom to stay with 'em, or I'd just have to stay home with 'em. The kids are so responsible now I don't have to worry about it. It makes a big difference.

Tom appears in the yard.

He's looking in the grill, and there's nothin' on it!

I'm so glad I have one little girl. The boys are great, but they're so different, boys and girls, it's nice to be able to experience them both. Emily--she's kinda special. I tell her, "Whatever you want to do, I'll support you, but I don't know anything about cheerleading. Don't ask me how you jump."

Now the girls have every chance a boy has, which is great.

When the kids were little, Tom could do anything with them I could do. Back then there was a lot of husbands that never did that. They wouldn't even change diapers. Tom fretted over Matthew when he was sick, all during those nights he couldn't sleep. He was always so good with them. The older the boys get, like with Jake and Matthew, I see them building more of a relationship with Tom. They're getting involved in the farming more. Tom is teaching them a lot.

I think Emily and I have a traditional mother-daughter relationship. It's kinda like it was with my Mom and me. There's just something different. I don't know how to put it. You can be with her and talk about things. As the boys get older, they're more associated with Tom, and she kinda gets closer and closer to me. It seems like that. I hope it stays. Of course, she's getting closer to the teenage years. She'll get a lot more independent. She's the type that whatever she sets her head to be, she can be. She's got the academic ability, and she's got the personality to get up in front of people.

When the kids were little, Tom could do anything with them I could do. Back then there was a lot of husbands that never did that. They wouldn't even change diapers. Tom fretted over

414

Matthew when he was sick, all during those nights he couldn't sleep. He was always so good with them.

When the kids were little, I was home with them most of the time. Tom was farming. During the spring and the fall, you call yourselves "farmers' widows." Every time you have any kind of family get-togethers, you always go with the kids by yourself, because your husband is in the field. I was home full-time and had more of an influence on them, I suppose, than what he did at that time.

Then, when I started working, when David was little, during the summertime, they spent more time with Tom. So, I guess, maybe, they got the best of both of us at different ages. You always just took your kids with you when you did stuff on the farm. They went and sat in the pickup while you filled up the corn, and they rode back and forth while you filled up the bin. They were too little to stay alone in the house.

My kids have always been with either me or my husband. We did have that luxury of being there. Seeing everything happen. Anytime your kids are involved in something and you go to watch them, doing something they really love doing, you get such a sense of pride.

I look out and I see them out in the field on a tractor, working. "Kay, you're getting old. Your kids are out farming." It really hits you. Things that I used to do, they're saying now, "That's all right, I'll take care of that." I'm getting shoved back. Pretty soon I won't be allowed to go on the tractor and go to the field and do anything, I don't suppose.

They feel like they're responsible for something. They are. It will help them when they get out on their own. You start working a big field. You get tired. You want to go home, but you keep going. You pull out of the field. You pull your cultivators. You look back, and the field is nice and clean. Hot day out there. A lot of hours, but look how nice the field is! Ready to plant. When you get done, you've got something.

Oh! it must be bath time. Davie's bringing the heifer out for a bath. We're doing it three times a day, because it's so hot.

I wish I could stay home with them still, even now. I dreamed . . . how it was supposed to be . . . when the kids were old enough that they were all in school, Tom and I would go off to the field and do what we had to do. Back to just Tom and me, again. The kids would come home, and I'd be there, again.

Tom and I had gotten so used to being partners. In farming you're together all the time, working the field together. We're really, really close. It was really tough with kids and not being there with Tom, anymore. I packed up the whole family and a picnic lunch and took it to the field. The babies you pack up in a car seat. Find a shade tree. Tom would come down on the tractor or the combine. The kids would get a chance to see him. He'd get to talk to the kids. They always begged to ride with him. Delightful. The good old days.

I love my job, but I'll get rid of it just as soon as I can. I was saying to Tom this morning, "If it rains, and we keep having the good cattle sales, I want to be back home on the farm, before I get too old to do any more farming."

Yesterday I was in the fields, looking at the cracks in the ground. It's so dry. It's kinda depressing. After dinner I went for a walk along the road, just to walk, and look at the stars, and remember what it's all about.

SERENA ROSS
Age: 46

"You can stand alone. That doesn't preclude standing next to somebody, but you need to be able to stand alone."

Serena is Jewish, the associate director of a social service agency. She is a single parent of three daughters: Heidi is twenty-four; Alisa is twenty-one; and Beth is nineteen. Serena's children live near her in California, but they no longer live at home. Serena has taught them to be strong, independent young women.

There is a certain strength in my mother. Even though I resent my Mom's being pretty fragile, there still is a strength. She's a survivor of the Holocaust. Her family got killed. She watched her parents being murdered, her sibling. She had a younger sibling at the time they were taken away to the camps.

My mother was fed sterilization chemicals in the camp. She never thought that she'd be able to have any kids. Then she got married. Actually the doctor had said to her, "Don't even try to get pregnant. You're too weak and emaciated." But she wanted to have a kid. She had me and then had temporary blindness. She was physically emaciated, so her system couldn't handle a pregnancy, I guess. Her strength came through all of that--and I was terribly spoiled as a result.

Throughout my own childhood a voice said, "Pay attention to the stuff you don't like in your interactions with Mom, because there are things you want to make sure you don't do when you become a mother." There's a lot tied to her being a Holocaust survivor. She's fearful of the world around her. The world is not a safe place. As a child I wasn't allowed to explore, because my mother was frightened. So, it was important for me to not frighten my kids by stopping them from exploring the world. I told the kids, "If I ever do this, please point it out to me, because I really didn't like when it happened to me."

There were other issues--allowing the children to be children, not relying on them to become my parent. Throughout much of my childhood I felt a responsibility to protect my parents, because of their experiences and their fear. I lied to my parents in order to protect them. I gave them what they needed, while I did what I needed. "If you can't handle what I'm going to do, I'm just not going to tell you."

As a mother I was concerned about lying in my kids. I told them, "I'm not comfortable if you lie to me. I need for there to be open communication. I may not always agree with you, but I would much rather we talk about something and see if there's a way to resolve it." That came more easily over time.

Fortunately I didn't go through the same experiences that my mother did, so that was an easier one to get rid of. The fear stayed though. I'd find myself getting panicky when the kids wanted to do things that might harm them. I overreacted to their taking risks. But through the adolescent years risk-taking is critical to development! Through taking risks they begin to take some ownership for the consequences of their behavior. Taking risks is empowering.

The first child was the hardest. I said to a friend in Heidi's presence, "With the first one, the first three years of puberty were hell, and then she grew up."

Heidi said, "It was hell for three years until you grew up, Mom."

She's probably right. I really struggled with her. It had to do with power. Who's in control? That's the bottom line. Her asserting herself as growing child, my asserting myself as parent and responsible party.

It was easier with Alisa and easier, still, with Beth. I relaxed more with each child. Things that had troubled me no longer troubled me. I think I began to feel more comfortable with myself as a parent and didn't need to be frantic about it. I didn't feel that there was The Right Decision that I needed to make. I began to trust more that I could make a right decision for that circumstance.

I can be an individual and a parent. I learned that over time. I didn't realize that until my oldest was in kindergarten, and I started coming back out. Before that I felt isolated from the world. It was a struggle to be a good parent and an individual with my own needs, simultaneously, to get these things to merge together rather than being two competing needs.

It became okay to say to my kids, "When I come home from work, I really need five minutes of quiet. Please. Then I will listen to all three of you." I felt guilty doing that at first. They resented it at first, but after a while they saw that it really made a difference. They discovered that if they asked me after dinner, they got a better response.

For a while after I got the divorce I felt more independent than I had at any point in my life. It was very exciting, but I also had three young children to take care of. They were nine, six, and five when my ex-husband moved out. I was like a nineteen year old kid going, "Wow! The world's out here!" I did a lot of things at that point that were for me, going back to school, getting involved in politics, getting a part-time job, and then a full-time job.

One big issue for me was to raise my kids to be independent, particularly because they are females, particularly because I wound up in a position where I was a single parent raising three kids on my own. The divorce was my choice, but it was a damn good thing I had gone to college. It was a damn good thing I had done some volunteer work, because I could go forward with my life.

I've wanted to be sure that my kids understand that they have to be able to be self-sufficient. You don't need to rely on males. You are capable and competent to do what you need to do. You can stand alone. That doesn't preclude standing next to somebody, but you need to be able to stand alone.

All three of my girls are determined to succeed. They are going to succeed, and they do succeed, in what they choose to succeed in. That's really exciting to see.

A new type of relationship emerges when they move out of the house. It is more of a friendship. There were rules when they lived with me, and I was an authority figure. I needed to know, for instance, where they were and when they would be coming home. Once they were no longer living with me, that struggle was gone. For some reason, once they moved out, the fact that they were out late was no longer a burden of mine. That freed up the relationship.

In some ways there's more communication with them now that they're not at home. It is more precious, more treasured.

My sense is that with each generation parenting gets better. You lose some of the shit and you build on what's positive. I think my kids are going to do even better as parents. I look forward to seeing them as parents. I want to see what wends its way through: what threads stay and what is discarded.

HAZEL KELSEY
Age: 89

"But they never told me not to give, so I kept doin' it."

Sweet, sweet. A twinkle in her eye. Hazel remembers her mother knitting mittens for the soldiers in World War I. Hazel was seventeen when she had her first child, and then, she "just kept having them," five more. She raised foster children along with her own. Three of Hazel's children are still living.

Hazel won an award for outstanding volunteer service in the county home, where she has lived for the last four years. When new people come to the home and are feeling down, Hazel goes to see them.

"Just last year they had me down to the junior high. I signed up. One of the girls wanted to know algebra, and I loved algebra. I said, 'I don't <u>think</u> I forgot it. I'll show her.' So I went down and helped her with the algebra."

Hazel smiled and chuckled as she talked. A mother to all, forever.

She calls me "Ma." She was my oldest daughter's child. I might as well tell you, this baby belonged to my husband. I didn't take her on account of that, though. I kept her because I wanted to. She says to me, "You're the only mother I got." Her mother didn't want her. She was going to give her up. I had a whole houseful of children anyway, because I had foster children. So, I got her. I brought her up. I'm "Ma" to them all, I guess.

I even had a little colored baby. I was supposed to keep them until they found a home for 'em. Then I missed 'em, of course. I'd had 'em so long, and then they'd come get 'em. And I'd miss 'em. I had him three years. They came and gave him

421

back to his mother. I didn't hear any more, so I guess he was all right. He was a tiny baby when I got him, only nine months old. But he was walking! He was so bow-legged that you could roll a little ball right between his little legs! I got his legs so they were a little straighter. I kept massaging 'em all the time. It doesn't make any difference to me whether they're black, white, or what they are. I like 'em just the same.

I raised an awful lot of children. My children took it all in good. I don't know how I happened to get all of 'em. The mothers had trouble or something with their husbands and--bang!--I get 'em all in my dish. I wouldn't turn 'em out.

I had six of my own. My daughter Rita, when she was born, she only weighed three pounds. I fell down the hill--she was a seven months baby. A little tiny bit of a thing. When she cried she sounded like a cat crying. When she got hungry, she'd make that funny little noise, and I'd go and feed her with an eye-dropper.

I never had a natural birth anyway. They called them "instrument cases." They gave me ether. My oldest son, they had quite a little time with him. He was active, I guess. They worked fast. He had two great big spots on his face and a gash up over his eye. It all healed right up. They said in a few minutes more he would have choked to death on his own cord.

My daughter that's in Maine, she named her first one after me. I thought, "Lord, help the poor baby! I hope she won't have to go through my life."

If I could only get up and walk around, I could do a whole lot more. They don't like to have me walk. I fell last week. That knee went out so quick, and down I went. Didn't hurt me though! I take all kind of chances, that's all. I always took lots of chances! Heaven sakes, yes! Even after I broke my hip.

About five years ago, I had my antenna on top of the roof, and the TV wasn't comin' in good. So, I went upstairs in the bathroom and went out the window, crawled out on the roof, and turned the antenna. My neighbor said, "I didn't dare to holler to you, Hazel. I knew you'd jump and fall, but I watched ya. You got out all right, and you got right back in that window all right."

"Yeah, I got the television going all right, too!" I said.

422

That was stupid, honest. But the children was findin' fault, because the television weren't comin' in good. I said, "You wait a minute, I'll see if I can fix it." But I didn't give it a thought, see? If I had fallen right down on that cement, there wouldn't have been nothin' left of me! So, I got it fixed, and I crawled back in and called down stairs, "How 'bout it now?"

"Oh, that's coming in good now, Ma."

I used to go out and play with the kids. That's why they say in here, "Hazel, you don't even talk like an old person." I was always with young kids. I'll be ninety years old my next birthday. I hate to think of that! I was the last of nine children in my family. For fifteen years I was a nurse. Lord help the poor devils now if I give 'em medicine, because I can't see that good. But I was good then.

I made all the clothes when the kids were little. I liked the little girls. You can dress them up cunnin'. Somebody'd give me a coat or something big. I'd rip it all up, and wash it, and then make it into little suits. 'Course I lived on a farm anyway. You'd buy grain. It would come in colored bags, handsome bags. I used to take them, and wash them all up, and make little dresses. Cotton. Pretty, they were.

I didn't have too much to do on the farm. We had cattle, Holsteins and Guernseys. I churned the butter. We did have some chickens. And I candled the eggs. We had some brooders. When they'd find something the matter with any of those brooder chickens, they couldn't walk or something, I'd gather 'em all up, and bring 'em in the house, and make their own little brooder for 'em. I put a flashlight in a box and got 'em so they'd fly around all right. Then I'd turn 'em out with the rest of 'em.

My husband was good. Oh, yes. He loved children too, so that made it easy.

People used to come in the house and say, "Hazel, how do you ever keep this house so good?"

I said, "You kind of have to when you have a whole houseful of children." But the children didn't bother my house. They had a great big play-room. Once in a while they'd take a little tricycle and sneak one round out in the kitchen or somethin'. I didn't say nothin', so they'd go right back. If I'd given the devil over it, they'd have come and done it anyway then, but I didn't say nothin'. They had all their toys there. A big toy box. They'd come in from school, and I'd help 'em with their school work. I liked it. I liked every minute of it.

I taught them everything good, anyway. And they are good. They turned out very good. And they're keepin' their own children. My granddaughter, she'd like to have me leave the home here and come to live with her. I said, "Yeah, I know it. You've got a five-year-old. You'd like to have me come take care of him, wouldn't ya?"

"No," she said, "not that, Ma. I'd just like to pay back some of the things you had to do for me."

The custodian here said, "What can I give you for Christmas, Hazel?"

"What can you give me? I don't want nothin,' Bob."

"I got to give you something. You must have been a wonderful mother." He was having trouble with his mother and father. I guess he's going to pick on me!

When he first asked me, I said, "Oh, give me a new leg, Bob."

He said, "I'd do that in a minute, if I could."

I was always givin' even when I was just a kid. My father brought me--oh!--a handsome pair of shoes, and I loved 'em. Then I went to school, of course. This family didn't have much money, and the girl said, "Oh, those are awful pretty. I wish my mother and father could buy me a pair like that."

I looked at her a few minutes, and I said, "What size do you take?" Well, she didn't know what size. I said, "Let me try on yours."

Oh God, they were all to and everything, but they fit me all right. I said, "Try mine on." So they fit her. I said, "Well, let's swap." I give her my new shoes, and I took her old ones and went home.

My mother said, "Hazel, where's your shoes?"

I told her who I give them to.

She never said it wasn't right. "Well, I guess your father will get you another pair."

424

I would take clothes right out of my closet, if some little kid didn't have 'em. If a kid wanted it, I'd say, "I'll bring it to you tomorrow."

'Course my mother would miss it. We were poor anyway. She'd ask. I'd say, "I took it to school and gave it to a little girl." But they never told me not to give, so I kept doin' it. I liked to give.

I guess my children thought an awful lot of me. And grandchildren and great-grandchildren do now. They call me up on the phone to talk. "Ma," they say, "it sounds good to hear your voice."

INDEX

The page numbers will lead you to the <u>first pages of stories</u> that deal with the following:

ABOUT THE AUTHOR

EMILY MOORE grew up in Springfield, Massachusetts. She graduated from Smith College in 1971 and later earned a master's degree in counseling from the University of New Hampshire. She is the mother of two sons who were teenagers when most of the work for this book was done. Now they are finishing college and entering the world of full-time work. Emily lives in Deerfield, New Hampshire with her husband Richard. She owns and operates Moore Designs, Inc., a jewelry manufacturing business, and paints watercolors.